BLOCK BY BLOCK

HISTORICAL STUDIES OF URBAN AMERICA
EDITED BY KATHLEEN N. CONZEN, TIMOTHY J. GILFOYLE, AND JAMES R. GROSSMAN

Also in the series:

BLOCK BY BLOCK

Neighborhoods and Public Policy on Chicago's West Side

Amanda I. Seligman

THE UNIVERSITY OF CHICAGO PRESS ▪ CHICAGO AND LONDON

Amanda I. Seligman is assistant professor of history at the University of
Wisconsin–Milwaukee.

The University of Chicago Press, Chicago 60637
The University of Chicago Press, Ltd., London
© 2005 by The University of Chicago
All rights reserved. Published 2005
Printed in the United States of America
14 13 12 11 10 09 08 07 06 05   1 2 3 4 5

ISBN: 0-226-74663-1 (cloth)
ISBN: 0-226-74665-8 (paper)

Library of Congress Cataloging-in-Publication Data

Seligman, Amanda I.
Block by block : neighborhoods and public policy on Chicago's West Side
/ Amanda I. Seligman.
    p.   cm. — (Historical studies of urban America)
Includes index.
ISBN 0-226-74663-1 (cloth : alk. paper) — ISBN 0-226-74665-8 (pbk. :
alk. paper)
1. Chicago (Ill.)—Race relations—History—20th century. 2. Chicago
(Ill.)—Social conditions—20th century. 3. Urban policy—Illinois—
Chicago—History—20th century. 4. African Americans—Illinois—
Chicago—Social conditions—20th century. 5. Whites—Illinois—
Chicago—Migrations—20th century. 6. Whites—Illinois—Chicago—
Social conditions—20th century. 7. African Americans—Housing—
Illinois—Chicago—History—20th century. 8. Whites—Housing—
Illinois—Chicago—History—20th century. 9. City and town life—
Illinois—Chicago—History—20th century. 10. Suburban life—Illinois—
Chicago—History—20th century. I. Title. II. Series.
F548.9.A1S45   2005
977.3'11043—dc22   2004016543

Parts of chapters 6, 7, and 8 appeared as "'Apologies to Dracula,
Werewolf, Frankenstein': White Homeowners and Blockbusters in
Chicago," *Journal of the Illinois State Historical Society* (Spring 2001):
70–95.

For my teachers

CONTENTS

ACKNOWLEDGMENTS

The work of the historian is anything but lonely. I am honored to have the chance to offer my gratitude to the people who have accompanied me on the journey toward this book. This book would not exist without them, but I alone remain responsible for its errors of fact and interpretation. I would like to begin by thanking my primary and secondary school and college teachers, who shaped this book in ways too deep to be completely recognizable. I also owe a debt of thanks to the people of Princeton Project '55, especially John H. Fish, who first introduced me to Chicago.

Henry Binford saw this project through from its inception to its completion in dissertation form. No graduate student could dream of an adviser who is a better model of the humane teacher. I am grateful for Henry's continuing professional support and friendship. In the years since I left Northwestern, I have become more and more appreciative of his contributions to my development. Joe Barton and Mike Sherry also served on my dissertation committee, and I thank them for their advice. Jared Orsi, Graham Peck, and Rebecca Shereikis provided invaluable support for this project over several years, as part of a dissertation-writing group. I learned much about how to be an urban historian from Ann Durkin Keating, who read the completed dissertation and helped me think about how to turn it into a book.

Scott Henderson deserves a paragraph of thanks all to himself. Since I met Scott, he has read and critiqued almost everything I have written, usually within twenty-four hours of receiving it. He read the entirety of this book as it evolved—not always in a linear order. Scott also generously provided citations in answer to my numerous queries. He always offered helpful advice alongside sustaining encouragement.

Many colleagues generously offered observations and encouragement about this project over the course of its gestation. I would like to thank the following people for their helpful comments: Robin Bachin, Roger Biles, Jim Campbell, Martha Carlin, Greg Carman, Lorna Dilley, Bruce Fetter, Carlos R. Galvão-Sobrinho, Michael Gordon, Victor Greene, Jim Grossman, Anne Hansen, Arnold Hirsch, Mike Homel, Douglas Howland, Suellen Hoy,

William P. Jones, Jennifer Jordan, Judith Kenny, Art McEvoy, Jeff Merrick, Michele Mitchell, Raymond A. Mohl, Carl H. Nightingale, Wendy Plotkin, Steve Reich, Joe Rodriguez, Marc Rodriguez, Beryl Satter, Eric Schneider, Helene Slessarev, Carol Summerfield, William B. Turner, and Merry Wiesner-Hanks. Diane Dillon kept me company through many long hours at the Chicago Historical Society. Margo Anderson provided astute advice at several crucial moments in the book's progress. My colleagues in the Department of History and Urban Studies Programs at the University of Wisconsin–Milwaukee have made my professional life most pleasant over the past several years. I would also like to offer thanks to the history department staff at UWM—Anita Cathey, Queen Crenshaw, Teena Rawls, and Louise Whitaker—for ensuring a congenial working environment.

I have been fortunate to present sections of this project in diverse venues. I would like to thank the audience members and other panel participants at presentations to the University of Wisconsin–Milwaukee's Department of History; the Great Cities Winter Forum at the University of Illinois at Chicago; the National Policy History Conference at Bowling Green State University; the Illinois History Symposium; and the Organization of American Historians. I am grateful to the members of the Newberry Library Urban History Dissertation Group, including Wallace Best, Dennis Cremin, Drew Digby, Sarah Fenton, Brad Hunt, Doug Knox, Tim Neary, Tracy Poe, and Edie Sparks, who offered early and lively critique of part of the dissertation. Material from chapters 6, 7, and 8 have appeared in the *Journal of the Illinois State Historical Society*.

Librarians and archivists provided indispensable support to this book, both while I worked on it and during many preceding years, as they gathered the materials on which it is based. I offer my gratitude to the staffs of the American Friends Service Committee Archives, the Chicago Historical Society, the Harold Washington Library Center, the Abraham Lincoln Presidential Library in Springfield, Illinois, the Newberry Library, the Northwestern University Library, the Richard J. Daley Library of the University of Illinois at Chicago, the University of Notre Dame Hesburgh Library, and the Regenstein Library of the University of Chicago. The reference and interlibrary loan staffs of the University of Wisconsin–Milwaukee Golda Meir Library have been unflaggingly helpful and inspiring in their research techniques. I would especially like to thank Gloria Hamilton of the Northwestern University Library for teaching me what librarians do. The loss of Archie Motley, who dedicated his life's work to the mission of the Chicago Historical Society, is a deep blow. I am thankful to be among those who benefited from his help in person, while generations of scholars to come will continue to profit from his work.

The people involved with this book through the University of Chicago Press have made its production as painless as possible. Tim Gilfoyle read several versions of the manuscript and offered helpful critiques, always in an astonishingly timely fashion. Robert Devens and Elizabeth Branch Dyson ushered the manuscript through the inner workings of the Press. Erin DeWitt offered the manuscript a more meticulous reading than I ever imagined was possible. I would also like to offer my thanks to the two anonymous reviewers of the manuscript, who read it twice, each time offering both critical feedback and encouragement for the larger project.

Several institutions provided financial and technical support for this project. I am grateful to the University of Wisconsin–Milwaukee for support in the form of two Arts and Humanities Travel Grants from the Graduate School and a yearlong fellowship at the Center for 21st Century Studies, which provided me time to revise the manuscript. The Illinois Historic Preservation Agency provided me a King V. Hostick award. Northwestern University offered me financial support while I was a graduate student. UWM's Learning Technology Center assisted with the illustrations. Donna Genzmer and Ann Runyard of UWM's Cartography and Geographic Information Science Center produced the maps.

The members of two religious institutions have consistently put me in mind of the larger project of racial justice to which this book aspires to make a modest contribution. I thank the members of the Unitarian Church of Evanston and the Unitarian Church North for building faith communities that have complemented my intellectual work.

Finally, I would like to thank the members of my family. In the year when I completed this book, several events reminded me how precious they are to me. Brynna, Carolyn, Dave, Fred, Kerry, Carly, Darryl, David, Jenny, Lara, Mandy, Marty, and Nikki all sustain me. My deepest thanks belong to Joe, with whom I now begin the greater project.

ACRONYMS IN TEXT

ABC	Austin Business Council
ACC	Association of Community Councils
ACO	Austin Community Organization
ATOA	Austin Tenants and Owners Association
BYNC	Back of the Yards Neighborhood Council
CAM	Christian Action Ministry
CCB	Community Conservation Board
CCCO	Coordinating Council of Community Organizations
CCHR	Chicago Commission on Human Relations
CPC	Chicago Plan Commission
CPS	Chicago Public Schools
CREB	Chicago Real Estate Board
CTU	Chicago Tenants Union
DUR	Department of Urban Renewal
FHA	Federal Housing Administration
GLCC	Greater Lawndale Conservation Commission
GPACC	Garfield Park–Austin Community Council
GPIA	Garfield Park Improvement Association
GPWCC	Garfield Park West Community Council
ICHR	Illinois Commission on Human Relations
JAC	Joint Action Committee
LCCC	Lawndale Conservation Community Council
LPCA	Lincoln Park Conservation Association
MHPC	Metropolitan Housing and Planning Council
NAREB	National Association of Real Estate Boards
NLCC	North Lawndale Citizens Council
OBA	Organization for a Better Austin
POCC	Property Owners Coordinating Committee
SCLC	Southern Christian Leadership Conference
SSPB	South Side Planning Board
THA	Town Hall Assembly
UPG	United Property Group

Block by Block

In the spring of 1966, a debate over the feasibility of residential racial integration broke out in the *Garfieldian*, a local newspaper serving the West Garfield Park and Austin neighborhoods on Chicago's West Side. Longtime residents and the leader of a defunct neighborhood group responded to a local Realtor's comments denouncing legislation proposed to prohibit racial discrimination in housing sales. Several letter writers, supporting the Realtor's position, claimed that evidence from the Chicago metropolitan area clearly demonstrated that whites and African Americans could not live alongside one another. A "40-Year Resident" wrote that whites who tried to remain in neighborhoods recently occupied by African Americans "were harassed, abused, beaten and forced to leave the neighborhood in which they had hoped to remain." A woman who lived in Chicago for forty-one and a half years added, "An old saying has it that 'no roof is big enough to house two women,' but then it could also be said that no neighborhood is big enough to contain two races of people either!" A few residents argued that sustained integration was a real possibility. Mrs. Stanley Plona rebutted, "I have lived over half my life in an integrated community and I can attest to the fact that not only can two races live together but they can do so in peace and harmony. The only prerequisite is their mutual concern for each other and for the neighborhood in which they live."[1]

Perhaps the most poignant comments came from "Homeowner," who had recently moved from West Garfield Park into Austin. "Homeowner" recalled the activities of a neighborhood organization to which he once belonged: "We considered ourselves a tightly-knit group. The children even put on a play if I remember rightly. And then it went to waste. Our block clubs couldn't stop us. We ran. I've never seen any of them since. Why did we do it? I really don't know. Perhaps it was all a dream, a nightmare. But the more I think about it, the more I have to admit that what seemed to be undying loyalty to one another was a farce." "Homeowner" questioned what the *Garfieldian*'s other correspondents meant by "integration": "From your words, one can only conclude that for you it is the time between when the first Negro family moves in and the last white family moves out. This, sir, is a modified form of run-rabbit-run."[2]

"Homeowner" further challenged the perception, common among whites, that the presence of African Americans inevitably caused neighborhoods to deteriorate. Instead, he suggested, whites neglected those areas into which blacks might move. He recalled, "I traveled through the block during the last stages of 'integration.' I was selling tickets for a raffle. I rang the bell of every person, somehow hoping that a traitor wouldn't be looked down upon. I wasn't beat or robbed sir! I was accepted warmly by a people who had every right to spit in my face. These people were cleaning their homes, after my kind had allowed them to grow filthy in the months before the planned exodus. In the years before, a steady accumulation of garbage had piled up in our alleys. We were ready to move and we didn't care. Tell me again, who is it that makes slums?"[3] If whites' slovenliness was to blame for local decay, then perhaps racial integration might not be so threatening.

This bitter exchange occurred as the Austin neighborhood was in the midst of a transformation from largely white residency to African American. As "Homeowner's" mobility suggested, Austin was not the first neighborhood on Chicago's West Side to experience this change. During and after World War II, in a revival of the Great Migration, tens of thousands of African Americans left the rural South and headed for urban centers in the North and West.[4] Many of those who migrated to Chicago found their way to the city's West Side. North Lawndale, the point of entry for many migrants, became home to large numbers of African Americans as early as the mid-1940s. Starting in 1959, African Americans found housing in West Garfield Park, directly to the north of North Lawndale. In 1963 African Americans began to move into the southeastern portions of Austin, which was just west of West Garfield Park. Together with sections of East Garfield Park and the Near West Side, where many African Americans also live, particularly in public housing, these neighborhoods are called the "West Side" in common Chicago parlance.

In the last quarter of the twentieth century, the black West Side was notorious as one of the worst parts of the city, a living embodiment of the urban crisis. Despite the efforts of a few vibrant community development organizations, most notably West Garfield Park's Bethel New Life, the residents were poor, the housing stock and infrastructure decayed, and the streets crime-ridden. In 1986 the staff of the *Chicago Tribune* published *The American Millstone*, a collection of articles that held up North Lawndale as a symbol of all that was wrong with urban America and the "permanent underclass": crime, violence, drugs, single motherhood, infant mortality, chronic unemployment, and welfare dependency.[5] When social scientists wished to demonstrate the devastating effects of racial segregation and economic inequality in America, they visited the West Side.[6] Even African Americans from the South Side, the older area of black settlement in Chicago, shunned the West Side. A 1990 study by the *Chicago Reporter* found that black South Siders regarded "their western counterparts [as] country ruffians with little class or ambition."[7]

In the years since African Americans moved into once all-white neighborhoods like those on the West Side of Chicago, historians have studied this transformation. Why did white Americans, around the nation, leave familiar neighborhoods—often at a financial loss—when African Americans moved into them? Historians have examined how religion and racism informed whites' decisions to leave or remain. Other scholars have documented the shame and bitterness whites felt about their departures. Despite the variations among local transformations, the ubiquity of the white suburban migration across the nation prompted urban historian Jon Teaford to characterize the postwar period as one of crisis in the cities and triumph in the suburbs.[8]

In popular culture, the decisions of whites to leave neighborhoods with increasing African American populations seem ordinary and inevitable, not a puzzle to be scrutinized. Teachers of urban history know that many students feel the phenomenon needs little explanation. Former residents of Chicago's South Side, interviewed by writer Louis Rosen in the 1990s, recollected their departures with images of natural disasters, actions as sensible—and as terrifying—as running away from lava flowing out of an active volcano. Observers frequently use the term "white flight" as shorthand for the retreat of whites from city neighborhoods to suburban havens. As Gerald Gamm notes, the phrase "simultaneously names and presumes to solve the riddle of the urban exodus."[9] Discussions of "white flight" are often coupled with reference to the rioting of urban African Americans that made the mid-1960s seem like a never-ending "long, hot summer." Whites left "changing" neighborhoods, so the explanation goes, to avoid the dangers presented by unruly young African Americans, and they took legitimate commercial enterprises with them. Mention of the 1960s riots functions as a shorthand explanation for the subsequent economic devastation of black neighborhoods like those on Chicago's West Side.[10]

The phrase "white flight" appeals to many ears, both popular and scholarly.[11] This pair of rhyming words, which the *Oxford English Dictionary* dates to 1967, does reflect the speed with which whites tended to abandon a residential block once African Americans moved onto it.[12] One witness to the process of racial change in Chicago observed, "The pattern moves much too swiftly to permit the 10-year census reports to detail the changes." The decennial census, although inadequate to track velocity or minute details, captured the thoroughness of whites' departures—many previously all-white areas on both the South and West sides of Chicago became all-black between the 1950, 1960, and 1970 enumerations. The Real Estate Research Corporation, a leading investigator of Chicago's housing market, calculated the extent of racial change by dispatching observers to make annual visual inspections of each block in the city. A July 1962 article in the *Saturday Evening Post* estimated that every week two or three blocks in Chicago changed from white to black occupancy.[13]

This book argues, however, that to summarize the behavior of white West Siders as "white flight" is to narrow the breadth of their struggles to preserve their neighborhoods. Describing whites' relationship to the city by examining only the moments of their leaving neglects their multiple sources of discontent with the postwar urban environment. In the years preceding African American settlement in their neighborhoods, whites offered a variety of responses to long-standing problems they perceived in their physical surroundings. When African Americans arrived in their immediate locale, West Siders also worked to try to keep them out. On some occasions, African Americans tried to move into the neighborhood in the midst of ongoing campaigns to improve the area's infrastructure; in such cases, white activists added to their list of the effort's potential benefits the deterrence of further black settlement. Rhetoric against the "blighting" of their neighborhoods by deteriorating housing, schools, and parks became suffused with racist assumptions about the effects of African Americans on their surroundings. When African Americans continued to arrive, whites finally departed, one block at a time. White West Siders' ultimate "flight" to suburbs was in fact only the capstone to a series of responses to transformations in Chicago's physical and social landscape.[14]

In the immediate postwar years, white West Siders were deeply concerned by fractures in the area's physical infrastructure, which was starting to show ominous signs of age and neglect. Before the movement of African Americans into white neighborhoods seemed likely—and even as their advent loomed—white West Siders poured considerable energies into the preservation and improvement of the local landscape. Almost invariably, though, their efforts to confront these tenacious physical problems were thwarted. Both the priorities of Mayor Richard J. Daley's Democratic machine and the mechanisms for implementing public policy in Chicago reinforced old grievances about the West Side's political insignificance. By the time white West Siders had to decide whether to remain in homes next door to black neighbors, they had already spent many years losing battles to shore up their deteriorating environs.

But even when African Americans did move into their neighborhoods, white West Siders did not immediately flee. Instead, their initial response to black in-migration was to defend their community's racial homogeneity. Their tactics ranged among mob violence, organized but peaceful resistance, hostility to individual African Americans, and appeals to other white residents to remain in the area. Some whites, like two of the correspondents in the *Garfieldian* colloquy, held out hope that their neighborhood might provide a model of integration for the rest of the nation's benefit. Others rioted, threatening physically the properties to which blacks dared aspire. Still others, who shared with the rioters the sense that African Americans should not be allowed into the neighborhood but found physical violence a repugnant tactic, organized hostile community groups instead. Both neighborhoods that white West Siders "defended," as well as those that they left "undefended," ultimately changed from white to black.[15]

Religious demographics explain some of the local experience of racial change on the West Side, but religion cannot account for its ultimate transformation. In a pattern noticed around the nation, a Jewish area, North Lawndale, served as the easiest point of entry for African American migrants. Rather than next moving southward into South Lawndale, a neighborhood dominated by working-class Polish and Bohemian Catholics, African Americans headed north into West Garfield Park and Austin.[16] In these neighborhoods, occupied by a mix of Protestants and Catholics, blacks met more formal and organized resistance to their presence than they experienced in North Lawndale. But almost all white residents of these areas also moved away eventually, despite having to leave their religious institutions behind them.

West Siders monitored the racial composition of their neighborhoods, but most tended not to move until there were African Americans living on their immediate block. As Arnold Hirsch notes in other Chicago neighbor-hoods, "Although there were widely shared assumptions regarding the undesirability of racial change, the various neighborhoods responded to it independently, reacting only as it actually touched them. The housing bat-tles, the struggles over 'turf,' were local by nature." They might have antic-ipated moving when African Americans reached the block where they lived, but West Siders rarely left before this eventuality came to pass. The racial transformation of urban neighborhoods might seem swift and inevitable in retrospect, but on the ground it was a slow and sometimes agonizing process.[17]

The various postwar activities of white West Siders, therefore, repre-sent not "white flight," but a futile struggle against a series of urban crises. Whites in Chicago, of course, were not the only people who experienced the postwar years as a time of urban crisis. Thomas Sugrue examined the experiences of African Americans in Detroit. The elements of their crisis, "joblessness, concentrated poverty, physical decay, and racial isolation," culminating in the riots of the mid-1960s, resulted from racial discrimi-nation and deindustrialization.[18] White West Siders, for their part, paid little heed to the processes of deindustrialization occurring around them in Chicago, probably reasoning that they could follow employment oppor-tunities to the suburbs if they chose.[19] The urban crisis of the postwar years was not a monolith. The problems that plagued urban African American communities—deindustrialization, poverty, and poor city serv-ices—were not the troubles that alarmed whites and to which they responded. This book reconstructs the failed efforts of white West Siders to address the nuisances that they perceived. For whites on Chicago's West Side, the urban crisis consisted of the twin threats of environmental decay and racial succession.[20]

West Siders hoped to fend off these threats, bringing both informal means and public policy mechanisms to bear on their problems. In order to achieve their goals, as well as to bring their neighbors into their efforts, they often coalesced into community-based organizations. Some of these groups, most notably the Organization for a Better Austin, followed the pre-cepts of Saul Alinsky, the legendary father of community organizing in the United States. Alinsky, who organized the Back of the Yards Neighborhood Council and The Woodlawn Organization in Chicago, called for ordinary people to use confrontational tactics and raw power politics. Other groups rejected Alinsky's abrasive style but nonetheless sought collective action.[21]

Not all West Siders, of course, participated in such organizations.[22] Many quietly watched the transformations around them, discussed their dismay with family members at the kitchen table, and left without consulting anyone else. Others, however, like the disillusioned "Homeowner," made common cause with their neighbors. Often it was men who provided the public face of such organizations. In the 1950s only a few women— well-educated liberals, for the most part—took leadership roles in such groups, where they often clashed with more conservative male officers. Increasingly in the 1960s, however, women founded and led organizations themselves, focusing especially on schools and real estate practices. For some women, this step onto a public stage was only a temporary departure from their attention to domestic responsibilities. For at least one— Gale Cincotta, who gained national prominence in the 1970s—local organizing was the start of a lifelong career as an activist.[23] White women activists were not bound by shared racial ideologies. They worked both sides of pressing debates and often clashed with one another. Some sought to accommodate their communities to limited numbers of African Americans, while others energetically tried to protect the racial homogeneity of their neighborhoods.

But in the end, this is a story about loss. White West Side groups won many small victories, but none of their campaigns fundamentally altered the underlying conditions that concerned them. White West Siders were potential beneficiaries of some of the laws that enabled residents of other neighborhoods to shape their futures. Yet careful examination of "the crucial process of policy implementation"[24] reveals the degree to which they were marginal to Chicago politics. In the case of plans for physical redevelopment—urban renewal and the University of Illinois campus—white West Siders persuaded officials that their area should be included in improvement plans. Formal recognition of the legitimacy of their claims, however, was rarely accompanied by actual realization. In the arenas of social policy—schools and housing—white West Siders also enjoyed enough rapport with city bureaucrats to influence minor features of public administration. Especially during the 1950s, white parents often convinced school administrators to set school boundaries that kept white children in racially homogenous schools; the consequence of their success was terrific overcrowding in the classrooms that served African American children. In the case of housing, whites tried to use a law intended to protect African Americans against discrimination in Chicago. But in neither arena did white West Siders successfully stymie the block-by-block pattern of racial change. Just as the federal Voting Rights Act and Civil Rights Act failed to end racial discrimination, neither did the passage of city ordinances guarantee their implementation to the liking of all local residents.[25] The difficulty that white West Siders had bending complex and confusing local governments to their will points to one of the sources of further deterioration in these neighborhoods when they were occupied primarily by poor, politically disconnected, recent African American migrants.

White West Siders' inability to manipulate public policy in their favor reveals both the enormous reach and the subtle limits of the power of Chicago's legendary mayor, Richard J. Daley. During his reign, Daley enjoyed popular acclaim as the uncontested political power in the city and, nationally, as a "kingmaker" in the 1960 presidential election. Recent scholarship has characterized Daley as an "American Pharaoh" who wielded "absolute power." Arnold Hirsch, however, found that Daley's major role in the infamous segregation of Chicago's public housing was as a caretaker rather than a creator.[26] As mayor, Daley had an absolute negative power, the capacity to veto any proposal that did not comport with his vision for the city's future. But Daley's positive powers were tempered. The mayor could not simply do anything he cared to; rather, he had to pick pragmatic courses of action.

In the absence of direct evidence, it is difficult to discern why Daley chose not to channel available resources to white West Side neighborhoods. Daley was a master of evasion who provided few advance clues to constituents whom he planned to disappoint.[27] The partial victories Daley allowed West Siders hinted that he was not unalterably opposed to their claims. But several conditions suggested that he had little intention of allocating scarce resources to the West Side. Daley's vision for renewing the city derived from architect Daniel Burnham's 1909 *Plan of Chicago*. The plan, which envisioned the entire region, imagined a downtown rebuilt on a grand scale. In 1910 the Chicago City Council adopted Burnham's plan as its own. Daley reportedly viewed the schoolchildren's textbook based on the Burnham Plan, *Wacker's Manual of Chicago*, as the best book he ever read. When Daley took the reins of the city that Burnham had proposed to redesign, he undertook to address pieces of "the tedious but essential business of the cost of carrying out [the] plan and of how it could be met."[28] Over the course of his two decades as mayor, Daley's choices demonstrated that his ambition was to rebuild as much of Chicago as he could. Rehabilitating and repairing deteriorating residential neighborhoods were less important to his goals.

Given that city and federal funds for redevelopment were finite, West Side neighborhoods, far removed from the downtown, could not have been Daley's highest priority. In addition, the South Side neighborhood of Bridgeport, where Richard J. Daley lived his entire life, probably also claimed more of his attention than the West Side. Finally, Daley was surely aware of the growing population of African Americans in Chicago whom neither the new public housing supply nor the existing South Side Black

Belt could accommodate. Black migration into the West Side's North Lawndale neighborhood was already under way when Daley became mayor in 1955. Rather than encourage African Americans to increase their pressure on the South Side neighborhoods around Bridgeport, Daley probably concluded that the West Side's plentiful supply of private housing could serve as an outlet for the second Great Migration. Had infinite monies been available to answer the demands of his white West Side constituents, no doubt the master politician would have included the area in his largesse. But short of such a marvel, and in light of Lawndale's function as a safety valve for the city's black migrants, white West Siders' requests for the means to preserve and rehabilitate their neighborhoods went unheeded.

The West Side that African Americans inherited, therefore, was shaped by several distinctive sources. The physical quality of the neighborhoods stemmed from the untreated deterioration of the early postwar years, a neglect sustained into the initial period of African American occupancy, as "Homeowner" observed. In contrast to Brownsville, Brooklyn, where a shabby housing stock built on the cheap served several successive generations,[29] the decayed state of Chicago's West Side was a relatively recent development. The deterioration nonetheless preceded the arrival of African Americans. Policies to improve the West Side's condition existed but were not employed, even while whites still occupied the area. For its part, the continuing racial segregation of the West Side resulted from the almost universal unwillingness of whites to live among large numbers of African Americans. Some white West Siders expressed willingness to live in neighborhoods that might be "integrated"—the meaning of which was ambiguous—but proved reluctant to become racial minorities themselves. As whites moved out, the West Side became once again as racially segregated as it had been before African Americans arrived. This ghetto[30] was not the result of active efforts to create it, as was the "second ghetto" of public housing described by Arnold Hirsch.[31] The West Side ghetto born after World War II was the product of the neighborhood's exclusion from postwar urban redevelopment, the political powerlessness of preceding white residents, and their racism.

Embedded in my attention to the efforts of white West Siders to combat their version of the urban crisis is an effort to attend to the specific local contours of racism. I hope, as George Fredrickson has written, "to understand this malignancy so that it can be more effectively treated, just as a medical researcher studying cancer does not moralize about it but searches for knowledge that might point the way to a cure." Actions that look quite distinct at a given moment can stem from the same motives, while similar actions can carry different connotations in different periods.

For example, as Gerald Gamm observes about Boston, the impulse to leave a neighborhood and to defend it are both racist responses to African American migration.[32] On the other hand, the racial significance of housing-code enforcement varies across time. In the 1950s, in the context of a narrow housing market for African Americans, the failure to enforce the housing code in black Chicago neighborhoods resulted in hundreds of fire deaths. In the twenty-first century, by contrast, in the context of gentrification, municipalities use their housing codes as a pretext for evicting poor people and people of color from lucrative real estate.[33]

Racism, like sexism, is a shape-shifter, a malleable and elusive monster that plagues American society under different guises at different times.[34] In this case, racism was a parasite, latching on to relatively benign visions for the city's future improvement. White West Siders rarely articulated their antipathy to African Americans in public forums,[35] but their deeds indicated the depth of their feelings. The racism of white West Siders was palpable to African Americans considering living there, but it manifested differently from other historical forms of American racism. The stings of "microinsults" that African Americans experience regularly in the twenty-first century are not identical with the lashes of nineteenth-century slave owners; both had the capacity to traumatize, but they are distinct historical phenomena.[36]

A word about the structure of the book is in order. After an initial chapter describing the nineteenth-century origins of the West Side neighborhoods, each subsequent chapter takes up an arena of public policy in which white West Siders sought to achieve their ends. Although the action in some of the chapters overlaps, the order is roughly chronological, following the basic order in which West Siders took up distinct causes. The book focuses initially on West Siders' efforts to control the physical environment, campaigns that occurred primarily in the 1950s. Like other Chicagoans in that decade, West Siders urged the use of the city's new housing code to improve their neighborhood. At approximately the same time, following the lead of the Hyde Park neighborhood, they sought urban renewal for the West Side. Realizing they had little hope of attracting the sort of funds that the University of Chicago could marshal, organizations in West Garfield Park and Austin sought to bring a new campus of the University of Illinois into their community. As whites were trying—but failing—to improve the area's physical environment, African Americans began arriving and making use of local public facilities. White West Siders turned a portion of their attention to policing the boundaries of the public schools, trying to sustain their threatened racial homogeneity. Finally, the last three chapters of the book examine how white residents of West Side neighborhoods responded to African American immigration. Some West Siders attacked black settlers and others welcomed them, while also encouraging their incumbent white neighbors to stay. West Side neighborhoods ultimately changed from white to black not because residents failed to defend them, but because they were politically impotent—white West Siders could not implement the kinds of neighborhood defenses they hoped to. White West Siders gave up their neighborhoods to escape African Americans, but they left the city, for suburban havens, to escape their powerlessness.

CHAPTER 1

Chicago's West Side

In March 1950 residents, businessmen, and activists from the Lawndale and Crawford neighborhoods gathered at the Chicago City Council for a hearing on the proposed construction of public housing apartments on Kildare Avenue between Seventeenth and Nineteenth streets. The audience "heartily applauded speakers" testifying in opposition to the project. Like whites in other parts of Chicago, they were hostile to the prospect of public housing residents moving into the neighborhood. In this case, they articulated their objections by arguing that the public housing site was long designated for a park. Dr. Andrew Toman, son of the area's late alderman, testified that the health of children who lived in crowded neighborhoods required the provision of public play areas. The incumbent alderman pointed out that his ward housed forty thousand children who were currently served by only one small park. In addition, real estate professionals objected that the site, an excavated clay pit, was too unstable to support residential construction. A banker claimed that he would refuse to finance mortgages for any private housing on the site. He concluded, "Lawndale-Crawford has long been the step-child of the city of Chicago, and it's about time that the other aldermen in the city council give our local alderman a little support in the betterment of the community."[1]

Other midcentury white West Siders shared this sense of beleaguerment, from time to time bemoaning the area's role as "the city's step-child."[2] The West Side was surely part of Chicago, but it rarely received the kind of attention—positive or negative—that might have inspired residents to feel the city government regarded their future as critical.[3] Founded primarily as residential and industrial suburbs, the West Side neighborhoods were annexed into Chicago proper over the course of the nineteenth century. West Side residents received city services and paid city taxes, but rarely exercised a proportional share of political power. The West Side's long-standing lack of influence in Chicago affairs laid the foundation for area residents' relative powerlessness in the postwar period. When they mobilized to confront impending decay and the in-migration of African Americans, they had few historical precedents to suggest that they would achieve their goals. But, at the same time, the relative stability and modest prosperity of the neighborhoods gave little hint that by the last decades of the twentieth century, the West Side would be notorious as one of the most devastated African American urban centers in the United States.[4]

The neighborhoods on the West Side of Chicago were neither the best nor the worst in the city. For Russian Jews, North Lawndale was a symbol of upward mobility, of escape from the teeming slums of the Near West Side. For other Chicagoans, the prime appeal of neighborhoods like North Lawndale and West Garfield Park was their proximity to blue-collar industrial jobs. For the most part, West Side neighborhoods remained outside the attention of other Chicagoans. They lacked the glamour of the emerging centers of commerce and wealth on the city's Near North Side and sections of the South Side. They were neither as lurid as the city's notorious vice district, the Levee, nor as promising as the lakefront park system planned by architect Daniel Burnham. In the twentieth century, Bridgeport, a South Side Irish neighborhood in many ways comparable to the West Side areas, became home to a multigenerational political dynasty that dominated the Democratic Party and Chicago politics. While a few West Side natives played prominent roles in the city's political machinations, their influence did little to enhance the West Side's prestige or condition.

Chicago in the Nineteenth Century

Chicago's West Side neighborhoods were settled in the middle period of the city's development. The city's original center, just north and south of the main branch of the Chicago River, remained the major focus of land use and speculation for decades after its foundation in the 1830s. Chicago initially grew northward and southward, with just a little additional settlement immediately to the west of the river's branches. Only after the Great Fire of 1871 did Chicagoans cast their eyes westward; the West Side neighborhoods of North Lawndale, West Garfield Park, and Austin filled with buildings and people between 1880 and 1920. After World War II, undeveloped areas within Chicago's boundaries, on the Northwest and Southwest sides, were built up with new housing. The desirability of West Side areas, which once seemed a haven of quietude and modest opportunity, waned by comparison.

Chicago's history as a settled area dates to the arrival of Jean Baptiste Point du Sable, a black fur trader of French Canadian and Haitian descent, who lived at the mouth of the Chicago River between the 1770s and 1800. The Potawatomi who occupied northern Illinois regarded the Chicago area as suitable for passage and temporary stays, but too swampy to settle permanently. In 1673 French explorers Jacques Marquette and Louis Joliet recognized Chicago's potential as a commercial hub for North America, envisioning the excavation of a portage between the Chicago and Des Plaines rivers that would enable continuous water transport between the St. Lawrence and Mississippi rivers. In 1803 the young United States government established Fort Dearborn to protect the land around the Chicago River ceded in the 1795 Treaty of Greenville, but the military abandoned it during the War of 1812. Rowdy settlers and traders returned to the area permanently in the 1820s.[5]

The town of Chicago was incorporated in 1833, after the Potawatomis' defeat in the Black Hawk War sealed their departure to areas west of the Mississippi River. With the arrival of the city's first permanent white residents, Chicago's future as a center of commerce manifested immediately. The city's first mayor, William B. Ogden, regarded his family's investment in Chicago land as a mistake until he realized how profitably he could resell the property. The tribulations of land speculation drove Chicago's economy for the first decade after it became a city in 1837, as investors anticipated the completion of the Illinois and Michigan Canal. Irish immigrants who went to Chicago to build the canal settled at its eastern terminus, in the area that became the Bridgeport neighborhood. Native-born migrants from New England and Ohio comprised the balance of Chicago's burgeoning early population.

The arrival of the railroads in 1848, the same year the canal opened, transformed Chicago into the hub of transcontinental transport. Both eastern and western railroad lines terminated in Chicago, making it the nation's most significant transfer point for goods being sold cross-country. Chicago became a center not only of transport, but also of local production and new forms of financial speculation. As historian William Cronon has detailed, Chicago's trade in grain, lumber, and meat drawn from the city's hinterland made traffic in commodities more important to the city's economy than the thriving real estate market. The construction of enormous grain elevators between the Chicago River's branches and the railroads made possible the sale of huge volumes of western corn and wheat to the East Coast and also inspired the sale of commodities futures in Chicago. Dealers sold the rich forests of Wisconsin and Michigan from acres of lumber yards along the south branch of the Chicago River, enabling the construction of wooden structures throughout the North American plains. Finally, the invention of the refrigerated railroad car allowed the transportation of slaughtered meat across great distances. In response, in 1865 Chicago's meatpackers established the Union Stock Yards south of the city limits. This area, which exported more meat throughout the United States than any other place, was annexed into the city in 1889. Manufacturers also began to locate in Chicago; Cyrus McCormick, inventor of the reaper, built a factory for his machines just north of the main branch of the Chicago River.[6]

People poured into Chicago in the mid-nineteenth century to try their hands at the city's new enterprises. Although migrants clustered by ethnicity, few lived in complete isolation from people of different origins. Chicago's small African American population, which was not segregated until the Great Migration of the World War I era, scattered into pockets on the South, North, and West sides of the city. German immigrants headed to the North Side, where they built small homes and businesses. Irish immigrants mostly settled on the South Side but also established "Patches" on the city's North and West sides. Chicago's elite, who owned the real estate and ran the companies of the city's capitalist engines, built fashionable homes on the South Side, on the 2200 blocks of Indiana, Prairie, Calumet, and South Park avenues.[7] A few of the rich also ventured west across the Chicago River toward Union Park. By the time of the Great Fire of 1871, Chicago was considerably built up and densely populated to the north and the south. Chicagoans of different classes had begun to discover the possibilities of investing in the Far West Side neighborhoods but had yet only sparsely settled it.

The Neighborhoods

In American cities, geographical designations mean different things to different people. In the late twentieth century, the "West Side" colloquially referred to those areas west of Chicago's downtown that were occupied by African Americans. For clarity, the areas that were immediately adjacent to the downtown were sometimes called the "Near West Side," and the neighborhoods of West Garfield Park and Austin, farther from the Loop, were sometimes collectively called the "Far West Side." North Lawndale, West Garfield Park, and Austin correspond to "community areas" within

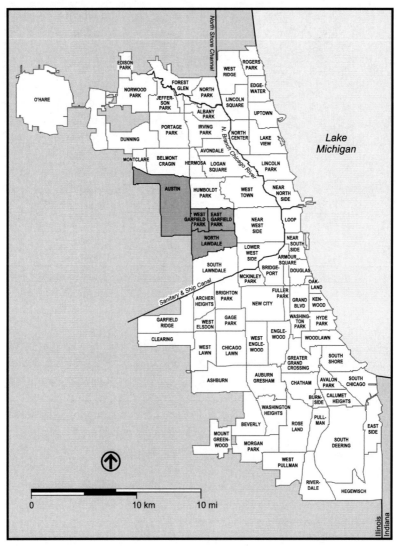

Fig. 1. Chicago community areas. Produced by the University of Wisconsin–Milwaukee, Cartography & GIS Center.

the West Side. Sociologists based at the University of Chicago drew the boundaries of the community areas in the 1920s. They were trying to create a map with permanent borders, in order to facilitate the study of populations and neighborhood characteristics across time. Members of the Chicago school of sociology understood cities to consist of "natural areas," whose overall character and class composition remained stable, even as

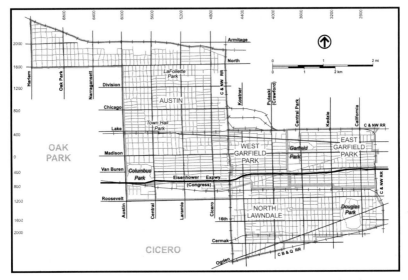

Fig. 2. West Side community areas. Produced by the University of Wisconsin–Milwaukee, Cartography & GIS Center.

their particular racial and ethnic populations changed. To demarcate boundaries, the sociologists and their staff interviewed venerable residents, researched local history, and observed phenomena such as railroad tracks that served as "natural" boundaries. In some cases, such as West Garfield Park, the delineated community areas corresponded fairly well to local conceptions. Other names, such as "New City," seemed more capricious. Despite the inadequacies of the community-area approach, much of the scholarship produced in subsequent years observed the general outlines demarcated in the early twentieth century. Statistical data are usually presented by community area, and many Chicago-area archives organize their collections under these headings. For the postwar period, the community-area names "North Lawndale," "West Garfield Park," and "Austin" reflected a general consensus on the ground.[8]

The three neighborhoods at the heart of the West Side—North Lawndale, West Garfield Park, and Austin—emerged as separate communities. Their populations were distinct; they became part of Chicago at different times; and their infrastructures connected up with one another only after their development was well under way. North Lawndale, which in the postwar years became the point of entry for African Americans migrating from the South, was one of two main centers of Jewish life in Chicago in the early twentieth century. West Garfield Park, a small self-contained neighborhood, was the site of the West Side's most prominent commercial district, which centered on the intersection of Madison and Crawford (Pulaski). Served by a few large Catholic parishes from early in its history, West Garfield Park remained a majority Catholic community after World War II. Austin, the largest of the three areas, marked the western edge of the city and housed more than 100,000 people. Austin's nineteenth-century residents established a wealth of Protestant churches; with the arrival of more working-class residents in the early twentieth century, Catholics became the most populous religious group in the area. By the 1920s these three distinctive neighborhoods had grown together into the West Side.[9]

North Lawndale

North Lawndale was founded as a suburb of Chicago. Within a few years of the appearance of the first clustered settlement, several roughly simultaneous developments made the area urban in legal fact, while the neighborhood's character remained "semi-suburban" until the twentieth century. First, the portion of North Lawndale east of modern-day Pulaski Road was annexed into Chicago in 1869, well before it was built up or had much population. Second, the purchase of land in the eastern portion of North Lawndale for the development of the West Side park system, including Douglas Park, spurred speculative interest in the area. Finally, the devastation of the Great Chicago Fire of 1871 drove the city's population and industrial concerns outward in search of new locations for settlement.[10]

The community areas later known as North Lawndale and South Lawndale grew out of two suburban developments. The first was Lawndale, a speculative subdivision built by A. C. Millard and E. J. Decker and reportedly named by Decker's daughter. In 1871 Millard and Decker platted the Lawndale subdivision, bounded on the east and west by Homan and Hamlin, and on the north and south by Twenty-second and Twenty-sixth. By 1873 several dozen houses dotted the area. Millard Avenue functioned as the subdivision's main street, containing several stores, a four-story hotel, and the area's first church. Residents founded a variety of community institutions, including one of the earliest Women's Clubs in the city.[11]

The second original subdivision within North Lawndale was Crawford, an area named for one of the first farmers to own large tracts of local land. In 1848 Peter Crawford, a Scottish immigrant, purchased 160 acres of land bounded by what later became Crawford, Kostner, Cermak, and Twenty-sixth streets. Crawford encouraged service from the Burlington Railroad by providing a strip of land for a depot in 1863 and donated land for the area's first school, the Crawford Academy. The development of the area accelerated after 1880, when the Crawford family sold off parcels of their property for small farms, which were further subdivided and resold.

Chicago's annexation of the Crawford area in 1889 brought the remainder of the North Lawndale community area into the city.[12]

Both Lawndale and Crawford lay at the southern edge of the area that later became the heart of North Lawndale. In the initial stages of their development, they were largely isolated from one another. An early resident remembered, "Lawndale and Crawford, in the old days, were absolutely separate communities. The folks here now can't appreciate it. There was a little group in Crawford and a larger one in Lawndale and a sidewalk in between." He described the layout of the settlements: "In the olden days, Crawford and Lawndale might have been likened in area to a dumbbell—I am not referring to the quality of the people but to the shape of the area." As more people came to the area in search of industrial jobs, the space between the two villages closed, causing them to "gr[o]w together."[13]

Lawndale's industrial work opportunities increased dramatically after the Great Chicago Fire of 1871, which devastated the city's downtown and North Side. The McCormick Reaper Company, whose original factory was destroyed in the fire, relocated to Twenty-seventh and Western; the placement of this new factory, technically within the Lower West Side community area, encouraged the migration of employees into the neighboring Lawndale area. Company executives later moved into Lawndale. Both North and South Lawndale, surrounded by railroads and their service yards and dotted with large swathes of property covered by industrial concerns, became centers of manufacturing activity. Living in the area saved workers the expense of commuting and facilitated job changes. Chicagoans of German and Irish extraction predominated among the area's new residents, occupying two-flat buildings; Polish and Czech migrants joined them later in the nineteenth century. The opening of the Western Electric plant in the neighboring suburb of Cicero in 1903 also stimulated migration to North Lawndale.[14]

In 1906 Sears, Roebuck and Company opened a national headquarters building—four city blocks long, occupying forty acres—along the northern border of Lawndale. The enormous complex, which was financed by the first public offering of Sears stock, cost $5.6 million. The new headquarters consolidated Sears' sprawling and complicated mail-order operations into a single location, enabling precision control over inventory and shipping. In addition to executive offices and large rooms where clerks processed mail orders pouring into the company in the early twentieth century, the North Lawndale Sears plant housed elaborate mechanisms that delivered a customer's diverse goods to a single point for simultaneous shipment. According to a description from the 1905 catalog, the plant's engineering included "miles of railroad tracks ... elevators, mechanical conveyors, endless chains, moving sidewalks, gravity cuts, apparatus and conveyors, pneumatic tubes and every known mechanical appliance for reducing labor." Eight thousand people staffed the West Side plant when it opened. To serve the needs of its North Lawndale employees, the Sears complex included medical facilities, a branch of the public library, a YMCA, and five restaurants. In 1925, under the leadership of General Robert E. Wood, Sears expanded its business into retail stores; one of its first experimental stores opened in the tower section of the headquarters building in North Lawndale.[15]

Both Sears' Homan Avenue complex and the construction of the Garfield Park Elevated line prompted settlement in the northern part of North Lawndale. In the second decade of the twentieth century, North Lawndale's population was dramatically increased by an influx of Russian Jews who headed westward from the Near West Side along Roosevelt Road. Their aspirations for upward mobility prompted some who remained on the Near West Side to mock North Lawndale as "Deutschland," a reference to the disparities in class status and religious orthodoxy between German and Russian Jews in Chicago. The construction of large apartment buildings, each accommodating ten to twenty households, also helped to shift Lawndale's center of gravity northward. North Lawndale's population ballooned, rising from 46,000 in 1910 to more than 112,000 in 1930. A student of North Lawndale estimated that in 1930, 75,000 of the area's residents were Jewish. North Lawndale in the interwar years was home to some of the city's most important Jewish cultural institutions. Numerous synagogues appeared along Douglas and Independence boulevards, while North Lawndale's residents patronized the Jewish People's Institute, the Hebrew Theological College, and Theodore Herzl Junior College.[16]

Jewish North Lawndale was densely populated and in relatively poor condition. Compared to other Chicago neighborhoods, including the adjacent West Garfield Park and South Lawndale, North Lawndale was not "above average in percentage of structures in better condition" at midcentury. The character of the housing allowed many people to crowd into the area. There were more two-flats than any other type of structure among North Lawndale's housing stock, but 14 percent of the area's residential structures were apartment buildings with between five and forty units each. Many of the residential buildings in North Lawndale were constructed between 1895 and 1914, but more than fifteen hundred still occupied in 1942 were built before 1895. The 1942 *Report of the Chicago Land Use Survey* found that two-thirds of the residential structures in North Lawndale needed minor repairs, while about one-quarter were in good condition. Property owners made some improvements after World War II. In 1950,

84.1 percent of the dwelling units in North Lawndale were in good condition, being neither dilapidated nor lacking toilets and hot and cold running water. Also, 84.1 percent of the dwelling units were not overcrowded (more than one person per room); ominously, however, only 63.6 percent of the units occupied by the area's growing African American population met that criterion. By 1960, while the percentage of substandard housing units remained about the same, 35 percent of homes in the entire community area were overcrowded, reflecting the efforts of large numbers of African Americans to squeeze into a fixed housing stock.[17]

West Garfield Park

Travelers passed through the prairie that became the West Garfield Park neighborhood for years before stopping to settle the area. Before the Civil War, stagecoaches drove west along Elgin Road (Lake Street) and Colorado Avenue (Fifth Avenue), delivering people and mail. After the war, in 1869, although still sparsely populated, the area was part of a large annexation into Chicago. The same year, responding to appeals from East Garfield Park property owners, the state legislature authorized the creation of the West Chicago Park Commission. The Park Commission assembled the land for a trio of large parks connected by boulevards: Douglas Park, Central (later Garfield) Park, and Humboldt Park. The assembly of land for Central Park prompted wealthy property owners to invest in the property just to its east, leaving an unusual legacy of "beautiful stone and brick residences" in the otherwise working-class East Garfield Park community area.[18]

The park also elevated land values to its west, without attracting elite residences. George Smith, who owned 240 acres, held on to his land until 1872, when the West Chicago Land Company offered him a terrific profit. In 1873, when the Chicago and Northwestern Railroad purchased land around Kinzie and Keeler for its shops, West Garfield Park began to acquire its first substantial population. The new Northwestern shops employed fifteen hundred people in its first months; these workers and their families formed the nucleus of the Village of Central Park. Institutions to serve this settlement emerged quickly. The first school, named in honor of shops superintendent G. W. Tilton, was constructed in 1874. The building doubled as a community center and house of worship until churches and clubs constructed their own facilities, which Protestants and Catholics did in quick succession during the 1870s. Lake Street emerged as the village's business center.[19]

Owners of land immediately west of the new park also held on to it well after the creation of the park. In 1878 a swath of land owned by the family of Lambert Tree, a judge and arts patron, became the Chicago Gentlemen's

Trotting and Racing Club. In addition to providing space for exercising horses, the club hosted boxing matches and the Illinois State Fair. In 1888 one Ed Corrigan leased the trotting park and converted it into a racetrack, bringing gambling, saloons, and beer gardens to the area. In 1891 Corrigan decided to relocate his business outside city limits, building the Hawthorne Race Track in Stickney and surrendering his lease on the Garfield Park Race Track. Regarding his former business as a rival, Corrigan was rumored to have offered a $50,000 bribe to have the Garfield Park track shut down; in 1892 Chicago police raided the Garfield Park Race Track three times. Three people died in the shootout at the final raid, and the track closed permanently. For several years the site continued as a venue for less controversial entertainment, hosting Buffalo Bill's Wild West Show and reenactments of the siege of Vicksburg, the last days of Pompeii, and the fall of Sebastopol. In 1908 the land was subdivided and built up with private homes and public facilities, including the first regional branch of the city's public library system.[20]

With the depressing effects of the seedy racetrack alleviated, West Garfield Park began to develop as a desirable working- and middle-class residential community. The link to the downtown provided by the Elevated line, built in the 1890s, made it possible for Loop commuters to take easy trips home to West Garfield Park. Some new residents sought work in the industrial concerns that embraced the neighborhood, such as those on its border with North Lawndale. Other people came to the community by way of their professional organizations; a "policemen's syndicate" sold most of its holdings on Wilcox to police officers, creating "Uniform Row." The housing constructed for new residents consisted mostly of small multifamily buildings, such as two- and three-flats. Most of the early twentieth-century population was of Irish descent, although Germans also moved to the area. During the 1920s and the 1930s, Italians and Russian Jews settled in West Garfield Park. St. Mel's Parish, which in the 1940s claimed to be "the largest Catholic parish in the world," served the area's many Roman Catholics.[21]

At the heart of the new West Garfield Park area was the intersection of Madison and Crawford (Pulaski), a burgeoning commercial district. The intersection's first building, constructed in 1882, was a tavern. After the closing of the Garfield Park Race Track in 1892, the neighborhood's "carnival atmosphere" dissipated and a broader variety of commercial establishments congregated near the intersection. The character of local commerce climbed considerably between 1914 and 1929. Developers constructed hotels, ballrooms, and theaters in the district. The Midwest Athletic Club, an imposing twelve-story building faced with brick terra-cotta and granite, opened at Madison and Hamlin in 1928. Several department stores located around the intersection in the mid-twentieth century, including Madigan's and Baer Brothers & Prodie; a Goldblatt Brothers store joined them after World War II. The intersection also became one of the most important retail centers on the West Side, although the *Garfieldian* was disingenuous when, reporting the district's annual $20 million in retail sales, it commented, "The Madison-Crawford shopping center is often referred to as the most prominent corner in the city." The Garfield Park Club, a merchant's association founded in 1920, petitioned for local improvements such as street lighting and sidewalks.[22] Perhaps comprehending that West Garfield Park's recent ascent to prosperity was tenuous, the businessmen who invested in this intersection vigilantly defended it from perceived interlopers. In two major midcentury campaigns against the intrusion of representatives of ethnic minorities and the poor, they sought to protect the emergent middle-class consumer identity of the Madison-Crawford business district. Although West Garfield Park residents never made an explicit connection between these efforts and their later attempts to prevent African Americans from living in the neighborhood, they did provide local practice in political mobilization.

They lost the first battle, waged over the name of the north-south street bisecting the district. In the process of rationalizing Chicago's street names in 1913, the city council renamed Fortieth Street for Peter Crawford, one of the West Side's early landowners. In 1933, in an effort to shore up Polish American support for the Democratic coalition assembled by the assassinated mayor Anton Cermak, the newly elected mayor Edward J. Kelly offered to rename Crawford Avenue for the Revolutionary War hero General Casimir Pulaski.[23] The Garfield Park Businessmen's Association, the successor to the Garfield Park Club, led a host of other local civic and commercial groups in vociferous objection to the proposal. The merchants were careful not to say that they objected to the ethnic resonance of Pulaski's name, emphasizing instead the material costs of printing new stationery and signs, as well as the intangible value of the commercial center's identification as the Madison-Crawford district. They launched a legal and public relations campaign against the change. The fight wended its way through the Chicago and Illinois legislatures and courts until 1952, when the Illinois Supreme Court finally ruled in favor of Pulaski Road.[24]

The Crawford-Pulaski case folded the same year that merchants succeeded in driving an Illinois state unemployment office out of West Garfield Park. In June 1952 the *Garfieldian* targeted the office, located on Madison between Pulaski Road and the park, and quickly rallied neighborhood residents and merchants. As with the campaign against Pulaski Road, it is difficult to tell precisely how much of the hostility to the office was rooted in race. Objections frequently cited the behavior of the unemployed, who competed with paying customers for parking spaces and lined up in public view on the sidewalk outside the office to collect their compensation. The *Garfieldian* scorned the arrival of unemployment compensation recipients in brand-new "Buicks and Mercurys" and taxis and complained that they left Garfield Park strewn with litter, feces, and whiskey bottles. These behaviors might well have been ones that racist whites articulated in connection with the growing population of African Americans on the West Side. But a 1949 photograph of unemployed people showed mostly whites waiting in line, with only one African American in view. Perhaps an increase in black patronage of the unemployment office sparked the protest against its location in West Garfield Park. The *Garfieldian* also critiqued the high rent the state office paid for use of the storefront, suggesting that any merchant who paid so much would quickly go out of business. In February 1953 the state director of labor agreed to move the unemployment office out of West Garfield Park.[25]

At midcentury West Garfield Park was in slightly better condition than North Lawndale. Almost half of the residential structures in West Garfield Park were two-flats, homes with one apartment stacked atop the other. A mixture of single-family detached homes and large and small apartment buildings made up the balance. Most of these structures were built around the turn of the twentieth century. The 1942 *Chicago Land Use Survey* found that about one-third of the residential structures in West Garfield Park were in good physical condition, while slightly more than half were classified as "in need of minor repairs." Fewer than two hundred needed "major repairs," and only seven seemed "unfit for use." The 1950 census confirmed the *Land Use Survey*'s assessment of the general good quality of West Garfield Park's housing stock, finding that 89.4 percent of the area's dwelling units were not dilapidated and were served with adequate plumbing facilities. Similarly, 86.6 percent of dwelling units were not overcrowded.[26]

Austin

The Austin neighborhood was the most affluent and most populous of the white West Side community areas. Several different residential sections constituted distinct neighborhoods within Austin. The housing stock in Austin ranged from small frame homes to mansions on large lots to small apartment buildings. During the nineteenth century, there was little sustained industrial development in Austin, but this pattern changed in the twentieth century. Like Oak Park, its neighbor to the west, Austin was part of Cicero Township until the end of the nineteenth century. Austin residents took pride in the neighborhood's distinctive qualities, making it the most suburban part of the West Side.[27]

Austin's topography set it slightly apart from the rest of the metropolitan area. Elevated several feet above the land to its east, a north-south ridge served as a highway for Native Americans traveling through the area. As in many Chicago neighborhoods, the land passed through several hands before being developed. The federal government obtained the property from the local Native American people for canal development in 1816. On the removal of the Potawatomi to the west in 1835, Henry L. DeKoven purchased 280 acres for farming. During DeKoven's three decades on the land, local infrastructure development consisted primarily of transportation improvements. The 1842 grading of Pennsylvania Avenue, which later became Lake Street, provided east-west travelers a small measure of relief from the muddy trails. Both mail coaches and the Frink and Walker stagecoach traveled along Lake.[28]

Formal local government arrived in 1857, when fourteen voters elected ten of their number as officials of the new town of Cicero. In 1865 Henry W. Austin purchased Henry DeKoven's land for speculative development. To entice a clock company and railroad depot to the area, Henry Austin and another local property owner donated forty acres of land and platted the town of Austinville in 1866. The clock factory failed, as did a subsequent series of efforts to develop local industry; the building became a shoe factory, a tannery, a rolling mill, and finally a foundry before it burned down in 1868. Anticipating the growth of Chicago to the east, Cicero Township officially incorporated in 1867 and made Austin the seat of local government. Township officials located their town hall—a structure whose symbolic importance endured into the late twentieth century—in the public square in 1870. Residents founded an array of other institutions, including commercial enterprises, schools, and a plethora of Protestant and Catholic churches.[29]

Austin's population grew gradually over the next several decades, reaching several thousand by the turn of the twentieth century. Many early residents of Austin were the families of men who commuted by train into Chicago on a daily basis. Early real estate developers advertised Austin's suburban virtues. For example, an 1874 map boasted that Austin "possesses many peculiar advantages for suburban residents, such as good drainage, pure water, and no liquor saloons!" In Central Austin several wealthy families occupied elegant mansions, including one that famed Prairie-style architect Frank Lloyd Wright designed.[30]

While developers promoted Austin as an elite suburban oasis, the growth of the metropolitan region siphoned working-class Chicagoans toward

Austin's edges. During the depression of the 1890s, Henry Austin endeared himself to residents by declining to foreclose on their mortgages. New centers of population grew up beyond Austinville. The Moreland community, populated primarily by Irish employees of the Northwestern Railroad shops, centered on the intersection of Lake and Cicero. A cluster of German railroad shop workers built Hamburg to the north of Moreland. Other sections, such as the farm owned by Abram Gale, remained undeveloped until well into the twentieth century.[31] Despite the increasingly diverse class and ethnic composition of Cicero Township, business leaders continued to identify Austin as fundamentally suburban.

Austin proper, however, did not remain legally suburban. Long-standing tensions between rival interests in Oak Park and Austin peaked in 1899. Austin voters approved the extension of the Lake Street Elevated as far west as Austin Boulevard, to the chagrin of Oak Park residents, who feared the arrival of inexpensive transportation would encourage working-class migration into Cicero. To punish Austin, the town board voted to detach it from Cicero and annex the community into Chicago. Austinites protested their urbanization but lost in court, making Austin one of the largest neighborhoods within Chicago.[32]

In the twentieth century, developers built up Austin but took care to insist that they were remaining true to the neighborhood's suburban history. In 1905 F. A. Hill & Co. advertised Austin as "The Place to Live, Without Saloons, Without Factories, Without Old Buildings, Without Smoke and Dust; Here There is Good Transportation, Good Schools and Churches, Good Stores and Markets, Good Neighbors; To be Enjoyed, Clean Improved Streets, Lawn and Trees, Clean Air and Breezes, Quiet and Comfort." The pamphlet argued that Hill's development would attract only the highest quality people to Austin, because, as he explained, "I build residences only and will not allow flats to be built in my subdivisions. Neither do I rent any of my houses. All of them are occupied by the owners; a fact which insures better care of the property, the logical result of which is pretty lawns kept in order, trees trimmed, houses neatly painted and kept so, the absence of dilapidation so often seen in homes occupied by renters, and a more home-like tone to the neighborhood. The surroundings have as much to do with the making of a home as the house itself." Such assertions belied the changing demographic mix in Austin. Increasing transportation connections to Chicago's downtown brought a diverse mix of people to Austin. Among the most visible new residents were German and Swedish migrants and their descendants, eastern European Jews, and people of English, Irish, and Scottish descent. They occupied a variety of housing units, including bungalows, two-family homes, and apartment buildings.[33]

Despite the increasing density of the neighborhood and the legal connection with Chicago, Austinites persistently promoted its distinction from the rest of the city. When the post office estimated in 1926 that Austin housed more than 140,000 people, a local newspaper pointedly remarked, "Austin's population is four times that of Evanston and is unequalled by any city in the state outside of Chicago." In 1940 the *Austinite* newspaper boasted, "To be considered a suburbanite, yet to realize all the advantages of the city is the privilege enjoyed by Austin residents. That is the general opinion of persons interviewed this week on the subject of why they prefer Austin to other parts of the city or to outlying suburbs." After World War II, the *Austinite* declared the area a "City within a City." As evidence, the paper mentioned that even four decades after annexation, "mail addressed to a local address, 'Austin, ILL.' is still sent—and delivered." Further, the paper remarked, a population of 123,000 made Austin "the largest [city] in the state excepting Chicago in its entirety. There are more people residing in Austin than in Peoria, in East St. Louis, Rockford, Springfield, or the combined cities of Moline and Rock Island."[34] In 1961 a woman recollecting her childhood affirmed the distinction between Austin and the rest of Chicago:

> When I was growing up in Austin, I was acutely aware of the conscious attempt to maintain the area as a separate entity linked to Chicago only by legal circumstances. Our boundaries were sharply defined, being indeed the old village boundaries. We had our own town hall, although in fact the Chicago Park District had long ago incorporated this edifice in its park program. Our local newspaper, "The Austinite[,]" published a periodical in form and content not unlike the neighboring "Oak Leaves," and quite different from the usual neighborhood paper. The telephone company abetted this civic self-deception by issuing an Austin directory in addition to the usual Chicago book. But by and large, it was the individual resident who lent support to the continuance of community apartheid. One never lived "on the west side"[;] one lived "in Austin."[35]

This persistent identification of Austin as suburban, however, did not mean that it remained an exclusively residential area.[36] Thousands of railroad employees settled in Austin, conveniently near the several railroad yards occupying local land. Over the first several decades of the twentieth century, pockets of industrial production sprang up in Austin, turning the landscape into a patchwork. Major employers in the area included Zenith Radio, Mars, Incorporated, Revere Copper and Brass, Nachmann Spring-filled Corporation, E. J. Brach & Sons, Edward Katzinger Company, Pettibone Mulliken, and Victor Manufacturing and Gasket Company. The arrival of industry in Austin increased the working-class population. Western Electric's Hawthorne Works in Cicero (directly south of Austin) campaigned for workers among Austin residents. In 1941 a real estate observer described the resulting social geography of Austin: "There is a general tendency, whether in north, middle or south Austin, for housing quality to improve from east to west. This change appears to be related to employment and income. In the eastern half of Austin a higher proportion of employed are in industry, while in western Austin employment in the Loop is much greater."[37] Several Roman Catholic parishes, as well as numerous Protestant churches, served Austin's residents. Austinites sometimes referred to their neighborhood as a "city of churches."[38]

According to the 1942 *Chicago Land Use Survey*, the Austin area was in relatively good shape. Of its 16,581 residential structures, 46.1 percent were single-family detached houses and another 35.2 percent were classic Chicago two-flats. Austin had grown steadily since the 1880s; the peak period of construction was 1915–19, but the neighborhood also added another 1,871 units between 1925 and 1929 and continued to see new construction even during the Great Depression. The 1942 *Land Use Survey* classified 44 percent of Austin's residential structures as being in good condition, with another 53 percent needing minor repairs. Also, 498 needed major repairs, and another twelve were unfit for use.[39]

As the undeveloped spaces between North Lawndale, West Garfield Park, and Austin filled up in the early twentieth century, the West Side became a physically continuous whole. The most dramatic transformation in the West Side's physical character during the mid-twentieth century was the construction of the Congress (Eisenhower) Street Expressway, which cut through the southern sections of East and West Garfield Park and Austin. Although anticipated in Daniel Burnham's famous *Plan of Chicago* (1909), construction on the Congress Expressway did not begin until 1949. Building the highway required the demolition of homes and other structures in its path. The expressway was constructed well before the era of the 1970s highway revolt, and residents raised little public objection to their displacement. The major concern expressed in West Side newspaper coverage of the highway's arrival was, in fact, the lengthy gap between periods of building demolition and road construction, which left eyesores, rubble, and other hazards visible in the neighborhood. The *Garfieldian* complained, "Organized hoodlums, vandals, morons and just ordinary scavengers loot the vacant buildings that are to be wrecked to make way for the Congress St. highway in broad daylight as well as at night time." Remaining residents applauded the expressway for bringing more people and business into the

area. Sears executives praised the highway as an improvement and a reason to keep their company headquarters in North Lawndale.[40]

The establishment of the West Side as a set of modest neighborhoods
did not deliver the area any special political influence. Residents of the
West Side occasionally rose to prominence in Chicago, but the area failed
to become a locus of clout. Much of the civic improvement money and
energy in Chicago in the twentieth century went toward fulfillment of elements of the 1909 Burnham Plan,[41] which focused on the aesthetic ration-
alization of the downtown and lakefront. West Side politicians used the
power of patronage to reward loyal supporters with employment but did
not translate their influence into dramatic material uplift for the West Side.
Mayors Carter Harrison I and II, who intermittently dominated turn-of-
the-century Chicago politics, lived at Ashland and Jackson, in the Near
West Side. Mayor Anton Cermak, the architect of the "house for all peoples"—the Democratic political machine that ruled Chicago for most of
the twentieth century—drew his original power from his fellow Bohemians
in South Lawndale. Cermak's close ally 28th Ward committeeman Patrick
Nash spent little time at his home base on the West Side. Jacob Arvey, an
alderman and mayoral power broker, represented the 24th Ward—including North Lawndale—in his official capacities and rewarded his supporters accordingly. Neither West Garfield Park nor Austin provided political
leadership in Chicago politics.[42] The West Side's relative lack of power was
accentuated in the second half of the twentieth century, when a succession
of Bridgeport residents—Edward J. Kelly, Martin H. Kennelly, and finally
Richard J. Daley—took control of the city's Democratic machine and the
mayor's office.

African Americans on the West Side

Despite the overwhelming racial homogeneity of the West Side in the first
half of the twentieth century, it was not absolutely without African
Americans. From the nineteenth century, a small cluster of African
Americans made their homes on the city's Near West Side and frequented
businesses, churches, and other institutions in the area. Young black residents enjoyed community festivals and supervised activities at Union Park,
where African American teachers and artists provided lessons in dance,
music, athletics, and sewing. In 1913 the *Chicago Defender*, the city's major
African American newspaper, hailed "The Great West Side" and advised,
"South Siders would do well to pattern after them." Although they remembered the area as relatively racially harmonious, longtime black residents
also acknowledged constraints imposed by their white neighbors: the lim-

Table 1: Population of Chicago[43]

Year	White	Black	Total	% White	% Black
1930	3,137,043	233,903	3,376,438	92.91	6.93
1940	3,114,564	277,731	3,396,808	91.69	8.18
1950	3,111,525	492,265	3,620,962	85.93	13.59
1960	2,712,748	812,637	3,550,404	76.41	22.89
1970	2,207,767	1,102,620	3,369,359	65.52	32.72
1980	1,490,216	1,197,000	3,005,072	49.59	39.83

its on black mobility in the area seemed to be Hubbard or Grand to the north, Western Avenue to the west, and Lake or Madison Street to the south. The Great Migration of black southerners to northern urban centers around World War I drew tens of thousands of migrants to Chicago's South Side and spurred a second African American settlement in the Near West Side, around Maxwell Street.[44] But Bronzeville, on the South Side, clearly remained the cultural heart of black Chicago.[45]

A handful of black West Side families scattered beyond the boundaries of the small Near West Side colony. The Jackson family purchased land in the Austin area in the last quarter of the nineteenth century, well before the neighborhood was annexed into Chicago. This family remained in Austin throughout the twentieth century and developed strong local ties, graduating several members from Austin High School. One son, Obern "Podgie" Simons, and another black alumnus arrived spontaneously at the school to help in the fall of 1965 when rioting erupted between white and African American students. Although local papers hailed the Jacksons as upstanding old settlers, the family encountered occasional racial animus. According to one family story, a white man offered Andrew Jackson $25 to move out of the neighborhood; Jackson turned the offer around, saying that the neighbors would surely prefer to pay the repugnant white man to leave.[46]

In the decades after World War II, the populations of East Garfield Park, North Lawndale, West Garfield Park, and finally Austin changed from white to black. The revival of the Great Migration after World War II brought hundreds of thousands of southern black migrants to Chicago and accounted for many of those who found their way to the West Side. The Travelers' Aid Society of Chicago, which tracked the number of train cars delivering new migrants and returning vacationers on the City of New Orleans, reported a shift in demand for services. Where the Illinois Central train stations on the South Side were once the main debarkation point for migrants, travelers increasingly arrived at the bus station on Randolph Street, in downtown Chicago. The location of the bus terminal pointed new arrivals as much toward the West Side as toward the South. In addition, Travelers' Aid

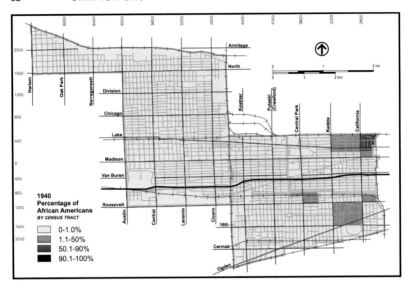

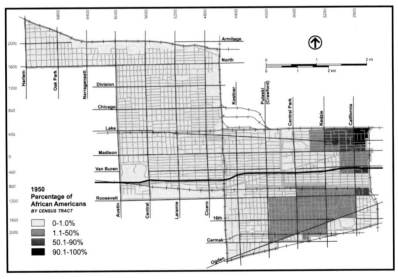

reported an increase in requests for help with automobile breakdowns, suggesting that some southern migrants were shunning both train and bus in favor of personal transportation.[47]

In addition to southern migrants, the West Side's growing African American population included Chicagoans displaced by urban renewal projects elsewhere in the city. It is difficult to say precisely how many black South Siders moved to the West Side; the city agency responsible for helping displaced residents find new homes failed to keep adequate records.

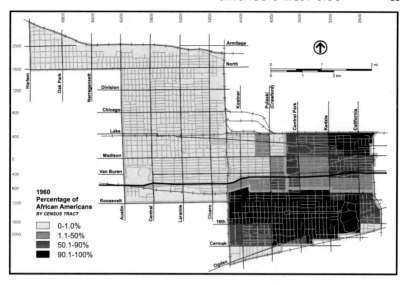

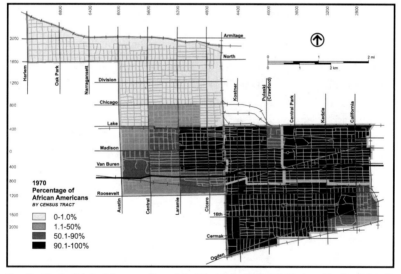

Figs. 3a, 3b, 3c, 3d. Racial composition of the West Side, 1940–70. Produced by the University of Wisconsin–Milwaukee, Cartography & GIS Center.

Anecdotal evidence, however, suggests that some African American West Siders had previously lived elsewhere in Chicago. In 1960 more than half of North Lawndale's residents, who were primarily African Americans, reported having lived somewhere else in Chicago five years previously.[48]

African Americans from the South and elsewhere in Chicago who moved to the West Side in the postwar years settled in one of three places. Some

Table 2: East Garfield Park Population[49]

Year	White	Black	Total	% White	% Black
1940	62,704	2,990	65,789	95.31	4.54
1950	58,144	11,695	70,091	82.96	16.69
1960	25,409	41,097	66,871	38.00	61.46
1970	883	51,121	52,185	1.69	97.96
1980	223	31,263	31,580	0.71	99.00

Table 3: North Lawndale Population

Year	White	Black	Total	% White	% Black
1940	102,048	380	107,470	94.95	0.35
1950	87,096	13,146	100,489	86.67	13.08
1960	10,792	113,827	124,937	8.64	91.11
1970	2,966	91,274	94,772	3.13	96.31
1980	1,038	59,370	61,523	1.69	96.50

joined the old settlement on the Near West Side, swelling the population there. Others moved into the family public housing that the Chicago Housing Authority constructed in the Near West Side and East Garfield Park during the 1950s, including Maplewood Courts, Rockwell Gardens, Harrison Courts, Henry Horner Homes and Extension, Leclaire Courts, and Ogden Courts.[50] Still others—those of primary concern in this book—moved into private housing in North Lawndale, West Garfield Park, and Austin. As they moved into private housing on the West Side, African Americans generally settled either in recently established black neighborhoods or on the edges of the territory that was expanding one block at a time. In general, this expansion moved in a northwesterly direction. The first West Side neighborhoods to receive African Americans were East Garfield Park and North Lawndale, whose black population grew tenfold during the 1950s, while its white population declined. Beginning around 1959, African Americans sought housing in the smaller neighborhood of West Garfield Park, just north of North Lawndale. By approximately 1963, most of West Garfield Park's population was black; with migrants continuing to arrive in Chicago, the next area of African American settlement was in Austin. Although many of the new residents of the West Side were working class or poor, middle-class and professional African Americans also took the opportunity to buy homes there.[51] In any case, the process of black migration into these neighborhoods was neither orderly nor, from the perspective of white residents, inevitable.

Scholars took note of the dramatic increase in postwar African American migration to northern urban centers like Chicago while it was under way.

Table 4: West Garfield Park Population

Year	White	Black	Total	% White	% Black
1940	48,392	24	48,447	99.89	0.05
1950	48,328	23	48,443	99.76	0.05
1960	38,152	7,204	45,611	83.65	15.79
1970	1,365	46,929	48,464	2.82	96.83
1980	246	33,475	33,865	0.73	98.85

Table 5: Austin Population

Year	White	Black	Total	% White	% Black
1940	132,004	60	132,107	99.92	0.05
1950	131,970	122	132,180	99.84	0.09
1960	124,916	31	125,133	99.83	0.02
1970	84,909	41,583	127,981	66.35	32.49
1980	28,649	101,831	138,026	20.76	73.78

David Wallace, author of a Ph.D. dissertation in regional planning, estimated that thirty thousand African Americans were arriving in Chicago annually by 1952. Sociologists investigated the effect of the arrival of so many migrants on cities' social landscapes and housing markets. They were primarily interested in two related phenomena: First, borrowing a metaphor from ecology, scholars investigated "succession," the process by which African Americans replaced whites in certain neighborhoods; and, second, they studied the dynamics of racial segregation, which were key to the inability of African Americans to find decent uncrowded housing. Robert Weaver's 1948 study, *The Negro Ghetto*, noted that "Chicago leads the way" in the growth of concentrated, racially segregated housing districts. Otis Duncan and Beverly Duncan's *The Negro Population of Chicago* documented the nuances of the process by which blacks replaced whites in housing, identifying five "stages of succession" that racially changing neighborhoods experienced. Karl Taeuber and Alma Taeuber's 1965 *Negroes in Cities* used a "segregation index" to compare the extent to which whites and African Americans around the country lived in isolation from one another. They cautioned, "Processes of succession by which a high degree of residential segregation is maintained in Chicago may or may not typify patterns and processes in other cities."[52]

African Americans were not the only migrants to Chicago in the immediate postwar decades. The city's increasing Latino population spilled out in a V shape, north and south of the West Side neighborhoods where African Americans settled. Chicago's Mexican population dated to the first quarter of the twentieth century, when approximately twenty-six thousand migrants moved to the factory complexes on the city's Far South Side. Some Mexicans made homes on the Near West Side, from which they were displaced by postwar urban renewal. During World War II, international labor agreements drew thousands of Mexican workers to Chicago, a transnational migration that continued well after formal recruitment stopped. Most of these new migrants settled south of the emerging black West Side, alongside former residents of the Near West Side. Together, these groups provided the Lower West Side and South Lawndale community areas with the city's greatest concentration of Mexicans.[53] In the late twentieth century, these neighborhoods were more popularly known as Pilsen and Little Village, respectively.[54] The northern arm of the Latino V embracing the black West Side was constituted primarily of Puerto Ricans, who moved into the West Town and Humboldt Park community areas. Humboldt Park also became home to a group of African Americans, who settled in the area's southernmost census tracts, adjacent to East Garfield Park.[55]

The West Side's long-standing lack of political influence hampered new residents' and merchants' efforts to shape the neighborhood's destiny. As African Americans moved to the West Side, the Democratic Party made a concerted effort to bring these thousands of new voters into the political machine. West Side wards were soon represented by black servants of the Democratic Party, known collectively as the "silent six" for their steady obedience to the dictates of their political bosses. Alderman Benjamin Lewis of the 29th Ward, the first of the West Side's black aldermen, was found assassinated in his office in 1963 in a murder that remains unsolved.[56] Whites who remained on the West Side also found themselves without strong political support. In 1965, due to a peculiar cascade of events, none of the three wards containing Austinites had aldermanic representation. When a staff member at the Board of Election Commissioners told Barbara Plona, a member of the Austin Community Organization, that no new elections would be scheduled until 1967, she coordinated a campaign to get elections called. In March she persuaded the mayor to set elections for June.[57]

Despite their political weakness and the scholarship that implied the eventual settlement of African Americans on the West Side, whites in those neighborhoods did not foresee their own departures. Between the time when African Americans started moving into North Lawndale after World War II and when they finally moved away themselves, groups of white West Siders advocated for a variety of policy initiatives that they believed were in their neighborhoods' best interests. Not all white West Siders participated in these organizations, and sometimes such groups managed to provoke dissent. But few if any whites publicly repudiated the hope of continuing to live and work on behalf of the West Side. As Richard J. Daley reminisced as he ran for mayor in 1954, "Chicago has always been a city of neighborhoods. Back in the early days it was neighborhood pride that created great projects and got them done. My own Bridgeport neighborhood, Hyde Park, Auburn Park, the Great West Side neighborhood and many others all had a wonderful spirit. People were proud of their neighborhoods and saw to it that those neighborhoods were deserving of pride."[58] How white West Siders and their organizations sought to shore up their neighborhoods, and how Mayor Daley directed resources to other sections of Chicago, occupies the remainder of this book.

CHAPTER 2

Housing Codes

In late winter 1961, "Willing Willie," a housing columnist and editorial gadfly for the *Garfieldian*, visited an eighteen-flat building at 146 South Hamlin. At the building Willing Willie observed an "amazing number of children hopping around in the mud" and mailboxes listing between two and six names for each apartment. An eighteen-unit apartment building should have, presumably, housed eighteen families, but Willing Willie estimated between forty and fifty families were in residence. The reporter, seeking official verification that the building was overcrowded, persuaded a city housing inspector to check the building for violations of Chicago's five-year-old housing code. To Willing Willie's chagrin, the inspector ruled that, technically, the building was not overcrowded—not even the six-room apartment occupied by thirteen people violated city standards. Willing Willie concluded, "The front of the building, of sturdy, red brick . . . still has a neat appearance, but it is only a question of time until the effects of the overcrowding on the inside make their way through to affect the entire building. It is of this sort of thing blight is made."[1]

The most unusual element of this story is the presence of the housing inspector. Although Chicago's housing supply was overcrowded, city inspectors and the courts only rarely, if ever, enforced the regulations prohibiting excessive numbers of people in residences. For almost a century, housing reformers in Chicago pushed for laws establishing safety and sanitary standards for the city's residences. In the early twentieth century, many of these activists, including Edith Abbott and Robert Hunter, were associated with Hull-House or the University of

Fig. 4. Multiple name tags on a mailbox indicated that several families were occupying an apartment constructed for one family. *Garfieldian*, November 9, 1960. Courtesy of the Special Collections and Preservation Division, Chicago Public Library.

Chicago. Housing reformers regarded a poor physical environment as the root of a broad array of urban problems and urged improvement in the living conditions of the poor as a humanitarian imperative. Although successful in their advocacy for increasingly stringent requirements, such reformers were consistently disappointed with the implementation of new laws. In the middle decades of the twentieth century, the Metropolitan Housing and Planning Council (MHPC) took center stage in the campaign for housing standards. MHPC also worked on several other initiatives to improve and reshape Chicago in the middle of the twentieth century, including efforts to create urban renewal and build a University of Illinois campus close to the downtown. In the mid-1950s MHPC led a successful charge to legislate Chicago's first formal housing code as a central piece of the city's postwar renaissance.

Richard J. Daley's ascent to the mayoralty in 1955 coincided with the emergence of a new era of redevelopment in the city. In contrast to housing reformers, Daley considered the housing code to be the legal cornerstone of Chicago's revitalization, rather than an end in itself. For Daley, the significance of the housing code was that its passage was a prerequisite for receiving federal urban renewal funds. Scholars and journalists have documented the series of infrastructure projects in Chicago that came to fruition during Daley's administration. The reintroduction of commercial skyscraper construction, the erection of high-rise public housing, the opening of O'Hare Airport, and the construction of major highways linking the city's downtown to its suburban hinterland all occurred during Daley's first years as mayor. The late 1950s also witnessed several less glamorous manifestations of Daley's physical agenda for Chicago. The mayor garnered accolades for reinvigorating Chicago's annual summer clean-up drive and supplying new streetlights to many city neighborhoods.[2] He also supported updating the city's zoning code. Daley threw his political weight behind advocacy for Chicago's new housing code, which was drafted by MHPC and passed in 1956. All of these projects reinforced Mayor Daley's ambitious agenda for the long-term restructuring and revitalization of Chicago.

For their own reasons, which overlapped in part with those of housing reformers, community groups on Chicago's West Side responded enthusiastically to the new housing code.[3] During the early postwar years, West Siders articulated deep concern about the deterioration of their local physical environment. Like professional reformers, white West Siders were particularly worried about a phenomenon they referred to as "blight." A term borrowed from the study of ecology, blight connoted a type of physical decay with organic qualities. West Siders believed that a deteriorating and neglected building was bad in itself, presenting health and moral threats to its occupants. In addition, a blighted structure had the potential to infect nearby properties with its decay, thereby threatening the vitality of the surrounding neighborhood. Finally, excessive numbers of people occupying a single home wore out their private domestic facilities quickly. As residents sought to escape crowded dwellings, they also put pressure on public resources, such as streets, schools, and parks. West Siders had been alarmed by the physical deterioration of their environs since the Great Depression, a condition exacerbated by wartime supply shortages and the postwar housing crunch. Accordingly, they sought to use Chicago's new housing code to root out buildings that endangered the health of their neighborhoods.

Eventually, West Siders also saw housing code enforcement as an important mechanism for preserving local racial homogeneity. When African Americans moved into their neighborhoods, West Siders intensified their code enforcement activities. As scholar Robert Beauregard has shown nationally, in the 1960s discussions of blight, physical decay, and other urban problems became infused with "a racial dimension."[4] Although West Siders could observe around them examples of deterioration that were entirely unconnected with African Americans, they often also reflexively attributed these problems to black people. Some West Siders argued simply that African Americans' propensity for living in overcrowded conditions was problematic; others argued more explicitly that blacks, especially southern migrants, were essentially incapable of healthy urban living. Getting the housing code enforced in their neighborhoods therefore assumed a special importance for white West Siders when African Americans appeared on the scene; it was not always clear to what extent they were supposed to improve the physical condition of a white neighborhood and to what extent whites' housing activities were intended to keep out blacks. With both these concerns in mind—the physical and the racial—white West Side community groups not only verbally endorsed the new housing code, but also worked hard to bring about its enforcement in their neighborhoods.

Both MHPC and West Side community groups, however, were frustrated in their hopes that the housing code would serve as a tool for improving Chicago's residential neighborhoods. Like generations of housing activists before them in Chicago and other American cities, West Siders discovered an enormous gap between the existence of a public policy on paper and its enforcement in practice.[5] While the 1956 housing code laid out standards that all residential units in Chicago could be required to meet, property owners routinely failed to bring their buildings up to code without suffering any adverse consequences. Inspectors did not systematically canvass all dwellings in the city to ensure their compliance with the code. Property owners hauled into court usually escaped with only minimal fines that did nothing to compel the remedy of their buildings. Increasingly during the 1960s, the housing code's major function was to justify the city's demolition of deteriorating buildings, leaving vacant lots in residential neighborhoods. In order to counter criticism of its unbalanced enforcement efforts, the Building Department sporadically swept entire swaths of neighborhoods for code violations. This practice, however, placed severe strains on small homeowners, especially African Americans without access to traditional mortgages. Under the Daley administration, the housing code primarily served the city government's agenda for the reordering of the city's space; it did little to remedy the physical crisis that West Siders feared in the postwar period.

Building inspection is a government function notorious for its vulnerability to venality. A small team of city inspectors, away from their offices and their supervisors, visiting a site whose owner was anxious not to invest any more money in the building, could easily overlook violations in exchange for a financial gesture. It might seem surprising that an examination of housing codes in Chicago has little to say about bribery and corruption in the inspection and enforcement process. Indeed, in the 1970s a series of corruption scandals broke open the city's Building Department.

An administrator told political scientist Bryan Jones that Chicago's Building Department was "probably the most corrupt municipal department in the country." There is little reason to believe that corrupt inspectors were not also on the job in the 1950s and 1960s as well.[6] That white West Siders devoted little of their attention to complaints about corrupt inspection practices is a measure of two distinct weaknesses: First, West Siders lacked the political influence—"clout," in Chicago parlance—to persuade officials that their neighborhoods merited special attention. Second, the West Side had more than enough buildings in need of repair; it was simply pragmatic to urge correction of buildings not protected by corrupt property owners and inspection officials, instead of waging a quixotic war against determined enemies.

History of Housing Codes

A city's right to regulate conditions in private buildings, including housing, grows out of its police powers and its right to control nuisances. In the nineteenth century, disasters devastated populations and property, even while city sizes and congestion grew. In response, city and state governments enacted legislation to control the composition and upkeep of buildings. The 1866 cholera epidemics in New York City, for example, prompted the state of New York to authorize a Metropolitan Board of Health with a mandate to regulate the unsanitary conditions that fostered disease. The ubiquity of fires in nineteenth-century cities also fostered prohibitions on wood construction within specified "fire limits" of most American cities. As historian Elizabeth Blackmar has argued, the major purpose of such regulations was to protect the health of the city as a whole, rather than its individual inhabitants, against the risks associated with their landlords' properties.[7] For a small but passionate group of housing reformers, however, the effects of terrible housing on residents cried out for further remedy.

The utter squalor of New York tenement conditions provided such reformers an entrée into housing regulation. The New York Tenement House Law of 1867 extended the authority of the Metropolitan Board of Health into properties inhabited by "more than three families living independently of another, and doing their cooking upon the premises" and set a precedent for state regulation of housing conditions. A new Tenement House Law passed in 1879 had the unintended consequence of promoting the widespread erection of the notorious "dumb-bell tenement," whose failures photographer Jacob Riis documented vividly in *How the Other Half Lives*.[8] The dangerous and dirty air shafts that characterized the dumb-bell tenements inspired reformer Lawrence Veiller to advocate for the Tenement

House Law of 1901. That legislation—which introduced the distinction between "old law" and "new law" tenements to New York City—required new tenement buildings to meet a series of sanitary, ventilation, and fire-safety standards. Veiller, who became the director of the new National Housing Association in 1910, promoted similar changes for other cities and states. Although few cities had a similar concentration of large apartment buildings, poor and working people in cities around the United States lived in unregulated, wretched conditions.[9]

The history of housing regulation in Chicago followed on the heels of New York City's innovations, although different types of buildings were the center of concern. While New York's tenements housed hundreds of people simultaneously, Chicago's poor often crowded themselves into smaller buildings. As early as 1835, just two years after the city's founding, the Chicago City Council created a Board of Health to regulate nuisances in the city; this body disbanded in 1860, and in 1867 the state of Illinois established a new Board of Health. The new Board of Health eventually claimed the right to regulate sanitary conditions in tenements, which in Chicago, as in New York City, were buildings housing three or more families. In 1879 the city council passed a Tenement and Workshop Inspection Act, which invested enforcement powers in a Department of Health. Over the course of the nineteenth century, the city council gradually increased this department's regulatory powers. In addition, in residential districts property owners could keep nuisances such as stables and slaughterhouses from their block by getting neighboring property owners to agree to a ban.[10]

While the Health Department incrementally acquired the right to regulate sanitary conditions, a separate set of regulations, administered by the Building Department, governed new construction in the city. As early as 1845, Chicago had some fire limits, ordinances that prohibited construction with flammable materials in certain areas of the city. In response to the Great Fire of 1871, the city council expanded the scope of these regulations; because the fire limits did not cover the entire city, working-class Chicagoans moved to the periphery, where they could build with cheaper, but flammable, materials. In 1881 the boundaries of the fire limits were temporarily coterminous with the city limits, but as Chicago's boundaries expanded through annexation, exceptions to the prohibition on building with flammable materials accreted. Over the rest of the nineteenth century, the city council passed a series of ordinances controlling construction standards for new buildings in the city; most notably, an 1875 ordinance required builders to seek a permit for their plans from the commissioner of buildings, and in 1898 the city council passed a new building code.[11]

While impressive on paper, these regulations changed little on the ground; as Edith Abbott noted dryly, "Certainly when one turns from the printed ordinances to look at the houses in which the poor are actually living in Chicago, it is clear that the standards of housing tolerated and the standards of housing as set forth in the letter of the law are very different." The City Homes Association, created by reformers associated with Hull-House, commissioned Robert Hunter to document local tenement conditions, which were appalling. In response to Hunter's 1901 study, the city council passed a law detailing standards for new construction of buildings intended to house two or more families; this Tenement House Act was revised in 1910 and again in 1920.[12] Despite these reforms, Chicago's Tenement House Act of 1902 and the other housing regulations were enforced erratically. While new buildings in Chicago were improved, the conditions in older housing remained wretched. By 1935 Edith Abbott revealed in *The Tenements of Chicago* that thousands of Chicagoans continued to live in dreadful circumstances, despite the existence of laws declaring their domiciles uninhabitable.[13]

In the middle decades of the twentieth century, housing conditions became a matter of national attention. Building codes, laws regulating all new construction whether residential or commercial, flourished in the 1920s when the federal Department of Commerce and the National Board of Fire Underwriters wrote model codes and lobbied localities to adopt them. But the state of much housing in the United States deteriorated during the Great Depression of the 1930s, as strapped Americans channeled their resources into survival rather than to property maintenance. With the onset of World War II, millions of Americans moved around the country in search of war production jobs. A national building code encouraging flexible housing arrangements responded to this great shift in population. In order to accommodate the tens of thousands of war production workers streaming into Chicago, property owners divided up their apartments into more numerous, smaller units, without adding new plumbing and electrical facilities. Space-efficient sinks and stoves enabled landlords to transform luxury apartments into "kitchenettes." The Edgewater and Uptown neighborhoods, on Chicago's North Side, were the most thoroughly transformed, as gracious luxury apartments became warrens of one- and two-room dwellings. Such subdivided apartments, sometimes referred to as "conversions," were separated from one another by glass doors. These "crash-panel" doors, legal since the 1890s and explicitly endorsed by the city council in 1940, theoretically provided converted apartments with a second exit that could be used in emergencies. Crash-panel doors became a bone of legal contention in the postwar years. After the war, when demobilized veterans and their brides searching for independent homes exacerbated the housing shortage, the city council extended the emergency provisions until a new code was adopted.[14]

With World War II concluded, several civic organizations and the city government decided it was time to review the building code. At least fifty American cities did the same. The major push to revise the code in Chicago came from the Metropolitan Housing and Planning Council, an organization dominated by business and civic elites and founded in 1934 to focus on housing conditions.[15] By 1948 the group expanded its mission to include broader concerns such as urban planning. Initially the new building code effort foundered, but when Mayor Edward J. Kelly appointed a former Federal Housing Administration staff member to coordinate the revision, it picked up steam. A proposal dividing the city into three districts with successively laxer standards made its way to the city council in 1948.[16] In the densely built-up center of the city, the proposal called for strict new controls on fire hazards; the second district, surrounding the downtown, would have maintained the existing moderate standards; and property owners in the less built-up areas of Chicago would have been permitted to construct frame and prefabricated housing. Chicago's construction unions objected fiercely to the provisions that would have permitted new homes to be assembled off-site, and they threatened to prevent passage of the proposals. After a lengthy debate, in 1949 the city council passed a building code revision that prohibited the use of prefabricated materials, except in small homes.[17]

The revised building code did little to ameliorate several administrative flaws that continued to concern MHPC. First, the code itself was confusing. The city lacked a single written resource that people interested in housing regulations could consult. Arguing a few years later for another code revision, an MHPC pamphlet commented, "The laws are scattered all over the municipal code; some of them are only in dusty volumes lying in law libraries." Even city inspectors lacked a handbook laying out the rules. The longtime director of MHPC recalled one Building Department inspector who "put together a kind of cookbook-like notebook. Every time he found another regulation, he would jot it down and add it to the notebook."[18]

Second, chaos ruled the enforcement process. In an effort to eliminate overlapping responsibilities, the city council transferred the Bureau of Housing Inspection, which had the authority to enforce the various provisions of the building code, from the Board of Health to the Building Department; but the two bureaucracies fit together poorly. Additional separate codes, entrusted to different enforcement agencies, still governed the condition of electricity, plumbing, and ventilation in Chicago's buildings. Authorities charged with enforcing the building code did so haphazardly.

Richard Smykal, a respected retired general called in from the suburb of Wheaton to reform the Building Department in 1953, found "utter chaos, disorganization, and demoralization." Smykal discovered that ninety thousand complaints were ignored annually; that reporters freely perused case files and left the office with records that intrigued them; and that staff members were underpaid, uncooperative, and corrupt. In the most dramatic example of the breakdown in formal controls, in 1954 an AFL Electrical Workers official took over the Bureau of Electrical Inspections. He directed inspectors to obey only his instructions and informed city officials of his coup by telegram.[19]

A third flaw in the 1949 building code revision was that it was not retroactive. Well before the passage of the 1949 building code, Edith Abbott argued that "our canvass in district after district showed that the provisions of the code which dealt only with new buildings would not in the lifetime of a generation affect the houses in the so-called 'congested districts.'" The exemption of old buildings from the 1949 code meant that the vast majority of existing housing in Chicago was not subject to the higher standards. Additionally, the Building Department was reluctant to take action against conversions that were illegal but in existence over a long period of time, arguing that "continued use and occupancy have sanctified present use of the property." Further, when inspectors did find violations, the resulting court cases rarely concluded with findings of guilt or in meaningful punishments, providing building owners with little incentive to comply with legal orders. Judges routinely granted continuances, in order to give property owners time to comply voluntarily with the regulations. Prosecution of building code violations, MHPC concluded in 1951, was "milk-toast."[20]

The *Chicago Tribune* editorialized, "The word is out: You can get by in Chicago. You can rig up any old junk hole basement or attic and call it home. Nobody will bother you—not much, anyhow." During the early 1950s, concerned civic groups and city officials began to study how to improve all housing conditions in Chicago, not just new construction. In 1952 D. E. Mackelmann, the acting Housing and Redevelopment coordinator, hired a staff member to cull from the building code all the provisions relating to housing. The next year a report commissioned from a private firm surveyed the state of city government and outlined a variety of recommendations for proceeding with conservation and slum clearance in the city. Critics from MHPC argued that the report gave inadequate attention to the unenforced building code.[21]

Meanwhile, Chicago's poorest apartment dwellers paid the price for the city's loose and ineffective regulation of housing. African Americans were especially likely to live in unsanitary and unsafe dwellings. In a revival of the pre-Depression Great Migration, African Americans poured into the city in great numbers after World War II. Because they were unwelcome in white neighborhoods, African Americans crowded into the traditional Black Belt on the South Side and the emerging ghetto in North Lawndale on the West Side. Apartments occupied by African Americans burned, through accident and arson, in alarming numbers after World War II. In a one-year period, more than seven hundred fires burned apartments in a small section of the South Side alone. The emergency crash-panel doors, many recently installed in converted units, failed to provide residents with safe exits from burning apartments; fire investigators often discovered curtains and furniture blocking the doors, and people who did manage to break the glass during a fire faced the difficulty of traversing an unfamiliar apartment through darkness and smoke. Between January 1947 and August 1954, 235 Chicagoans died in tenement fires. From time to time, the print media drew attention to Chicagoans' continuing vulnerability to fire. In June 1953, drawing on information provided by MHPC and confirmed by a team of investigative reporters, the *Chicago Daily News* published a ten-part series of articles that "shocked an entire community into action" and inspired the creation of the Citizens Committee to Fight Slums.[22]

Over the next several months, the Citizens Committee to Fight Slums studied the state of housing in Chicago. In February 1954 the committee recommended the consolidation of all regulations pertaining to housing into a single code. The proposed housing code would be distinct from the general building code, which applied to all construction in the city. The housing code, the committee urged, should apply to all facilities used as residences, regardless of their age. The committee further suggested that all city agencies charged with oversight of housing should eventually be consolidated. MHPC then assumed responsibility for drafting detailed provisions for Chicago's first housing code. An MHPC committee, led by University of Chicago law professor Allison Dunham, drew up a proposal and submitted it to city officials. During the first half of 1955, the proposed housing code circulated among city officials for comment and revision.[23]

In 1954 the federal government provided Chicago officials with an external incentive to create a systematic housing code. The United States Housing Act of 1954, a vital instrument for Chicago's development over the next decade, granted cities substantial funds for the purposes of urban renewal and conservation. In order to obtain these monies, city governments had to submit applications demonstrating that they had in place a "workable program," including a housing code to reinforce redevelopment efforts. A city official explained, "Without such a Workable Program, there can be no loans and capital grants for renewal projects (CLCC and CCB), no mortgage insurance under Section 220 of the National Housing Act, no annual contribution for public housing." During 1955 and 1956, Chicago received federal urban renewal funds in anticipation of passage of its housing code.[24] Beyond the possibilities of preventing deaths and improving the city for its own sake, the availability of a federal bonanza provided a clear political impetus for the passage of Chicago's first formal housing code. Eventually, under the guidance of Richard J. Daley, the housing code's potential role in protecting housing occupants was subordinated to his larger goals for redevelopment in Chicago.

Immediately after his election as mayor in April 1955, Daley began to promote the code sponsored by MHPC. Daley wanted the new code settled on by the end of the calendar year. In January 1956 the parties reached a deal on the code and began moving it through the city council's adoption process. Only one alderman, who objected to the provisions requiring the elimination of the infamous crash-panel doors within five years, opposed the code. He argued that the code would cause a hardship for property owners, especially those who had recently paid to install crash-panel doors, on the assumption they would continue to be required. He suggested the code would prompt the displacement of families and offered a series of nine amendments to soften the financial blow to property owners. In June the city council passed the new housing code, without the nine amendments, to go into effect on the first day of 1957.[25]

Beyond assembling regulations governing residences into a single document for the first time, the new housing code made several significant changes to provisions about living space in Chicago. The code regulated all housing in the city, regardless of the date of its original construction; MHPC argued in its transmittal letter to Mayor Daley that the code "applies to future occupancy for housing and is prospective in operation. If an owner desires to use his building for housing he must comply with this Code, even though before he was not required to do so. Even if this be said to be retroactive, it is not unconstitutional." The code defined obligations of both property owners and tenants, making each legally responsible for certain aspects of residential safety and sanitation. Property owners could no longer install crash-panel doors and were required to remove existing ones within five years. The new code required the provision of hot and cold running water. In an important innovation, the housing code regulated the crowding of living quarters by demanding a certain number of square feet for each resident of a dwelling. In contrast, the old occupancy limit, more concerned with providing air to unventilated apartments, set a minimum of cubic feet. Describing occupancy in terms of cubic feet meant that an elevator shaft—with lots of oxygen but mostly unusable space—might have met the old requirements. Suddenly in 1957 thousands of residences in the city were in violation of the new housing code. Authorities had no immediate plans to evict residents from substandard units, but MHPC applauded Mayor Daley for ushering into law almost precisely the code that it recommended.[26]

The city launched its new housing code with great fanfare. A conference held at the LaSalle Hotel in mid-January 1957 featured an overview of the elements of the code, academic papers contextualizing Chicago's code within a national framework, and a review of the importance of enforcement to the code's success. Alderman William T. Murphy told the audience, "In the housing code *and its enforcement*, Chicago has the single most important tool for elevating housing standards throughout the city." An official from Ohio emphasized the importance of dedicated staff members to effective code enforcement, bragging, "We have 25 high-type, intelligent and enthusiastic inspectors already on our staff in Cincinnati, and I should rather keep those 25 from now on, than to have unlimited numbers of blockheads and goons added to our payroll." The new Chicago building commissioner, George Ramsey, cautioned that code enforcement was not a "magic wand" for improvement of housing, but promised that it was "a high priority job of this department and we intend to go forward with it." Mayor Daley put muscle behind Ramsey's promise in March, sending out teams of inspectors to investigate neighborhoods on the South Side. The teams consisted of inspectors from several different offices, including the city corporation counsel and specialists on the building, housing, electricity, fire, and health codes. Another group surveyed six buildings in North Lawndale, on the West Side, pronouncing them "all very bad."[27]

The Daley administration did not launch the new housing code in a vacuum. The housing code was offered simultaneously with other reforms intended to better control land use in the city and to improve deteriorating parts of the physical environment. Alongside the new housing code, Daley promoted a new zoning code, which the city council passed in May 1957. While the housing code was an innovation, the new zoning code was a revision of previous codes. By the late 1930s, city planners regarded the original 1923 zoning code as a failure. The city council amended the zoning code in the early 1940s, but, according to Harry Chaddick, the central figure in postwar zoning in Chicago, attention to the war effort made moot the new provisions. The 1957 zoning code allocated the land in the city by its status as residential, industrial, or commercial and classified appropriate densities for each parcel.[28]

Daley followed the zoning revisions with enactment of a "dwelling registration ordinance," which required property owners whose buildings contained three or more residential units to make themselves known to the city.

It might seem surprising that Chicago officials had no other ready means of knowing who owned which parcels of land in the city. But Illinois law permitted property owners to conceal their identities in a "blind trust." Beneficiaries of a blind trust could have their names discovered through legal proceedings, but causing unknown people to appear in court was a slow effort, which Daley and others argued hindered the process of housing code enforcement. The city council refused to pass Daley's initial proposal applying to all buildings with at least two units but passed a revised plan after the mayor made an extraordinary appeal to the committee.[29]

Local Response

Community organizations on the West Side welcomed the housing code as a potentially invaluable tool in their war against deterioration, well before African Americans moved into the area. The West Side's upward trajectory in the 1920s halted during the Great Depression, when homeowners could spare little money for property maintenance. Although the West Side's housing stock was not so bad that Edith Abbott's staff canvassed it for *The Tenements of Chicago*, local conditions worried some observers. Like city officials, West Siders understood that the mere existence of the code was insufficient to guarantee good housing conditions. The *Garfieldian* hailed the new housing code but cautioned "that all of the codes in the world will not help stop the blight unless they are enforced." In contrast to New York City, where tenants groups in this period pressured absentee landlords to improve their rental units, in Chicago property-owning residents brought this concern to bear on one another, in an effort to protect their neighborhood from the physical threat of blight.[30]

As early as World War II, West Side residents expressed concern about the area's future. An Austin observer carefully delineated the state of "neighborhood deterioration." He lamented two kinds of properties threatening the area's health. First, he disparaged many small frame houses that already "closely approach a blighted position." Further, he commented wryly, "The average quality of the neighborhood is raised distinctly by the presence of many brick two-flats and apartment buildings, yet ironically it was the admission of these types of structures into the neighborhood which set in motion the trend of deterioration." In 1943 one civic-minded newspaper columnist argued that residents needed to give attention to postwar planning. Among the problems that West Siders should address, not "even a very small part of what is possible at reasonable cost has been covered. Things like plastering cracked and broken ceilings and walls, repairing sagging porches and stairs, installing windows for light and air in almost windowless rooms—these are a few more that come to mind quickly." In 1946 the *Garfieldian* routinely publicized the presence of filthy conditions and rats in West Garfield Park alleys. Conditions immediately after the war gave West Side property owners little incentive to improve their properties; instead, increases in population inspired a continuing practice of sub rosa conversion of large buildings into smaller apartments and rooming houses.[31]

At the end of the war, the magnitude of the housing crisis in Chicago became apparent as veterans and their families sought to establish households independent from their relatives' homes. The Chicago Housing Center registered the names of 175,000 veterans looking for places to live, most of them unable to afford rents above $60 a month. Local newspapers ran page after page of "housing wanted" classified advertisements placed by veterans desiring homes. The *West Side News* explained that it offered the advertisements as a free service "with the knowledge that the housing situation is extremely critical and will tend to get worse before it gets better." The *Garfield News* cited as typical the case of a veteran who spent a year and a half living at the Austin YMCA while his wife and three children stayed elsewhere. In the spring of 1948, MHPC estimated that in Chicago there were still 70,000 families living with other families and 100,000 families living in "units in serious disrepair or unfit for use." While the city had a zero percent vacancy rate, fewer than 6,000 new dwellings were authorized the previous year.[32]

Beginning around 1948, as new housing opportunities for whites opened up in the Chicago suburbs, the housing crunch on the West Side began to ease. The fact that potential white residents could locate affordable homes, however, did not ensure the quality of those properties. A reporter for the *Garfieldian* investigated the range of housing available in the neighborhood in 1953, concluding that locating "an apartment on the West Side these days is not a difficult as it was, but it's still quite an experience." The investigation identified wide and inexplicable variations between units, noting, "It's not uncommon to find a nicely furnished two-room apartment for $65 right next door to a two-room dump for $90 a month." Conversions were ubiquitous, resulting in apartments with shared toilets and "amazing" floor plans. The reporter observed, "It's not too unusual in these places to have to walk from the kitchen through the bedroom to get to the living room."[33]

West Side neighborhoods in the postwar years seemed to be in fair condition—mostly intact but with pockets of decay that threatened the entire area. Henry Chaddick, Chicago's zoning czar, cautioned West Side residents in 1956 that the housing stock of West Garfield Park and Austin, which

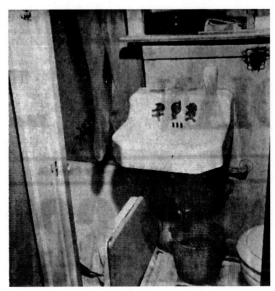

Fig. 5. Owners of converted apartments squeezed equipment and utilities into whatever spaces they fit. The *Garfieldian* reported that these bathroom facilities were placed in a former pantry. *Garfieldian*, April 14, 1965. Courtesy of the Special Collections and Preservation Division, Chicago Public Library.

included substantial numbers of small apartment buildings, made the area "suspectible [*sic*] to slum and blight." In Austin a few blocks just northwest of the town hall were a perennial source of worry during the 1950s and 1960s. The leaders of the Garfield Park–Austin Community Council, extrapolating from a small survey taken in 1956, estimated that approximately 1,100 out of the 5,000 buildings in the neighborhood remained converted from their original layouts. A resident of a furnished converted apartment warned, "Our West Side is fast decaying and becoming a slum area—we can now call it a blighted area. Converted apartments and rooming houses have made it at most unrecognizable from what it used to be."[34]

West Siders felt anxious that the area's deteriorating physical environment suggested that they might be living in a slum.[35] They knew from their experiences in densely populated, neglected neighborhoods how buildings could go from bad to worse. They encapsulated their fears with the word "blight," a term that carries different connotations in different times and places.[36] On Chicago's West Side immediately after World War II, "blight" referred primarily to the poor physical condition of a property. In particular, West Siders were concerned about the consequences of existing decay and how excess population accelerated the wearing out of a neighborhood and its facilities. Blighted buildings jeopardized the health and well-being of residents, who suffered from the physical threat presented by the decay and the moral hazard of living in a degraded environment.

In addition to the threats a blighted building presented to its occupants, West Siders also regarded blight as a contagion, possessing organic qualities and capable of spreading and infecting neighboring properties. The *Garfieldian* elucidated this logic in a 1953 editorial, explaining that "like any disease, community decay starts small and grows larger. It strikes like cancer, not like a heart attack. And, like cancer, it must be fought at the very earliest stages if it is to be licked." A pamphlet produced by the Greater Lawndale Conservation Commission (GLCC) explained, "Overcrowding means overuse. It means that plumbing wears out faster than normal wear and age. Garbage disposal is commonly inadequate. Soon the building 'runs down.' Delinquency, disease, and crime often result." The pamphlet concluded, "If one owner overcrowds his building, or lets it deteriorate, or fails to provide adequate garbage disposal and lighting, we all suffer." A North Lawndale resident offered a more specific account of the logic of overcrowding in public testimony; he agreed that extra uncontained garbage in a neighborhood "led to rats and disease." Moreover, he observed, children suffered important consequences from overcrowding. "With no space to move around inside the house and yards, they spent more time on the streets. This, in turn, has led to vandalism and delinquency." Additionally, city officials did not provide facilities for neighborhoods in proportion to unsanctioned over-occupancy. Schools quickly became oversubscribed in crowded neighborhoods. For example, when city officials acquired one two-flat building in North Lawndale, they discovered it housed eighteen families with forty-two children attending public school. Adults who owned automobiles learned that in crowded neighborhoods, parking and traffic problems increased.[37]

West Side property owners also showed disdain toward people renting crowded dwellings. The presence of increasing numbers of renters was, in itself, a problem for some West Siders, who believed that property owners automatically had a greater commitment to a neighborhood than tenants possibly could. The owner of a two-flat argued, "When there are more renters than property owners in a block, most everyone does not respect private property." An active West Side Realtor emphasized the responsibility of children for bad conditions: "The hard fact is that any objective study of slum conditions must take note that a high percentage of abuse in our housing results from misconduct by children who are not under proper disciplinary control of their parents and this occurs far more in rented quarters than in owner-occupied homes." The zoning laws in effect until 1958 designated certain sections of the West Side, including West Garfield Park, as rooming house districts. Some property owners converted apartments into single-room units but did not put locks on the doors, enabling their legal classification as rooming houses. The Garfield Park–Austin Community Council took the position in 1957 that "the restriction against rooming houses [was] a prime weapon in its fight against the spread of blight." Sometimes the objections to renters carried racist subtexts. When property owners complained about tenants as "barbarians on a rampage" and people who needed education in "the customs of metropolitan living," they were referring to southern migrants, most of whom were African Americans.[38]

Yet white West Siders also expressed concerns about the physical deterioration of their local housing stock well before African Americans began moving into their neighborhoods. In 1949 the *Garfieldian* editorialized, "Although Austin and Garfield Park have no slum problem at present, evidence of the minor variations and violations which put a neighborhood on the down grade and eventually result in the blight come to us nearly every week." The paper advocated enforcement of existing building codes, fearing that structures violating such codes "will ruin property values in a district and generally put it on the skids." In 1950, in response to a flurry of concern that the area near LaFollette Park in North Austin might be used for public housing, one resident tartly described "the Waller ave. [*sic*] slums" as "rat-holes." In 1953 a resident of 1139 North Long warned that Austin might turn into a "shanty town" if new property owners continued to convert "one family, five room bungalows" into multi-unit buildings. The *Garfieldian* concluded in 1954 that "everyone knows, in a general way, that illegal conversions, zoning violations, an increase in rooming houses, and a general lethargy among property owners in keeping their buildings in tip top condition threaten the communities." In response to this condition, the newspaper urged, "The first step in the campaign to halt the blight should be a survey of actual housing conditions in the communities. By that we mean a block-by-block, house-by-house check of the actual number of conversions, zoning changes, building violations."[39]

Although their fears about blight preceded black residence in the area, white West Siders also inferred a connection between African Americans and deterioration. The arrival of African American tenants in the vicinity prompted white neighbors to step up their calls for city officials to correct long-standing code violations. One resident of Austin hoped that "by developing a community spirit and enforcing the housing code, perhaps the Negro in-migration will not occur in Austin." In 1960, shortly after African Americans first moved into West Garfield Park, the *Garfieldian* reported to its readers the terrible condition of the Mona building at 4400 West Jackson.

The building, originally a six-flat, had been converted to more than two dozen separate units. A reporter, visiting the building on the pretense of seeking an apartment, discovered a "foul smelling, roach infested interior" and was shown a room "with a light bulb dangling from a ceiling cord, a small sink and a gas plate. Dead cockroaches littered the floor and shelves." In response to this publicity, a building inspector visited and identified 273 separate violations of the housing code. The United Property Group (UPG), a West Garfield Park organization formed in direct response to the arrival of a black family in the neighborhood, approached the building's owners in an effort to win their cooperation in correcting the violations. The owners agreed to make a superficial clean-up, "washing windows in the building, covering garbage cans, removing torn screens and painting the front hall," but refused to deconvert the building, a process they estimated would cost $10,000. The building inspector, noting that the violations were not new, informed the *Garfieldian* that "the building probably would have been brought to court a year or two ago if neighbors and/or tenants had complained to the building department then about blight." Because of the extremely poor state of the building, the city's corporation counsel expedited its path to court. But in March a fire damaged the building and required the evacuation of its tenants. UPG complained that "the building is not only an eyesore, but constitutes a menace since it attracts derelicts." After several years of litigation that proceeded while the building sat vacant, it was renovated and returned to use in 1963.[40]

West Side community organizations asked their constituents to report intelligence about blight in the neighborhood to their officials. The *Garfieldian* advised, "Every citizen, and especially property owners, should consider it their civic obligation to report abandoned or run-down buildings." In a 1953 editorial, the paper also quoted city Housing and Redevelopment coordinator James G. Downs, who urged citizens, "Keep your eyes open. Every building change you see may not be a violation, but it's your privilege and duty to inquire about it and find out if it is legal. And if everyone does this, no illegal conversion will slip by." West Side property owners took this responsibility seriously, especially when they believed they had a financial interest at stake. One homeowner reported to the Garfield Park West Community Council (GPWCC) that his home had lost value, despite his investment of thousands of dollars in renovations; his neighbor converted a two-flat building into six apartments, which included the basement and porch as separate units. Residents of Lawndale asked a GLCC staff member to check out a nearby apartment building where for the first time 2.5- and 3.5-room apartments were being advertised for rent; their sudden appearance suggested a "sneak" conversion.[41]

West Side community organizations did not rely exclusively on residents' intelligence gathering to combat conversions and deterioration in the neighborhood. They also initiated actions consistent with their broader missions. The Garfield Park Good Neighbors Council—which believed that "stability had nothing to do with race, religion or ethnic considerations, but had a great deal to do with family incomes"—hoped to welcome property owners who could "complete payments without illegally converting homes to double or triple occupancy." By contrast, GPWCC, renamed the Garfield Park–Austin Community Council (GPACC), had less interest in promoting neighborly relations. GPACC solicited irate homeowners who would be pleased to sue the city for allowing an illegal conversion next door to degrade their property's value. The *Garfieldian* and the United Property Group, whose special mission was to dissuade African Americans from moving into West Garfield Park, conducted a survey to identify overcrowded apartments in the neighborhood. Counting the numbers of doorbells to ascertain the original numbers of dwelling units on an eight-block stretch of the neighborhood, they compared the building's intended occupancy with the numbers of names on mailboxes. UPG forwarded to city officials the addresses of buildings housing as many as three times the number of expected families. When an organization's budget allowed, it hired staff devoted to housing issues. The Greater Lawndale Conservation Commission, which enjoyed substantial financial backing from Sears, employed a housing and zoning enforcement officer to investigate housing conditions, educate residents about their rights and responsibilities, and report code violations to the appropriate city authorities. The GLCC housing officer claimed that he once obtained $400,000 worth of improvements in a one-month period. In 1955 the city's deputy housing coordinator, D. E. Mackelmann, congratulated West Side neighborhood organizations for reducing the number of new illegal conversions in the area.[42]

In a few instances, West Siders created new community organizations in response to local events that fed directly into their worst fears about physical deterioration. In the summer of 1953, for example, the conversion of an apartment building at 3352 Van Buren galvanized residents of the western section of East Garfield Park into action. The owner of the property, neighbors alleged, was evicting his tenants and subdividing the building into small apartments. His neighbors responded rapidly when they noticed ten families, with a total of twenty-four children, moving into five of the vacated units. In a case of stunningly quick official action, the area's incumbents filed complaints with city officials. Inspectors identified two hundred building and health code violations; within a month a judge heard the complaints and fined the property owner $400. These attentive residents formed the Garfield Park Improvement Association (GPIA) and elected officers. For the next half decade, GPIA operated in the vicinity to "maintain a clean and decent neighborhood in which to live."[43] The same year, middle-class black residents of a small section of North Lawndale organized the Central Civic Improvement Association in response to the conversion of a local building from an apartment into a hotel.[44]

Because the Building Department's inspection units were understaffed, the city depended on the cooperation of local organizations to report suspected violations. City officials did not, however, readily reciprocate by returning information about active cases to complainants. In 1960 the Association of Community Councils (ACC) published a pamphlet outlining how to report buildings that appeared to violate the housing code. Individual citizens could file complaints directly with the Building Department or with the Mayor's Office of Inquiry and Information, a service established by Mayor Daley shortly after his inauguration. Although the city accepted complaints from individuals, the only information it furnished in return was its initial response to the violation. Community organizations, however, could receive more detailed information about the progress of a complaint through the city's bureaucracy—but only if the organization's representative made an appointment a week in advance requesting a briefing. The ACC's pamphlet advised, "Patience and persistence are important ingredients for effective citizen action in code enforcement. Some administrative procedures are long and tedious and many require some time before a problem is finally resolved." William Bonner, the GLCC housing officer, made a practice of reinspecting buildings after the Building Department declared cases closed; on his departure from GLCC in 1960, he estimated that he had returned to the department for reopening between twenty and twenty-five of the three hundred cases he had reported.[45]

How local organizations handled the information the city made available to them varied. On Chicago's North Side, the Lincoln Park Conservation Association (LPCA) waged an aggressive war against deteriorating properties. LPCA's newsletter included a column listing the current court status of every building its staff reported for code violations. GLCC's housing officer was charged with reporting violations to the city and cultivating a relationship with the Building Department. In contrast to LPCA, whose reports indicated specific buildings under official scrutiny, GLCC published a monthly "scorecard" in its newsletter. The scorecard indicated how many complaints were at which stage of the investigation process but did not subject the owners of given buildings to the same kind of potential public humiliation that LPCA did. For its part, the Austin Tenants and Owners Association, which was most active in 1966, used the community newspapers as a means of publicizing the deteriorating buildings it hoped to have cleaned up.[46]

Although West Siders greeted the housing code enthusiastically, they by no means embraced the notion that government should as a matter of course provide services that citizens might perform privately. With equal vigor, West Siders argued that individuals, particularly property owners, had a significant share of the responsibility for protecting the local physical environment. For example, the *Garfieldian* editorialized, "Eyesores should not be permitted to stand to detract from the value or beauty of property. In addition, removal of the eyesores will encourage property owners who have been negligent to join the clean-up drive." The chairman of the Bradley and Honore Neighborhood Association, writing a guest editorial in the same newspaper in 1958, argued that "decent and proud neighborhoods . . . must be cherished by the active, enlightened and determined people who live in them or else they will become a field of operations for unscrupulous real estate operators and other fast buck manipulators who will milk a neighborhood for profit, thereby turning a good neighborhood into a slum."[47] The laxness of official enforcement meant that private efforts were sometimes the only ones improving a neighborhood.

Accordingly, white West Siders engaged in a wide variety of private upkeep activities, even as they agitated for the city to do its bit by enforcing its housing code. A favorite approach was a community-wide sanitation drive that aimed for a dramatic improvement in an area's overall cleanliness. For example, in 1955 the Garfield Park Improvement Association sent almost four hundred landlords letters announcing a coordinated drive to clean up local alleys and eliminate rats. The Off the Street Club publicized clean-up campaigns with parades featuring children marching through the community alongside garbage trucks borrowed from the Department of Streets and Sanitation. West Side groups sometimes coordinated their activities with official events; in 1957 the Garfield Park Citizens Committee for a Cleaner Community surveyed the condition of the area in advance of Mayor Daley's annual clean-up drive, which was run by the Citizens Committee for a Cleaner Chicago. On other occasions, groups ran improvement programs for their immediate vicinity. The Associated Block Committees of Garfield Park–Austin urged residents to pick up litter and cut weeds on their blocks. In 1959 residents of the 3200 and 3300 blocks of Washington agreed to "plant flowers and beautify their lawns as a living memorial to the deceased who used to live in those blocks." Groups also sponsored seasonally appropriate activities, urging residents to participate in "plantup" contests in the springtime and Christmas lighting competitions in December.[48]

White West Siders also took part in a beautification campaign run by the Chicago Real Estate Board (CREB). CREB's annual Better Neighborhood Crusade invited participants to compete for $20,000 in prizes for improved and beautiful properties. The chairperson of the campaign argued explicitly that the private voluntary program was a means of preempting expensive government intervention in the urban landscape, such as that characterized by "the 'bull dozer' and the subsidized redevelopment project." He concluded, "The practical and economically sound way to conserve the desirable properties in old sound communities is through city-wide voluntary groups—property owners, banks and savings and loan associations, real estate men, and residents." CREB's notion of a voluntary and private campaign, however, did not mean that it respected the privacy of contest entrants; the fact that the judges for the Better Neighborhood Crusade expected to inspect the interiors as well as the exteriors of homes entered in the contest discouraged some African American residents of North Lawndale from participating.[49]

Not all Chicago property owners welcomed the housing code as warmly as the activities of West Side neighborhood groups might suggest. MHPC staff were kept busy fighting efforts to loosen the requirements of the housing code in the years after its passage. Some owners of rental buildings never reconciled themselves to obeying the terms of the housing code and challenged the city's right to intervene in their property. The Chicago Property Owners Association, hoping to demonstrate that the housing code was unconstitutional, sued the city. After several years of litigation, in 1963 the Illinois Supreme Court upheld the legality of a variety of provisions. Having lost the battle over the code's legality, the Chicago Property Owners Association then set out to weaken it. In November 1963 they proposed a variety of amendments, including removal of the provisions outlawing crash-panel doors and requiring separate baths for each apartment. The group won permission for city council hearings on their proposals, but the code remained unchanged.[50]

Enforcement

Despite the ambitious start made by the city government and community groups, critics soon realized that the 1956 housing code offered no panacea for the city's housing problems. As the authorities emphasized at the conference launching Chicago's new code, enforcement was critical to its success. And, they learned, under the new regime, enforcement was little better than under the old. As early as September 1957, the *Garfieldian* expressed dismay at the Building Department's lackadaisical attitude toward implementing the new housing code.[51] Having a new housing code for Chicago was, by itself, insufficient to create a safe housing supply.

Building Department officials proved reluctant to enforce the limits on the number of people permitted to reside in a given unit. In public and in private, city officials discouraged reports of overcrowding in neighborhoods where alternative housing was unavailable. An MHPC activist reported in 1958 that no overcrowding complaints had yet been processed in court; even on those occasions when staff inspectors wrote up accounts of crowding, their superiors censored them, sending forward for prosecution only a subset of the violations. Building Department officials claimed to be unable to demonstrate how many people lived in a given unit. The numbers of names on mailboxes and lists of registered voters were suggestive rather than definitive. William Bonner, the GLCC housing enforcement officer, did not bother submitting such complaints because, as he explained, "I was told at the Building Department that they can not enforce overcrowding." Once, GLCC requested that Alderman Benjamin Lewis intervene with the Building Department to get enforcement on the crowding rules in a particular section of Lawndale; the building commissioner turned down Lewis's request, asking instead for information about apartment buildings in the area with other sorts of violations. The *Garfieldian* responded with scorn to such evasions from the Building Department: "If this is true, then the time and tax money spent to draft the ordinance was an appalling waste."[52]

City officials were particularly unwilling to enforce the crowding rules in African American neighborhoods lest they incidentally encroach on white neighborhoods. Reporting to his mentor Saul Alinsky, Nicholas von Hoffman noted bluntly, "A concerted effort to enforce the code would result in an increased pressure by the unhoused Negro population to move into areas which are now occupied by whites." Von Hoffman also noted that Building Commissioner Ramsey frequently announced his intention not to enforce the code's occupancy standards "in spite of the fact that it throws him open to prosecution for malfe[a]sance since the law does not give the Commissioner of Buildings the power to administratively decide which sections of the law he shall enforce and which he shall ignore."[53]

Treating illegal conversions was also a conundrum. On the one hand, such apartments were created without official permission, and therefore illegal, regardless of when the conversion occurred. Illegal conversions sometimes contributed to violations of the housing code's provisions against crowding. On the other hand, compelling owners to deconvert an apartment, especially when occupied, was extraordinarily difficult. An MHPC activist noted, "Even though there may be inspections, notices, suits, and fines, the matter ends there. The illegal units are occupied and remain in use."[54]

To some critics of the new housing code, the city's refusal to prosecute cases of overcrowding indicated an unfair disparity in treatment of property owners and their tenants. In this view, tenants who allowed friends and relatives to live in their apartments without permission from the landlord contributed to overcrowding as well as other sanitary problems. The *Chicago Daily News* agreed with this critique, editorializing in 1961 that "not once has a tenant been sued for a violation as landlords have been countless times." The new housing code for the first time imposed legal obligations on tenants for the maintenance of the units they occupied. Tenants were responsible for maintaining their living quarters in a sanitary condition and disposing of garbage properly. One real estate dealer asked rhetorically, "If a person is willing to live in his own filth, can you ask a landlord to always keep coming in and cleaning the place up for him?"[55]

City officials reluctant to enforce the code passed some of the blame for their inaction on to the courts, which also failed to cooperate with the housing code, and how property owners worked the system. Although the housing code gave judges a variety of means for obtaining property owners' cooperation, the threat of fines for code violations—the most serious of these tools—remained hollow. The *Chicago Sun-Times* reported that only half of the fines levied by the housing courts in code violation cases were ever collected. Property owners who failed to pay their fines were not otherwise punished. Even the very rare imposition of high fines did not necessarily prompt offending owners to correct the code violations. In a case believed to involve the highest fine in Chicago housing court history—$107,600 (538 violations, each assessed at the maximum fine of $200)—the property owner simply boarded up the building without fixing it.[56]

In a detailed study conducted for MHPC, Mary Bolton Wirth corroborated the criticism, explaining why the courts systematically failed to put teeth into the housing code. While she acknowledged improvement in the system since the passage of the housing code, several factors contributed to the housing court's continuing weakness. Crafty owners might, of course, try to avoid court altogether by bribing inspectors. Chicago's system attempted to subvert such corruption with a "team inspection" plan, in which several people attended each building in order to present a "unified case" to prosecutors. All these inspectors, however, were expected to appear in court, in case defense attorneys refused to accept the testimony entered into the inspection records and demanded the right to cross-examine them as witnesses. After one particularly frustrating case in which fifty-five inspectors spent the day in court only to have the judge continue the case to another time, someone commented bitterly, the "enforcement arm strikes out blindly in all directions." The presence of inspectors in court might have made a legal case strong, but the time constraints reduced the total number of buildings they could visit and violations they could identify. In addition, Wirth noted, the physical space of the courtroom was awkward and noisy; the method of transferring cases to different judges was disorganized and often resulted in the absence of attorneys and inspectors from the right room when a case was called. Further, housing court duty was not a desirable assignment for judges, who continued to rotate around the ranks of the municipal court; as soon as a judge became knowledgeable about housing procedures and notorious landlords, he left for another position. Additionally, the several judges who heard cases tended to levy different punishments for the same violations, prompting shrewd property owners to request a transfer of their cases to the lenient judges.[57]

Even property owners found guilty of housing code violations had a variety of techniques for avoiding both payment of fines and compliance with court orders. If a building owner transferred the property to a new owner—such as a relative—the inspection process had to start all over again. Judges exhibited some leniency toward small property owners who lived on-site and were not frequently in court. The judges also were responsive to "the magic word," a promise to deconvert a unit to its original structure. In such cases, property owners were given time to complete the repairs before the fine was dismissed.[58]

If the heralded new housing code therefore contributed little to the actual improvement of buildings in decaying neighborhoods, the city nonetheless made effective use of the housing code for its own purposes. The existence of the code was critical to Chicago's ability to obtain federal funding for urban renewal; improving or preserving existing infrastructure was much less important. In addition, the city used the housing code to force the demolition of especially deteriorated buildings in neighborhoods not designated for urban renewal. Each year between 1960 and 1964, the city increased the number of deteriorated buildings it demolished by approximately one hundred. By October 1964 the city was on pace to demolish almost five hundred such buildings. One MHPC member complained, "Code enforcement in poor neighborhoods is 'non-existent until buildings are about ready to be demolished.'"[59] The subordination of the housing code to urban renewal illustrated the Daley administration's commitment to rebuilding the city over its rehabilitation.

The deficiencies of the 1956 housing code prompted MHPC and other activists to seek yet another round of reform. Beginning in the summer of 1966, MHPC began studying and promoting a set of tougher requirements and better enforcement for residential dwellings in Chicago. In this effort, however, MHPC did not enjoy the same cooperation from city officials that it had during the prior round of code reform. Building Commission officials denied that new measures were needed to make housing code enforcement more effective; further, they claimed, the backlog of unprosecuted cases had disappeared, so no new measures were needed. Without support from the city government, MHPC's recommendations languished.[60]

Given the failures of enforcement and the mayor's apparent indifference to further code reform, community organizations concerned about blight in their neighborhoods shifted their attention away from formal complaint procedures during the 1960s.[61] Some organizations sought out the owners of deteriorated local properties, but, increasingly, they did so in hopes of negotiating directly with the responsible party for improvements. The possibility of prosecution for housing code violations, they knew, was a threat that carried little weight. But being called publicly to account inspired some owners to improve their properties. The Austin Community Organization (ACO), whose tactics followed the precepts of Saul Alinsky, made a practice of inviting neglectful property owners to their meetings. In 1964, for example, ACO activists held a "tense session" with a man who managed a two-flat converted into eight apartments, telling him that "transient accommodations" were not welcome in their neighborhood. A few years later, ACO's successor, the Organization for a Better Austin (OBA), used a similar approach. Frustrated with court proceedings that dawdled while "tenants are forced to live in unbelievably bad conditions," OBA regularly called negligent property owners to "compliance meetings" and compelled them to agree to fix up their buildings.[62]

In 1966 members of the Austin Tenants and Owners Association (ATOA) focused their ire on a building at Cicero and West End that they considered to be a slum, calculating that publicity and humiliation would prompt the owner to make improvements. Lacking the resources to report all the troubling buildings in the area, they decided to try for a big win that would inspire their neighbors. One of the group's leaders explained that "if they succeed in forcing him to correct the violations . . . the building would stand as an example of what could be done to renew the area. And this success would automatically encourage the area residents to greater effort to rehabilitating their properties." After the building's owner failed to respond to several invitations to meet with the group, two dozen ATOA members marched over to view the property themselves, inviting along a local reporter. According to the reporter's subsequent article, the visit to the building's backyard revealed "rusty and torn screens on some windows and none at all on others; a basement entrance with no stairway leading to it with a mound of debris blocking the approach to the door; and a downspout from the eaves that does not meet the sewer opening and funnels rain water into the yard. An ice chest with the door still attached stands on the porch, a hazard to children, and slats are missing on some porch railings." A local block club, also disgusted with this owner's unwillingness to meet with them or repair his properties, made the issuance of an invitation to their next meeting a standing item of unfinished business on their agenda. In the early winter of 1967, after half a year of trying to summon the owner, an inter-racial group of ATOA members went to him. Carrying signs reading "Austin Residents Fight Slum Landlords," several dozen activists picketed his house twice. The pickets finally got his attention; he met with the activists in February and initiated repairs on his property.[63]

Groups like ATOA, OBA, and ACO, which were white-dominated organ-izations, were not the only ones working on improving the physical state of housing in Chicago in the mid- to late 1960s. African Americans, as well, sought to remedy conditions of the buildings where they and their neigh-bors lived. When Martin Luther King Jr. lived in Chicago for an extended stretch of 1966, he made housing conditions the focus of his activism. King's effort to create a northern civil rights movement had two main aims, both intended to liberate African Americans from slum buildings: better condi-tions in black neighborhoods and unfettered access to housing in white neighborhoods. While the marches for open occupancy garnered King much attention, including a rock in the head flung by an angry white Southwest Sider, the staff of the Southern Christian Leadership Conference (SCLC) fanned out in East Garfield Park and North Lawndale, organizing black tenants to pressure their landlords to improve their buildings. A flyer inviting residents to find out about SCLC's plans declared, "A slum is a com-munity where folks are cheated."[64] Like their white counterparts, SCLC and the tenants' organizations recognized that the courts did little to enforce the statutes requiring certain standards of housing; instead, they used other forms of pressure—rent strikes and picket lines—to pressure offending landlords to fix their properties. King's effort to generate a northern civil rights movement focused on housing, however, failed, and he left town with only token accomplishments.[65]

If the attention drawn to the housing code by dissatisfied community groups did little to improve how the courts enforced housing regulations, it might have inspired a few extra enforcement efforts by the Building Department. Occasionally, the Daley administration responded to the crit-icism of housing code enforcement with sweeps of neighborhoods that suf-fered from high concentrations of deteriorating buildings. In March 1966, for example, the city announced inspections for fifteen thousand structures on the West Side, including the area where Martin Luther King Jr. had set up shop. These sporadic sweeps, while generating good publicity for city officials, adversely affected poor homeowners, particularly African Americans, who often lacked the financial resources to make the repairs to bring their properties into compliance with the housing code.[66]

African American homeowners in Chicago frequently had to stretch their finances further than whites in order to purchase property. Because banks routinely refused loans in black neighborhoods, African Americans turned to usurious land contract sales to finance their purchases.[67] In order to raise money to pay off their contracts, black Chicago property owners often rented out a portion of their space to tenants or relatives, a practice used by previous generations of working-class European immigrants to Chicago. Some properties, such as the ubiquitous two-flats, were built for occupation by more than one family. But buyers who were unaware of the strictures on conversions and the details of the new housing code also anticipated rental income from space in basements and attics. Further, pre-closing property inspections were not a standard procedure, so sometimes home buyers discovered that their new house needed repairs only after they moved in. Finally, because contract buyers did not hold legal title to their home until they paid off the balance of their obligation, they were foreclosed from borrowing money to pay for repairs after inspections. So when city officials decided to canvass entire neighborhoods rather than investigate particularly egregious buildings that activists complained about, they usually caught in their net well-intentioned homeowners.[68]

African American homeowners required to meet the terms of the housing code often found themselves in financial straits. Rosa Scott, a resident of Woodlawn, on the South Side, explained, "Our houses cannot comply with the present codes. It is like forcing a Cadillac motor into a Model-T-Ford. It just won't work." As an example, she cited her sister, who "paid over $5,000 for improvements in her basement[;] now they have her in court for non-compliance after she went to the expense and trouble to meet urban renewal requests." South Side civil rights activist Robert Lucas, speaking on behalf of Protest at the Polls, testified before the City Council Committee on Building and Zoning that "the building inspectors gleefully descend upon Negro property owners who have no influence and no ready cash. The discriminatory inforcement [sic] of the building code has been responsible for many a thrifty and frugal family losing their life savings in one month." Concluding that "no law is just which applied sanctions indiscriminately to the rich and the poor, or the strong and the weak alike," Lucas urged that "grace periods and lower penalties" be offered to small property owners.[69]

Groups more sympathetic to enforcement wanted the Building Department to crack down on slum landlords who allowed their properties to languish unrepaired. But they could not at the same time suggest code exemptions for resident homeowners, whose stake in the community they wished to reinforce, not diminish. Instead of arguing that small property owners should not be held responsible for the same sorts of repairs as big property owners, such groups argued in favor of open occupancy legislation. By enabling African Americans to purchase homes wherever they could afford them, such a law would ease the crowding in black neighborhoods.[70]

Chicago's housing code grew out of efforts by reformers to protect the entire city from fire and the health of poor people with few housing options. The letter of the law, however, was distinct from its practice. Throughout the history of efforts to regulate housing conditions in Chicago, official exemptions and reluctance to enforce were routine. In the much-ballyhooed new housing code of 1956, the city had a means for improvement that it wielded only selectively, toward the ends favored by the mayor and his officials. The existence of the housing code allowed the city to pursue grander dreams of transformation, including a new tool: federally funded urban renewal. The housing code thus was transformed from a tool for general urban rehabilitation and the protection of the poor into a particular weapon wielded in service of a localized redevelopment. As officials turned toward new means of ridding the city of undesirable buildings and stretches of neighborhoods, white West Siders followed along. They, too, wished to tap into the new sources of money available to wipe out the hazards in their surroundings.

CHAPTER 3

Conservation and Urban Renewal

In April 1959 Ira J. Bach, commissioner of Chicago's two-year-old Department of City Planning, arranged a bus trip through Chicago for heads of other city departments. The trip was a tour of the city's urban renewal program. The route ran north to south through the city, highlighting 158 acres of old railroad tracks at the south end of the Loop that Mayor Richard J. Daley intended for a campus of the University of Illinois, as well as new Chicago Housing Authority buildings, the Prairie Shores apartment complex, the construction site of the McCormick Place Convention Center, and new townhouses in Hyde Park. Parts of Chicago in the late 1950s were abuzz with redevelopment, but the city's West Side was entirely absent from the tour's itinerary.[1]

The omission of the West Side resulted not from local aversion to urban renewal, but from the reluctance of city officials to incorporate the West Side into their plans. Chicagoans of many stripes had ambitious ideas for preserving and renewing the city. In the immediate postwar years, institutions on the South Side, seeking to protect their physical plants against decay and the migration of African Americans into the surrounding neighborhoods, lobbied for and then used new legislative tools that enabled them to acquire, clear, and rebuild on the sites of deteriorating properties. The University of Chicago put its surrounding neighborhood of Hyde Park forward as a locale for experimenting with redevelopment practices. In the mid-1950s, under Mayor Richard J. Daley, the city government developed plans to apply these techniques on a wider basis.

Daley's administration envisioned renewing the city with a ring of clearance and redevelopment around the downtown. That buffer area would protect existing businesses and new government buildings in the Loop and also spread remedial effects outward into the city's residential neighborhoods. This downtown-oriented program placed the West Side—which in the mid-1950s was neither as decayed nor as densely populated by African Americans as the South Side—low on the priority list. Officials did not preclude outright working with the West Side but repeatedly postponed action there. By 1960 the possibility of expanding Chicago's urban renewal program was attenuated by shortfalls of money, ineffectual staff, administrative redundancy, and the financial sinkhole of the prototype conservation project in Hyde Park.

Nonetheless, white West Siders saw in Chicago's conservation and urban renewal programs an opportunity to improve the state of their neighborhoods. The same complex of anxieties that prompted West Siders to support implementation of the new housing code inspired their eagerness for urban renewal. Like the South Side institutions that pioneered urban renewal, white West Siders operated from a combination of fears about the physical and racial conditions of their environments. The physical deterioration of their environment, which they interpreted as blight, represented a material threat to the neighborhood. In addition, such decay seemed to repel desirable white residents and allow the admission of undesirable African Americans to the neighborhood.

Accordingly, during the postwar decades, especially the 1950s, West Side community groups and institutions actively agitated to be included on Chicago's agenda for conservation and urban renewal. The most sustained effort to obtain urban renewal for the West Side emanated from Sears, Roebuck and Company, the giant retailer whose national headquarters occupied a large swath of North Lawndale. While Sears' effort focused primarily on removing African Americans from the neighborhood, residential community groups from West Garfield Park and Austin had more mixed motives for seeking inclusion in Chicago's urban renewal program. White residents of Chicago's West Side imagined for themselves a future within the city's borders; after decades during which it was exceedingly difficult to afford private local investments, they hoped at last for an improved physical environment. The Far West Side was not gravely affected by deterioration, but small untreated pockets of decay worried neighborhood groups. In addition to improvement's intrinsic benefits, they hoped that signs of local physical rejuvenation might inspire white residents to stay, which would help keep African Americans out.[2]

In most of these cases, West Side organizations eventually succeeded in winning formal recognition of the legitimacy of their requests for urban renewal. Repeatedly, however, the city declined to pursue specific action on West Siders' petitions, illustrating their relative lack of influence in Chicago's political power structure. One West Side newspaper concluded in 1970, "So far as the West Side is concerned, urban renewal has always been confined to promises. Nothing whatsoever has been accomplished in the area." As officials' neglect of the 1956 housing code also showed, the existence of desirable public policies did not guarantee their uniform implementation. No direct evidence indicates why the Daley administration allowed West Siders' requests to fall by the wayside, but the area was clearly not a high priority.[3] It is possible that Richard J. Daley anticipated the settlement of participants in the second Great Migration in precisely those neighborhoods. The sure result was that the West Side neighborhoods, where African Americans sought refuge in the postwar years, were among the most deteriorated and neglected in the city.

As they urged that some form of rehabilitation program be granted to their neighborhood, West Siders only occasionally differentiated urban renewal and conservation. This distinction, however, mattered to the Daley administration, which envisioned the wholesale remaking of Chicago. "Urban renewal" came to refer to the large-scale clearance and rebuilding process that dispossessed and displaced tens of thousands of Chicagoans from their homes. "Conservation" was the more moderate form of property rehabilitation; conservation projects generally funded the repair of existing properties without requiring residents to depart. During the postwar years, several different city agencies administered such projects for the city. In each case, white West Siders wanted access to whatever monies and tools were available to enable them to improve their neighborhoods. West Siders were so consistently thwarted in these requests that they rarely had the opportunity to articulate in detail what a renewal project in their area might look like.[4]

In retrospect, given that many Americans now regard urban renewal as anathema, often remembering it particularly as "Negro removal," it is startling to think that there was a time when people sought any version of it for their own neighborhoods.[5] In the early 1950s, when white West Siders began their drive, it was not clear that their desire for modest specific rehabilitation projects did not mesh with the Daley administration's broad agenda for rebuilding. By the mid-1960s, in part because of examples from Chicago, the term "urban renewal" developed a fearsome reputation, and professional planners began suggesting that conservation was preferable to large-scale clearance. But as urban renewal went out of fashion, the seeds sown for urban renewal in the 1950s finally began to bear fruit in the mid-1960s. As the city government overcame financial and bureaucratic hurdles, Chicago at last seemed poised to initiate some form of urban renewal on the West Side. In response, activists speaking on behalf of the West Side's new African American population, like their counterparts in other cities, mobilized *against* its implementation.[6] The officially constituted urban renewal advisory committee for North Lawndale explicitly called for the alternative of "human renewal," and a citywide coalition moved to stop the city council from executing any plans not approved by local residents. As a result of the combination of their predecessors' struggles and the dilatory character of city action, black West Siders inherited neighborhoods that were both deteriorated and also newly threatened by the prospect of drastic action from the city government.

History of Urban Renewal in Chicago

From the onset of urban renewal programming in Chicago, officials structured their efforts to benefit and protect the downtown—which they argued was a means of renewing the city as a whole. The city's postwar urban renewal program operated on four simultaneous fronts. First, University of Chicago officials influenced the state legislature to experiment with possible tools for urban renewal in the Hyde Park area. Second, the city itself used those tools to clear out acres and acres of deteriorated properties around the Loop in select neighborhoods. These cleared and rebuilt areas were to buffer the Loop against further decay. Third, new public buildings were erected within the Loop to ensure the downtown's attractiveness to the city's power brokers. Fourth, the city erected massive public housing complexes to contain some of the displaced slum dwellers at a suitable distance from the downtown. With these priorities, all of them costly, the Daley administration had few resources to spare for the entreaties of white West Siders.[7]

Chicago's government and business elites, a classic "pro-growth coalition," became quite concerned about the physical state of Chicago during the Great Depression. New commercial development in the Loop came to a standstill when the national economy crashed in 1929. Real estate dealers, downtown businesspeople, and politicians worried about the possible consequences of the increasingly neglected and decaying structures. From the point of view of urban planners and city officials, Chicago's once-booming downtown was under a dual threat. First, the economic crisis undermined their ability to foster commerce. Second, because they seemed blighted, the decay of neglected, unrepaired buildings surrounding the downtown had the potential to spread to other structures and undermine the stability of the Loop as Chicago's business center. As early as the 1920s, the beginnings of a residential shift to the suburbs suggested there were viable alternatives to centering business in the downtown.[8] Without appropriate legislative tools, officials could do little during the 1930s to protect the downtown directly, but they began collecting data to support long-term redevelopment plans.

Two local agencies exercised authority over the physical restructuring of the city. The Chicago Plan Commission (CPC), created in 1909 to implement the city's first master plan, took little action during the Depression. In 1939 CPC's numbers were reduced and its functions absorbed into the city government. Provided with monies from the federal Works Progress Administration, CPC researched and documented Chicago's physical condition. The second agency, the Metropolitan Housing and Planning Council (MHPC), was a quasi-official body formed in 1934 and charged with investigating the city's housing needs. MHPC members dismissed CPC as an "apathetic creature of the aldermen." MHPC, dominated by a board of governors with financial interests in Chicago's downtown, took the lead in anticipating the city's future development. Using data assembled by CPC staff, MHPC fashioned new legislative tools that made postwar urban renewal possible.[9]

In the early 1940s, the city administration began translating the information gathered about Chicago during the Depression into concrete plans for postwar revitalization. A series of wartime CPC publications documented the extent of decline throughout the city and recommended a general approach for redevelopment.[10] The studies carefully distinguished the areas of the city that were blighted beyond rehabilitation from those that could be conserved. In 1942 and 1943, the two volumes of the *Chicago Land Use Survey* detailed the residential and industrial uses of every block within the city. Using this data, in 1943 CPC issued the *Master Plan of Residential Land Use of Chicago*. The *Master Plan* calculated that 10.7 percent of the city's area was "blighted" or "near-blighted."[11] It called for the complete demolition of buildings in such areas so that "new residential neighborhoods can be created." The *Master Plan* found an additional fifty-seven square miles, or 26.6 percent of the city's area, in need of "conservation," that is, selective demolition, rehabilitation, and reduction of population densities.[12]

In aggregating data about the condition of housing into geographically distinctive clusters, Chicago's city government took an analytic step more sophisticated than many of its contemporaries. During the Depression and

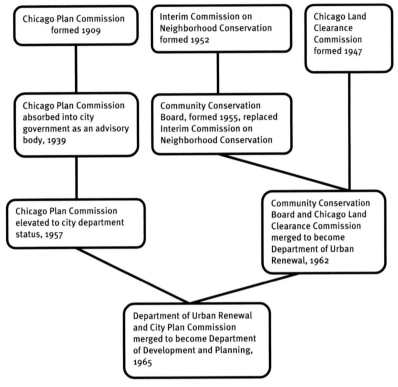

Fig. 6. Chicago's planning and urban renewal agencies.

World War II years, most cities around the United States had, at most, only partial inventories of their housing stocks. The peculiar interests and energies of private reformers and official plan commissions dictated the timing, location, and thoroughness of local knowledge about housing. The 1934 Real Property Inventories, compiled by the U.S. Department of Commerce, provided the most comprehensive examination of housing conditions in American cities. These inventories made a "complete census of dwellings" in sixty-four cities of diverse ages, including one from each of the forty-eight states. The cities ranged from Cleveland, Ohio, with 232,170 separate dwelling units, to Santa Fe, New Mexico, with only 2,720 dwellings. Edith Elmer Wood interpreted the significance of the Real Property Inventories and assembled the partial data available for other cities in her 1935 study, *Slums and Blighted Areas in the United States.* Where she lacked strictly comparable data about conditions, Wood used the asking price of rental housing as a proxy for its physical state.[13]

Because the Real Property Inventories did not include Chicago, comparisons between its housing stock and that in other cities must be made with caution. The data for Chicago, however, suggested that its physical condition was not anomalous. The 1942 *Chicago Land Use Survey* identified 7.8 percent of the total residential structures (buildings) and 19.8 percent of the dwelling units (apartments and houses) as inadequate.[14] This state of affairs made Chicago appear similar to the other cities in the national 1934 Real Property Inventories. Residents of such small cities as Providence, Rhode Island, and Syracuse, New York, where less than 10 percent of the structures were "in bad condition," inhabited the healthiest housing stock discovered in 1934.[15] The largest cities on the 1934 list, Cleveland, Ohio, and Minneapolis, Minnesota, saw larger percentages of their residential structures "in bad condition," with 18.6 and 13.5 percent so indicated.[16] Wood also argued that Chicago's conditions were similar to New York City, where in 1934 the New York Housing Authority made its own property inventory. In New York as a whole, 7.7 percent of the residential structures needed "major repairs" or were "unfit for use," while in Manhattan proper, 20.2 percent of residential structures fell into these categories.[17] Because all of these data described the conditions of buildings only, without consideration of human crowding, they probably understated the number of people directly affected by them. In Chicago, however, where authorities operated under the assumption that such conditions threatened not only building occupants but also the surrounding environment, the concentration of poor residential structures in certain areas was alarming.

Chicago's *Master Plan* identified the areas that encircled the city's downtown as the sections that most needed complete redevelopment, which was neither an economic nor historical coincidence. Settled relatively early in the city's history and left intact by the Great Fire of 1871, the areas immediately south and west of the Loop were among the oldest built-up and continuously populated parts of Chicago. Most of the residents were African Americans or the working-class descendants of late nineteenth-century European immigrants. The buildings they inhabited were dangerously overcrowded and deteriorating.[18] Because these decaying areas circumscribed the Loop, officials worried that they could easily blight the rest of the downtown.

Members of the pro-growth coalition considered the rebuilding of the areas around the downtown crucial for protecting Chicago's economic future. They reasoned that clearing and reconstructing decayed areas would prevent blight from impinging on the business district. In a protected downtown, businesses and wealthy customers would continue to engage in commerce, preserving both the tax base for the city and the appeal of the downtown to the tourist trade. Thus, although Chicago's postwar plans might have served the city as a whole, they centered on protecting the downtown against the decay seen as threatening from the south and west. When the tractable Mayor Martin Kennelly took office in 1947, business leaders supplied him with a legislative agenda for revitalizing the city through a combination of slum clearance and public housing.[19]

The first postwar redevelopment projects were carried out on the South Side. At the north and south ends of African American settlement, private institutions took the initiative in clearing out old dilapidated buildings. Having decided not to leave the city for suburban grounds, Michael Reese Hospital and the Illinois Institute of Technology initiated the process at the north end of the Black Belt by improving their own facilities during the war. To protect their investment in physical plants against the contagion they perceived around them and to bring new, healthy building to the area, these institutions created the South Side Planning Board (SSPB) in 1946. SSPB attracted investment from the New York Life Insurance Company, which replaced acres of nearby "slum housing" with the middle-income housing developments of Lake Meadows and Prairie Shores.[20]

South Side institutions also pushed for state legislation that created a new group of redevelopment agencies with overlapping authority and increased powers to control chunks of private property in the city. The 1947 Illinois Blighted Areas Redevelopment Act authorized the creation of local Land Clearance Commissions with the power of eminent domain over properties deemed cheaper to clear than to rehabilitate. The Chicago Land Clearance Commission could take blighted properties larger than two acres, clear them of buildings, and resell them to private developers. In 1952 the city created an Interim Commission on Neighborhood Conservation to begin a coordinated effort. The next major piece of state legislation, the 1953 Urban Community Conservation Act, allowed Chicago to establish a Community Conservation Board (CCB), which it did in 1955. This act, which included districts that were not yet blighted, added slum prevention to the growing list of reasons a city could take private property. CCB had the power to designate areas of forty or more acres as "conservation areas." The mayor appointed Community Conservation Councils, local organizations charged with representing the interests of conservation areas. Also in 1953 the Neighborhood Redevelopment Corporation Act of 1941 was amended to make its use feasible. The 1953 amendment allowed small groups of citizens to file for state recognition as Neighborhood Redevelopment Corporations. Such corporations, on obtaining the cooperation of owners of 60 percent of property in a designated conservation area, could take the rest by the power of eminent domain and then clear and rebuild on the site.[21]

The University of Chicago, in the Hyde Park area at the south end of the Black Belt, was the first institution to take advantage of this legislation. In 1953 MHPC released a study commissioned by the university recommending Hyde Park as the setting for an experimental effort. In the Hyde Park program, university and city officials collaborated to work out how urban renewal and conservation could be implemented elsewhere in the city. When existing laws proved inadequate for the project, the university persuaded the state legislature to enact the 1953 Urban Community Conservation Act, which provided "the tools to preserve Hyde Park." Acting through the South East Chicago Commission, the South West Hyde Park Neighborhood Redevelopment Corporation, and the city council, the university proceeded with clearance and rebuilding in the western portions of Hyde Park. This expensive project, which used $24 million in public funds, was well under way by 1958 and mostly completed by 1960.[22]

As the Hyde Park, Lake Meadows, and Prairie Shores experiments proceeded, city officials' attention turned to securing the downtown's future more systematically. As mayor, Richard J. Daley moved aggressively to step up Chicago's renewal efforts. Part of Daley's political agenda was to implement measures that MHPC had long advocated. Daley pushed through the state legislature a reorganization of the city's renewal agencies, a change that delayed some of the low-priority projects but streamlined a redundant bureaucracy. Daley also sponsored the revision of Chicago's zoning ordinance in 1957. In addition, under Daley's watch, Chicago also saw a spurt of construction of public buildings in the downtown; a new federal complex at the south end of the Loop; and a new Civic Center, at the north end graced by a sculpture by Pablo Picasso.[23] All of this construction ensured that a steady stream of attorneys, at least, would make their presence felt downtown for decades to come.

Simultaneously, officials sought to rid the city of the ring of slums surrounding the Loop and replace them with a buffer zone for the central business district. North of the Chicago River, the city authorized two distinct renewal projects intended to make the city attractive to white middle-class professionals who might work in the downtown. The first project was Sandburg Village on the Near North Side, built under the authority of the Blighted Areas Redevelopment Act. Sandburg Village replaced an old rooming house area that divided the legendary Gold Coast from one of Chicago's most notorious slums, sometimes called "Little Hell." A group of developers led by Arthur Rubloff underbid all other prospects for the cleared land and then built luxury high-rise apartments on the site.[24] Just north of Sandburg Village, the influential Lincoln Park Conservation Association

(LPCA) won recognition from the CCB as a conservation area. LPCA attracted urban renewal monies for a program of selective demolition and rehabilitation. These projects laid the foundation for Lincoln Park's subsequent status as one of the city's most appealing residential neighborhoods for young white professionals.[25] South of the Loop, the city built one of the nation's largest convention centers, McCormick Place. And on a 300-acre site on the Near West Side, the Chicago Medical Center Commission, an independent state-authorized agency, razed homes and replaced them with hospital facilities.[26]

The construction of public housing for poor African Americans supplemented the redevelopment of deteriorated areas immediately around the downtown in the city's plans. Most of the urban renewal projects that "cleared" land also displaced hundreds or thousands of people who lived in the buildings that occupied the property.[27] Although the Chicago Land Clearance Commission initially kept no records, in 1961 the Tenants Relocation Bureau of Chicago estimated that since 1948, 43,418 families and 15,250 single people had been displaced by urban renewal and other redevelopment projects. The key to evicting residents from renewal areas was the 1947 Relocation Act, the "companion measure" of the Blighted Areas Redevelopment Act.[28] The Chicago Housing Authority's program of high-rise building offered public "relocation" housing for families evicted from condemned areas. The new public housing complexes were systematically located on sites already populated by African Americans, in order to pacify whites who did not want the government to introduce blacks into their communities.[29] The Robert Taylor Homes on the South Side, the Cabrini-Green complex on the Near North Side, and the combination of Harrison Courts, Maplewood Courts, Rockwell Gardens, and Ogden Courts at the western edge of the Near West Side delineated the black ghetto that existed when they were planned.[30] In what Arnold Hirsch has called a "ferocious application of a domestic 'containment' policy," African Americans were locked into badly maintained and poorly landscaped buildings, a "second ghetto" of public housing, removed from both the downtown and the outlying white residential areas.[31] Thus, the city administration used the bulk of the money authorized for conservation and urban renewal during the 1950s to build a protective ring around downtown business interests.

Daley's actions revealed his commitment to the vision of revitalizing Chicago from the center out—protecting and renewing the Loop area, while expecting the benefits of the center's reinvigoration to spill outward in the city. His Department of City Planning laid out Daley's priorities in its first official report, issued in 1958, the *Development Plan for the Central Area of Chicago*.[32] As an enthusiastic consumer of the new federal and state tools of the postwar era, Daley might have spent any leftover monies and energies on the city's outlying residential wards. But a series of unfortunate developments scuttled Daley's ability to share the wealth, if that was ever his intention. Funding shortfalls after 1960, periodic administrative reorganizations, and perhaps official indifference all fettered the expansion of the projects to neighborhoods such as those on the West Side.

Many residents of the city's outlying residential neighborhoods shared the concerns of city officials about the contagious dangers of decay and blight. They hoped to benefit from the windfall of state and federal monies for local improvement through urban renewal and conservation. On the West Side, local organizations won formal acknowledgment that their neighborhoods merited assistance, but the city's emphasis on protecting the downtown and channeling most urban renewal programs to that end limited official response to simple recognition, not any substantive programs or funds.

North Lawndale

The comprehensive and most sustained effort to bring urban renewal to the West Side originated in North Lawndale. Initially, a small group of liberals who envisioned creating an improved and interracial community sponsored the effort under the auspices of the North Lawndale Citizens Council (NLCC). A subsequently constituted group—the Greater Lawndale Conservation Commission (GLCC)—charged with pursuing urban renewal for the area, however, received the lion's share of its funding from corporate giant Sears and other neighborhood businesses. As was the case in Hyde Park, the institutional interests of Sears overwhelmed the racial liberalism of NLCC's founders. The influence of business interests over GLCC frequently put the organization at odds with local residents—both the departing Jewish residents and the in-migrant African Americans. Nonetheless, tensions within Lawndale's population ultimately had little bearing on the success of GLCC's program. North Lawndale was not a high-enough priority for city officials to bother shepherding the area through the urban renewal machinery. By the time it might have provided a specific program for Lawndale, the city was entirely out of money for any sort of new urban renewal projects.

In 1950 a small group of citizens hoping to address "the problems arising out of the changing community" organized NLCC. Middle-class African Americans had been moving into North Lawndale steadily since the end of World War II. The leaders of NLCC aspired to create, in their words, "an interracial community able to maintain harmonious living and decent

standards . . . a 'pilot community' of an interracial makeup." To achieve
these ends, NLCC leaders sponsored a variety of local activities. In its first
years, NLCC organized a block club program, screened residents for tuber-
culosis, investigated illegal conversions, and sponsored employment counseling. An NLCC officer explained that the group was arranged along the
same lines as the Back of the Yards Neighborhood Council (BYNC), a South
Side group that was the first community organization founded by the legendary Saul Alinsky. In contrast to the racially homogeneous BYNC, NLCC
intentionally cultivated both black and white leaders and participants.[33]

In 1953 NLCC's focus narrowed to the physical environment. Two years
earlier the city's Building Commission singled out Lawndale for special
attention, finding that about half the buildings inspected had serious code
violations. NLCC leaders, however, complained about the difficulties of correcting such code violations. NLCC shared with other people in the period
the sense that both blight and improvement were "catching," so a more concentrated rehabilitation program seemed to be in order. Following a meeting with James Downs, chairman of Chicago's Neighborhood Conservation
Commission, the group decided to explore the possibility of getting the city
to certify Lawndale as a "conservation area," the necessary precursor to any
urban renewal program.[34]

From their first interactions with North Lawndale leaders, city officials
cautioned that other sections of the city were already further along in attracting such funding. In his October meeting with NLCC, Downs explained that
his commission intended to choose six areas of the city for experiments with
conservation. Administrators had already selected four South Side neighborhoods, and they intended to pick one West Side and one North Side community for the other two pilot projects. Institutions on the Near West Side
had already organized a proposal. Downs explained to NLCC leaders that in
order to demonstrate their earnestness, they needed to raise money and set
up a full-time staff and office dedicated to the effort of bringing conservation to Lawndale. At the end of November, participants in an NLCC meeting agreed to set up a local community council, and an executive of Sears
offered to provide stationery for the new organization. By January 1954 the
Greater Lawndale Conservation Commission held weekly meetings at the
Sears YMCA.[35] The creation of GLCC spelled the end of NLCC.[36]

The transfer of the renewal impulse from NLCC to GLCC provided Sears,
Roebuck and Company an opportunity to insert its corporate interests into
the local planning process. Although it was neither the reason for
Lawndale's existence nor the only company in the area, Sears represented
one of the most significant corporate investments on the West Side and
exercised a corresponding influence on local affairs. By 1957 some four-

teen thousand people, including roughly two thousand company executives, worked at Sears in North Lawndale. Because "an organization and an investment of this magnitude are not very mobile," the company's vice president of public relations explained, Sears had a stake in the racial and economic changes occurring in North Lawndale during the mid-1950s.[37]

Sears executives were indeed worried about Lawndale's future, although their concerns were not those of the physical environment to which NLCC responded. The primary source of their concern was the migration of African Americans into Lawndale. Sears officials associated African Americans with blight and feared that the recent crowding of blacks into the neighborhood was spurring the deterioration of Lawndale into "a rock-bottom slum." Because of the facilities that Sears provided within its headquarters, company employees did not have to spend much money or time in other Lawndale commercial enterprises. But the company's white employees were increasingly reluctant to come to work in an area inhabited by African Americans. A decade after the company moved its headquarters to Chicago's downtown, a journalist studying the company learned that employees believed that "the neighborhood surrounding the plant had become so dangerous that Sears employed the third-largest police force in the state of Illinois. The three-block walk from the elevated-train station to the red brick complex had become a picket line of uniformed policemen." Significantly, Sears executives did not see in black Lawndale residents a pool of potential employees. Before the 1954 retirement of chairman of the board Robert E. Wood, a plantation owner and "typical Southern gentleman," only a few African Americans were employed at Sears headquarters, even in manual and clerical positions. Only an intense campaign by the American Friends Service Committee persuaded Wood's successors to hire African Americans in public contact and white-collar positions.[38]

Sears executives were so concerned about the future of Lawndale that early in the 1950s they explored the possibility of moving their headquarters elsewhere, "perhaps to some pleasant location in the suburbs." Considerations of corporate responsibility and publicity, however, prompted the company to stay in Lawndale. Sears had a long-standing practice of providing charitable goods and services to communities the company served. As the company's national customer base shifted at mid-century from its traditional rural mail-order catalog sales to urban and especially suburban consumers who shopped in stores, Sears' philanthropy followed. Accordingly, in the 1950s, in a series of addresses and popular pamphlets, Sears instructed executives and store managers around the nation to offer civic leadership in the area of urban renewal. Sears chairman Theodore V. Houser explained, "Neighborhood deterioration represents the same kind of need in the case of the cities that poor live-stock breeds and poor crop yields represented a generation ago on the farms. Unquestionably, it is one of today's most urgent national problems, and our interests as businessmen and citizens coincide as they do in many other areas." In this context, abandoning its urban headquarters, a move that executives feared might also "sound the death knell of the area," would be disastrous to the company's reputation. So Sears poured large sums of money into the Greater Lawndale Conservation Commission, hoping it would generate a solution to Lawndale's problems. In an effort to prevent GLCC from appearing to be a puppet of the company, Sears kept the size of its contributions to the organization secret.[39]

With substantial financial backing from Sears, GLCC focused its early efforts on winning the support of other local business interests and generating a broader consensus for the group's goals. Julian Levi, the director of the South East Chicago Commission and therefore the man responsible for much of the urban renewal program in Hyde Park, advised the GLCC leadership to begin fund-raising with local businesses and mer-chants, and then move to building relationships with other local institu-tions. Levi cautioned that a "house-to-house canvass for funds" would not raise enough money to be worth the effort. The motto carried on the GLCC letterhead, "Neighborhood Insurance: Costs Little, Protects Much," sub-tly reflected the organization's assumption that local businesses were its primary constituents.[40]

GLCC did little to cultivate local residents. Even in the absence of spe-cific projects, both white and black groups in the area were suspicious of GLCC's motives. Local organizations with white constituencies assumed that GLCC's primary mission—like NLCC's—was the promotion of inte-gration, which they regarded as the first step in their own displacement. African Americans already in the Lawndale area, on the other hand, sus-pected that GLCC's urban renewal ambitions were a cover for dispossess-ing them. The president of the Douglas Park Federation of Neighborhood Clubs and Churches criticized the temporary leaders of GLCC so fiercely that they hesitated to serve as the group's permanent executives. In July 1954 the "Federation Clubs and Churches" called a public meeting to protest GLCC's still amorphous plans. In a flyer edged with swastikas, it warned against allowing a group of businessmen who "do not even live in this area to foist a so-called conservation program that will cause the eviction of ten-ants and the loss or property." Although GLCC leaders dismissed the fed-eration as "a tiny, though vociferous segment of the community," they hastened to include a few prominent black citizens on the board.[41]

African American members of the organization's board of directors voiced some of the most sustained criticism of GLCC. When L. C. Branch, the owner of the House of Branch Funeral Home, failed to win high office in GLCC in 1956, he publicly lambasted the group for inattention to grassroots reservations about its plans. GLCC's board members and executive director lived outside the area and did not understand the "social or physical problems confronting the community." Gloria Pughsley, a GLCC vice president and president of the Greater Lawndale Association of Block Clubs, repeatedly clashed with other officers. After she finally left the board, she explained, "They don't want to fan any sparks of progress. Again, it's the technique of keeping the Negro begging. As long as he is begging, he's under your thumb." Branch and Pughsley both maintained that the African American residents of Lawndale were deeply concerned with the area's physical condition and that they welcomed conservation programs. But they feared that GLCC might really be after a large-scale clearance project that would displace many African American homeowners.[42]

So, despite the sponsorship of corporate giant Sears, the Greater Lawndale Conservation Commission entered the citywide competition for urban renewal monies with several distinct disadvantages. GLCC presented to the city an unusually narrow base. It successfully persuaded local business interests to cooperate but made only the most superficial effort to win support from local residents, who in fact gave evidence of their hostility to the organization's purposes. Additionally, GLCC was subject to internal dissension that sometimes spilled out into public venues. Finally, none of the signals they received from city officials suggested that the group had managed to persuade the local government that Lawndale should receive priority treatment. Lawndale's representatives were warned from the start that the Near West Side was better organized to serve as the West Side's pilot project. And as they proceeded, GLCC officials heard little to indicate that the Daley administration wanted to advance Lawndale's claims. In other policy arenas, West Siders often received at least a small measure of encouragement from city officials, even when their projects were ultimately denied. It seems likely that city officials had little intention of allocating renewal monies to a section of Chicago ill-positioned to support the rehabilitation of the downtown, but that they were willing to string Lawndale along in case extra money serendipitously manifested.

Despite these multiple disadvantages, GLCC forged ahead. In September 1954 the president of GLCC wrote to James Downs, requesting formal recognition of Lawndale as a conservation area. Downs's deputy responded with a polite letter that welcomed GLCC's efforts but cautioned that a recent state supreme court decision required the reorganization of the administration of urban renewal in Chicago. About eighteen months later, after the creation of the city's Community Conservation Board, GLCC submitted to the new body a four-page list of "Lawndale Leaders" for appointment to the required local advisory council. CCB did not forward that list to the mayor, suggesting that it anticipated little specific action for North Lawndale. Nonetheless, the city began the process of recognizing the area as formally eligible for conservation.[43]

In September 1956 General Richard Smykal, commissioner of the CCB, announced a public hearing of testimony relating to the designation of a "West Congress Conservation Area," consisting of sections of three distinct neighborhoods: North Lawndale, East Garfield Park, and West Garfield Park. GLCC officers would have preferred an area coterminous with their organization's boundaries, but for expediency's sake they accepted a conservation designation covering part of the North Lawndale area. The minutes of the board of directors meeting held after the hearing conceded, "Obviously, improvements cannot stop at a certain street or alley lines, and any improvement made in one section will affect the whole area." In fact, GLCC had little say in the matter, as CCB selected the boundaries for consideration without consulting GLCC executives. Smykal's official reason for selecting the West Congress area was that it would "permit faster action in preparing a conservation plan . . . than would be possible if each of the three were treated as an individual conservation area."[44] In fact, he was honoring a request from West Garfield Park activists that their aspirations for community conservation be appended to Lawndale's effort.

Even with this wrench in the works, GLCC made a conscientious effort to demonstrate local institutional enthusiasm for conservation in the West Congress area. At the hearing, held on October 9, 1956, at the Gold Dome building in Garfield Park, GLCC turned out speakers from a wide range of local institutions, including representatives of the area's industrial concerns, small business owners, churches, and hospitals. All testified on behalf of the conservation designation, but GLCC was still disappointed. Local newspapers paid more attention to a man who collapsed and died at the hearing than they did to the conservation proposal itself. By mid-December it was apparent that CCB was going to exclude Lawndale from this round of conservation. In public comments, Commissioner Smykal reportedly "glossed over" the recommendation for the West Congress area. West Siders heard various reasons for the decision, but GLCC directors suspected that "some people in high places" considered Lawndale blighted beyond salvation.[45]

These events prompted GLCC leaders to conclude that they had a "local publicity" problem and to think about how they might obtain at least a facade of popular support for their plans. The communities in Chicago that successfully courted urban renewal—like Hyde Park and Lincoln Park—mobilized active groups of citizens who spoke publicly in favor of the clearance programs.[46] In early 1957 Sears commissioned a secret report on GLCC's relationship with the local community, concluding, "The citizens [*sic*] action arm of the GLCC must enlist general neighborhood citizens [*sic*] support and the program must be adaptable to the variety of characteristics among the population in the area." The report recommended that GLCC use action on housing code enforcement and block club creation to persuade residents that it had their interests at heart. A member of CCB reinforced this new direction in June. He told the directors of GLCC that in their zeal to cultivate support from business and industry, they had neglected the "grass roots." If GLCC met with Italian American and African American residents on issues of concern to them, such as the enforcement of the housing code, then the board might reconsider its decision.[47]

As these messages accumulated, GLCC began to make more of an effort to involve Lawndale's residents in their program. In December 1956, in order to "provide a direct means of communication between the residents and the Commission," GLCC began actively soliciting individual members, who paid between $1 and $5 for the privilege. In July 1957 GLCC sponsored a new Ladies Auxiliary, a small group consisting primarily of African American professional women.[48] The Ladies Auxiliary took over the membership drive, raising the number of individual memberships from 25 in 1957 to 1,250 three years later. GLCC also hired a community organizer to act as a liaison with the area's growing African American population. Such links with Lawndale residents, however, did not transform GLCC into a community-based organization or a general outlet for local concerns. In 1959 the executive director insisted to dissenting staff members that the purpose of the community-organizing effort was "to enlist support for a plan for Lawndale," not to plan whatever other projects residents happened to find appealing. As late as 1966, an observer characterized GLCC as "dependent on and controlled by conservative business."[49]

CCB rewarded GLCC for taking steps toward cultivating community cooperation. The electorate's passage of a bond issue in June 1957 freed up new funds for conservation and urban renewal in Chicago. In November the board held new hearings on whether Lawndale should be designated a conservation area, and in December it announced that the area was now technically eligible for conservation funding. In the short run, this designation did nothing to change Lawndale's landscape. By the summer of 1958, the executive director and president of GLCC appreciated the significance of the mayor's failure to appoint the required Community Advisory Council. That step was a prerequisite to the initiation of local planning surveys and the receipt of federal funding. Without it, urban renewal in Lawndale could not proceed.[50]

The appointment of a local advisory council, however, would only have created an official body empowered to pester an unresponsive city administration. Even if Mayor Daley wanted to channel urban renewal funds to Lawndale in the early 1960s, he could not have. Chicago was out of urban renewal funds and entirely dependent on the federal government to provide more. The Federal Housing Act of 1961 made new monies available, but Chicago failed to meet the law's conditions. Under the terms of the act, Chicago could receive $2 in federal funds for every dollar it contributed to the process or that local institutions such as hospitals or universities spent on public works in urban renewal areas. This federal largesse had the potential, thought observers, to double the city's attack on decay or even eliminate slums altogether.[51]

But Chicago was in no position to contribute even one-third of the cost of new urban renewal programs. In 1961 a former city urban renewal official acknowledged that Chicago was "out of cash." It had been since 1960. A $66 million bond issue put before the voters in April 1962 might have triggered the federal windfall. But for the first time in the postwar years, responding to abuses in the urban renewal program that included the infliction of the University of Illinois campus on a residential community that did not want it, voters rejected the bond and strangled plans to expand Chicago's urban renewal and public housing programs.[52]

Further, federal officials were displeased with certain aspects of urban renewal. Monsignor John Egan, who watched urban renewal policy and politics carefully, observed that "the rehabilitation program in Hyde Park has fallen flat on its face and has not developed over the last two years, and the Federal people feel that until there is an adequate program, they are not going to move on the other projects." In effect, only projects initiated between 1953 and 1957 were enacted. So Lawndale, which was just low enough on Mayor Daley's agenda to have been rebuffed without being rejected altogether, was not treated to the dubious benefits of urban renewal. Residents of West Garfield Park, who also hoped to use city and federal funds to preserve their neighborhood, found themselves similarly ignored. In 1963 an MHPC observer wrote caustically that urban renewal "has degenerated into a holding action, an attempt to bring to fruition the dynamic plans made when urban renewal was popular. But the popularity, the optimism, the dynamism—and the cash—are gone. Urban Renewal in Chicago has become stagnant."[53]

West Garfield Park and Austin

African Americans were present in the South Side areas where local institutions pioneered urban renewal techniques. In group discussions and public discourse about the rehabilitation of blighted areas, whites routinely conflated the presence of blacks with the deterioration of the site in question. Monsignor John O'Grady of the National Conference of Catholic Charities ruefully acknowledged, "When people in our parishes talk about conservation, they are talking about Negroes." Earl Dickerson, counsel for the Supreme Liberty Life Insurance Company, told a group of Hyde Park residents, "Some of us get mighty tired of hearing what a menace we are . . . and of having people talk of slums and Negroes as if they were tied together by edict." The University of Chicago's expensive program of urban renewal in the Hyde Park neighborhood was premised on the removal of poor and working-class African Americans from the area, alongside the physical redevelopment of the site.[54] Sears' promotion of the Greater Lawndale Conservation Commission, likewise, had the significant purpose of protecting its employees against the intangible threat of working in an African American neighborhood.

By contrast, residents of West Garfield Park who agitated for their inclusion in the city's urban renewal and conservation efforts did not share in the immediate purpose of "Negro removal." When they made their initial requests for urban renewal, there were almost no African Americans living in West Garfield Park to be cleared out by the process. They were no doubt aware of discussions elsewhere in the city that routinely associated the presence of African Americans with blight, and when blacks did move into the area, the *Garfieldian* printed variations of this argument. But in requesting conservation programs for their neighborhood, West Garfield Parkers employed a different logic from their counterparts in Hyde Park and North Lawndale. One West Garfield Park leader critiqued the Hyde Park effort as a "unilateral, unrelated, piecemeal redevelopment which will never, under any circumstances, provide decent housing for all of our citizens nor improve the living standards of our many, worthwhile family neighborhoods." West Garfield Parkers instead asked for programs to shore up decaying buildings in the neighborhood with a minimum of residential displacement. This process, combined with an array of other local improvements, they hoped, would reinforce private investments in property and encourage white residents to remain in the area. Their effort for

Steps to Stem Decay

Fig. 7. This cartoon appeared in local newspapers twice, first in 1958 and then in 1970. In 1958 the *Garfieldian* headed it, "First Steps toward Conservation." In 1970 the *Austin News* ran it under the line "Steps to Stem Decay." "First Steps toward Conservation," *Garfieldian*, November 19, 1958; "Steps to Stem Decay," *Austin News*, May 6, 1970. Courtesy of the Special Collections and Preservation Division, Chicago Public Library.

urban renewal was not "Negro removal," but rather aimed at building the confidence of established white neighbors in the future of the area through rehabilitation of the physical environment. Their secondary agenda was to prevent blacks from having the opportunity to move into West Garfield Park.[55]

For several years before organizing a formal conservation effort, residents of West Garfield Park heard complaints about incipient deterioration. The *Garfieldian* vigilantly reported "evidence of the minor variations and violations which put a neighborhood on the down grade and eventually result in the blight." For example, the paper praised the decision to tear down some car barns owned by the Chicago Transit Authority, noting that "the 'Chinese Wall' has separated the 3800 block of Madison st. [sic] from the rest of the business district and provided a breeding place for crime, slums and honky-tonks." In 1954 the paper editorialized against "illegal conversions, zoning violations, an increase in rooming houses, and a general lethargy among property owners in keeping their buildings in tip top condition."[56]

In addition to these complaints about all-white sections of the West Side, residents also encountered descriptions of blight that might as easily have been allusions to African Americans. For example, in 1946 the *Garfieldian* wrapped up a seven-part series on the history of West Garfield Park with the observation that "a revitalized community life can stop the spread of blight, which approaches the community dangerously close on the east, and [become] a model for the conservation of similar neighborhoods throughout Chicago." A pair of letters to the editor, appearing in July 1956, illustrated the ambiguities of the rhetoric of blight. One woman, alarmed that West Garfield Park needed to be rescued from becoming a slum, blamed city officials for permitting rooming houses in the area. As the city built public housing, it cleared out slum areas, displacing residents who then sought inexpensive accommodations in rooming houses. As "transients," these neighbors were difficult for other property owners to bear, for they "are dirty, have no manners or respect for anyone else and are noisy." She concluded, "The housing project can accommodate some of these people but not all and another neighborhood is ruined." In all likelihood, this writer was thinking of African Americans as the source of the impending slum in West Garfield Park, since all new public housing in Chicago was being built in black neighborhoods. On the other hand, an "Austin Property Owner" decried absentee landlords' practice of renting small apartments to large families in his neighborhood. "It is impossible for a family of adults and children over five in number to live decently in three and four room apartments which have only one bedroom. . . . It isn't fair to the responsible property owner who is endeavoring to keep his property up and who consistently turns away undesirable tenants, many times at a financial loss."[57] There were only a handful of longtime African American residents in Austin in 1956, so this writer was probably genuinely concerned about the overcrowding of white apartment dwellers.

Responding to the accumulating worries about the state of West Garfield Park, in March 1954 a group of residents organized a new community group to address juvenile delinquency, code violations, and crime; to centralize information on local affairs; and to "end the creeping blight which has been attacking the area." Interpreted by many of its early members as an improvement association, the Garfield Park–Austin Community Council (GPACC) swiftly attracted members and money.[58] Its first membership drive netted more than two thousand individual members, sixty-one member organizations, eighty-five block club captains, and $5,800 in dues. GPACC's early activities reflected members' willingness to solve neighborhood programs with local tools: the organization tried to chase a pool hall out of the area, and members participated in Mayor Daley's citywide clean-up campaign in 1955, investing their time and sweat in the area's appearance.[59] Soon, however, GPACC turned toward a strategy of harnessing government legal and financial tools for the preservation of the neighborhood. Among the projects the organization undertook were influencing zoning regulations, winning a conservation program, obtaining federal mortgage insurance for housing rehabilitation, and bringing a campus of the University of Illinois to Garfield Park.

GPACC began its effort to win a conservation program for West Garfield Park with a bang. Rather than wait for the city bureaucracy to notice their neighborhood's needs and take slow action, GPACC prepared a survey of the area. In March 1956 GPACC presented CCB commissioner General Richard Smykal with the results of their study. The report found that 98 percent of the structures in the area were in good condition, but that problems such as "illegal conversions, rooming houses, overcrowding, unsanitary conditions and transiency" threatened the neighborhood. They estimated that 20 percent of the area's buildings were converted from their original uses and that almost a quarter were held by absentee owners. Smykal's praise for their initiative heartened GPACC's leaders. Usually, Smykal said, city staff took months documenting such conditions. GPACC officials were, accordingly, disappointed when Smykal rebuffed them in their next meeting. All funds for conservation in Chicago were already committed. The Hyde Park–Kenwood project was already under way, with federal help; a project for the Near West Side was just getting started; and Lincoln Park and Englewood would be next. Any big conservation program for West Garfield Park would have to wait for the "distant future," but, acting on his influence as the city's former commissioner of buildings, Smykal could promote a crackdown on illegal conversions. In the meantime, perhaps they should follow the lead of the South Shore and Uptown communities in requesting Federal Housing Administration support for local rehabilitation loans. GPACC representatives met with Smykal again in August and learned that CCB might, at some undetermined point in the future, conduct its own study of the area.[60]

The Garfield Park–Austin Community Council sought a way around the board's delays. If they were unable to bring conservation to West Garfield Park, then they would try to attach West Garfield Park to another area with—from their perspective—better prospects for obtaining renewal money: North Lawndale. Although Lawndale was not on the list of areas that Smykal cited as administration priorities, it was at least adjacent to West Garfield Park and already had a public hearing scheduled on its designation as a conservation area. Smykal agreed to change the area under consideration, suggesting that it might be possible to violate the city's usual practice of respecting the physical and social boundaries between communities. As we have seen, he did not ask representatives of the Greater Lawndale Conservation Commission for their approval. On October 6, 1956, approximately six hundred West Side residents, business owners, and community leaders gathered at the Gold Dome building in Garfield Park for the hearing.[61]

Although these local representatives testified enthusiastically in favor of government-sponsored conservation in the area, they did not unanimously support the boundaries of the proposed "West Congress Conservation Area." The president of the Roosevelt Road Businessmen's Association, for example, argued that "it is only fair to extend such services . . . to the whole area of Lawndale. Such services would not function as effectively if they were restricted to the area within the boundaries which have been drawn." In December Richard Smykal reported that CCB declined to recognize a West Congress Conservation Area. He explained that the lack of community consensus informed the decision, but the shortage of funds for city staff to conduct further studies was also relevant.[62]

GPACC's chairman, Timothy Tuomey Jr., was disappointed with the decision to bypass West Garfield Park. He complained that this omission was an unwarranted punishment for cooperating with repeated CCB requests for their patience. When, next July, the daily papers reported that Smykal had named East Humboldt Park and Lawndale as the next two neighborhoods on the city's priority list for conservation, Tuomey dashed off a scathing letter reminding Smykal of West Garfield Park's efforts. Smykal's response amounted to "little more than a polite acknowledgement" of Tuomey's letter. Tuomey followed up by writing to Ira Bach, the city's commissioner of planning, but the *Garfieldian* did not report a response, suggesting that Tuomey never received one. GPACC learned from these efforts that they could not pin their hopes for improving the West Side on programs that required the sponsorship of city officials. When the chance to build a new University of Illinois campus appeared, GPACC leaders began to focus their efforts on attracting the campus to preserve West Garfield Park, a lobbying effort that centered on state government.[63]

Even as they diverted most of their energies to the University of Illinois campaign, GPACC pursued one last opportunity to obtain federal support for local improvements, an effort that again reinforced the lesson of city indifference to their concerns. The group followed up on General Smykal's suggestion that the community might be eligible for Federal Housing Administration section 220 loans. These loans derived from an obscure provision of the 1954 Federal Housing Act. Under the terms of section 220, in designated areas the federal government insured the mortgages of individual homeowners who borrowed money for improvements on their homes or other buildings. Residents could borrow money for rehabilitation at a 5 percent interest rate, and they had thirty-nine years to pay back the loan. In advocating local support for the 220 program, Tuomey took pains to explain that use of the loan money did not signify that West Garfield Park was blighted. Rather, neighborhoods eligible for 220 money were of "sufficiently high character so that private individuals can preserve them with a helping hand from the government." The generous terms would, Tuomey hoped, inspire young white couples to stay in the city instead of moving to the suburbs.[64]

In seeking a 220 designation for West Garfield Park, GPACC did not violate recognized neighborhood boundary lines, as it had with the request to piggyback on to North Lawndale's urban renewal program. This time, GPACC asked for a conservation designation for the northwest corner of the neighborhood, the area of the original nineteenth-century settlement of Central Park Village. The district had developed in the early 1870s, when employees of the Northwestern Railroad built homes near the company's shops. The names of the area and the local elementary school honored the shops' first superintendent, G. W. Tilton. The area housed St. Mel's Roman Catholic Church, which served the entire West Garfield Park community. The structures in the area were a hodgepodge of single-family houses, two-flats, apartment buildings, and a few scattered industrial sites. A census-based study of the Tilton area, made to determine its eligibility for section 220 loans, found that most of the area's 3,167 dwelling units were in good condition. Only 3.3 percent were dilapidated, 15.9 percent were officially substandard, and 7.7 percent were overcrowded. After granting preliminary approval of the request in May 1958 and holding a public hearing where it heard unanimous support for the designation, in July 1958 CCB granted its full approval to the section 220 designation for an expanded Tilton area.[65]

West Garfield Park residents eager to rehabilitate their properties, however, learned that even this level of cooperation from city officials was insufficient to ensure that the conservation program turned from a paper policy into action. Tilton residents began to wait for the administrative processes necessary to release the rehabilitation funds. Periodically, they read reports in the *Garfieldian* that the area was still under study. The church bulletin at St. Mel Holy Ghost Parish blamed the city's concentration of effort in Hyde Park–Kenwood for the delays. In January and July 1959, West Garfield Park residents learned that detailed maps and surveys were being prepared. Despite these signs of progress, they would have to wait until the federal government approved the section 220 plans made for the South Shore–O'Keefe area on Chicago's South Side. Finally, in 1963 Lewis W. Hill, the assistant commissioner of urban renewal, visited West Garfield Park for another purpose. In an aside, he mentioned that flaws in the section 220 legislation prevented its use anywhere else in Chicago other than South Shore.[66]

Thus West Garfield Park residents who hoped to use conservation and urban renewal mechanisms to shore up their private investments were repeatedly disappointed. Even when the city recognized the legitimacy of their claims, nothing in their physical environs changed. While West Garfield Park was in better condition than many other neighborhoods, there was certainly room for improvement. Tuomey concluded as early as 1959: "From time to time, as you know, the City goes through the motions of designating sections for conservation projects. However, this is done for the sake of appearance and is slanted for public consumption. All of this show is meaningless and misleading. Nothing ever gets done." Tuomey and the GPACC Board of Directors urged the Housing and Home Finance Agency to suspend all federal funding for urban renewal from the city until Chicago committed the money to "the benefit and welfare of the total community." City officials and white West Siders were consistently at odds with one another over the urgency of using urban renewal money to improve the area. As early as 1956, D. E. Mackelmann's office tried to caution GPACC members "that federal funds alone will never be sufficient to solve the city's conservation problems." But Monsignor John Egan thought that the problem was not simply funding shortfalls, reflecting, "I have long felt with others that apart from the Medical Center the west side has been much neglected in the city's plans."[67]

Mobilizing against Urban Renewal

After more than a decade of frustrating white West Siders with their hesitation to include the area on Chicago's active urban renewal agenda, in the late 1960s city officials suggested that North Lawndale's time had finally come. The passage of a $195 million bond issue in 1966 enabled the city once again to authorize new projects. Official proposals and rumors of secret plans circulated. The affected Lawndale residents, however, were no longer whites optimistic about the benefits of urban renewal. The middle-class African Americans skeptical of GLCC's motives in 1954 were now joined by thousands more migrants from elsewhere in the city and the South. Some had experienced firsthand the results of clearance, and others feared that any local urban renewal might simply displace them all again. The owner of Ivery's Grocery wrote in 1965, "Urban Renewal in any form cripples or destroyes [sic] a small business. There is no plan that can be worked out to take the place of a stable neighborhood. I know of no way of combating urban renewal." As urban renewal suddenly loomed, black West Siders offered an alternative people-oriented vision of improving the city, and they mobilized to prevent any disruption of their neighborhood.[68] Departing white residents had left them not only a deteriorating environment, but also fostered the seeds of a public policy that might remove them from their new homes.

In 1964 the Department of Urban Renewal (DUR) issued its first reports on the prospective redevelopment of North Lawndale. The plans, affecting four-and-a-half square miles, described how the area might look in the future. They called for separating out the mix of residential, commercial, and industrial functions in the area. New street arrangements would keep traffic from the residential sections, and fewer strips of stores would disrupt the area's balance of land uses. A close reading of the reports, however, raised questions about the information on which these plans were premised. DUR's population figures stated that three-quarters of the people in the conservation area were white, which had not been true since the mid-1950s. A reliable study issued in 1967 estimated that Lawndale's population was more than 91 percent African American in 1960 and had reached 94.6 percent African American in 1966.[69]

Despite the outdated data in the reports and the continuing unavailability of funds for renewal, the mayor finally appointed the long-awaited Lawndale Conservation Community Council (LCCC) in January 1965. The council's function was to serve as a "liaison group" between local residents and city officials in the planning process. Chaired by Hazzard Parks, the director of a local social service center, the council's original members consisted of seven African Americans and two whites; two members represented the GLCC Board of Directors. Over the next fifteen months, LCCC held hearings and met with community groups in the Lawndale area. Parks instructed LCCC members that their responsibility was to listen to and ask questions about residents' views, without attempting to rebut anyone's positions.[70]

When LCCC issued its report in August 1966, it did far more than express the concerns of Lawndale residents that the area's physical rehabilitation should protect their homes. LCCC might well have chosen to focus solely on the physical environment, as a survey by the Dangerous and Hazardous Building Section of the city's Department of Buildings had recently identified 143 buildings in Lawndale as eligible for demolition. Instead LCCC's plan explicitly repudiated the traditional dedication of urban renewal monies to physical restructuring. Echoing the rhetoric of the ongoing War on Poverty, LCCC opened its report with the claim that "urban renewal is human renewal—the maximum participation of *all* of its citizens in attaining the greatest benefits for *all* of its citizens. It cannot be regarded merely in terms of bricks and mortar. . . . [T]he social, economic, psychological, and physical factors must receive equal attention in achieving these aspirations." LCCC recommended not only code enforcement and building rehabilitation, but also a wide array of improvements in social, educational, employment, and medical services to the area.[71]

In September LCCC members again emphasized their preference for neighborhood rehabilitation that balanced physical redevelopment with social needs. When the new federal Model Cities program was announced, Hazzard Parks offered up North Lawndale as a "demonstration area." This play for increased social services fell on deaf ears when Chicago sent the nation's first request for Model Cities funding to the federal government six months later. Black West Side activists criticized the city's plan for demonstrating "more of the same disregard for the needs of the poor and near-poor and the crowded, underserviced neighborhoods to which they are restricted."[72]

Publicly presented plans for the renewal of Lawndale were not the only ones residents heard about. In 1967 political aspirants raised allegations of a secret large-scale clearance and redevelopment project. Luster H. Jackson, an independent black candidate for alderman of the 29th Ward, charged that the real estate firm Draper and Kramer was developing a project that might require the displacement of "hundreds of thousands of Lawndale homeowners." Although his estimate significantly inflated Lawndale's total population, Jackson tapped into a genuine fear. "The plans," he asserted, "include luxury high rise apartments like those in Lake Meadows and other types of buildings for high and 'moderate' income families." Lawndale's black residents, he implied, not only would have to move to make way for the project, but also would be unable to afford to buy their way back into the neighborhood once construction was complete. Jackson produced documents that, he said, showed that the firm's proposal would cost $220 million. A report about a slightly different version of the plan specified that it called for the relocation of 66,000 people from 2.06 square miles of property. West Side Federation activist Lew Kreinberg found evidence that the plan projected not only 12,500 new high-income homes, but also a 45-acre golf course. Ferd Kramer denied that the project was an independent secret plan. The papers that Luster Jackson exhibited, Kramer said, were draft versions of a Model Cities proposal the firm was preparing at the city's request. Indeed, just a few months later, city officials called a meeting for West Siders to examine a plan for "intensive development in Lawndale" and other local communities; in the middle of 1967, various city and corporate officials met with Vice President Hubert Humphrey and staff of the federal Model Cities office to discuss the viability of their plans.[73]

With an eye toward the history of urban renewal in Chicago and the impending official and secret plans for Lawndale, African Americans' objections coalesced into group action. The specific object of their wrath was Mayor Daley's proposal for a $179 million urban renewal package. In March 1967 representatives of eight South and West Side groups linked to the Chicago Freedom Movement gathered and resolved that "the only effective way to stop Urban Renewal from taking over our communities is through a joint effort." They formed a "City-Wide Urban Renewal Committee" and proposed a set of principles for urban planning that reflected "the needs of these we represent—the poor, the near-poor, the racial, and the ethnic minorities—the third of our population that remains today ill-housed, ill-fed, and ill-clad." Instead of clearing occupied buildings and displacing residents, the committee advocated using vacant lots; building high-quality housing for the poor; experimenting with single-unit homes and walk-up apartments on scattered sites; making it possible for people with low incomes to purchase their homes; and citizen participation in the planning process.[74]

Hoping to halt urban renewal that did not incorporate their principles, the City-Wide Urban Renewal Committee took their concerns to the Chicago City Council. Aldermen Collins and Biggs declined to present a resolution on their behalf, so approximately 150 protesters from the committee appeared at a Chicago City Council meeting. The group's press release said that they intended to use the mechanism of a citizen petition to get their resolution heard. When the aldermen raised the topic, the crowd began chanting, "Stop Urban Renewal." Police arrested three people for trespassing on the council's main floor and expelled the rest of the protesters from the building. After these disruptions, the city council postponed further action on pending proposals for Lawndale and Woodlawn. This victory was only temporary; later in June the city council's Committee on Housing and Planning authorized further study of both areas.[75]

At a People's Planning and Action Conference in the same month, Lawndale residents collectively formalized their objections to having urban renewal imposed on them. Called by the West Side Federation, the conference featured national experts on urban affairs, most notably Jane Jacobs and Charles Abrams. The most important feature of the conference was its articulation of a proposal for authorizing urban renewal in Lawndale, including a denunciation of any decisions taken without the participation and consent of local residents. The conference also spun off a community development corporation, the North Lawndale Economic Development Corporation, which later became known as Pyramidwest.[76]

City officials continued to pursue some urban renewal and Model Cities proposals for Lawndale, but with little cooperation from residents. The Department of Urban Renewal issued new proposals for the Lawndale area in 1968 and 1970. A $38 million Model Cities program was authorized for Lawndale and three other neighborhoods in 1970, but Judge Richard Austin's order in the famous *Gatreaux* case held up the release of most of the funds until the city built three-quarters of its public housing in white residential neighborhoods. The call of Lawndale residents for comprehensive social and economic services for their neighborhood went largely unheeded. The War on Poverty's local Urban Progress Center, which might have provided some such programs, also failed to win enthusiasm from residents. Pearlie Mae Robinson, president of a Lawndale block club, cited the lack of community control as she dismissed the War on Poverty's branch office: "It's for the birds."[77]

Mayor Richard J. Daley remained focused on downtown redevelopment, beginning in the late 1960s to "wage war" on bad spots within the Loop itself. Perhaps the most famous symbol of Daley's successful efforts to revitalize the downtown's economy was the construction of the Sears Tower in the early 1970s. When Sears officials finally gave up hope of redeveloping Lawndale, they struck a deal with Daley to build the world's tallest building just west of the Loop, a structure that one writer described as "no architectural gem; it is your average, run-of-the-mill office building on a Brobdingnagian scale." Sears did not completely abandon the old West Side complex; the company's laboratory facilities remained open, and executives occasionally used the empty spaces to test retail display designs and house data-processing computers. Even though only a few African Americans were ever hired in the Lawndale offices or store, the retailer's departure from the area signaled a new phase in the West Side's transformation and was a potent symbolic blow. During the 1970s and 1980s, North Lawndale's population declined both numerically and economically. In 1983 *Chicago Tribune* reporters singled out Lawndale as an "American

Millstone," the living incarnation of all that was wrong with urban America. Only at the close of the twentieth century did new hopes for a humane and effective economic redevelopment reappear in Lawndale.[78]

In the 1950s white West Siders called on city officials to help them marshal the financial resources to improve the area's physical infrastructure and environs. They shared with the Daley administration the assumption that physical redevelopment was the key to the preservation and revitalization of any area, but the mayor channeled the available funds to the downtown. Daley's policies resulted in an often-traumatic—but fairly effective—redevelopment process in the neighborhoods just north and south of the Loop, and the almost complete neglect of the infrastructure of outlying areas like the West Side. In the long run, these policies meant that African Americans sought private housing in one of the most physically deteriorated portions of Chicago. In the short run, however, the city's neglect encouraged white West Siders to cast about for other mechanisms for preserving their neighborhoods. As it became evident that their schemes for urban renewal were unlikely to bear fruit rapidly enough to serve their purposes, white West Siders focused some of their energies on another opportunity to control their environs: they tried to lure a new campus of the University of Illinois into their midst.

CHAPTER 4

A Chicago Campus for the University of Illinois

I n 1946 the University of Illinois established a temporary campus to serve Chicagoans. The university trustees obtained accommodations on Navy Pier, a long, thin structure just north of the downtown, projecting a mile out into Lake Michigan. The facility proved entirely inadequate to the booming postwar student enrollments.[1] To get from class to class, students and faculty had to travel the lengthy pier's crowded, narrow corridors. The simultaneous use of the pier by shipping companies caused constant interruptions. Instructors often resorted to yelling to make their lessons audible. Lost truck drivers sometimes stuck their heads through classroom windows to get directions. Student protests against the site's deficiencies became commonplace. In 1954 the Trustees of the University of Illinois decided that it was time to locate their own permanent dedicated campus to serve the Chicago metropolitan area.[2]

Authorizing a new university campus was much easier than figuring out where to put it. Fearing displacement from their homes, few Chicago-area residents wanted the university located nearby. Community groups in the Harrison-Halsted area where the University of Illinois Chicago Circle (UIC) campus was finally constructed in the mid-1960s appealed the decision to the United States Supreme Court before surrendering to the bulldozers. Only residents of the Far West Side of Chicago—West Garfield Park and Austin—wanted the campus in their own backyard. Beginning in 1957, they ran a spirited but futile campaign to "trade" away Garfield Park in exchange for the university.[3]

West Siders sought the university campus for two reasons. First, they envisioned the campus as a remedy for the physical decay that threatened their immediate environs. They hoped that the campus—like urban renewal—would inspire physical and economic improvements in the neighborhoods west of the campus. If they could not obtain direct assistance from the city government for conservation, they might instead attract an engine of revitalization from the state. Second, they hoped that the erection of a large and vital institution in the path of the block-by-block migration of African Americans might disrupt their westward trajectory. Residents of the Far West Side saw in the university's inadequate campus an opportunity to alleviate the twin elements of the urban crisis that was undermining their attachments to their neighborhoods.

The chance to bulldoze Garfield Park was attractive to West Siders precisely for this pair of reasons. By the 1950s Garfield Park, once a West Side treasure, had fallen into a severe state of decay, like some of the nearby housing stock. At the same time, African Americans living east of the park were beginning to use its facilities. Removing the park and installing a campus full of middle-class white educators and their clientele might inspire African Americans to move elsewhere. In the context of rising white anxiety over the state of the entire Chicago park system, eliminating the liability of the park and attracting an amenity like the university might solve several problems simultaneously.

Far West Siders, however, lacked political power.[4] They were sufficiently organized to persuade university trustees that the campus ought to go in Garfield Park, but they could not budge Chicago's power brokers from their focus on the downtown. Mayor Richard J. Daley's vision for the redevelopment of Chicago imagined a revitalization beginning with the center of the city and then spreading outward. His administration's blueprint, the *Development Plan for the Central Area of Chicago*, identified the new university campus as a cornerstone of redevelopment and recommended its placement just to the south of the Loop, on a site occupied by several railroads. The Metropolitan Housing and Planning Council (MHPC) concurred with Daley's vision and in 1959 created a Joint Action Committee (JAC) to advocate the selection of the South Loop site and block any alternative locations, especially Garfield Park. Mayor Daley was unable to close the deal for the railroad terminals, but JAC threw enough obstacles in the path of the acquisition of Garfield Park that Daley selected his second-choice site, the Harrison-Halsted area, just west of the Loop. Residents of Chicago's Far West Side watched bitterly as residents of that neighborhood failed to fight off the institution that they had wanted for themselves.

West Siders' Motives

In calling for the placement of the new University of Illinois campus within their neighborhood, West Garfield Parkers staked out a unique position as the only community in the metropolitan area trying to attract the institution. Many of the surviving documents that reflect their goals are propaganda produced to entice authorities to select Garfield Park; they express the advantages of the West Side to the university, rather than revealing how the area would benefit from the campus. Further, as political scientist James W. Ford discovered, West Side community groups had some motives they were willing to offer for "public consumption" and some less palatable hopes that they expressed only in private.[5] Nonetheless, between the lines, Far West Siders offered a few glimpses of their conviction that the campus might aid in the preservation of the local environment.

What did Far West Siders hope to gain from an institution to which residents elsewhere said, "Not in my backyard"? Activists had both environmental and racial reasons for campaigning for the university. They began their campaign in concert with their general effort to prevent the area's physical and economic decay.[6] As with their drive for urban renewal, they anticipated that the university's presence would spark the physical and economic rejuvenation of the area's neglected landscape. They quickly grafted on to these aspirations the possibility that the presence of the university campus would deter African Americans from moving any farther west within the city. They seized on Garfield Park as the site for the campus because in its declining maintenance and increasing use by African Americans living to its east, it seemed the local embodiment of wider dismay about the state of large parks in the city of Chicago.

West Siders' campus campaign originated with the Garfield Park–Austin Community Council (GPACC) as an effort to restore the area's status as a desirable residential neighborhood. GPACC's first public statement on the possibility of winning the campus recognized that the Daley administration's plans for the city's improvement began with the center and anticipated an eventual spread to the outer ring of neighborhoods. Oddly, in light of the subsequent assumption that the university-in-the-park might divert the arrival of African Americans, GPACC initially read the city's plans as an "unconscious master plan" to industrialize the Far West Side. "Deteriorated residential properties, for the most part, are being swallowed up for industrial projects. . . . If this official policy continues," GPACC suggested, "Garfield Park and Austin will only be good for slum clearance." Another Garfield Park campus supporter concluded that the campus would become "an oasis barrier against blight and deterioration."[7]

Further, the campus would have a multiplier effect. Park-site supporters argued that the campus, operating as a "self-help conservation program," would spur owners of private property to make improvements, persuade entrepreneurs to open new businesses, and generally improve neighborhood morale. The campus might "provide a nucleus for preservation and rehabilitation of the entire West Side." A leader in the campus campaign told Mayor Daley, "We haven't asked for government help. We don't want free money. . . . If we get the university we can take care of our own problems." The establishment of such an important cultural institution on the West Side might also pressure city officials to enforce the local zoning and housing codes. In contrast both to the conservation program they were unable to obtain and also to the expensive urban renewal plan operating in the Hyde Park–Kenwood neighborhoods on the South Side, the university campus would not function as a simple handout, but as an active incentive for redevelopment.[8]

Additionally, residents of the Far West Side hoped that the presence of a university campus would alter the pattern of racial change on the West Side. When the university campaign began in 1957, West Garfield Park had experienced the very first hints of racial change, but the associated turmoil was concentrated south and east of the park. Only a few African Americans had ventured west of Garfield Park and north of the Congress Expressway, into West Garfield Park proper. For the moment, both the park and the highway seemed to be "natural barrier[s]" preventing blacks from "jumping" into West Garfield Park. But in 1959, when the campus campaign was well under way, a black family moved into the interior of West Garfield Park, violating the usual pattern of steady block-by-block racial turnover. Thus the possibility that the campus might also affect the composition of the local population took on a new immediacy midway through the campaign.[9]

Park-site supporters were loath to reveal the hope that putting the university atop the park would keep African Americans out of West Garfield Park. Instead, they emphasized the potential of the campus to stem the tide of departure of whites to points elsewhere, thereby "stabilizing" the neighborhood. Mrs. Michael Burkin told a reporter that many "old residents" were already leaving the area but that the new university campus "might improve the situation." The author of a letter to the *Garfieldian* envisioned a process of racial stabilization in West Garfield Park that allowed room for some new people in the area. On the one hand, the university would inspire existing residents to stay in the area; on the other hand, it would bring into the area a "great influx" of people associated with educational achievement, "thereby aiding and stabilizing the neighborhood both in a business and residential aspect."[10]

GPACC's original proposal, offered in April 1957, envisioned placing the campus within the regular street grid. The site in the northeast corner of the West Garfield Park neighborhood required the land under some "car barns" owned by the Chicago Transit Authority and about twenty acres of parkland. By December, however, the possibility of giving up the park entirely in exchange for the campus emerged, as a headline in the *Garfieldian* proclaimed: "Give Up All of Park to UI, Say Many W. Side Leaders." Evidently, the discussion about whether any of the parkland would be available for the university triggered the possibility of placing the campus entirely within property that was already publicly owned.[11] Far West Siders were much more candid about the sources of their willingness to give up the park than they were about their eagerness to bring the campus in the first place. There were two reasons for the proposal to place the university within the park: First, the state of Garfield Park itself; and second, a general climate of fear about the parks that arose precisely while the University of Illinois site decision was debated.

During the first half of the twentieth century, Garfield Park had been a jewel in the community's crown. The West Chicago Park Commission established three large parks to serve the people of the city's West Division in 1869—Humboldt Park to the north, Douglas Park to the south, and Central Park in between. Boulevards connected the three parks into the West Park System. Central Park was rechristened to memorialize President James A. Garfield after his assassination in 1881.[12]

In contrast to the parks of the city's South and North divisions, the West Park System remained underdeveloped and unattractive. The seedy Garfield Park Race Track abutting the grounds of Garfield Park created an unsavory atmosphere. Architect William Le Baron Jenney drew up designs for the West Side parks in the 1870s, but the notoriously corrupt board of directors of the West Park System authorized their implementation for only about a quarter of the space in the three parks. Park engineer Oscar F. Dubuis managed some improvements, but not until the reform of the board in 1905 was the landscaping of the West Side parks completed. The new president of the board hired as general superintendent Jens Jensen, a landscape architect who had been previously fired from his position as superintendent of nearby Humboldt Park in 1900 for refusing to allow coal dealers to deliver short weights of fuel.[13]

Under Jensen's direction, Garfield Park acquired its modern design. Jensen blended Jenney's European pastoral plans with the forms of Frank Lloyd Wright's Prairie school. Like other large city parks laid out in the United States during the nineteenth century, Garfield Park contained a pleasure ground, a broad expanse of green carefully landscaped to evoke pastoral sensibilities. The park also housed an internationally renowned conservatory that was a center of horticulture in the Midwest. The original building, erected in 1886, was replaced by a modern facility in 1907. The conservatory contained eight separate houses to provide appropriate climates for its disparate floral exhibitions, including one that recapitulated the geological development of the midwestern prairie. A large lagoon, where children sailed handmade rafts and adults rowed about in larger boats, was another park amenity.[14]

After its improvement under Jensen's direction, the park became the pride and joy of West Side boosters. The Gold Dome building was constructed in the northern section of the park in 1928. Named for its most prominent feature, the structure served as the park's administrative headquarters. It contained gymnasiums, auditoriums, swimming pools, and assembly rooms. Jackson Boulevard, which the Works Progress Administration improved in 1937 to allow better flow of automobile traffic, bisected the park. The southern portion of the park, once a cow pasture and later a bicycle track, contained a golf course. Garfield Park also was a Jim Crow park: West Side African Americans, who lived just a mile or two east, were welcome only in Union Park, a much smaller, older park on the Near West Side. Different white ethnic groups informally claimed for themselves the three great West Side parks: Humboldt Park for the Germans, Douglas Park for the Irish, and Garfield Park for the "Americans."[15]

After the Second World War, however, Far West Siders began to be dissatisfied with the maintenance of Garfield Park. For reasons that were never clear to residents, park administrators neglected it during the 1950s and 1960s. The *Garfieldian* editorialized as early as 1952 that the West Side park system needed repairs and new facilities. In 1961, when African Americans regularly frequented the park, the *Garfieldian* enumerated the accumulated abuse of Garfield Park: children waded in the lily pond, which was both unsightly and dangerous to their health; a portion of the lagoon filled in for use as a parking lot amounted to a trash heap; litter floated in the water remaining in the lagoon; the old boathouse, whose existence the prohibition of boating made superfluous, was covered with graffiti; and the lagoon shores were used for burning trash. The Park District cooperated in cleaning up the park after this editorial, but noted that there was no money for new facilities without a new bond issue authorizing such spending.[16]

In addition to the increasing unsightliness of Garfield Park, during the 1950s people living to its west began to think of it as a dangerous place that attracted disreputable people. In 1949 the police warned that while "drunks" were not yet making use of Garfield Park, they were using parks to the east in increasing numbers. The potential threat loomed again in 1952, when

West Garfield Park merchants launched their campaign against the state Unemployment Office located in the shopping district at 3841 Madison Street. Their chief complaint was that it brought "undesirable" people to the area. Probably mixed among those receiving unemployment compensation were people whose black or brown skin readily marked them as outsiders, not residents of the all-white West Garfield Park. Angry business owners accused the unemployed people who came to Madison Street for relief checks of lingering in the park and littering it with human excrement and empty bottles of whiskey.[17]

West Siders nostalgically remembered sleeping in parks on hot summer nights. But by the end of 1960, assaults in several of Chicago's large parks gave them all a shared aura of danger. In 1955 a Detroit serviceman raped and killed a woman in Calumet Park. In 1956 a sunbather was strangled in Lincoln Park. A man wielding a knife threatened a young woman vacationer and a blind man in Grant Park in May 1960. The next month, after nine people were attacked in the North Side's Lincoln Park during a thirteen-day period, the *Chicago Sun-Times* ran an editorial entitled "Public Parks—or Urban Jungles?" While the *Sun-Times* urged the reclamation of the city's large parks from criminals, the *Garfieldian* more pessimistically announced that the incidents marked the end of the era of the large city parks and that "decent citizens" no longer used them. In July, while Vice President Richard Nixon was in the city for the Republican National Convention, a group of teenagers attacked five people in Lincoln Park, raping two women and beating their husbands. A vacationing British schoolteacher was beaten and almost raped in Grant Park in August. This last attack, in the city's "front yard" in broad daylight, so jeopardized Chicago's international reputation that the city offered to make amends by subsidizing her two-month hospital stay.[18]

White West Garfield Parkers were increasingly reluctant to use park facilities where they might encounter such dangerous people. As one upset resident lamented, "The race track attracted bums and it was thrown out. The bums are back, hiding in the bushes and preying on women so that they are afraid to go there." A letter to the editor of the *Garfieldian* complained of drunken, threatening men and women using the park and worried that it might become a skid row. By the end of the 1950s, West Side residents charged that misbehavior in the park included dope use, purse snatching, sexual offenses, and gang activity. Columnist Jack Mabley reported that Garfield Park was called "Robbers' Roost." Residents of West Garfield Park repeated their complaints often, emphasizing the danger that the park presented to women and children. As parks historian Galen Cranz notes, in this period Americans who were contemplating moving out of cities tended

'Like I've Been Telling You'

Fig. 8. The *Austin News* revived this older cartoon in 1970 in response to a plan to build a high school in Humboldt Park. *Austin News*, April 8, 1970. Courtesy of the Special Collections and Preservation Division, Chicago Public Library.

to think about parks as "part of the urban crisis rather than its cure." Some sentiment that Garfield Park was a community resource remained in the 1950s, when a representative of a pro-integration group called it "a wonderful park," but the numbers of whites who shared that sense diminished as more African Americans used the park.[19]

By 1960, when more than half the residents of East Garfield Park were African American, some of white West Siders' fears were realized in direct confrontations with black park users. The mother of boys whose softball and catcher's mitt were stolen by "older boys" asked, "Just for whom are we saving Garfield Park?" She said that girls no longer used the park at all and called for greater police protection in the park. Another mother who escorted seventeen children to the park in August 1960 felt pressured out when a group of African American boys threw stones at her charges. A park employee advised her that these boys were "looking for trouble" and that she ought to leave. A Japanese American man described the extortion of his son by "a group of boys with knives" at a Garfield Park day camp. In the summer of 1961, the owner of the Graemere Hotel, a reputable residential hotel located just east of the park, was chased out of the park by a group of twenty youngsters shouting racial insults at him.[20]

These episodes reinforced a rising sensibility among white Chicagoans that they must dispute African Americans' use of public spaces such as "schools, playgrounds, parks, and beaches." On the city's Far South Side, for example, white resistance to black families in the Chicago Housing Authority's Trumbull Park Homes included conflict over use of the eponymous park. Whites also attacked blacks using forbidden sections of Calumet Park on Chicago's Far South Side. When in 1961 black and white students held a series of "wade-ins" to protest de facto segregation at Rainbow Beach, angry whites repeatedly assaulted them.[21]

Garfield Park was a psychologically significant site for white West Siders. Early urban sociologists in Chicago emphasized the existence of "natural areas" within the city, divided by natural or human-made barriers into distinct neighborhoods. In laying out the city's official community areas, these scholars interpreted Garfield Park as a divider between the East Garfield Park and West Garfield Park community areas. Although some of the judgments of these scholars later proved arbitrary, inaccurate, and historically dynamic, their observations about the role of Garfield Park as a partition were sound.[22] Rather than share Garfield Park with African Americans or contest its use, whites on the West Side resolved to get rid of it altogether. The University of Illinois trustees' search for a site for a Chicago-area campus presented West Siders with a rare opportunity to replace an obsolete urban resource with a fresh foundation for neighborhood improvement.

The Campaign for the University

As the shortcomings of the Navy Pier facility became undeniable in the mid-1950s, University of Illinois trustees began searching for a permanent campus location. A site several miles beyond the Chicago city limits quickly emerged as their favorite: Miller Meadows, a Forest Preserve District plain nestled along the west bank of the Des Plaines River. Although the site had promise, the Forest Preserve District steadfastly refused to betray its public trust by selling the property. As Chicago's population expanded outward in the postwar years, the forest preserves became increasingly important

regional recreation resources. The Forest Preserve advisory board, dominated by bankers and businesspeople financially invested in Chicago's
downtown, proved instrumental in preventing the sale of the Miller
Meadows land to the University of Illinois. At the same time, Chicagoans
increasingly held that the new university campus should be convenient to
its urban student body.[23]

The trustees' attention turned to other sites. Although some officials continued to hope for a campus in a peripheral location, including a golf course
in Riverside adjacent to Miller Meadows, most new sites under consideration were near the city's "center of population" but not within the downtown itself. One location proposed on the Near West Side immediately drew
criticism because the land-clearance process would displace too many residents.[24] The basis of this objection, however, was also the source of its
appeal. All participants in the site-selection process understood that the new
campus had the potential not only to provide a new service to the city, but
could at the same time free it of some undesirable land uses and renew its
infrastructure.

Certainly Richard J. Daley, elected mayor early in the site-selection
process, understood the double opportunity embedded in the decision.
Mayor Daley was partial to a site in the South Loop, on land owned by several railroad corporations. Daley viewed the South Loop location as an
anchor for the redevelopment of the rest of the downtown. According to the
Development Plan for the Central Area of Chicago, the first major planning
document his administration issued, the railroad terminals "contributed to
the growth of blight and decreased land values in adjacent areas . . .
obstructed the continuity of public roads and streets and created traffic congestion." Placing the University of Illinois campus on this site would not
only "assist in the large scale redevelopment of vacated railroad land and
blighted portions of the area immediately south of the Loop"; it would also
provide university students with ready access to the cultural, intellectual,
and employment opportunities of Chicago's downtown. Over the next several years, Mayor Daley consistently threw his support to the South Loop
site for the university campus, even as he prepared for the eventuality that
he would be unable to wrest control of the land from the railroads.[25]

One of the contingencies that Daley occasionally acknowledged—probably never intending to accede to it—was the possibility of locating the
university within Garfield Park. In April 1957 leaders of the Garfield
Park–Austin Community Council proposed bringing the campus to the West
Side as an element of their program of urban renewal and conservation.
According to James W. Ford, Timothy Tuomey, who was GPACC's director, first thought of the possibility when discussing the Miller Meadows site

with the president of the Park District. GPACC officers initially imagined the campus replacing deteriorated housing and some property owned by the Chicago Transit Authority, just to the west of the park. While the area was not yet a slum, GPACC suggested, the car barns had "traditionally stagnated the full residential development of this unfortunate sector." In the original version of their proposal, the amenities afforded by the nearby park were a reason to construct the campus next to it: "Every building would command a view of the park's greensward, lagoon, botanical gardens, band stand and football and baseball fields, all of which could be used to foster the enjoyment of the area and encourage the participation of the student body in every form of sports from crew to curling."[26]

Timothy Tuomey presented the initial case for bringing the campus to the "middle West Side." Tuomey criticized the center-out approach to urban renewal favored by the Daley administration as "financially foolish, absurd and unconscionable," arguing that pouring money into the needs of institutions such as "Lake Meadows, Michael Reese hospital, Illinois Institute of Technology and the University of Chicago . . . the Medical Center . . . [and] the still un-approved Fort Dearborn project" left the "worthwhile residential neighborhoods . . . virtually unprotected from the physical and moral decay of blight." Instead of using urban renewal to clear out existing slums, the city ought to "prepar[e] . . . fire-breaks," like the university campus, to "save the realty tax structure of the city and prevent the astronomical cost and long fruitless years of total redevelopment."[27]

Tuomey's statement enumerated the advantages that the Far West Side offered to the university. If construction on nonresidential properties began immediately, Tuomey optimistically claimed, part of the Garfield Park campus could be open to students as early as the fall term of 1958. Further, the West Side was centrally located, and therefore accessible to students commuting via both public and private transportation, and also convenient to the Loop. West Garfield Park's business district, centered on the intersection of Madison Street and Pulaski Road, offered many part-time employment opportunities for students. Additionally, the university could use the existing Park District power plant instead of spending money to build a new one. Tuomey noted that there was good housing available in West Garfield Park and Austin for faculty seeking to live nearby.[28]

When he specified where members of the university community might find jobs and homes, Tuomey betrayed the underlying racial assumptions of the campaign. He did not anticipate that residents of the eastern section of the West Side, by now primarily African Americans, might be constituents of the university. Similarly, he assumed that neither students nor faculty would find an African American neighborhood a congenial place to live. It does not seem to have occurred to Tuomey, or other Garfield Park site supporters, that an urban campus of the University of Illinois might attract substantial numbers of African Americans into the student body. Garfield Park site supporters likewise showed little concern that transforming a corner of the park into part of a university campus might deprive East Garfield Park residents of a public resource they used. Indeed, in December 1957, when Far West Side activists learned that the university's chances of coming to the area hinged on the availability of the parkland, they suggested placing the entire campus on park property. When Far West Side sentiment converged on using the park for the campus, what had been indifference from the east turned into active opposition. Institutions speaking on behalf of East Garfield Park residents condemned the taking of recreation space from a neighborhood that already lacked adequate play space.[29] But organized groups and ordinary residents of the Far West Side expressed largely unified enthusiasm for putting the campus in the park.

The *Garfieldian*, itself a leading proponent of the Garfield Park campus campaign, identified substantial support for attracting the campus to the neighborhood.[30] The paper polled its audience to illustrate the consensus. The weekly found in 1957 that 80 percent of West Siders were willing to trade away the park for the university and pointedly noted that none of the respondents who objected to the change lived in its vicinity. Two years later the *Garfieldian* reported that 90 percent of people polled in the immediate area of the park supported its use for the university campus. The *Garfieldian* proceeded to argue that the extent of local support was itself a reason for putting the university in the park. The chairman of the university's site-selection committee encountered similar affirmative responses when he asked West Siders if they were willing to give up the parkland.[31]

Although the *Garfieldian*'s polling methods were questionable, the paper bolstered its claim of local support by printing many favorable letters from readers. Ray Wolfram, for example, argued that banks had stopped making loans to the area. A new university would restore lenders' confidence. He also suggested that the new campus would inspire the renovation of the large apartment buildings east of Pulaski Road for use by students and faculty. Anna Goldberg, one of the *Garfieldian*'s most persistent correspondents, argued that the university would encourage the "base characters" who frequented the park to "display more respect." Another letter writer called the university a "boon" and described Garfield Park as a "large, debris littered park, frequented mostly by unsavory people." Even after the campus was lost to the Near West Side, the *Garfieldian* continued to print letters claiming that Garfield Park would have been a better choice. As the historian of the campus site decision later observed, Garfield Park was the only potential site whose residents wanted the campus.[32]

Local fervor for the park location, however, did not translate into organizational solidarity. As James W. Ford observed, Garfield Park site supporters failed to form a "super-organization for political action," working instead "as a loose confederation." Possibly because of personality conflicts, the cooperative efforts of the Bradley and Honore Neighborhood Association, the Garfield Park Improvement Association, and other groups excluded Timothy Tuomey of the Garfield Park–Austin Community Council, who originated the idea. Rather than build a coordinated organization, Garfield Park site supporters concentrated on accumulating statements of public support for the West Side location. In this aim they succeeded admirably, garnering support from local neighborhood organizations, including the United Property Group and its rival, the Garfield Park Good Neighbors Council; larger local institutions such as Sears, the Greater Lawndale Conservation Commission, and the Midwest Community Council; civic organizations including the Austin YMCA, Kiwanis, and groups claiming to represent forty thousand Greek Americans; and seven state legislators and two aldermen. Their aversion to coordinated action hampered Garfield Park activists' ability to influence Chicago officials; by contrast, supporters of Mayor Daley's preferred South Side location formed a well-coordinated and financed organization to block the selection of Garfield Park.[33]

Once the possibility of locating the campus in suburban Miller Meadows dissolved, Mayor Daley's administration sought to ensure that the university would be located within Chicago. Addressing university trustees with qualms about the high price of land within Chicago, Daley promised to use federal urban renewal money to make up the difference between the cost of suburban and city properties. His administration floated several proposals. One plan placed a new campus on Lake Michigan, atop an artificial island recommended in Daniel Burnham's 1909 *Plan of Chicago*. The idea of putting a university on Northerly Island, the home of the Meigs Field Airport, had "dramatic potentiality," but on the advice of Ira Bach, Daley abandoned it as impractical. The South Loop Terminal Railroad site, whose consolidation the *Plan of Chicago* also recommended, emerged as the Daley administration's main target. Acquiring the railroad land, however, required complicated simultaneous negotiations with several different corporations. Perhaps most worrisome was the risk that if the railroad corporations recognized the depths of Daley's desire for their property, they would raise their asking price. These factors gave Daley reason to appear to hold his options open and provided Far West Siders hope that they might win the campus after all.[34]

Despite the obstacles of powerful opposition and poor coordination, Far West Siders forged ahead with their campaign to win the university. Tuomey's group designated a council of businessmen to press the case for the campus with the trustees. They organized a bus tour of the site for University of Illinois and city officials. By October 1958, when the Real Estate Research Corporation released a report on choice sites for the university, Garfield Park was among the final four. In February the trustees voted to make acquisition of either the Riverside Golf Club or Northerly Island their top priority but remained willing to consider the railroad terminals or Garfield Park. The *Garfieldian* lambasted the trustees for recommending the two sites that least met the criteria of "accessibility, availability and nearness to part-time jobs."[35]

Hoping to sway the trustees' votes, Garfield Parkers swung into high gear in the spring of 1959. Local cars and store windows sported stickers that read "University of Illinois for Garfield Park. Have you written to Mayor Daley?" In April the Bradley and Honore Neighborhood Association and the Garfield Park Improvement Association held a rally at the Gold Dome building in the park. Dozens of Garfield Park residents took a bus trip to Springfield to lobby the state legislature. They asked legislators to reverse their approval of the Riverside site and demand the campus be located within city limits, which the state House of Representatives did.[36]

To promote their case, the Garfield Park Improvement Association and the Bradley and Honore Neighborhood Association prepared a pamphlet entitled "The Garfield Park Area: Where the City and the Suburbs Meet" and distributed four thousand copies. The brochure touted what the Far West Side could offer the university, including "accessibility, central location, and fine buildings." In addition, it argued that the Garfield Park area had "all the advantages of suburban living without the inconveniences and insufferably high taxes common to so many of the suburbs far removed from the city and the center of things." The brochure transformed the precarious position of Far West Siders, who understood both the push to the suburbs and also the continuing pull of the city, from a quandary for themselves into a benefit for the university.[37]

These multiple efforts convinced university officials. On May 16 the university trustees voted to pursue the Garfield Park site as its first choice for the new campus. The trustees' report envisioned a campus occupying the half of the park to the south of Madison Street, as well as some five acres of adjoining private property. A public hearing on Garfield Park's future turned out twenty-three speakers in favor of placing the university there, with nineteen opposed. West Garfield Parkers supplemented their favorable testimony with a petition signed by twenty thousand West Side residents. The Garfield Park–Austin Community Council also showed a color movie, "The Case for the U. of I." The president of the university assured West Garfield Parkers that the trustees would not back down from their new commitment to the park site. The *Garfieldian*, flushed with its evanescent victory, crowed that none of the opposition was local.[38] This notion of "local" neglected the opposition that came from the east side of the park.

But before the trustees decided to go ahead with the park campus, significant obstacles loomed. As was the case with Miller Meadows, Garfield Park served a public function that would end with its metamorphosis into a university campus. Colonel Jacob Arvey, a leading figure in the Cook County Democratic Party who sat on the Park District Board, opposed the sale of the parkland. The Park District Board president also declared himself against selling any land. Further snarling negotiations, neither the Park District Board nor the university trustees wanted to make the first move: without a formal request, the Park District was reluctant to express willingness to sell its land; the university trustees, for their part, had no wish to replay the embarrassing experience of the "Miller Meadow fiasco," so they hesitated to make the request without a prior assurance that the park would be available. After the trustees decided to pursue the site, Park District officials implied that there were no insurmountable barriers to the conveyance of the land but indicated that they wanted to move slowly. In June the state legislature passed a bill explicitly permitting the Park District to sell its land to the university; in July Governor William G. Stratton signed the bill into law.[39]

The strongest objection to replacing the park with the university campus was the enormous loss of recreation space. Scholar Carl Condit later echoed this idea when he condemned the proposal's potential for "damage to the urban fabric." Opponents of the Garfield Park site argued that large parks remained integral to the regional recreation system. The Illinois Audubon Society denounced the trustees as "Neanderthal" for even considering the site. Other opponents, mostly suburban residents, argued that the park belonged to all the people in the Chicago region. The *Garfieldian* answered these criticisms with the claim that the founders of the park system intended for local residents to have a voice in its disposition. The *Garfieldian* noted the sudden appearance of park "saviors" and dismissed them out of hand. The opponents of the park site, the paper suggested, simply preferred a campus in the Loop.[40]

The Sisters of Marillac House, an East Garfield Park social service organization, offered a concrete example of the park's continuing significance for some West Siders' lives. The women religious explained that their summer recreation program depended on the availability of the park. Families living in overcrowded housing badly needed the space and beauty that Garfield Park provided. The sisters often took the African American children in their day-care programs to Garfield Park, a practice that dismayed whites living to its west. Some Far West Side residents also expressed fears about the loss of valuable recreation space but suggested that the city substitute small parks for the campus.[41]

The opponents of the West Side location saw their strongest allies organized in the spring of 1959, in response to the trustees' selection of the park. In March the Metropolitan Housing and Planning Council organized the Central Area Action Committee, which it "created for the purpose of generating public support of the Central Area Plan," whose "first crucial test" was the conversion of the railroad terminals into the university campus. Three days after the University of Illinois trustees voted to pursue Garfield Park, MHPC convened an "emergency session of the groups committed to the South Side site." A political insider assured the assembled group that "the Mayor is still definitely for the South Side site *and willing to fight for it as long as it seems to have a chance....* His seeming acceptance of the Garfield Park site is politically expedient since it assures the city of the university campus." Collectively called the Joint Action Committee, participants plotted to identify alternate sites, "purely to avert using Garfield Park," and to generate public enthusiasm for the South Side site.[42]

The most effective tactic in JAC's arsenal was delay, an approach in which its members were practiced. Leaders hoped to slow implementation of the decision for Garfield Park long enough for Mayor Daley to conclude the delicate negotiations with the owners of the railroad properties. While the university trustees and park officials took the initial steps toward exchanging the parkland, JAC organized a lawsuit to test whether the property was in fact legally available to the university. MHPC and JAC staffed and led the effort, with substantial financial assistance from member organizations.[43]

In March 1960 representatives of the Park District staff and board, the university, the city, and the state's attorney met with the corporation counsel for Chicago and agreed to generate a "friendly lawsuit" testing the parkland's legal availability. Commissioner Jacob Arvey took pains to assure the public that agreeing to participate in the lawsuit was by no means the same as consenting to sell off the property. The university, for its part, disclosed its offer of $3.25 million to the Park District Board, without mentioning that the purpose of the move was to trigger the lawsuit. The trustees made the offer to Mayor Daley, who did not forward the request to the Park District Board, raising public suspicion that the purpose of the entire maneuver was to retard the process. The university then stunned West Siders by suspending planning for the Garfield Park campus, explaining that it was unwilling to expend further monies without a guarantee of the land's availability.[44]

This legal engagement provided precisely the obstructions that JAC and Daley desired. In April the Illinois Supreme Court ruled that the thirty acres included in the lawsuit could be sold to the university, which Garfield Park campus advocates took to mean that the rest could be obtained as well. The case returned to the circuit court in June, however, when three owners of property near the park sought a permanent injunction against the use of the land.[45] In August Judge Cornelius Harrington held that the 1959 Illinois law authorizing the sale was in fact unconstitutional, and that only a referendum could overturn the original 1869 law creating the West Side parks.[46] The backers of the Garfield Park campus site expressed outrage, pointing out that the Chicago Park District had shown no such qualms when it sold land to the Chicago Board of Education for an elementary school on the South Side.[47] In January 1961 the Illinois State Supreme Court agreed with these protests, reversing entirely Harrington's decision and again making the land in Garfield Park available for conversion to a university campus.[48]

Daley, however, used the intervening months to arrange an alternate site for the new university. The mayor never said outright that he would seek a different site closer to the downtown if the deal for the railroad terminals fell through, instead making carefully noncommittal comments like, "Everybody is working under the assumption it (the university campus site) is Garfield Park." James W. Ford reported that a member of a West Side delegation who met with Daley found him "cordial, as he always is, diplomatic, and opposed to us every step of the way!" Daley's affect, sometimes adopted in order to put off making a decision, reminded several observers of the Buddha.[49]

While the Garfield Park litigation proceeded, city staff worked behind the scenes to find a site other than the railroad terminals that would similarly fortify the Central Area Plan. An urban renewal clearance area on the Near West Side surfaced occasionally as a possibility during the campus discussions. The Harrison-Halsted area was a working-class, multi-ethnic district that Jane Addams's famous Hull-House had served since the late nineteenth century. The site was close to the downtown and could undergird the Loop's renewal, just as the railroad site would. During the summer of 1960, Daley's staff began floating the area as a potential location for the campus, possibly as a way of putting pressure on the railroads to cooperate with the city. In September the Department of City Planning announced that Daley formally recommended the Harrison-Halsted site to the university trustees, in case the best location, the terminals, ultimately proved unobtainable. In February 1961 university trustees and city officials held a meeting with the mayor and concluded that getting the Garfield Park site—and the necessary replacement parkland—was impossible, despite the latest ruling from the Illinois Supreme Court. If he had to swallow the bitter pill of losing the railroad site, Daley was pleased to authorize the Harrison-Halsted location instead.[50]

This new decision infuriated residents of both the Near West Side and West Garfield Park. The *Garfieldian* editorialized about the irony of a neighborhood that did not want the university having it "jammed down the throat," when another neighborhood desperately wanted it. West Garfield Park residents launched a letter-writing campaign asking the trustees to reconsider. The United Property Group, leading this phase of the campus campaign, accused the city's urban renewal plan of operating for the benefit of downtown merchants and real estate dealers. One angry resident fulminated against the "conspiracy to make the West Side a ghetto," reminding *Garfieldian* readers of the campus's potential to prevent white out-migration.[51]

The residents of the threatened Harrison-Halsted neighborhood reacted even more vigorously. Florence Scala, a local activist who emerged as the leader of the protest, complained that residents of the area were denied the chance even to express their opinions, a courtesy granted Garfield Parkers. The Harrison-Halsted Community Group, however, had only a month to organize before the city council vote required to condemn their neighborhood. Near West Siders took their plea to every organization they could reach but persuaded no one. Scala later remembered that it was "as though we were talking to a stone wall, a mountain." After the aldermen's perfunctory vote, Harrison-Halsted residents held a sit-down strike outside the city hall. They then turned unsuccessfully to the courts. In 1963 the U.S. Supreme Court declined to hear their appeals. When construction began, most of the Hull-House complex and surrounding residential areas were demolished. By 1965 the first classes started at the University of Illinois Chicago Circle campus.[52]

Small Parks

The losing campaign for the University of Illinois campus provoked a secondary debate that illustrated Far West Siders' expectations of remaining in the city, despite their continuing losses in the public policy arena. In the course of arguing that the park was dangerous and should be replaced by the campus, West Garfield Parkers began to wonder where else they might go for recreation. While the West Side had several other large and small parks, they seemed few and far between.[53] The editors of the *Garfieldian* revived an idea popular among Progressive reformers in the first part of the twentieth century: that there should be a small park within walking distance of all city dwellers.[54] The newspaper proposed using the money collected by the Park District from Garfield Park's sale to build small neighborhood parks throughout the West Side. Various West Side organizations, including members of the Bradley and Honore Neighborhood Association and the United Property Group, enthusiastically took up the cause of small parks and gave the movement an independent life. In December 1960 a delegation headed by 30th Ward alderman Daniel Ronan took to the superintendent of the Chicago Park District a formal proposal for a system of playgrounds, play lots, wading and swimming pools, and athletic fields for the West Side. The visitors emphasized that small parks were "an absolute necessity," and that their creation should be independent of the final decision on the university site.[55] These parks would provide Far West Siders with a physically improved but still racially segregated city.

In advocating small parks as a permanent alternative to the city's large park system, white West Siders reflected their desire to create an urban landscape composed of pieces small enough to manage. As parks historian Galen Cranz notes, in large spaces such as Garfield Park, "minorities had to interact with one another." In small local parks, however, white West Siders could control the social and physical use of their environment. In the early part of the twentieth century, historian Thomas Jablonsky has argued, the new neighborhood parks in Chicago were instrumental in providing the children of working-class immigrant families with an expanded sense of a "home range" within the city. Small parks drew children out of the self-contained enclaves of their immigrant parents and introduced them into a larger urban community. In the second half of the twentieth century, as large parks appeared dangerous and unmanageable, white West Siders tried to use small parks to reverse this process, so that they could retain a racially homogeneous slice of the city for their own benefit.[56]

Other people in the city and the nation agreed with white West Siders that smaller parks suited postwar urban landscapes better than large ones. In 1965 Mayor Richard J. Daley said that the days of large parks in Chicago were over and declared that the city would be better off with small parks located near all residents. An "open space movement," beginning in the early 1960s, sought to tuck small parks into odd lots and unused parcels of urban land around the country. But whereas the Progressive-era playground movement stemmed from a coherent ideology that structured the design of the parks and informed the activities held in them, the playground movement of the 1960s lacked such a clear philosophy. In fact, this lack of coherence prompted Galen Cranz, working as a playground designer for Chicago's Neighborhood Improvement and Beautification Program in 1969, to write a history of American park design.[57] Some of Cranz's difficulty in locating a clear philosophy behind postwar parks stemmed from the fact that the movement had multiple incompatible sources, including the impulse to eliminate Garfield Park.

African Americans who lived on the West Side during the 1960s were, if anything, even more active in the pursuit of small parks than were whites, but their motivations were entirely different. Many African American homeowners, block club members, and community organizations devoted great energy to creating new recreation spaces on the West Side. In some cases, they tried to solve the problems associated with the growing numbers of lots left vacant by absentee owners. In other cases, they wanted to find wholesome outlets for youth with too much leisure time and too few recreational opportunities.[58]

The problem of youth with too many unsupervised hours stemmed in part from the policies of the Chicago Public School system. During the 1950s the board of education shortened the school day for many black children in Chicago; in the 1960s it sent African American students back to school full-time, but in the process occupied much of the available play space on the West Side. In both the cases of the University of Illinois campus campaign and the neighborhood schools debate, white West Siders regarded educational institutions instrumentally. They understood that school facilities, as much as residential buildings and commercial enterprises, shaped the city's racial landscape.

CHAPTER 5

Public Schools

Just as the University of Illinois Chicago Circle campus prepared to open in January 1965, white residents of Austin protested a Chicago Board of Education plan to "cluster," or mix, the student bodies of Marshall and Austin high schools and May and Sumner elementary schools. Although the boundaries of the paired schools abutted one another, their populations were distinct. Of the four schools, three were almost entirely racially segregated; only May School, whose population was approximately one-quarter African American, counted as integrated. White Austin residents, whose opinions on racial intermixing varied to a surprising degree, objected vociferously to the plan, many on the grounds that it violated a long-standing board commitment to neighborhood schools. "I wonder," wrote Helen L. Dewsberry to school board member Cyrus Adams, "if the two gentlemen who prepared these very illustrous [sic] reports, think we people are stupid to the point of jamming things down our neck, without our fighting for our rights." Although the board quickly dropped the cluster plan, the racial composition of the white schools changed over the next few years. By 1970 both May Elementary and Austin High School were overwhelmingly African American.[1]

During the 1960s white Chicagoans had frequent opportunities for protest, as the board of education struggled to dispel accusations of deliberate segregation. White opposition to school desegregation efforts in Chicago was fierce, although less dramatic than the showdowns in other parts of the country. In southern states white segregationist legislatures, governors, and school officials creatively evaded the U.S. Supreme

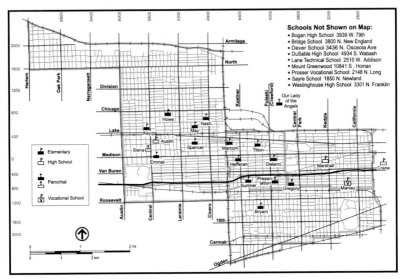

Fig. 9. West Side schools. Produced by the University of Wisconsin–Milwaukee, Cartography & GIS Center.

Court *Brown v. Board* decisions for years. Angry white southerners stood on the front lines against black children integrating previously all-white schools with full confidence that the local and state governments shared their views. Most famously, of course, in 1957 President Eisenhower provided federal military protection to nine black students in Little Rock, Arkansas, before they could attend Central High School. In New Orleans the four six-year-old girls who were the first black children to attend formerly whites-only schools faced enormous hostility. Ruby Bridges, the only black student assigned to the Frantz school in 1960, traveled daily through threatening crowds into a school that was shunned by her white classmates for the entire year. In Virginia white citizens rallied around journalist James J. Kilpatrick's call for "massive resistance" to school integration. For five years, from 1959 to 1964, officials in Prince Edward County simply shut the public schools rather than comply with the Supreme Court's ruling.[2]

Chicago's schools, by contrast, were periodically integrated and resegregated as the racial composition of neighborhoods changed. In de jure segregated southern school systems, black children suffered the indignity of traveling past all-white schools on their journeys to distant, inferior all-black schools; the celebrated *Brown* decisions effectively established integrated local schools as the legal standard. In the North, however, the practice of requiring children to attend the public school nearest to their homes perpetuated de facto segregation. White northerners recognized that as long as children were assigned to neighborhood schools, residential segregation in housing kept the populations of neighborhood schools racially homogenous. White northerners focused their protests not on the admission of tiny groups of African American children to white schools, but on policy shifts that threatened to undermine the principle of the neighborhood school. In Boston in 1974, for example, white parents offered violent and prolonged objections to a judge's order that the school system bus children all around the city in order to achieve immediate desegregation.[3] No court order for school desegregation provided whites in Chicago with such a clear focus for their protests. Instead, white Chicagoans reacted against a series of small-scale decisions. Consequently, white objections to school desegregation in Chicago were shrill and frequent, but not as sustained as in other northern cities.

Most white West Siders, like their counterparts around Chicago and the North, valorized the neighborhood school policy. As long as African Americans lived at a distance, white West Siders' support for the neighborhood school policy served their interest in racially homogenous schools. A few African American schools in Chicago, most notably the South Side's DuSable High School, had faculties committed to the success of their students, even if their facilities were deficient.[4] But most black children in Chicago attended crowded, poorly maintained schools with inadequate supplies and inexperienced teachers. When white parents imagined black pupils in their children's classrooms, the specter of these conditions compounded their anxieties about interracial schooling. In contrast to the physical and moral degradation of the environment represented by a blighted landscape, racially integrated public schools represented the disruption of the social homogeneity of neighborhood life. The potential for black children in white schools signaled a new kind of crisis to West Siders, one that they lacked the ability to put off effectively. Both racial hostility and awareness of the neglect of schools that black students attended prompted white West Siders to resist school integration, however it came about.

But West Siders' allegiance to the concept of the neighborhood school left them in a quandary when African Americans moved into the neighborhood. Having proclaimed the right of children to attend the school nearest their home, they could offer few credible objections when African American children legitimately enrolled in their local public school. Whether they were racists who objected to any form of integration or racial moderates[5] who personally abhorred the conditions that school officials allowed to flourish in majority-black schools, most white parents eventually responded to the arrival of black students in the local public school by withdrawing their own children. By the time it dawned on some, such as those whose children attended May School, to ally with African Americans in protesting the conditions that flourished at schools attended by black children, the process of residential racial change on the West Side was largely complete. On the West Side, whites' tenacious commitment to neighborhood schools undermined their hopes of maintaining all-white communities.

The abortive plan to cluster pairs of West Side schools marked one of the first efforts by the Chicago Board of Education to shake off the thrall of school superintendent Benjamin C. Willis. From his arrival in 1953 until the unsettling 1963–64 school year, Willis unambiguously controlled the operations of Chicago's public schools. Mayor Richard J. Daley shrewdly maintained a public distance from school affairs, allowing Willis to bear the brunt of the criticism of his administration. During the 1950s white West Side parents kept an attentive eye on policy decisions, like the ones that set the boundaries of their local schools. On the rare occasions when decisions displeased them, West Siders intervened with officials to protect the racial homogeneity of their schools. During the early 1960s, however, civil rights activists succeeded in putting so much pressure on Willis that the board of education began to shift out from the superintendent's influence. Where the unchallenged Willis had avoided policies that intentionally drew black and white students into the same schools, the board now introduced programs, such as the cluster plan, that nibbled at the edges of de facto segregation and undermined the neighborhood school policy. These experiments aroused white West Siders who regarded the intentional desegregation of their schools as harbingers of their own ousters from their neighborhoods.[6]

During the mid- to late 1960s, West Side activists—sometimes joined by opponents of integration from other parts of the city—vigorously protested the board's efforts to promote integration in the schools that moved ahead of changes in residential population. These efforts were sufficient to head off wholesale change in the approach of the public school system to integration but were ineffective at slowing the arrival of African American children in the schools that white children attended on the West Side. One group of white West Siders with an unusual commitment to the possibilities of integration pushed the board from the other side, encouraging the administration to ameliorate the conditions that prevailed in black schools. Their efforts succeeded in generating temporary solutions to the problems at their particular schools but failed to introduce a systemic commitment to integration in the Chicago Public Schools.

Chicago Public Schools in the 1950s

For most of the first decade of the Willis administration, white West Siders were largely satisfied with the state of their local public schools and so had little reason to protest. The budget shortfalls and corruption of the 1930s and the 1940s were over, and the top administrators had regained control of the school system. A new school superintendent cleaned out the "Augean Stables" of the system, and his successor, dubbed "Big Ben the Builder," appeared committed to erecting new schools to address the perennial problem of overcrowding.[7] The Willis administration contained problems within their local environs. When the population of black neighborhoods swelled, white schools remained unaffected. As the area of African American settlement expanded westward, the Willis administration left intact policy mechanisms that permitted white students to leave the schools where black children enrolled. On a few occasions, white West Siders felt impelled to lobby school officials to reconsider decisions that accelerated the entrance of black students into white schools. The relative rarity of these episodes testified both to West Siders' general contentment with the state of schools in the 1950s and also to their willingness to mobilize to protect that condition.

As long as the Willis administration kept African American pupils out of their children's schools, white Chicagoans were largely pleased with his superintendency. Until the 1940s, the operations of the Chicago school system and city politics were deeply intertwined, usually to the benefit of the Democratic Party's patronage machine. Especially during the mayoralty of Edward J. Kelly (1933–47), the schools were mired in political controversies over decisions about promotion practices, textbook purchases, and curricula. Herold Hunt, Willis's immediate predecessor, did much to begin the process of cleaning up the system. Willis, who held a doctorate in education from Columbia University, left the superintendency of Buffalo's public school system to take over in Chicago in 1953. Willis's response to the controversies that engulfed his predecessors was to insist on the complete separation of school governance from city politics.[8]

Both his personality and the structure of his office enabled Willis to treat the school system "as his own principality," in the view of one of his critics. With a salary that reached $48,500 in 1961, the superintendent of the Chicago Public Schools (CPS) was reputed to be the fourth-highest paid public official in the United States, following the president of the United States, the governor of New York State, and the mayor of New York City.[9] Willis wielded tight control over the entire operation of the school system.

In 1963 the *Chicago's American* newspaper called him "a high-handed, self-willed official who seemed to regard all opposition as spiteful and all cri[t]icism as sabotage." School administration staff reportedly found it difficult to question Willis's decisions from within, "because any attempt at examination is labeled an act of disloyalty." Even his supporters considered the authoritarian Willis "brusque" and "dictatorial." One of the only complimentary things that a *Chicago Tribune* reporter found to say about Willis on his retirement in 1966 was that he "always had an undeniable way with children."[10]

Willis and his subordinates carefully managed the release of information about the operations of the schools. While appearing to provide much data, they made it very difficult to obtain the evidence necessary to critique the system. On the one hand, Willis was notorious for his "charts and graphs" approach to presentations, overwhelming his audience with details. On the other hand, Willis also insisted that sensitive data not be available to the public. For example, he refused to release school-by-school reports of the standardized tests taken by Chicago pupils, information that would have allowed potentially unfavorable comparisons and criticisms. Similarly when the U.S. Office of Education demanded that students take national achievement tests, Willis declined to administer them. He also refused to release information about the capacity and enrollment of the schools, data invaluable for documenting disparities in the use of facilities in different neighborhoods. Discerning racial disparities in school facilities was particularly difficult, because CPS took no racial head counts of the pupil population until ordered in 1963 by the state legislature. Even members of the board of education also found Willis's high-handedness exasperating. After Willis's departure in 1966, Cyrus Adams complained that he was "very chintzy about giving out facts and statistics and was adamant at not releasing anything even to the Board Members which would in any way reflect inadequacy on the part of the school system."[11]

Despite these criticisms, Willis won approbation from white parents around the city, whose children he buffered from some of the effects of population changes in the schools. In the years just after World War II, internal shifts in the city's population worsened school crowding. Population increases caused by war production, migration, and the baby boom gave Chicago the largest average class size of all the big American cities in 1953. As residential development on the Northwest and Southwest sides of the city opened up new housing opportunities, white Chicagoans who moved there found that school construction had not kept pace, temporarily leaving their children with overcrowded, albeit all-white, classrooms. At the same time, African Americans faced deeper and more sustained school overcrowding structured by the city's residential segregation. In black schools the annual in-migration of tens of thousands of African American southerners exacerbated the space crunch. Even as they gained access to West Side housing, African Americans arrived in far greater numbers than the whites who left. While casual observers assumed that African Americans overpopulated their new neighborhoods and schools because their families consisted of women with many children, crowding in racially segregated housing accounted for much of the difference.[12]

The neighborhood school policy contributed to the crowding in Chicago's black schools. Like school administrators around the United States, Chicago officials viewed the education of children in local neighborhood schools as the best possible practice (although children with disabilities often traveled far to classrooms with specialized facilities). Arguing that children's psychological development depended on remaining within a small and comprehensible world, Willis insisted on educating them where they lived, rather than sending them to schools that could offer enough seats or complete school days. Further, school planners based their decisions about where to locate new schools on the numbers of building and conversion permits for each area of the city. Strict reliance on official data failed to account for the illegal conversions that created shelter—and crowding—in many black neighborhoods.[13] Willis's refusal to account for illegal conversions stemmed from his broader conviction that the business of the schools and the city should not mix.

Schools in black neighborhoods bore the most visible consequences of the neighborhood school policy. As African Americans piled into North Lawndale in the 1950s, the schools that served their children frequently became alarmingly crowded. The first response of school officials to severe crowding was to hold classes in all the available rooms in their buildings. When the William Cullen Bryant School enrolled two hundred extra students in 1956, for example, officials pressed the gymnasium and book storage rooms into service as classrooms. The practice of holding classes in space designed for other purposes drew intense scrutiny, however, after a fire devastated the Roman Catholic Our Lady of the Angels school in December 1958, killing ninety-five students and teachers. Much more commonly, administrators in crowded schools drew on the prewar practice of splitting oversubscribed grades into split, or "double," shifts. Children on split shift were invited to attend school for a portion of the normal day.[14]

Parents of children attending double shifts worried about the effects of the split shifts on children's education and their time not spent in class. High on their list of concerns was that the truncated school day fostered juvenile delinquency. In crowded, poor neighborhoods, families often sent

Fig. 10. Schools serving African American children were often overcrowded and under-supplied, both before and after the departure of Superintendent Benjamin C. Willis. Here children at Emmet West share books. *Austinite*, September 23, 1970. Courtesy of the Special Collections and Preservation Division, Chicago Public Library.

both parents into the paid workforce, leaving children without adult super-vision while they were out of school. James King warned, "Children play in the streets with the house key dangling from their necks. By the time they are ready for school their clothing is soiled, they may not have had lunch; their older brothers and sisters who are responsible for them may have gone their individual ways." Reverend Warren Kelly asked board of education members to "assume moral responsibility" for future gang members who learned vagrancy when forced out of school. Carmen Torres, concerned that her children were learning so little at their elementary school, considered sending them "to live with relatives [in Puerto Rico] so that they may receive a more adequate education." Another Spanish-speaking mother worried that the shortened school day slowed down the speed with which her chil-dren learned English.[15]

Critics of the double-shift system suggested a range of alternatives to school officials. Some urged the board to build new schools or buy existing facilities in crowded areas, a recommendation consistent with the neighborhood schools policy. Others recommended that the board bus children to vacant classrooms in adjacent neighborhoods. After the fire at Our Lady of the Angels, the Chicago Public Schools system leased thirty-five vacant classrooms to the archdiocese, so that surviving pupils could continue to attend school while replacement facilities were constructed. Claude Peck, the president of the Greater Lawndale Conservation Commission in 1959, pointed out that those classrooms could have been used to educate public school students from neighboring Lawndale in less crowded, full-time conditions.[16]

Willis's administration repeatedly rebuffed these suggestions. Officials insisted that pupils could still receive a full "educational program," despite spending less time in the school building. A Lawndale teacher explained that a "well trained teacher, equipped with good educational skills, can teach in four hours what would be taught in six hours, minus recesses. However, the shift problem is magnified by new teachers, crowded rooms and many educationally retarded children from other sections of our country." Willis told one concerned audience, "I am convinced that lack of proper health clinic facilities is more of a problem than is double shift in Lawndale." Sargent Shriver, the president of the Chicago Board of Education in 1957, argued, "The number of vacant seats in the Chicago public schools at this time is a very small percent of the total classroom seats in the city. In fact, if any industrial concern were utilizing its plant as well as we are utilizing ours, I think they would receive an award for efficiency." The Willis administration and the board adamantly refused to consider busing, citing the cost, a failed transportation effort in New York City, and rampant misinformation about the availability of vacant rooms.[17]

Especially after the fire at Our Lady of the Angels, the board preferred constructing new buildings over adapting old facilities to new purposes and higher safety standards. As part of the building program, the board authorized several new schools for the Lawndale area and other crowded spots around the city, although Willis cautioned that the fluidity of the city's population complicated the task of accurately estimating future enrollments. While waiting for new schools, children were not permitted to transfer outside of their neighborhoods. Faith Rich, a desegregation researcher and activist, complained, "They are making a fetish out of the district." Gregory Elementary School, which served Lawndale students, became so crowded that officials considered placing the pupils on triple shifts. Rather than resort to this drastic measure, however, the board shrank Gregory's boundaries, sending some of the pupils to nearby schools also already on double shifts.[18]

The neighborhood school policy, however, was not administered in an entirely consistent fashion during the 1950s. The main mechanism that enabled white students to evade crowding was the "neutral zone" policy. In subsections of several school attendance zones, parents were permitted to choose between adjacent schools. Because white and black children attending a temporarily integrated school did not usually live side by side, the policy worked differently for each group. White children on the West Side could transfer to a school to the west or north, where African Americans had not yet reached. Black children in neutral zone areas, by contrast, were offered the choice between attending a newly crowded resegregating school or a recently crowded black school. Further, principals had the discretion to permit or refuse transfers, allowing the whimsy of school staffs to reinforce existing segregation. Willis's predecessor, Superintendent Herold Hunt, had eliminated the neutral zones in all but eighteen areas of the city in 1948, but not until 1959 were certain West Side schools removed from the list of exceptions. Finally in 1962 the policy was eliminated altogether.[19]

Thus, during the 1950s white West Siders only rarely had to confront policies emanating from the Chicago Public Schools that upset their ability to send their children to racially homogenous schools. A few occasions, however, when the board of education considered changes in school boundaries that had potential to create racially integrated classrooms illustrated that white West Siders could mobilize to protect what they saw as their interests, and that they could influence some decisions. Hints that the board of education might send black children to white schools sent white West Side parents into a frenzy of communication. They scrutinized proposed boundary changes to determine where their children would be sent and who would be coming into local schools. If they did not care for the results, school and city officials heard from them. They took care, however, not to speak in racial terms. Instead, they allowed the geography of the urban landscape to stand in for race.[20]

White parents demonstrated their facility with spatial rhetoric when Gregory Elementary became overcrowded in 1957. In order to accommodate the surge in students, administrators assigned several dozen seventh and eighth graders from Gregory to Manley Vocational School, a mile to the east, and put first and second graders on double shifts. White parents at Gregory responded quickly. The Garfield Park Improvement Association (GPIA) insinuated that the sudden increase in Gregory's enrollment resulted from "outsider" students who falsified their addresses in order to gain admission to the school. GPIA enlisted the help of Alderman Thomas Burke in communicating with school officials. The group's initial complaint criticized the methods used to notify parents that their children were transferred. But their reluctance to permit their children to mix across racial lines became evident as they objected to the assignment of the older children to classrooms in Manley. They specifically protested sending their children to a school nine blocks to the east—that is, into an area already inhabited by African Americans. An editorial in the *Garfieldian* suggested that the assignments to Manley were causing some parents to consider moving out of the area.[21]

White parents again demonstrated their potential for mobilization when African American students arrived at Sumner School. In September 1959 a new community organization began lodging complaints with school officials that African American students going to and from school were extorting money from and beating up white children. Like parents at Gregory Elementary, whites from Sumner expressed the racial basis of their fears only cautiously, but again the local racial geography betrayed them. The organization suggested that teachers supervise students' dispersals at the end of the school day, to make sure that they headed home, instead of going into areas where they did not belong. This group did not expect teachers to remember the address of every single student. Instead, they anticipated that the teachers would rely on race to determine the children's destinations, urging, "Have the teachers walk their classes out the door and to the corner . . . making sure that students who live east and south go east and south and those living north and west go north and west." White children had to be from the west and north; black children lived to the south and east. The alderman also betrayed the underlying racial conflict when he suggested that a solution lay in a meeting between white and African American parents. White parents did meet with Sumner's principal. They told him that fifty white families had already withdrawn their children from Sumner and were instead sending them to Presentation, a local Catholic school. Apparently, tensions eased after this meeting, and the next week the leader of the organization said that the problem was getting better.[22]

White West Garfield Park parents also took swift action when the board of education proposed changing the boundaries of several local elementary schools. As African Americans began to move into the southern section of West Garfield Park in the early 1960s, the elementary schools began to experience severe overcrowding. Hefferan School, built to supplement Tilton, Delano, and Sumner schools, opened in the fall of 1961; by December the school enrolled more than twice as many students as its official capacity, with more students arriving daily. In August 1962 the board of education proposed adjusting the attendance boundaries of four West Garfield Park elementary schools—Delano, Tilton, Marconi, and Hefferan—to redistribute the crowded students. The proposed changes mixed up the racial composition of the schools, a change that alarmed the United Property Group (UPG), an organization of activist whites who opposed African American migration into the neighborhood. UPG responded with vigor to the board's proposal, promising "an 'all out' fight" to return the schools to their former boundaries, which (for the moment) confined the crowding to majority-black schools.[23]

UPG offered a severe, but carefully worded, critique of the proposed boundaries, arguing that the "zig-zag boundaries" violated the spirit of the neighborhood school policy. For the convenience and safety of students, UPG argued, schools ought to be located in the "approximate center" of their attendance areas. Among their list of seven specific objections to the proposal was that "children who live across the street from Hefferan school, 4409 Wilcox, are forced to go to Tilton school, 4152 West End, or Marconi, 230 N. Kolmar, a distance of eight or nine blocks in some cases." They also complained, "Tilton students south of Jackson must cross three busy streets—Jackson, Madison and Washington." UPG representatives were very careful not to mention that race was salient to their protest of the boundary changes. Again, the key to understanding their protest lies in the racial geography of West Garfield Park. Until 1965 Madison Street, which ran east and west through the area, functioned as "an imaginary Mason and Dixon line," north of which all the residents were white.[24] In 1962 African American children were majorities at Delano and Hefferan, in the southern part of West Garfield Park, while Tilton and Marconi were white schools north of Madison. The proposed changes compromised the segregationist function of Madison Street by sending black children to the white part of West Garfield Park. UPG members concealed their objections to a school policy that sent children across the racial dividing line of Madison Street behind the superficially neutral terms of geography.

UPG members did not simply stew in their objections. Members immediately circulated petitions supporting the original boundaries among white West Garfield Park residents. When the schools reopened for the fall session, women picketed at each of the schools involved in the realignments. A delegation from UPG persuaded school officials to spend an entire day meeting with them about their concerns. Although this meeting did not result in any immediate alterations, school officials took the unusually solicitous step of providing UPG with "school population statistics" so that the group could draft a counterproposal. Superintendent Willis agreed to hold public hearings to consider alterations in the plan, without committing to reversing the decision. Disappointed with the superintendent's lack of complete deference to their concerns, UPG officials turned to city hall, where they met with an assistant to Mayor Richard J. Daley to express their anger over the "ridiculous" boundaries. They also demanded that the board of education inform other city officials about any overcrowded housing it identified. UPG apparently found the mayor's staff more cooperative than the superintendent; in early November the local newspaper congratulated the board of education for "'un-zigging' the zig-zag boundaries."[25]

School System in Crisis

The accumulated policies that trapped black children in crowded schools and allowed whites to escape convinced African American activists and their white allies that the Willis administration's approach to education was racist and intentionally segregationist. As the 1950s wore on, they frequently said so. In the wake of the U.S. Supreme Court decisions in the *Brown* cases, activists had legitimate hope, denied to their early twentieth-century predecessors, that the accusation of racial injustice could precipitate change.[26] The Willis administration's adamant denials of problems, however, prompted African American activists to push harder. Their first step in demanding reform in the system was to obtain information documenting the extent of racial disparities among the public schools.

The leading independent researcher into the racial composition of the Chicago Public Schools was Faith Rich, an extraordinary white woman who moved into Lawndale along with tens of thousands of African Americans and pronounced the West Side "more real and alive th[a]n the white areas." Rich, who earned a Ph.D. in classics from Bryn Mawr College, devoted her life in Chicago to community and racial activism, especially to the work of the National Association for the Advancement of Colored People and the Congress of Racial Equality. For several years Rich loaned her skills to the Schools Committee of the Greater Lawndale Conservation Commission.[27] In 1957, frustrated with the unchecked swelling of the local school enrollments, Rich set out to document the number of unused classrooms in the system.

Rich's task was not an easy one. In contrast to the members of the United Property Group, Rich received no information from the Willis administration, which refused to make available records that indicated either the racial composition of the schools or the numbers of classrooms. Instead, she relied on parents and school staff, who were in short supply during the summer when she conducted her investigation. Starting with figures published for the 1930 school year, Rich calculated the amount of classroom space added to the physical plant under the New Deal with federal Public Works

Administration funding. She concluded that while Lawndale proper was short eight thousand seats, there were thirteen thousand vacant seats within a three-mile radius of the neighborhood. Rich published her results in the NAACP's national journal, *Crisis*, and provided details to GLCC officers for testimony at board of education budget hearings. With Rich's help, GLCC argued that if the board of education authorized appropriate transfers through the public school system, *"the full use of the existing school plant could eliminate [the double shift] twice over."* School officials disputed the accuracy of Rich's figures without providing firm numbers of their own. The Chicago Urban League experienced a similar response to its quest to catalog the available space in public schools.[28]

The construction program of "Big Ben the Builder" failed to eliminate the double shift. The combination of continuing high—and unpredictable—enrollments in black neighborhoods and rising criticism of the crowding of the schools in black neighborhoods prompted the board of education to begin using mobile classrooms. In March the portable classrooms debuted at crowded schools around the city, including at Sumner and Delano elementary schools on the West Side. By 1964 there were 250 portable classrooms in use in Chicago. Willis's critics immediately protested the segregatory function of the "Willis Wagons." The Woodlawn Organization sent "Truth Squads" armed with cameras into public schools to document the disparities between the facilities offered to white and black students. The Congress of Racial Equality picketed and leafleted at Sumner School when the portable units debuted. They offered several objections, including their cost, the drain on the facilities of a single school staff, and their placement in the playground, which was a gratuitous blow to a community already short of open recreation space. Anger at Willis's denials that the mobile units were segregated and wasteful grew during the summer of 1962.[29] By the fall of 1963, the schools were in crisis.

In addition to the mounting anger over the "Willis Wagons," the crisis of the 1963–64 school year had several additional sources that culminated simultaneously. First, a desegregation lawsuit brewing for several years was settled with an agreement to produce a study of integration in the school system. Second, an independent overview of the school system affirmed some of the complaints of civil rights activists. Third, a difference of opinion between Willis and the members of the board of education resulted in Willis's abrupt resignation from—and quick return to—his position as superintendent. Finally, civil rights activists instigated a pair of boycotts of the school system. While none of these efforts produced substantive systemic change in the Chicago Public Schools, they loosened Superintendent Willis's authority over the board. Consequently, in the lat-

Fig. 11. Civil rights activists picketing Hefferan School. *Garfieldian*, April 8, 1964. Courtesy of the Special Collections and Preservation Division, Chicago Public Library.

ter years of the 1960s, the board conducted a series of experiments in classroom integration.[30]

Two studies criticized elements of Willis's administration. The 1964 Hauser Report stemmed from the settlement of a lawsuit with South Side parents. The report, authored by University of Chicago sociologist Philip Hauser, found that the Chicago Public Schools were thoroughly segregated, with almost all African American students in the system attending schools with almost no white classmates. The report recommended carefully locating new schools so that they did not perpetuate racial divisions and combining, or "clustering," the attendance areas of pairs of schools on the verge of racial transition so that students could be allocated between them in a deliberately integrated pattern. The Hauser Report did not repudiate the neighborhood school policy; rather, it tweaked the concept of "neighborhood" to include both blacks and whites in the same locale. For its part, the Havighurst Report rebuked Willis's administration more thoroughly. This survey argued for a flexible neighborhood school policy. Most students should attend a local school, but the board should permit students to attend the schools best suited to them, even if they had to travel a distance from their homes to do so. Among the report's recommendations for ameliorating segregation was that the school administration select several neighborhoods to experiment with creating "stable integration" through active and astute management.[31]

The third element in the schools crisis came to a head in October 1963. In late August, acting on Willis's recommendation, the board of education approved a plan to allow the best students in crowded schools lacking honors programs to transfer to schools that could provide them with an education suited to their abilities. At all-white Bogan High School on the city's Southwest Side, white parents protested the anticipated arrival of African Americans as transfer students under this policy. Bogan parents rallied near their homes and marched on city hall and the board of education, demanding that their school be exempted from the new transfer policy. After meeting with parents from Bogan, Willis promptly reduced the list of schools receiving transfer students from twenty-four to nine. The board of education, in turn, ordered Willis to return two of the eliminated schools to the proposal, and parents of black children from the Southeast Side won a court order directing Willis to obey the board. Rather than comply, on October 4 Willis dodged bailiffs attempting to serve him with these orders and submitted his resignation, claiming that the board had overstepped its authority. African American activists hoped that the crisis might finally rid them of the superintendent. To their disappointment, the cowed board refused to accept Willis's resignation and voted to cancel the transfer orders.[32]

In the wake of the board's capitulation to Willis, African American activists forged ahead with plans for a one-day school boycott, billed as "Freedom Day." The boycott echoed those conducted by white parents in the American South, in response to federal court orders to integrate their schools. The Coordinating Council of Community Organizations (CCCO), which led the effort, urged parents to send their boycotting children to alternative classes held in churches. CCCO issued thirteen demands, including a call for Willis's departure, integration of students and school staff, and an end to the use of portable classrooms for purposes of segregation. On October 22, 1963, more than 224,000 children—about half of the system's students—stayed out of school. Board president Clair Roddewig met with CCCO representatives but refused to negotiate with them. Frustrated by the boycott's failure to change the system, CCCO called a second boycott for February 25, 1964. Less successful than the first, the second boycott drew only 175,000 students.[33]

Although the boycotts did not produce wholesale change in the Chicago Public Schools, the multiple upheavals of the 1963–64 school year unsettled the relations between the board of education and the superintendent. Although they asked Willis to stay in his job, some board members resented his imperious conduct. With further legal challenges to the segregation of Chicago's schools looming,[34] the board launched some experimental efforts in classroom integration. These efforts would have achieved token desegregation at best. But the slight loosening of the anti-integration policies of the Chicago Public Schools in the late 1960s aroused white West Siders who would not subject their children to the conditions that flourished when African Americans entered a school.

West Siders Aroused

As the board of education moved away from the neighborhood school policy, white West Siders stepped up their protests against the pending integration. Having learned from their own experiences, testimony in newspapers, and the bitter criticism of civil rights protestors that conditions in public schools deteriorated when black pupils arrived, white West Siders sought to hold them off as long as possible. Through the mid-1960s, however, the actions of white West Siders exhibited a certain myopia. Taking their cues from opponents of desegregation in other states and elsewhere in Chicago, they focused on keeping the schools as white as possible. Only in the late 1960s and early 1970s did it dawn on West Side activists to join forces with African American parents in objecting to the conditions that plagued black schools. White parents at a few Austin schools had some success in alleviating the crowding and other shortcomings that officials permitted in African American schools; but their efforts were insufficient to impress their neighbors who opposed integration altogether.

The first of the board's experiments in integration grew out of the Hauser Report of 1964. In April 1964 the board voted to adopt the Hauser Report "in general principle" and directed a subcommittee to study its recommendations for student integration. The head of the subcommittee, Frank M. Whiston, was one of Willis's reliable supporters. Together, the two drafted the Willis-Whiston plan, which permitted fifth- through eighth-grade students at schools with more than thirty-five students per classroom to transfer to schools with fewer than thirty in each class. Because Willis adamantly refused to fund transportation for students attending schools beyond their home neighborhoods, few schoolchildren ever took advantage of established transfer plans, and few were likely to exercise the Willis-Whiston option. A Chicago Urban League researcher pointed out that the plan emphasized crowding and entirely failed to recognize segregation as a problem. After some politicking and Whiston's elevation to the board's presidency, the reconstituted subcommittee passed the Willis-Whiston plan in June.[35]

Civil rights observers feared that the board had forgotten Hauser's recommendations for integrating schools. But Cyrus H. Adams, who became the new chair of the subcommittee, summoned Hauser to address members on the differences between his recommendations and Willis's plan. In late August the board adopted a new proposal to mix mostly white and mostly black schools together and redistribute their student populations. In November Willis submitted a list of ten pairs of schools to be clustered in the second semester of the school year. The schools included several on the city's South Side and four on the West Side: May and Sumner elementary schools and Austin and Marshall high schools. Kindergarten through eighth-grade students in each pair of schools could choose which to attend. Willis explained that the pairs were those that seemed likely to promote "additional interracial association of students." Board member James Clement disagreed, arguing that the plan should pair an overcrowded white school with an underused integrated school, thereby offering white students an incentive to mix with African Americans.[36]

Cyrus Adams and his colleagues on the board of education quickly discovered almost uniform and vehement opposition to the plan from white parents at the schools concerned. Black parents from Sumner and Marshall schools demonstrated little interest in the plan, not attending the general information meetings the principals offered. Part of white parents' opposition stemmed from fear rooted in a widespread misapprehension that white children would be compelled to attend school in black neighborhoods, but they also opposed the deliberate integration of the schools. Betty Larsen wrote to the *Garfieldian* that she would neither allow her daughter to enter the neighborhood around Marshall High School nor "permit said master-planners to cheat her out of an education." A white parent of children at May School, who feared the African American children already among their classmates, wrote that if the cluster plan was implemented, "you will have ruined 2 good schools. . . . We don't want the Negro shoved right down our throat." A parent at Austin High School contended, "I believe it is my constitutional right to send my children to the school of my choosing." A few people mixed nonracial concerns amid their assertions that it was not "the fault of the Austin Community" if black neighborhoods were overcrowded. A white teacher at a mostly black public school pointed out among his other concerns that the distances children had to travel in clustered schools "would result in more tardiness and, ultimately, in greater truancy." Some parents mentioned that they had intentionally purchased homes near the schools they wanted their children to attend; others cited the long distances children would walk to their new schools, decrying in particular the inconvenience to those who escorted their children to class each day.[37]

Some parents warned that they would move out of the neighborhood rather than allow their children to be part of the cluster plan. The Property Owners Coordinating Committee (POCC), a group of homeowners and real estate dealers, threatened that if the cluster plan was implemented, they would organize a "Drastic Action Plan," consisting of a coordinated exodus of whites from Chicago. POCC's head charged, "Anyone who sends their children to Sumner from the May school, which is already 25 per cent integrated, are not fit parents." The United Property Group chair Robert Bacigalupo proclaimed that "the people of Austin will not stand for sending their children to schools in communities where there exists a higher crime rate or the racial manipulation of their children." He further warned that Austin residents "will leave the city en masse if the neighborhood school policy is dropped."[38]

Even moderate groups, which under other circumstances tried to promote integration in housing, expressed doubts about the cluster plan. Lorraine Greenhouse, who was pushing the Austin Community Organization (ACO) to endorse open occupancy laws, wrote to members of the board of education of her dismay at "the hysteria which has been stirred up in our community." ACO also adopted a resolution against the cluster plan, on the grounds that "it has created considerable panic in Austin." Gale Cincotta, whose subsequent activities in housing issues gained her national fame, spoke against the cluster plan on behalf of the Parent-Teacher Association of May School, which some of her children attended. Noting that May's student body was already one-quarter African American and "subject to increase," the May PTA preferred that integration "should be all over the city and in every school, not just pushed in one school and in one area." Cincotta testified, "The white people here are already in a state of panic and if this new cluster plan is allowed to go into effect, you are going to have one more totally segregated 100 per cent Negro school."[39] Exacerbating the anxieties of whites about schools undermined the ability of people like Cincotta and Greenhouse to persuade their white neighbors that peaceful unforced integration was feasible.

Faced with overwhelming opposition, in early January the board of education backed away from the cluster plan. The decision not to implement the plan, however, did not end concern among white West Siders about how to cope with the continuing arrival of African American students, particularly in the high school. Because high schools drew their students from larger geographic areas than elementary schools, they felt the effects of black in-migration simultaneously with the first grammar schools in each area. Although Austin High School had few black students enrolled when the board of education proposed the cluster plan in the fall of 1964, that situation was changing. Three factors contributed to the increasing presence of black students in Austin High School. First, the school was underutilized in the 1950s and the early 1960s, prompting the board of education to extend the boundary between Austin and Marshall high schools from the Belt Line Railroad eastward to Keeler Avenue, well into the western section of West

Garfield Park. Within a few years, many African Americans lived inside the new boundaries. Secondly, the citywide transfer program for honors students allowed a couple dozen black students to enroll in Austin rather than their neighborhood schools. Finally, African Americans were starting to move into Austin proper.[40]

For most of the 1964–65 school year, while Austin High School's population remained approximately 96 percent white, few people expressed concern. The only troubling incident that reached the local newspaper occurred when police arrested forty-five youths for "mobbing" outside the school the week before the African American transfer students registered. In the spring, however, an episode at the nearby school store suggested the existence of ongoing low-level racial tension among the students. On Wednesday, May 12, a group of white youths chased a black student out of the store. On Thursday a cross-racial fight ensued after a white girl reportedly stepped on a black girl's foot. The store's owner tried to stop the fight but succeeded only in driving it outside, where the girls were arrested after inflicting scratches and bruises on one another. Police also arrested several male students, including the brother of one of the arrested white girls, for seeking to escalate the conflict with knives and pellet guns. Increased police patrols in the area apparently quelled further outbursts during the 1964–65 school year.[41]

The fall term opened much more noisily. Austin received additional transfer students for the 1965–66 school year, bringing the number of black students up to three hundred. School officials requested that the Chicago Transit Authority supply extra bus service to accommodate the commuting students. One day in early September, however, too few buses appeared. When the delayed buses finally arrived, students shoved one another to board first. The police who broke up the dispute blamed youthful "boisterousness," but the fighters divided along racial lines. Moreover, this episode was only one of several fights between black and white youths.[42]

The confrontations did not end. On October 7 a fight between girls in nearby Merrick Park attracted police attention. The girls fled, but the next day fighting broke out in the high school parking lot, reportedly in retaliation for the park incident. Police arrived and managed to herd students into their classrooms, but the bell rang almost immediately, drawing the entire student body back out into the halls. Fighting between students then erupted in the lunchroom and the hallways. Rioting students wielded chains, knives, chairs, dishes, and bottles. When groups of students of one race came upon isolated students of the other race, they attacked them. One police officer escorting a group of black girls out of the chaotic school witnessed a group of one hundred white students spot his charges and run at them, shouting

Fig. 12. A student injured in the riot at Austin High School. *Garfieldian*, October 13, 1965. Courtesy of the Special Collections and Preservation Division, Chicago Public Library.

"Let's get 'em." The officer drew his gun to disperse the threatening mob. Fourteen youths were arrested on Friday, and the next Monday police arrested twelve black students from Crane High School for loitering around Austin High School.[43]

Community response to the riot was swift. School officials blamed a small group of "troublemakers" who were quickly transferred, but parents were not appeased. On Sunday forty participants in the biracial Parents Committee for Action at Austin met at Olivet Methodist Church to draw up recommendations for improving the racial environment at the school. They, and more than one hundred white parents, showed up at the school uninvited, voicing discontent and demanding solutions. The parents were hustled into the assembly hall to meet with the principal, the local police district commander, and school officials. Gale Cincotta, who had two sons enrolled at Austin, expressed dissatisfaction with the reassurances the officials offered. She wondered how she could continue to tell her children to take their problems to the "proper authorities," when these officials were so unresponsive. Some in attendance regathered at the Austin Town Hall on Monday night. At an official parents' assembly on October 22, attended mostly by whites, school administrators reported that they had implemented several measures suggested at the spontaneous meeting.[44]

The local newspapers reported calm at Austin High School for the remainder of the year. In May Superintendent Willis startled Chicago by announcing abruptly that he would retire in August, despite a previous agreement that he would retire on his sixty-fifth birthday, in December 1966. The new superintendent, James F. Redmond, who returned to Chicago in September, had overseen the first year of school desegregation in New Orleans. School in Austin opened without incident in the fall 1966 session, which the principal, Dorothy Martin, attributed to "many meetings, great effort, work and cooperation."[45]

Fig. 13. After the riot at Austin High School, white students protest the racial integration of the school. *Garfieldian*, October 13, 1965. Courtesy of the Special Collections and Preservation Division, Chicago Public Library.

The peace between the students, however, did not imply resignation among white parents. In autumn 1966 seven hundred members of the student body at Austin High School, almost one-quarter of the total, were African American. A disproportionate number of black students were reported to be in the freshman and sophomore classes; since African Americans moved into the neighborhood in 1964, some white children graduating from public elementary schools enrolled in the city's vocational or private schools instead of Austin High School. White Austinites anticipated that with the continuing arrival of black students, the percentage of the school population that was African American would only increase. Although they were fairly scrupulous about not objecting publicly to the presence of those black students who lived within the school's formal boundary lines, they expressed fears about future educational standards and crowding at the school, which was already operating at 125 percent of its formal capacity. White activists noted that the residential population of the traditional attendance zone for Austin High School was 90 percent white, while the school was already one-quarter black. They warned that if the school became further unbalanced racially, the white residents of the neighborhood would move out to the suburbs.[46]

The Austin Business Council (ABC), which was formed in February 1965, led the effort to restrain the accelerating enrollment of African American pupils. The solution ABC envisioned was to return the boundaries of Austin High School to their pre-1964 location—to retract the eastern boundary westward back to the Belt Line Railroad. Instead of sending potential Austin High School students from West Garfield Park back to the abominably over-crowded Marshall High School, ABC urged building a new school or sending the students from the zone of contention north to Westinghouse High School. To achieve these goals, ABC sought not only the cooperation of the board of education, but also the endorsement of Mayor Richard J. Daley, with whom a delegation met in December 1966. ABC encouraged civic organizations and residents of Austin to write letters to the board of education "in favor of restoring the old boundaries of Austin High School" and prevailed upon the *Austinite*'s editor to print the full text of their resolution on the front page.[47]

Cooperative Austinites deluged school officials with a flood of letters in favor of the boundary restoration.[48] Parent-Teacher Associations from North Austin elementary schools feeding into Austin High School enthusi-astically endorsed the proposal, with the caveat that the four hundred black students already attending Austin from this area should be allowed to remain through their graduations. Even organizations that were bitter rivals in other circumstances, the Organization for a Better Austin and the Town Hall Assembly (THA), agreed—for different reasons—that the retrac-tion of the boundaries was a sound idea.[49]

Only a few local groups opposed the retraction of the Austin High School boundary. The main opposition came from the Christian Action Ministry (CAM; the forerunner of the famous Bethel New Life), based in West Garfield Park. CAM's representatives pointed to the problem's origins in res-idential segregation and asked whether the Austin Business Council would simply request another change in the boundaries of the high school when black pupils moved yet closer. Only two Austin-based groups, the Austin Tenants and Owners Association and the Austin Women for Community Good Will, opposed restoring the school's old boundary line. White Austin residents who hoped that Superintendent Redmond might support their desires, as Benjamin Willis had, were disappointed. School staff assured CAM that the new boundary line would be retained. Additionally, Redmond recommended to the board of education that they exclude Austin High School from the city's permissive transfer plan, in order to prevent the departure of white students and the resegregation of the school. The board of education delayed making a firm decision on Austin's boundaries before the start of the 1967–68 school year.[50]

White Austin parents began "frankly and openly casting about for" ways to enroll their children in the city's other public schools. Trying a series of slightly varied approaches, THA urged the board to approve voluntary transfers for white students. In one remarkable line of argument, the group claimed that by allowing Austin High School to resegregate into a majority-black school, the board was depriving the *white* pupils of an integrated education, "in violation of the U.S. Constitution which provides that children must attend an integrated school." Therefore, they continued, the board should allow students from North Austin to transfer to schools with empty seats. Beginning in the summer of 1970, THA pressed the board to open enrollment at two of the city's all-male selective high schools—Prosser Vocational and Lane Technical—to girls for the first time. In response, the board authorized the admission of two hundred girls to Lane Tech's sophomore class for the fall of 1971. About twenty girls from the Austin area enrolled in Lane Tech's first coeducational class. Some parents withdrew their children from the public school system altogether. The Catholic school system, however, became a less amenable choice when in 1967 John Cardinal Cody opened archdiocese schools to systemwide transfers. In 1971 the Town Hall Assembly debated whether a group of parents should collectively rent one or two apartments in an all-white section of the city, allowing their children to register for schools there.[51]

The members of the Town Hall Assembly, in their persistent and ingenious efforts to remove white students from Austin High School, reflected a dawning realization among whites on Chicago's West Side that advocating for neighborhood schools did not necessarily serve their perceived racial interests. In a city where the system of residential segregation ensured that newly black schools overcrowded rapidly, an inflexible adherence to the principle of local schooling inhibited whites' abilities to respond to the conditions that surfaced when blacks moved into the schools. Thus, whites who did not want their children to attend interracial schools, but who continued to live in the city, sought other locales for their further education. But THA and their ilk were not the only whites who began to understand the limitations of the neighborhood school policy. In the late 1960s, a different cluster of activists discovered that it was possible to ally themselves with black parents upset by the conditions that the slow-moving board of education allowed to flourish in schools serving African Americans.

The school where white parents explored the possibility of interracial activism was May Elementary School. As African American children moved into the May School area in the mid-1960s, some whites in the area offered the standard hostile reactions to their presence. But not all whites connected with May School understood their own withdrawal as an appropriate response. Gale Cincotta, an officer in the May School PTA, criticized her neighbors for thinking too locally: "We're all Chicagoans. We're all Austin residents. But we're divided into small groups, separate block clubs, different PTA groups, local church congregations. And when there's a problem anywhere, the groups say, 'That's not our territory. Our jurisdiction ends at such and such a boundary.' When there's trouble anywhere it affects the whole community."[52] Cincotta led May School parents in an effort to correct the deteriorating conditions at the school. In some cases, as with their opposition to the cluster proposal, that stance meant trying to keep more black students out of the school. In other cases, the parent-activists at May School called for better facilities. In still other cases, they urged that May students be bused to other schools in Chicago, a position that stirred an enormous controversy throughout the city. The innovations of May School parents reflected a small but significant alternative to the wholesale anti-integration stance of many white West Siders. These parents sought specific targeted remedies to the problems that their neighbors reflexively blamed on African Americans.

White parents of children at schools experiencing black in-migration sometimes expressed fears of a decline in educational standards. At May white activists urged the board to offer "preventive medicine" to the school, "rather than waiting until the entire district had been reduced to a point where remedial action would be necessary." Testifying before the board of education in the spring of 1966, they asked for a series of measures that would improve teaching and services at the school. They recommended that administrators apply for federal aid, assign African American teachers to West Side schools, hire "master teachers" for the school, and add extra mathematics and reading classes to May's summer session. Later, as she continued to push the board for improvements to May, Cincotta urged the hiring of a truant officer and the establishment of summer programs to keep children constructively occupied.[53]

In early 1967 a new addition was completed at May, restoring the average class size to thirty-six (down from forty-seven). The existence of the May addition, however, proved a tempting target to school administrators. Because the new facility lowered class sizes at May below those of surrounding schools, officials treated May as a resource for alleviating their crowding. Shortly after the addition formally opened, administrators announced their intention to expand May's boundary northward, effectively transferring 170 students out of nearby Spencer Elementary, which suffered from a variety of troubles and shortages. This boundary proposal presented several administrative challenges. In particular, it required the retention of the controversial mobile units at May; the school lacked teachers for the five additional classes; and the two elementary schools were technically in different administrative districts. Incensed May parents immediately convened a meeting to protest the change and then organized a new community group, the May School United Committee. Gale Cincotta complained, "This was the pattern in East Garfield, West Garfield, and now Austin. . . . Everyone talks about integration, but they keep right on changing boundaries so the ratio of Negroes goes upward."[54]

The new organization won a meeting with school administrators. But this conference proved to be a resounding failure. Personality clashes aggravated the underlying differences of opinion between administrators and the parents' delegation. The always-brash Cincotta, who later recalled her refusal to "bow and scrape, or be awed" by school officials, so annoyed Francis McKeag, the administration's representative, that he called the group "insane" and a "tribe" with whom he would not speak. Before the meeting fell apart, McKeag charged the group with the task of designing an alternate plan for schooling the crowded pupils. The members of the May School United Committee replied that their proposed change was "none."[55]

Cincotta then approached board member Cyrus H. Adams, disputing McKeag's figures about the amount of space available for classes and decrying the administrator's treatment of their group. She explained, "If we are successful in creating and keeping Austin a stabilized, integrated area, we will have helped the surrounding communities and also the entire city." Adams assured Cincotta that the board would not authorize any changes without consulting both the May PTA and the United Committee.[56] In May administrators notified the May School United Committee that because of increasing enrollments within the area, they would not change the school's boundaries. Indeed, in the fall 1967 semester, Cyrus Adams acknowledged the growth of the student body at May as "fantastic," and the PTA petitioned the board of education to contract the school's boundaries.[57]

Instead of shrinking the school's catchment area, in the winter of 1968 the board of education launched one of its most controversial desegregation efforts, centered on May School. Just before the new year started, Superintendent Redmond announced that at the end of January he planned to transfer five thousand elementary school students from crowded segregated schools in the Austin and South Shore neighborhoods into unused classrooms in distant schools. Redmond asked the board of education to authorize him to spend $150,000 on bus transportation for the students. Redmond explicitly linked his plans with the goal of creating integrated schools. His proposal had two components. In the South Shore neighborhood, black students would be bused out and white students bused in, creating schools in both areas with "a viable racial balance." In Austin black students would be bused to the city's Northwest Side, but in this case he was not requesting "reverse busing of white children."[58]

Redmond's proposal to bus children around the city aroused a citywide tempest of opposition, foreshadowing the storm half a decade later in Boston. By the first week of 1968, letters from angry Chicagoans poured into the board of education offices. Many came from the Hegewisch neighborhood on the Far South Side, whose white residents did not want to send their children to "the South Shore Jungle or anyplace else." Most simply protested being compelled to mix their children with African Americans on racist grounds; but a few parents offered nonracial concerns as well, like the mother who asked, "What happens if one of them becomes ill in school, do they have to wait until 3:00 to come home on the bus? I could not go to get them as my husband takes our car to work and I have an 11 month old baby that I can not be dragging around the city." An African American parent on the South Side objected that "to bus children from the immediate vicinity of a good school with gym, library, reading and band facilities to a school having none of these things, is utterly absurd." School administrators quickly dropped the plan to bus the white pupils, and the board eliminated the South Shore plan from consideration altogether.[59]

The board still intended to bus children from May and Spencer elementary schools, both now more than 80 percent African American, to eight all-white schools on the city's Northwest Side. Redmond's modified proposal for the West Side, considerably scaled back from the original five thousand children, identified twelve blocks from May School's attendance area and six blocks within Spencer's boundaries. The proposal assigned those blocks as noncontiguous parts of the attendance areas of eight Northwest Side receiving schools. The eighteen West Side blocks housed a total of 573 students, most of whom were African American. Kindergarten children, as well as seventh- and eighth-grade students, were excluded from the transfers, and no white school would become more than 11 percent black as a result of the busing.[60]

As on the South Side, these plans stimulated the wrath of white Northwest Side residents, who lived well beyond the parts of the city that were experiencing residential racial change. Northwest Siders wrote letters assailing the proposal, testified at public hearings held by the board, and participated in protests. Parent-Teacher Associations at all of the receiving schools took formal votes of almost unanimous opposition to the plan. Residents joined in several public demonstrations against the plan, including rallies in their neighborhoods and a motorcade through Chicago's downtown. They turned out local politicians to express their objections. Northwest Side congressman Roman Pucinski offered lengthy critical testimony, complaining that "it is a tragedy of our time that men cannot have honest disagreements without immediately being attacked as 'racists' and 'bigots,' and even 'un-American.'"[61] Henry J. Hyde, then a state representative from Illinois's 16th District, received a standing ovation for his argument against mixing black students with his constituents' children:

> The real heart of the matter, and we all know it, is that the family as a unit has no effective existence in the inner city. The destruction of the neighborhood school system further removes the family unit from any effective impact on the young plastic lives being shuttled around the city. . . . Taking children out of the ghetto for a few short envious hours a day does not take the ghetto out of the children. They must get up in and return to a ghetto environment that has far more effect on that young life than a daily bus trip to a strange school can have.[62]

State legislators, taking a page from the book of their counterparts in Louisiana, threatened to make the board of education an elective office if members passed the busing plan.[63]

Northwest Siders' objections were as virulent as those expressed by white South Siders. A mother who mistakenly believed that the West Side plans involved busing of white students threatened, "If my children are going to be bused to a school that is already overcrowded, I will sell my house and move to the suburbs where such dictatorship is not allowed."[64] A mother with seven children in both public and private schools cast her protest in terms of "equal rights," wondering why African American children set to attend Locke School should enjoy privileges denied to white students:

> The children at Locke School have never been able to eat their lunchesat [sic] the school because the school does not have these facilities.

No matter how bad the weather or how far these children live they have to walk home for lunch. Now you want us to approve the right for these colored children to have lunchroom facilities at this school. Where do you see equal rights in this situation[?][65]

Homeowners in the Bridge School area wrote to Superintendent Redmond, "We pay more taxes than most city areas; why should we not receive a higher quality of education than the slums? The Northwest side has subsidized the slums long enough."[66]

Although Redmond originally intended the busing plan for implementation in late January, the passion of the objections forced the board to postpone its vote several times.[67] Mayor Daley forced further delays when he urged the board to hold hearings in all of the affected neighborhoods. A crisis in a Southwest Side school in February emphasized the political delicacy of the situation, as a handful of carefully screened black students tried to enroll in Mount Greenwood Elementary School under the permissive transfer plan. The vitriol of the mob at Mount Greenwood prompted a *Chicago Daily News* reporter to draw comparisons to Little Rock and New Orleans and frightened the students into withdrawing. Cyrus Adams recognized that the fervor of whites' antagonism to the plan stemmed not only from antipathy to the arrival of blacks in their children's schools, but also to fear that the precedent might subsequently require their children to attend school in an African American neighborhood, as occurred in Boston a few years later. Reasoning that white parents would object less if they did not fear the mandatory transfers of their children in some future busing program, Adams insisted on altering the plan to allow African American parents to decline participation in the program. At a pair of tense board meetings, Adams brokered a deal that made the busing program voluntary instead of mandatory. On March 4, by a vote of eight to one, the board passed the plan, to begin a week later.[68]

Activists on both sides swung into a frenzy of preparation for the March 11 implementation of the plan. Members of the May and Spencer United Committees rounded up replacements for students who declined to participate. They were gratified by an unsolicited offer from friendly Northwest Side whites to provide home care for transferred children who got sick during school hours. Hostile Northwest Siders cast about for ways to express their anger. Mothers considered holding a "mop-up campaign" in front of the incoming buses. Efforts to persuade Catholic school students to transfer into the receiving schools and occupy the seats destined for the Austin students dissipated. More than half the students from the receiving schools staged a two-day boycott in protest of the transfers,

Fig. 14. The May and Spencer United Committees staged a rally to demand that students from overcrowded schools be bused to underused schools on the Northwest Side. Courtesy of Thomas A. Gaudette Papers (CSLA-18), Department of Archives and Special Collections, Charles Von der Ahe Library, Loyola Marymount University.

attending alternate classes in private homes and a public park's field house. Phone calls threatening violence, however, dimmed the fervor of the head of Greater Northwest Civic Association, a group created in response to the busing proposal. Aware that the busing protest had attracted the attention of a Southwest Side group, Operation Crescent, which sought to "keep a ring of all-white neighborhoods around the Negro ghetto," local organizers urged calm on opening day and "implored all outsiders and agitators to stay away from our schools today."[69]

Despite these pleas, March 11 was not entirely without incident. Several of the Northwest Side schools received bomb threats, and a Molotov cocktail slightly damaged the principal's office at Dever School. Jeering crowds and picketers gathered at several of the schools, greeting transfer students with signs reading "Goodbye Chicago, Elmwood Park here we come." At Sayre School, after the children entered the building, white parents chanted, "Vote Republican." After the first few days, public protests dropped off. For a short while, Northwest Side parents ran a rotating boycott among the schools and worked with allies in the state legislature to punish Superintendent Redmond. In order to meet its goal of 573 students on buses, in late March 1968 the school board voted to expand the number of blocks included in the program. But when riots broke out across the nation after April 4, in the wake of the assassination of Martin Luther King Jr., the school board voted to cease recruiting any new students.[70]

Fig. 15. Modular buildings, constructed quickly to serve crowded schools, were more acceptable to black parents than classrooms housed in trailers. *Austinite*, February 2, 1972. Courtesy of the Special Collections and Preservation Division, Chicago Public Library.

While the initiation of the busing program represented a moral victory for May and Sumner activists, the effort did not fundamentally change conditions on the West Side. Overcrowding and segregation continued to sweep through West Side schools as African Americans sought homes farther west and north in Austin. Beginning in 1970, the board of education began constructing semipermanent buildings known as "demountables," or modulars, for students at crowded schools. With ten to nineteen classrooms, demountables required approximately three months to construct. Like conventional school buildings, they occupied large plots of land, whose acquisition could be a protracted affair requiring litigation. In a few cases, school officials authorized the erection of the demountable buildings alongside portable classrooms on the playgrounds of crowded schools, but in other circumstances the demountables became branches of the original schools, with separate teaching and administrative staffs. Parents regarded the demountables as more acceptable than portables, because they were "semipermanent and give the children attending them a building with which to identify."[71]

White parents in Central Austin schools learned well from the examples of their neighbors in South Austin. After watching the board of education allow crowding at schools like May go unchecked until reaching a crisis point, parents at Emmet, Key, Howe, and Nash elementary schools tried to

preempt the problems that their neighbors encountered. When they realized that their children's schools stood next in the line to receive African
American students within their boundaries, parents agitated for the board
to provide mobile classrooms or, preferably, demountables at their
schools.[72] Emmet School, the most crowded school in the city between 1968
and 1970, received half a dozen demountables. When in 1970 the student
body was only 20 percent African American, the president of the Key School
PTA urged the board to build a demountable, "before, not after, the problem reaches the crisis state." Although the board did not agree immediately,
by 1971 members authorized demountables for each of these schools.[73]

The focus of Chicago Public School policy and white parents' activism
on neighborhood schools preserved a consistent pattern of demographic
change from the 1950s through the 1970s. The population of the public
schools in the path of residential racial change went from all-white, to temporarily integrated (and crowded), to all-black over the course of a few years.
During the late 1960s, whites promoted measures to improve conditions
within racially changing schools. This advocacy, however, neither solved
the basic problems of black-white interactions within the schools nor undermined the basic pattern of segregation. Neither Superintendent Redmond
nor his successor, Joseph Hannon, proposed or implemented an effective
desegregation plan for Chicago. Only in 1981 did the board of education
negotiate a school desegregation consent decree with the U.S. Department
of Justice.[74]

But as long as the neighborhood schools remained at the center of public policy, the degree of integration in each school was tightly linked to the
degree of residential integration in the neighborhood and in the city. The
1974 U.S. Supreme Court decision in *Milliken v. Bradley* ruled against the
necessity of desegregating schools across metropolitan areas. Thus most of
the racial mixing that Chicago's schoolchildren experienced in the third
quarter of the twentieth century occurred at the same time as their parents
confronted racial integration on their blocks.

CHAPTER 6

Blockbusting

In July 1962 the *Saturday Evening Post* ran an article with the incendiary title "Confessions of a Block-Buster." The recently coined term "blockbusting" referred to the decades-old practice of upsetting the racial homogeneity of all-white residential blocks in order to profit from the difference between the prices African American and white urbanites paid for housing.[1] Author Norris Vitchek freely described himself as a "blockbuster" operating in Chicago but shielded his identity behind a pseudonym. Vitchek rationalized the subterfuge, explaining that the practice was nothing more than real estate speculation. "Confessions" detailed Vitchek's tactics for convincing white homeowners in Chicago to sell their homes to him, so that he could resell them to African American buyers at inflated rates. Vitchek described blockbusters' earnings as "abnormal," claiming, "I know that I make four times the profit I could for the same amount of effort in all-white real estate. If anybody who is well established in this business in Chicago doesn't earn $100,000 a year, he is loafing."[2]

The appearance of Vitchek's "Confessions" outraged readers of the *Post* around the nation. A San Antonio resident asked, "If Vitchek felt so justified in his greedy crusade for money at the expense of his fellow white man, why did he bother to use a nom de plume?" A Realtor from San Francisco wrote, "Your deliberate aim at generating hate and misery and increased racial tension is nauseating." Edwin Berry, the executive director of the Chicago Urban League, however, recognized the article's real purpose: the author intended it as an exposé of blockbusting, not a justification. Berry's letter to the *Saturday Evening*

Post congratulated the magazine for publishing "an accurate picture of what goes on in racially transitional areas." He concluded, "It is this kind of real-estate operation that has made the word 'integration' a bad one."[3]

Chicago's daily newspapers offered only minimal coverage of the controversial article. The *Garfieldian*, however, whose West Side audience was familiar with the selling practices and steady racial change described in the *Post* article, gave "Confessions" extensive coverage. The *Garfieldian* focused on discovering the identity of "Norris Vitchek." Their suspicions quickly settled on Mark J. Satter, a white attorney who lived in the city's South Shore neighborhood. Satter was waging a one-man educational campaign about the consequences of the shortage of housing available to black Chicagoans. His legal practice represented African American clients in lawsuits over foreclosures on their properties in formerly white neighborhoods. Both of these activities suggested to white West Siders that Satter aimed to place African Americans in their neighborhoods and homes, and to displace them. After a few weeks of hedging, Satter admitted that he was indeed Alfred Balk's source but adamantly denied that he was a blockbuster.[4]

Angry white activists lured Satter on to a local television program to defend the *Post* article. There they accused him of filling the West Side apartment buildings he owned with black tenants in order to drive whites out of the neighborhood. These allegations amounted to a charge that Satter was a blockbuster. In addition, they said, Satter was fined for building code violations in those apartments. Satter acknowledged that African Americans lived in his buildings but insisted that he was motivated by principle, not by profit. Blacks, Satter argued, "have as much right to live decently as we have." The true blockbusters were those real estate dealers whose classified advertisements in the *Chicago Defender* offered homes to African Americans in all-white neighborhoods, with only a small down payment required. These were the blockbusters that "Confessions" meant to expose, for such brokers advertised homes to which they did not yet have access.[5]

The controversy over whether Mark Satter was a "blockbuster" reflected an emerging and confused debate in Chicago about how to deal with residential integration. In the early 1960s, a wave of newspaper articles and community organizations' newsletters documented "unscrupulous" real estate dealers whose sales tactics played on whites' fears and who took financial advantage of the constricted housing market for African Americans.[6] The few legal remedies to blockbusting comported with descriptions that newspapers offered; they were geared toward ameliorating the most egregious of blockbusters' tactics. Such approaches did not address racial change per se. This failure, in a period when both South Side and West Side neighborhoods were steadily changing from white to black occupancy, meant that a major element of whites' postwar urban crisis ended up unchecked.

Racial change, not sales tactics, stood at the heart of what most white West Siders counted as blockbusting. As far as many white homeowners were concerned, it was the willingness to change the city's racial boundaries that made a real estate dealer a blockbuster. Thus, even a man like Mark Satter, who abhorred the exploitation of black consumers inherent in blockbusting tactics, found himself under fire for promoting wider housing opportunities for African Americans. While white West Siders were uniform in their hostility toward blockbusters, they did not unanimously agree that African American neighbors should be treated as antagonistically as the real estate dealers who enabled them to find new homes. But the movement of African Americans onto a block occupied exclusively by whites represented a crisis that they had to confront. Black Chicagoans, for their part, expressed more mixed attitudes toward the real estate dealers and apartment owners who made housing available at the edge of the ghetto. Many were pleased with the opportunity to live in less crowded conditions, but others resented the psychological and financial costs associated with this housing. Blockbusting and its concomitant practices that exploited African Americans might have constituted a portion of their urban crisis as well, but the fact that blacks needed adequate housing so desperately meant that getting access to their own property was as much a welcome solution as it was a problem.

Blockbusting Practices

Change in the racial composition of residential blocks in Chicago was nothing new in the postwar period. Ever since the consolidation of the South Side African American ghetto in Chicago in the second decade of the twentieth century, blacks sought ways out of its crowded confines. Working-class whites jealously guarded the western boundary of the ghetto at Wentworth Avenue, so blacks with financial means looked southward for better housing.[7] Recognizing that crowding combined with new migration from the South meant some African Americans would seek homes outside the ghetto's limits, the Chicago Real Estate Board (CREB) moved to control the process. In 1917, following national guidelines, CREB stated a new policy: members could not permit African Americans to move onto a white block until the adjacent block was completely filled with blacks.[8] CREB's hand in the process was frequently invisible. Sociologists from the University of Chicago, already working under the assumption that cities were organisms, treated the pattern of block-by-block racial change as a natural feature of Chicago's development.[9]

CREB's policy envisioned a steady process of urban racial change that members would manage. Realtors were allowed to sell property to African

Americans, but only on blocks that blacks already occupied. CREB's members, however, lacked a monopoly on the sale of real estate in Chicago. The National Association of Real Estate Boards (NAREB) reserved the title "Realtor" for its members. Throughout the nation, local real estate boards excluded African American real estate dealers from membership.[10] Additionally, the majority of real estate salesmen and brokers who were licensed by the state of Illinois were not members of NAREB, and thus were not bound by CREB's code of ethics.[11] With Realtors enjoined from selling property to blacks on "white" blocks, other real estate dealers developed their own mechanisms for doing what NAREB forbade: initiating the change in the racial composition of Chicago blocks. These real estate dealers' activities alarmed white West Siders in the postwar period, when African Americans were migrating to Chicago at ten times the rate of the interwar years. Variously referred to as "speculators," "blockbusters," and "panic peddlers," brokers who sold homes to blacks in previously all-white sections of Chicago disrupted CREB's slow and steady reconfiguration of the city's racial demographics.[12]

Real estate dealers who made a living selling to African Americans did not wait passively for interested white home sellers to seek out their services. Instead, they used a variety of means to solicit property listings for resale to African Americans. Their tactics were so troubling and consistent that the president of one Southeast Side community organization speculated that "these people hold workshops on how to break a block."[13] Once a few African Americans had moved onto a Chicago block, their new white neighbors routinely concluded that a complete change in local racial composition was now inevitable. The process of racial succession on city blocks, which occurred in cities around the United States, became simultaneously notorious and ordinary in the 1960s. In a succinct summary that echoed the memories of many whites who witnessed the transformations of urban neighborhoods in this period, the narrator of Jeffrey Eugenides's 2002 novel *Middlesex* recollects the transformation of the Detroit neighborhood where his Greek immigrant grandfather opened a bar: "In the inevitable chain of cause and effect, as soon as the first black family had moved onto the block, the white neighbors immediately put their houses up for sale. The oversupply of houses depressed the real estate prices, which allowed poorer people to move in, and with poverty came crime, and with crime came more moving vans."[14] In fact, the dynamics of racial change were neither as inevitable, nor as simple, as this short description allows.

In October 1959 the *Chicago Daily News* described a three-phase process for blockbusting. First, during the "softening up" phase, blockbusters notified white homeowners that racial change was impending. They recruited

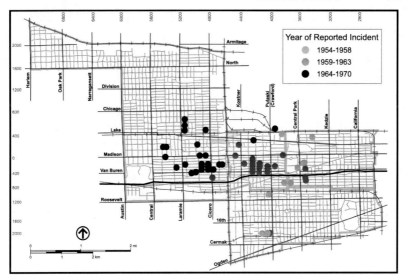

Fig. 16. Blockbusting episodes, 1954–70. Produced by the University of Wisconsin–Milwaukee, Cartography & GIS Center.

blacks to walk and drive through the neighborhood, signaling their interest in the area.[15] In one South Side neighborhood, real estate salesmen scared whites by bringing African Americans into the yards of absent residents and spreading stories about residents who were mugged on the Illinois Central line. Brokers sent homeowners letters soliciting their business. Some letters were generic "Dear Homeowner" invitations; the salutations on others, such as the letter to a widow addressed "Dear Mr. and Mrs.," indicated that the brokers did systematic research in official, if sometimes outdated, title documents. The letters usually advised homeowners that they would be wise to sell quickly. A letter sent to 4732 West Flournoy, for example, urged, "We earnestly feel that the time to sell is now, so that we can get you the best possible price, before there is a downward trend."[16] On the West Side, three thousand homeowners received a letter implying that the potential buyers were whites departing from racially changing neighborhoods elsewhere:

> For example, (there's) the problem of whether or not to sell your property. As we all know these are changing times. Many neighborhoods in Chicago are in the midst of a turbulent, changing population situation.
>
> We've had many calls from folks who have recently sold property in the so-called fringe areas, and are looking cash in hand, for homes in your neighborhood. With this active market in your area, we can help sell your property profitably and swiftly and find you a new location close by or in the suburbs.[17]

On the rare occasions when they responded to homeowners' complaints that such mailings were inflammatory, brokers defended them as standard advertising techniques.[18]

Some speculators were not particularly discriminating as they worked a block—one irritated African American homeowner finally posted a "Sold" sign on his building in order to give notice that the block was already "busted." (His white neighbors, concerned that the "Sold" sign might lure more speculators onto the block, persuaded him to replace it with one that read "Not for Sale.") Residents of the 4400 block of West End reported that a broker who was rebuffed during a personal visit retaliated by running an unauthorized advertisement in the *Defender*, Chicago's leading black newspaper. The planted ad reported the availability of a two-flat for sale on the block. The building's owner denied that it was for sale, but the advertisement nonetheless triggered calls to his neighbors soliciting their homes, on the assumption that the softening-up phase was nearly concluded.[19]

Once speculators made their intentions clear, they stepped up the pressure on particular homeowners in order to frighten them into being the first to sell, initiating the second phase of busting a block. A retired police officer complained, "I tell you, they drive you nuts. It gets so bad at times that you can't even go out and rake up your leaves without having some guy in a big Cadillac drive by and try to talk you into selling." Residents received early morning telephone calls claiming that their neighbors had sold their homes and that blacks were moving in. Other callers asked for "Johnnie Mae," a name that whites associated with southern blacks. A Lawndale resident wrote, "One sharpie taunted the owners with: 'What do you need, a house to fall on you? When are you going to get out?'" Speculators identified vulnerable property owners and used strong-arm tactics to obtain their buildings. A seventy-five-year-old widow who owned a fourteen-unit apartment building at the intersection of Gladys and Pulaski reported that a real estate dealer spent three uninterrupted hours pressuring her to sell her building. When she said that she needed to talk to her lawyer, the broker told her that the lawyer was out of town. Finally, she related, "my stomach started to hurt and I just couldn't take it any longer." Once she signed, the speculator told her that he would not release her from the contract unless she paid him the promised $3,000 commission.[20]

Panic peddlers sometimes used large apartment buildings such as the elderly widow's fourteen-flat instead of single-family homes to "bust" a block. Once they owned a building, speculators imposed substantial rent raises on the incumbent tenants and advised them that African Americans would be moving in soon. These tactics signaled to the residents that it was time to find other accommodations elsewhere. African Americans escaping from overcrowded expensive ghetto properties were accustomed to paying higher rents than whites and readily moved into such newly available housing.[21] Often, the new absentee owners of such buildings neglected their maintenance, which contributed to the impression of local deterioration and the popular belief that African Americans decayed neighborhoods. The charges leveled against Mark J. Satter during the "Confessions of a Blockbuster" episode included the allegation that he induced his white tenants to leave by hiring a black building manager and refusing to make repairs. A white West Garfield Park resident, who was grieved by white hostility to African Americans, warned, "There is nothing that depreciates an area so fast as the apartment building purchased by a rapacious 'businessman.'"[22]

Once someone agreed to sell, the successful broker could finally make honest reports to other neighbors that the block was going to change, initiating the final phase of blockbusting—buying up the rest of the block. Panic peddlers usually rewarded the first person on a block to sell with a price approaching its "market value." After the first sale, white homeowners began to "panic," accepting lower and lower offers for their houses. They complained that bankers and brokers who bought their property at depressed prices added insult to injury by acting like they were doing the homeowners a favor by giving them a chance to get out of the neighborhood while they could still recoup some portion of their investment. One black West Sider observed caustically that blockbusters were "selling to the white homeowner his own panic and getting paid for it."[23] The financial loss that whites experienced when they sold their homes facilitated the perception that blacks lowered property values.

This interpretation, however, ignored the phenomenon that scholars call the "dual housing market." African American buyers paid higher prices than whites for property because the supply available to them was smaller, a fact that Mark Satter explained as a "ruthless and wicked speculator's tax that has been added as a burden only upon the Negro people." Real estate brokers took advantage of the geographic restrictions on blacks' ability to move. A Jesuit seminarian active in Lawndale wrote about panic peddlers who bought buildings from whites for $15,000 and resold them to blacks at $28,000. An article that Mark Satter published in the *Chicago Bar Record* on the topic gave as a typical example a case in which a home purchased for $5,000 was quickly resold to an African American buyer for $14,000. The *Chicago Daily News* cited an example of black home buyers who paid $95 a month more than the mortgage held by the sellers. A study by the Chicago Commission on Human Relations documented one area of the South Side where prices of homes bought from whites by African Americans increased between 34 and 115 percent.[24] This process—buying the first property for a reasonable sum, then making successively lower and lower offers to those white property owners who remained and charging African Americans a premium—constituted the busting of a block.

Blockbusters made enormous profits from these practices because they inserted themselves into the transactions in two separate ways. First, they brokered transactions between sellers and buyers. Second, they helped buyers finance their purchases. Sometimes, brokers bought whites' property for themselves and concealed their ownership in a secret, or "blind," trust. While no state statute established blind trusts as a legal mechanism for concealing the true identities of property owners, Illinois courts recognized and legitimated the practice.[25] By holding property in trust for themselves rather than brokering conclusive transfers between buyers and sellers, speculators gained leverage in setting the prices and terms for subsequent sales; they not only received the original commissions, but also maximized their profits during the resale. Attorney Mark J. Satter warned readers of the Greater Lawndale Conservation Commission's newsletter to protect themselves: "If the broker tells you that the seller has moved away already, or the seller does not live on the property, then it is very likely that the seller is really the broker and has already purchased the property at his own price with the sole purpose of reselling it for a very high profit. A simple rule would be 'don't buy unless the seller lives on the premises.'"[26] Property purchased from an anonymous seller might well have been sold at least once already to an unsuspecting black buyer.

Repeated reselling was made possible by installment land contracts. Blockbusters profited from banks' refusal to lend mortgage money in racially changing areas, a practice legitimated since the 1930s by the Federal Housing Administration.[27] African American buyers often could not purchase property outright because they could not get mortgages. Instead, most property sales to African Americans were made "on contract." In a sale financed by a mortgage, the buyer secured a loan from a bank and bought the property outright, receiving title to the land and paying the lender back over a period of time, usually fifteen or thirty years.[28] By contrast, contract sales, which often carried high interest rates, allowed the *seller* to retain title to the property until the buyer paid back the entire purchase price. If a buyer missed a payment, he or she forfeited the property. The seller regained control of the property without reimbursing previous payments made on time, evicted the buyer, and found a new "purchaser." One black contract buyer resignedly told the *Chicago Daily News*, "It's like anything else. If you miss the payments, they take it away." In contrast to mortgage buyers, contract buyers had little legal recourse if they felt exploited, a vulnerability that enabled speculators to repeat the process over and over again with impunity. Contract sellers reaped enormous profits; as Arnold Hirsch pointed out, it usually took only two years to recoup the entirety of their original investments.[29]

The most famous example of how real estate speculators profited from contract sales appeared in print at the beginning of the twentieth century.[30] In *The Jungle*, Upton Sinclair's novel about Lithuanian immigrants ground to pieces in Chicago's stockyard district, the Rudkus family was gulled into signing a contract on a purportedly brand-new house. To their great dismay, they quickly discovered that the house was previously occupied by several other victims of the land company, and that they had to pay interest in addition to the balance. Eventually, the Rudkus family lost the house. A neighbor who finally met the terms of the contract boasted that she had "fooled the company."[31] Although *The Jungle* prompted national reform in the regulation of meatpacking, the legal mechanisms allowing contract sales in Illinois remained in place. Postwar blockbusters who were also contract sellers prospered as their properties revolved from one buyer to the next.

The practices of blockbusters took psychological advantage of both whites and blacks. African Americans who purchased homes on contract were often reluctant to admit it. Whites who sold their homes to blockbusters were embarrassed by their own actions. Louis Rosen found that none of the whites he interviewed during the 1990s were willing to talk about the actual process by which they sold their South Side properties, even three decades after the fact. Sometimes, whites who were the first to sell to a black buyer left their homes under cover of darkness, lest their neighbors chastise them for their betrayal. Others placed the blame on banks for refusing financing to whites who tried to get mortgages in areas experiencing racial change. One white homeowner said, "The banks actually are forcing the white home owner to deal with blockbusters."[32]

The shame that whites associated with selling their property to blockbusters derived from their failure to protect their own and their neighbors' investments in their homes. Although African American buyers paid inflated prices, white home sellers did not pocket the difference. Further, according to a contemporary study by sociologist Rose Helper, whites believed that "when property is transferred from white to Negro hands, it is lost to the white group forever. Hence the opportunities for future gain that that property might offer to white buyers are lost, and all possibilities for future control in the community by ownership of the land and property are also lost." Accordingly, groups opposed to the admission of African Americans to white neighborhoods argued that white homeowners had a significant set of mutual obligations. Whites should think of their neighbors before they sold their property, just as they were obliged to maintain the upkeep on their own premises lest the entire neighborhood fall into physical decay. Even if they felt they had to leave, the least they could do for their remaining neighbors was to protect their financial investments by selling "only to people who will take pride in their new community and become active in promoting its general welfare." Whites who sold their property to African Americans violated this standard of neighborhood protection by transforming its financial status. Blacks lowered property values for whites not by any failure to maintain local standards of physical upkeep, but by the simple act of moving a piece of property from one side of the dual housing market to the other. Mark Satter observed, "The speculator-broker causes deterioration in the community and brings civic decay in his path."[33]

Although blockbusting was a legitimate activity within the sphere of market capitalism, whites criticized such speculators for unfair disruption of the market. White anger at blockbusters for depriving them of profits associated with their erstwhile homes sometimes resonated with contemporary accusations of communism leveled at advocates for African Americans. Thomas J. Sugrue has noted that during the cold war, homeowner organizations in Detroit red-baited advocates of public housing and open occupancy, both of which whites saw as benefiting African Americans at their expense. Similarly, a white community leader on Chicago's West Side argued that taking away a property owner's right to discriminate on the basis of race "is unconstitutional and violates the principle of private property." Just as communists threatened to deprive everyone of private property, so did blockbusters' practices seem to steal the value of real estate from white homeowners without recompense or due process.[34]

White opprobrium of blockbusters was widespread, deep, and emotionally charged. One of the *Garfieldian*'s frequent correspondents lambasted them as "human vultures." Another resident said that blockbusters should be strung up "like horse thieves." The *Garfieldian* declared speculators "Public Enemy #1." In September 1959, as West Garfield Park whites began to grapple with blockbusters in their midst, the paper ran a cartoon of a monster labeled "Real Estate Speculator" stomping on communities of single-family homes. In addition to the warning "Beware This," the cartoonist offered "apologies to Dracula, Werewolf, Frankenstein" for slandering them by associating them with blockbusters. One salesman indicated his awareness of the hostility of residents when he answered a blunt question about whether he was a blockbuster: "No, I want to die with my head on." To protect themselves against this anger, blockbusters sometimes operated under false names, making them hard to locate if they suddenly aban-

Fig. 17. The cartoonist's caption suggested to the *Garfieldian*'s readers that blockbusters could do worse damage than a series of legendary monsters, including Dracula, a werewolf, or Frankenstein. *Garfieldian*, September 10, 1959. Courtesy of the Special Collections and Preservation Division, Chicago Public Library.

doned local operations. Such real estate dealers also readily changed the names and addresses of the businesses they operated.[35]

African Americans expressed more ambivalent views of blockbusters than white West Siders did. Some African Americans made a good living helping other blacks find homes in restricted housing markets.[36] Black real estate dealer Dempsey Travis, also a prolific author, made millions of dollars serving African American clients. Oscar C. Brown, another African American real estate broker, answered the *Chicago Daily News* series on panic peddling with the comment, "We wholly reject the terminology 'blockbusting,' which you employ to describe the movement of a Negro family into a community whose residents were formerly all white. . . . It is our business to find qualified buyers for desirable properties who are willing and able to purchase on terms acceptable to the sellers."[37] The African American director of one of the state's enforcement agencies expressed skepticism about the practicality of prosecuting people accused of blockbusting and panic peddling, phrases that he noted were "clichés" rather than legal terms.[38]

For those African Americans who gained access to much-needed housing through the process, the negative connotations embedded in whites' use of the word "blockbusting" probably made the concept irrelevant, except insofar as it anticipated the treatment they might receive from their new neighbors. Raymond A. Mohl has suggested that in Miami, Florida, African Americans regarded real estate developers who opened up new areas of housing to them as "community builders." There is evidence that some black property owners in Chicago had friendly relationships with some white speculators. Black hotel owner Julia Fairfax, for example, explained that many African Americans could buy property only with the help of Jewish intermediaries.[39] But the exploitative character of the installment land contracts with which most working-class African American home buyers in Chicago financed their homes probably attenuated any gratitude they might have felt toward white real estate brokers.[40] And some black property buyers understood that blockbusters profited from exploiting both parties in the transactions they brokered. An African American homeowner in Austin expressed pity for the previous owner of his property, who had sold at a loss of $6,000, saying, "The real estate men had gotten to him."[41]

Such real estate men got to many white West Siders in the postwar decades. They could not have flourished without thousands of property owners deciding that they no longer wished to hold on to homes in neighborhoods systematically neglected by city officials, populated by African Americans, and no longer appreciating in value. As blockbusters moved block by block through the West Side, white families finally decided to end their confrontations with the urban crises of the postwar years and seek new homes elsewhere. A significant subset of the population, however, did not leave until they had made some final efforts to stop the processes of blockbusting or find a way to live in an integrated community. White West Siders found inventive ways to make their last stands against their ultimate departures.

CHAPTER 7

Keeping African Americans Out

At a pivotal moment in Lorraine Hansberry's play *A Raisin in the Sun* (1959), the Younger family receives a visit from Karl Lindner, the chairman of the New Neighbors Orientation Committee of the Clybourne Park Improvement Association. Lena Younger has just used the insurance money from her husband's death to buy a house at 406 Clybourne Street, in the all-white Clybourne Park neighborhood. Lindner hopes to dissuade the Youngers from moving out of their small apartment in the South Side ghetto into Clybourne Park. He assures the disbelieving family:

I want you to believe me when I tell you that race prejudice simply doesn't enter into it. It is a matter of the people of Clybourne Park believing, rightly or wrongly, as I say, that for the happiness of all concerned that our Negro families are happier when they live in their *own* communities. . . . Our association is prepared, through the collective effort of our people, to buy the house from you at a financial gain to your family.

The Youngers decline Lindner's offer and set out for their new lives, despite the difficulties they might reasonably anticipate after this greeting.[1]

Hansberry's Clybourne Park was fictional, and only rarely could white neighborhood groups raise sufficient funds to buy out new black homeowners, who paid a premium for their properties.[2] Nevertheless, this scene neatly captures one of the myriad tactics whites used in postwar Chicago to protect the racial homogeneity of their communities. Like their counterparts in other cities, white West Siders sought to "defend" their neighborhoods from integration. The reflexive responses to black entrance into a white neighborhood were loud and sometimes violent demonstrations, a venerable tradition in Chicago. White West Siders also organized community groups to offer more temperate tactics for preventing African Americans from moving into the neighborhood. Finally, they participated in attempts to influence public policy mechanisms, trying both to punish blockbusters and also to preserve their right to exercise racial discrimination in the sale of property.[3]

A portion of West Siders' reaction to African American in-migration was entirely consistent with historical responses to black presence in "white" Chicago neighborhoods. Since the second decade of the twentieth century, white South Siders patrolled the boundaries of their neighborhoods, threatening blacks who entered for any purpose. African American banker Jesse Binga, who suffered multiple bombings of his property, was only one of dozens of blacks who were targets of such domestic terrorism. Such practices continued well into the 1950s, as African Americans sought homes in white West Side neighborhoods. Although much of the violent conflict over space in Chicago shifted to public venues such as parks after 1957, even during the 1960s some blacks who moved into white areas met violent resistance to their persons and property.[4]

Some white West Siders repudiated violent tactics but shared the ideal of racial separatism. Those inclined to activism hoped to hold the line against black migration into their neighborhoods through community organizations, like the United Property Group (UPG), based in West Garfield Park. The actions of groups such as UPG echoed their ideological cousins, the popular "improvement associations" that sponsored racially restrictive property deeds and neighborhood covenants during the first half of the twentieth century. Despite their energy, white West Siders were largely unsuccessful in halting change in the area's racial composition. The minister of a South Side church, observing a parallel movement in the early 1970s, said, "When I see a block club being formed . . . I say to myself, 'Look out, there goes the block.' It seems to me to be the final stage in a white homeowner's efforts to cope with the change."[5]

West Siders also participated in citywide efforts to change local laws, as a part of their effort to control the racial composition of their neighborhoods. Community groups and other organizations repeatedly sought to use local, state, and federal laws to achieve their vision for the city's future. For example, a lengthy struggle over the creation of a fair housing ordinance for Chicago resulted in a law that whites tried to harness to their own goal of stopping blockbusters. In 1964 West Siders supported a peculiar petition drive in hopes of preventing a statewide open occupancy law. As was the case with the other policy venues, white West Siders never successfully imposed their will upon the occupancy of private housing.[6] Even when supportive legislation was enacted, West Siders proved unable to use the new laws to keep African Americans out of their neighborhoods.

During the late 1950s and 1960s, white West Siders received a steady stream of information that suggested to them that African Americans were about to try to move into their neighborhoods. Chicago's newspapers frequently reported on blockbusters' systematic advance through the West Side. In 1957 Otis and Beverly Duncan published *The Negro Population of Chicago: A Study of Residential Succession*, which identified private housing on the West Side as one of the primary sites of new African American migration into Chicago. And, eventually, white West Siders met blockbusters and then African American neighbors on the blocks where they lived. When queried about their experiences three decades later, whites who left "changing" neighborhoods in the 1960s remembered the experience as inevitable. They used the language of natural disaster—"a shock wave," "tidal wave," "lava"—to describe their departures. "It was an exodus," wrote interviewer Louis Rosen, whose family moved out of a changed South Side neighborhood.[7]

Neither the historical fact of the steady white exodus from the West Side nor the memories of those who left should be taken to mean that at the time white West Siders regarded their eventual departures as inexorable. White West Siders imagined numerous tactics for keeping their neighborhoods to themselves.[8] Alongside the stream of outward migration, an inventive and persistent resistance played itself out. Many white West Siders were determined not to share the local urban landscape with African Americans. Only rarely did they spell out their racial logic as explicitly as Lorraine Hansberry's Karl Lindner character. Sometimes they spoke a murky language of property values. On a few occasions, such as the formation of the United Property Group, participants articulated the assumption that African Americans could only be bad for neighborhoods. The actions based on these ideas may have temporarily delayed a few families' decisions to leave, but the out-migration continued. Their wholesale departure from the West Side—treated by subsequent observers as "white flight"—represented the final stage in their struggles again the multipart postwar urban crisis.

Violence

During the late 1940s and early 1950s, Chicago's news media reported little violence by whites against African Americans in response to their arrival in private homes and their use of public facilities in white neighborhoods.

Despite this public silence, Arnold Hirsch discovered that the period was "an era of hidden violence."[9] Especially during the 1940s, whites in Chicago responded to black "move-ins" by gathering outside the homes of the newly arrived families, harassing and threatening them. Typically, these unreported riots "involved thousands of participants and continued for days." At the Chicago Housing Authority's Trumbull Park Homes, in the South Deering neighborhood on the city's Far South Side, whites spent an entire decade harassing a few black families. Their persecution was so severe and systematic that the Chicago Police Department structured its schedule around the need to keep approximately twelve hundred officers posted in Trumbull Park simultaneously.[10]

White residents of other parts of Chicago resented the concentration of so much police protection in one neighborhood, for a purpose with which they were not sympathetic. In 1953, six years before blacks moved to West Garfield Park, the *Garfieldian* editorialized against the diversion of half of the local Austin and Fillmore police officers to South Deering. The paper complained that the shortage of staff left West Side children unprotected crossing the street on their way to school. When "a light-complected Negro" attacked a white woman in Austin in 1954, the *Garfieldian* asked its readers, "Why should hundreds of police protect several families on the South Side daily when thousands of West Siders are afraid to walk their own streets at night?" In 1957, when white teenager Judy Anderson was brutally murdered by an unknown assailant, the paper took the opportunity to remind its readers that the local police station was understaffed because 30 of its 148 officers remained on duty at Trumbull Park. Charles X. Clancy, the chairman of the Apollo Savings and Loan Association, angrily wrote that the West Side was left "absolutely unprotected from hoodlums, thieves, and hold-up men while 900 police officers are forced to stand idly around this project." Clancy demanded that the "parties involved"—that is, the African Americans whom the police were detailed to protect—pay the $45,000 per day cost of keeping them on duty.[11]

Noting a decrease in the number of African Americans requesting police help in the late 1950s, Hirsch argues that most of the large-scale white-initiated disorder in Chicago was shifting away from housing toward "the perquisites of neighborhood control . . . schools, playgrounds, parks, and beaches." By the time the Far West Side began experiencing large-scale racial transition, he writes, "it was apparent that once the pattern of resistance in a given area was broken, and the first few black families were safely entrenched, subsequent move-ins were quickly and peacefully conducted." Hirsch's analysis, however, should not be taken to mean that African Americans could move into white sections of the West Side free from the prospect of racial violence. The Chicago Council against Racial and Religious Discrimination reported eleven incidents of "terroristic attacks" and seven locations of "repeated attacks" between August 1945 and April 1948 on the West Side alone.[12] Even after the racial turf battles shifted to public facilities, nonwhites moving to the West Side in the late 1950s—as well as the real estate brokers who enabled them to do so—continued to encounter threats and violence as frightening as that in other areas of Chicago, if ultimately not as sustained. Blacks received little help from the police who witnessed this treatment, suggesting that the extent of continuing harassment of African Americans was probably underreported.

At the end of July 1957, a crowd of six to seven thousand whites attacked black picnickers in Calumet Park on Chicago's South Side, initiating several days of disturbances. The news media provided more coverage of these events than previous confrontations, focusing new attention on de facto racial segregation in Chicago's public facilities.[13] As the Calumet Park riot drew to a close on July 31, a crowd of about a thousand whites gathered around a building at 3714 West Polk in North Lawndale, an area described by a local observer as a "pretty tight Italian community." The home was occupied by its new African American owner, who rented the second floor to another black tenant. A black family had also just purchased the house next door. Members of the white North Lawndale mob broke windows in the house before black Park District police officers arrested three people. The next night a smaller crowd of approximately two hundred teenagers gathered nearby shouting, "We want blood." After about two hours, someone threw bottles at city police observers, prompting ten arrests. For the next two nights, several dozen police officers patrolled the street and mingled with the crowd, but there was no more violence. Although there were no further reports of harassment at that address, the tone of relations between West Side police and African Americans over move-ins was established. The Greater Lawndale Association of Block Clubs and Organizations complained that "police had to guard the area and protect the attackers NOT THE FAMILY."[14]

William L. Glover and his wife also experienced violence after moving to the southwestern section of East Garfield Park. In February 1957 they purchased a two-flat building at 328 South Homan. When they first moved in, their furnace and boiler were destroyed. They were left alone until September, when renewed attacks frightened them. The Glovers' garage was burned down. Then their car, parked on the street, was set afire. Finally, large staples were shot through their windows on several successive nights. The Glovers felt that the police protection of their block, which housed two other black families, was inadequate. They set up their own twenty-four-hour watch and kept a loaded shotgun ready to use.[15]

Nathan and Lorine Freeman had similar difficulties in September 1957 when they bought a home at 4107 West Cullerton, in the southwestern section of North Lawndale. Without the help of a mortgage, the Freemans bought their home from a white couple who had lived in the house for three years. The Chicago Commission on Human Relations (CCHR) and the Lawndale police were notified ahead of time that the Freemans planned to move in on October 28, and again when they actually arrived. The Freemans' first night in their new home apparently passed without incident, but on the night of October 29, a crowd started gathering outside. At 8 P.M., in response to an anonymous call, the police arrived, but they reported nothing amiss. At 8:10 Mr. Freeman called a CCHR representative to complain that he had been chased out of his house and was unable to raise the police on the telephone. CCHR called the police for him. When the police returned, they again found no crowd. Instead, they ticketed Mr. Freeman for parking his car on the wrong side of the street. Ten minutes later police stopped him for making a U-turn and then arrested him when they saw a pistol on the seat of the car. The police were summoned a third time after 11 P.M., when a rock thrown through the window of the house injured a woman inside. At this point, police dispersed a crowd of about seventy-five whites gathered two doors away.[16]

The harassment of the Freeman family did not cease after their second night in Lawndale. They experienced "intermittent terror activities" over the next several months. On Valentine's Day 1958, a small bomb exploded in the alley next to their home. The Chicago Police Department subsequently suspended the pair of police officers who were assigned to watch the Freemans' house that night. At the time of the bombing, they were in their squad car, asleep or keeping warm. In March 1958 the head of the civil rights division of the Chicago Commission on Human Relations reported that more police officers were assigned to guard the Freemans' home than were on duty in Trumbull Park. A fire flared in a vacated building across the street as rumors swirled around the neighborhood that the rest of the buildings on the block were about to be sold to blacks.[17]

Episodes combining harassment of new black homeowners and police neglect were not isolated incidents. Nonwhites who occupied West Side property frequently suffered hostile greetings from their neighbors. Arsonists threw a torch on the roof of a building at 3449 West Lexington rented to African Americans. When a childless black couple bought a home at 3526 Jackson, the upstairs tenants agreed to remain, but other neighbors threw stink bombs and broke windows. Another house purchased by blacks was set on fire twice the first night of their occupancy. A family with children was firebombed twice during their first week in Lawndale. A black family in North Lawndale complained that over a four-year period they were consistently harassed by white hoodlums and ignored by the local police. An apartment building purchased by blacks in 1954 had its windows broken so often that the owners could not attract tenants. Such harassment continued in the 1960s. The "Tensions Bulletin" issued by CCHR reported examples of window breakage during both 1964 and 1965. Nor did violence automatically fade once a black family settled in a neighborhood; the Burnett family of 3106 West Taylor reported repeated assaults over a four-year period after their arrival in 1953.[18]

Quaker activists, famous for their anti-racist activities, were frequent targets of angry white neighbors on the West Side. Mary Louise Yoshino and her husband, John, a Nisei veteran of the United States Army, bought a home at 3504 West Harrison Street in East Garfield Park in 1946. The house was stoned twice, two months after their arrival. Mr. Yoshino joined the local neighborhood organization, the Bradley and Honore Neighborhood Association, but white members showed their unhappiness with his presence. The American Friends Service Committee's Project House—where students resided while pursuing community service internships—located at 3543 West Jackson, was subject to frequent attacks between 1956 and 1962. Project House residents assumed that the attacks were connected to their religious commitment to racial tolerance and their hosting of nonwhite visitors. Like increasing numbers of their black neighbors, Project House residents hesitated to involve the police "both because of their ineffectiveness and because of their methods." Racial harassment was not confined to the West Side; a 1957 CCHR report estimated that property damage was roughly the same in the South Side Englewood neighborhood as it was on the West Side.[19] But violence was not the only method of reminding African Americans that they were not welcome. Many more whites responded to the presence of blacks in the neighborhood by organizing community groups for sustained nonviolent action for segregation.

Organizing for Segregation

When Josh and Barbara Hargrave bought a house at 4338 West Jackson in 1959, neighbors initiated one of the swiftest and most thorough responses to racial change that the West Side witnessed in the postwar era. The Hargrave family was typical of postwar black residents of the West Side: southern migrants, displaced from their prior home in Chicago by urban renewal and unable to obtain a conventional mortgage despite their steady income. They had migrated from West Virginia at the end of the war, just in time to experience the city's postwar housing crunch. Their difficulty finding a landlord willing to accept their four children strengthened the Hargraves' resolve to buy their own home. The adults scrimped and saved their money; the children did odd jobs to help the family finances. Barbara Hargrave explained, "We neglected buying nice furniture, clothing for ourselves and our boys; sometimes we even cut down on necessities so we could save up enough to get a nice place and be happy together." They eventually found a home at 2649 West Fulton, but the city condemned that property for industrial urban renewal.[20] When the Hargraves moved into West Garfield Park, several thousand whites responded by mobbing their home. Once the violence petered out, residents formed the United Property Group, a group dedicated to keeping West Garfield Park and Austin white through legal means.

While searching for a home to replace their condemned property, the Hargraves met Harry Gaynor, a Jewish real estate broker who was decidedly not a panic peddler. Gaynor and his wife, Anne, welcomed black tenants in the building they themselves occupied and were once nominees for a Chicago Commission on Human Relations award.[21] In 1959 Harry Gaynor sold them Irene Rosen Lande's house, which had been on the market without a taker for the previous two years. The Hargraves made a $9,000 down payment on the three-flat building. The deed was held in a trust, however, suggesting to attorney Mark Satter that the Hargraves obtained the $20,000 balance through a contract purchase. Gaynor said that he had not handled the financial arrangements in the transaction and acknowledged the possibility of a contract sale that allowed for the transfer of the title to the Hargraves when they had paid off 50 percent of the balance. The purchase of the building at 4338 West Jackson by the Hargraves on Saturday, August 1, 1959, made them the first black homeowners west of the 4100 block. In buying a house more than two blocks west of that line, the Hargraves violated the usual block-by-block pattern of racial change in Chicago.[22]

Before the Hargraves moved in, whites in the area exploded in outrage at the news of the purchase. On Wednesday, August 5, and again on Thursday and Friday, a mob of between one and four thousand people gathered outside the building. Some threw stones and bricks. For once the police responded vigorously, sending in several hundred officers, who barricaded the street at both ends and arrested more than two dozen men and boys for taking part in the disturbance. The court ordered fourteen demonstrators held on $2,500 bonds, the maximum permitted, a move that the Chicago Urban League singled out for praise. The police maintained a strong, visible presence outside of the Hargraves' home for several weeks.[23]

Whites' anger focused on Harry Gaynor for enabling the Hargraves to buy property in West Garfield Park. As was the case with the appearance of "Confessions of a Blockbuster" in the *Saturday Evening Post*, West Garfield Park residents treated anyone who allowed blacks to enter a previously all-white neighborhood as a blockbuster. They did not differentiate between a profiteering speculator and a local broker acting out of a commitment to civil rights. Gaynor received obscene telephone calls and a death threat in the mail. The letter opened with an ominous reference to the recent unsolved murder of Mario Melchiorre, a West Side real estate dealer also suspected of blockbusting, and warned, "24-hour protection by the police for yourself, your office and your employees won't do you much good." The Federal Bureau of Investigation requested a copy of the threatening letter, and the police put an around-the-clock guard at Gaynor's home and office.[24]

Gaynor adamantly denied the charges of blockbusting: "It was not and was never intended to be." He elaborated, "If an owner calls me up, I will handle his building, but I won't encourage people to sell their homes because an area is changing. I have never done this and I never will." Gaynor wrote to Mayor Daley, urging him to make a public statement that "citizens have a right to purchase property; to live where they want to; and that legitimate brokers have a right to sell property." Gaynor claimed that he, like other reputable brokers, never solicited property owners to sell their homes. Several other brokers also had the listing for the building at 4338 West Jackson, and all had shown it to African Americans. Gaynor said the only solution was for the city to pursue an open occupancy ordinance, which would forbid property sellers to discriminate against potential buyers on the basis of race.[25]

Many of Gaynor's neighbors, however, wanted to retain the right to discriminate against potential African American property owners. Many channeled their energies into the United Property Group, founded by Gordon Mattson, a thirty-nine-year-old bachelor from Minnesota. For six years UPG sought to keep white West Garfield Parkers and Austinites in their homes. In mid-1965 a *Garfieldian* columnist criticized UPG for its narrowly focused goal of keeping "the whites from moving out or in, however you want to put it."[26] Mattson taught management and finance at the University of Nebraska before moving to Chicago to become a management consultant and care for a sick relative. He took up residence at 4422 West Jackson. Although he did not personally hold title to the home, it had belonged to other members of his family since 1919.[27]

Mattson denounced "mob action" of the sort that took place outside the Hargraves' home. He argued that such violent displays played "into the hands of the speculators who want the neighborhood to panic so that they will be able to make big profits in buying and selling property." He issued an eight-point plan of action that urged emotional and financial calm on his neighbors. Mattson channeled the hostility and disorder of the white mob into a community organization that sought more orderly methods of keeping whites in and blacks out of the neighborhood. Although he expressed the organization's purpose in a variety of ways—protecting property values, preventing violence, stopping blight, improving the community, and promoting fellowship—the primary goal of UPG members was to keep West Garfield Park an all-white community.[28]

In contrast to whites' efforts to disguise their sentiments against black students in their children's schools, the racism of this new organization was transparent. A critical West Garfield Park resident observed that UPG's leaders "seem to be determined not to let Negro fellow-Americans go beyond a certain point in their neighborhoods" and called their efforts "not only disgustingly racist but utterly futile." Mattson articulated his own aversion to African Americans in a long letter printed by the *Garfieldian*, which was sympathetic to the new organization's goals:

> Few of us would feel comfortable in neighborhoods made up exclusively of people with significantly higher or lower incomes than we earn, or in communities made up primarily of people who speak different languages than we speak, or in neighborhoods which are different from our standards of orderliness and neatness.
>
> When we force ourselves into environments different than those to which we have been accepted, we have no right to expect preferential treatment over others, and should expect to meet substantial prejudice. And we never improve our situation, nor further understanding by accusing others of being prejudiced against us or against the people whose interests we are trying to further.[29]

Like the critics of the African Americans who moved to the South Side's Trumbull Park, Mattson placed the blame for the trouble in West Garfield Park squarely on the shoulders of the newcomers and their supporters, whose "risky endeavors" were "forcing so-called integration" on an unwilling community. Reversing the rhetoric of Lorraine Hansberry's fictional Karl Linder, Mattson continued, "People are being led to believe that it is a gross sin to discriminate and to have prejudice. But the real truth is that so long as there are human differences there will always be discrimination and prejudice."[30]

Mattson envisioned UPG as an umbrella organization that coordinated active block clubs. Because meetings of more than eighty people were unwieldy, he urged property owners to organize initially with others from their own block. The *Garfieldian* published maps dividing West Garfield Park and eastern Austin into small sections and provided information on reaching Mattson for instructions on starting block clubs. Within three weeks of the Hargraves' purchase, three dozen such groups formed. By November the United Property Group had a name, elected officers, and a formal dues structure. In July 1960 UPG extended its organizing effort westward into neighboring Austin.[31]

UPG's first major effort was a collective statement that blockbusters were not welcome to continue working in West Garfield Park. Like white neighborhood groups in other parts of Chicago and the nation, UPG encouraged residents to put "Not for Sale" signs in their windows. Mattson explained that the signs were an "effective means for individual property owners to show they are cooperative with their neighbors and to tell visitors in the area that they plan to stay put and will not panic." He reported that by September 30, 1959, West Garfield Park residents posted four thousand such signs in the neighborhood. UPG also distributed to its members a red, white, and blue decal with the slogan "Improve Our Block." In June 1961 UPG distributed a second decal bearing the acronym "NFS," which stood for "Not for Sale," and the warning, "Real Estate solicitors are promptly reported to UPG."[32]

This last message reflected one of UPG's main functions: information control. Mattson regarded rumors about racial change as especially damaging to neighborhood morale. He suspected that blockbusters planted them as a way of inducing panic-stricken property owners to sell. He reasoned that UPG could serve as central clearinghouse for all information and dispel false rumors about real estate speculation in West Garfield Park. He urged residents approached by blockbusters to listen politely to their pitches in order to gather intelligence, and then to report what they learned to UPG. The group also kept track of local property ownership records in order to preempt blockbusters from lying about who had already sold their homes. Rather than give up the West Side to African Americans, UPG consistently argued, whites "must stay and hold their community."[33]

Most of UPG's activities in West Garfield Park focused on protecting the racial homogeneity of private housing and the public schools. The organization also sought to boost local white morale by sponsoring a variety of activities that advertised the area's virtues, such as rallies, mass meetings, public forums, surveys, and petition drives. UPG joined the campaign to bring the University of Illinois campus to Garfield Park. Despite these forays into broader community concerns, UPG's emphasis remained on protecting the racial homogeneity of West Garfield Park. In 1964 the Chicago Archdiocese's Chancery office denounced UPG and directed West Side

Fig. 18. The United Property Group urged white West Garfield Park residents to post decals in their windows illustrating that African Americans were not welcome to move into the neighborhood. *Garfieldian*, February 19, 1961. Courtesy of the Special Collections and Preservation Division, Chicago Public Library.

Catholic churches to withdraw financial and logistical aid. The Town Hall Assembly (THA), which was effectively UPG's successor in Austin, was perhaps more attentive to the risks of appearing narrowly interested in racial discrimination. While THA advocated many of the same positions as UPG, the leadership made sure that their other activities, such as its tutoring project and symphony orchestra, were well publicized.[34]

Mattson ran a losing battle in West Garfield Park. Although he won significant support and publicity, his efforts could not dissuade white residents from leaving. One of his neighbors received the call that indicated the imminent success of blockbusters in West Garfield Park. In April 1962 Mr. and Mrs. Herbert Brown were solicited by a real estate dealer who convinced them to sign a contract to sell their home at 4450 Monroe. Amid the usual pressure tactics for persuading whites that they should move, the solicitor sealed the deal by proclaiming that Mattson, who lived four blocks to the south of the Browns, had sold his home to African Americans. The charge turned out to be false; because Mattson did not own the property outright, he could not authorize its sale.[35]

That blacks had moved farther west into the area, however, was not at all implausible. In 1960 African Americans in West Garfield Park represented 16 percent of the population; by 1965 blacks constituted between 65 and 85 percent of local residents. In the middle of 1963, the UPG leadership acknowledged that the organization no longer had a constituency in West Garfield Park and shifted its energies to Austin. In December 1963 UPG officially withdrew to the west side of the Belt Line Railroad, formally changing its boundaries to make West Garfield Park's western border its own eastern limit. UPG's new leader, Robert Bacigalupo, the owner of a funeral home in Austin, succeeded in keeping the organization in the spotlight. But UPG's most likely recruits—white Austinites who feared living among African Americans—chose not to join a single-purpose organization condemned by religious authorities. In September 1965 the few remaining members of UPG formally disbanded.[36]

Defending Property Rights

The United Property Group and similar organizations did not try to maintain the West Side's segregation through their persuasive powers alone. Such groups also attempted to use legal mechanisms to achieve their goals. In the first half of the twentieth century, white Chicagoans excluded blacks from their neighborhoods by placing racially restrictive deeds on their own properties and forming racially restrictive local covenants with their neighbors. After the U.S. Supreme Court ruled in 1948 that the enforcement of such covenants and deeds was unconstitutional, white Chicagoans relied on neighborhood improvement associations to put up a hostile front to potential black neighbors. Groups like UPG urged neighborhood residents to refuse to sell their property to African Americans. The hostile response Southwest Siders offered to the open housing marches led by Martin Luther King during the summer of 1966 illustrated how entrenched the opposition to integration of Chicago neighborhoods remained.[37]

Despite the odds, however, civil rights activists sought ways to outlaw discriminatory practices in housing, appealing for the passage of laws to protect the rights of black citizens to live wherever they could afford. As it happened, advocates of segregation found some of their most promising tools for perpetuating racial discrimination amidst the emerging fair housing and open occupancy laws. Once Chicago passed a fair housing law in 1963, white residents tried to use its anti-blockbusting provisions to slow the pace of racial change. West Siders also participated in a peculiar effort to put an open occupancy referendum to a statewide vote in Illinois—in order to create the opportunity to reject it. Legal tactics, however, failed to interrupt the progress of the blockbusters—and their African American customers—through the West Side during the 1960s.

White Chicagoans tried to use the legal system to outlaw blockbusting itself. Alderman James Condon, investigating how other American cities dealt with blockbusting, found in 1961 that only Baltimore had an ordinance condemning the practice. Baltimore's law threatened to revoke the licenses of brokers who engaged in blockbusting tactics. Condon proposed to fine or imprison real estate dealers who solicited property in Chicago with "scare tactics," a practice that included making references to changes in a locale's racial or religious composition. Condon's proposal drew immediate fire from black real estate dealers and liberal 5th Ward alderman Leon Despres, who argued that the law would be "ineffective, vague, unenforceable and unconstitutional." Indeed, legal assaults on panic-peddling practices were hampered by the federal Constitution's provision for freedom of speech, which protected blockbusters' most effective tactics.[38]

White neighborhood groups also urged state officials to control blockbusting by exercising their established power to license real estate brokers. In Illinois the Real Estate Brokers and Salesmen Law empowered the Real Estate Examining Committee of the state's Department of Registration and Education (DRE) to test and license real estate brokers. UPG's leaders identified Frank Petrone, a West Sider employed as a technical adviser to DRE, as a potential ally in stopping blockbusters in West Garfield Park. UPG referred to Petrone's office detailed information on the practices of several blockbusting real estate firms. Among these cases was the solicitation of the

Brown family, at 4450 West Monroe, which prompted UPG's ultimate retreat into Austin. DRE declared the 4450 Monroe case out of its jurisdiction, on the grounds that the accused salesman had not yet received a license at the time of the solicitation. The fruitlessness of DRE's blockbusting investigations discouraged the *Garfieldian*'s editorial staff. The newspaper complained that the department "insists on the most detailed evidence, takes no initiative to do any investigating for itself and seems to require forever to get anything done. We have a feeling that if we did not prod them nothing would be done." When in 1963 DRE for the first time revoked a license issued to a South Side real estate broker, the *Garfieldian* applauded the unprecedented action but noted that the successful investigation took more than two years.[39]

Whites contesting blockbusters next turned to Chicago's Fair Housing Act, which the city council passed in 1963 after more than a decade of agitation, ostensibly as a protection for African Americans. In 1949 the Chicago City Council defeated Alderman Archibald Carey's proposal for an ordinance to outlaw racial and religious discrimination in private housing on land provided by the Chicago Housing Authority and the Chicago Land Clearance Commission. In March 1961 the Chicago Real Estate Board successfully fought a proposed Illinois law requested by the Chicago City Council to prohibit racial discrimination in the sale and rental of housing with five or more units.[40] The fate of fair housing legislation began to turn in 1962, when CCHR released *Selling and Buying Real Estate in a Racially Changing Neighborhood*. This study documented the character of the dual housing market in the South Side neighborhood of Englewood. After the study's release, CCHR held public hearings to discuss remedies for the inflated prices paid by buyers and the excessive profits made by real estate dealers. A delegation of African American aldermen normally obedient to Mayor Daley's party line warned him that the city needed to do something to conciliate their discontented constituents.[41]

In 1963 the city council considered a pair of ordinances to prevent both property owners and real estate brokers from discriminating on the basis of race. Public hearings on the bills held in August attracted both advocates and opponents. The Chicago Real Estate Board (CREB) led the opposition, arguing that "to restrict the right of choice in property sale or occupancy is a restriction on human rights." White neighborhood organizations, including UPG, joined CREB's vehement opposition to the bills. UPG president Robert Bacigalupo echoed CREB's sentiments, insinuating, "This is something the Communists are interested in fostering in trying to destroy the rights of the individual." Alderman Robert Massey tried to weaken the proposals with an amendment restricting application of the law to buildings with fifty or more units, a move that would have made the ordinance irrelevant on most of the West Side.[42]

In September the city council passed a fair housing ordinance that disappointed both opponents and proponents. The new law forbade real estate brokers from discriminating on the basis of race but stopped short of giving Chicago a full-fledged open occupancy law. The new ordinance failed to prohibit property owners from using race to discriminate against buyers. Additionally, the ordinance outlawed panic peddling. The Chicago Commission on Human Relations had responsibility for enforcement. CCHR's coordinator for housing and community services, an African American named Hal Freeman, said that the agency would observe both the anti-discrimination and anti-panic-peddling provisions of the ordinance. Freeman served notice that he had a narrower view of the definition of blockbusting than the one many white Chicagoans held. He cautioned that selling a home to an African American in an all-white neighborhood did not automatically make a broker a blockbuster.[43]

Once the law was enacted, white West Side groups tested the provisions against panic peddling. Just as they encouraged the Department of Registration and Education to police licensed brokers, West Siders took the opportunity to report speculators to CCHR. The United Property Group accompanied constituents to CCHR offices to help them file formal complaints. As in so many other public policy arenas, however, white West Siders were displeased with the execution of the anti-blockbusting portion of Chicago's Fair Housing Act. Two women who went with UPG leaders to CCHR offices left convinced that the city administration "couldn't care less about blockbusters" and was uninterested in fighting panic peddling.[44]

Quantitative reports of CCHR's enforcement efforts suggest why West Siders found the agency ineffective. By July 1964 CCHR received a total of twenty-eight complaints under the provisions of the Fair Housing Act. Twenty-three complaints charged brokers with racial discrimination, one each charged religious and national ancestry discrimination, and three charged panic peddling. By 1967, of 386 complaints, CCHR had dismissed half for lack of jurisdiction or probable cause. CCHR counted most of the rest as "satisfactorily resolved," although only seven reached the stage of a public hearing. CCHR answered criticism of the lack of litigation by explaining that its primary goal was reconciliation of citizens' complaints, not punishment of offenders. Staff resolved many complaints by obtaining assurances from brokers that they would cease using the offensive tactics.[45] The combination of case-by-case dismissals and the nonpunitive reconciliation process left West Siders with the sense that the statute was useless in stopping blockbusters active in their neighborhoods.

Simultaneous with the practical tests of the city's Fair Housing Act, a new group organized to prevent any further encroachments into white Chicagoans' right to dispose of their property however they wished. Fair housing laws prohibiting whites from refusing to sell their property to African Americans constrained the absolute rights of property owners. During the summer of 1963, as debate over passing the fair housing bill heated up, the Property Owners Coordinating Committee (POCC) emerged on the scene. The scanty available evidence leaves POCC's origins obscure. Some observers were convinced that POCC was nothing but a subsidiary of the Chicago Real Estate Board, while one of the leading fund-raisers suggested that a South Lawndale neighborhood organization spawned POCC. The group was initially announced as "a new division of the Chicago Real Estate Board." POCC consistently represented itself in public as a homeowners group, eventually claiming the membership of 170 organizations and more than 250,000 individuals. Several West Side groups participated in POCC's activities. Robert Bacigalupo, who assumed the mantle of UPG leadership from Gordon Mattson, sat on POCC's board of directors. Although its name suggested that POCC represented property owners, the Chicago Real Estate Board was the moving force behind the organization, providing office space and logistical support for its efforts. They had separate fund-raising mechanisms and formal activities, but POCC and CREB shared an address, a telephone number, and staff.[46]

POCC's primary purpose was to avert the enactment of an open occupancy law in Illinois. Casting the debate in terms of "forced housing," to emphasize how anti-discrimination laws impinged on property rights, POCC launched a campaign to put the question of open occupancy directly to Illinois voters. During 1964 POCC and its member organizations sought to gather several hundred thousand signatures on petitions requesting that the question of open occupancy be placed on the November 3 statewide ballot. In particular, the proposed referendum asked voters whether the Illinois legislature should pass an open occupancy law, and whether the state should permit municipal governments in Illinois to pass such ordinances on their own. One supporter of POCC's campaign offered a disingenuous interpretation of the referendum, suggesting that a statewide open occupancy law would force suburbs to share in the "burden" of a black population. She argued that if an open occupancy law regulated all municipalities across Illinois, effectively allowing blacks to move anywhere in the state, no single city with a fair housing law would suffer a concentration of blacks and the sort of rapid racial succession that Chicago had been experiencing. POCC's purpose in seeking the referendum, however, was not to encourage Illinois voters to approve open occupancy. Instead, POCC anticipated voters' rejection of both propositions, thereby preempting any further action on open occupancy by the state legislature.[47]

Community groups in white neighborhoods around Chicago arranged for members to distribute and collect signed petitions. But the referendum did not garner universal support. Most significantly, the Chicago Conference on Religion and Race issued a pamphlet, "Why the Three Major Faiths Oppose the Proposed Referendum on Open Occupancy Legislation." The pamphlet characterized the referendum questions as "inflammatory and misleading" and called on congregations to refuse to sign the petitions. This pamphlet infuriated S. T. Sutton, a POCC officer. Sutton wrote a letter to the editor of the *Chicago Sun-Times* that vehemently denounced the authority of clergy to direct citizens' positions on open occupancy. Sutton's prose was so intemperate that POCC issued a bulletin clarifying that his "extremely provocative" rhetoric represented only his personal views and was not an official statement. Illinois citizens never voted on open occupancy; the Illinois Electoral Board ruled that that the petitions improperly asked voters to decide on unrelated questions and removed the referendum from the November ballot. Nonetheless, in the short run, POCC's program turned out to be superfluous. In June 1967 both houses of the state legislature scuttled a proposed Illinois Fair Housing Practices Act.[48]

Further efforts to block open occupancy laws in Chicago and Illinois became moot with other developments in state governance and federal legislation. In 1963, despite a flood of constituent mail opposing any open occupancy legislation, Governor Otto Kerner issued an executive order prohibiting brokers in the state from accepting or acting on discriminatory listings. The Department of Registration and Education tried to implement this rule, but the Chicago Real Estate Board sponsored a lawsuit that held up the order in the court system, until it was finally upheld by the Illinois Supreme Court in 1967. At the same time, civil rights activists in Chicago drew attention to the closed housing market by marching through white Southwest Side neighborhoods. On one of these marches, a rock thrown by a hostile bystander wounded Martin Luther King in the head. Finally, the federal Fair Housing Act, passed in the wake of King's assassination in April 1968, made irrelevant the creation of open occupancy legislation specifically for Illinois. The 1968 Fair Housing Act and the U.S. Supreme Court's decision in *Jones v. Mayer* banned both blockbusting and racial discrimination in real estate dealing across the nation. A new Illinois constitution, adopted by a convention in 1970, built into state law new protections against racial discrimination in housing and employment.[49]

In the second half of the 1960s, the emergence of new attitudes toward racial questions helped soften the rhetoric about how to deal with African

American migration into Austin. Several national and international developments in the mid-1960s shook up Austinites' sense of how they ought to express their anxieties about the city's future. The legal landmarks of the civil rights movement and the international earthquake of the Second Vatican Council helped Austin residents find new ways of expressing their positions. Both proponents and opponents of integration spoke in a language of "stabilization," arguing for keeping whites in the neighborhood rather than for keeping blacks entirely out. A few organizations, like the Town Hall Assembly, remained committed to racially homogenous local institutions. At the same time, however, a few advocates of interracial living found a voice and an audience.

CHAPTER 8

Keeping Whites In

In February 1958 an unusual group met at the American Friends Service Committee Project House in East Garfield Park in observation of Brotherhood Week, a program of the National Conference of Christians and Jews. One of the meeting's purposes was to encourage "each member of the group [to] talk to as many neighbors and local leaders as possible, in an attempt to promote better understanding between people, cut down on some of the violence and strengthen the neighborhood in general." The Garfield Park Good Neighbors Council emerged from this meeting. Few records remain documenting this group's activities, but the organization articulated a rare sentiment in favor of interracial cooperation. When white West Garfield Park residents rioted in response to the Hargrave family's purchase of a home, the organization called an emergency meeting and condemned the violence. Their newsletter argued that residents should not worry about the onset of racial change in the neighborhood, as the area had been settled by successive groups of immigrants who together built a "clean, decent, friendly community, which soon welcomed new minorities—Italian Catholics and European Jews." The newsletter claimed that "virtually every Negro family in Garfield is a model tenant or homeowner" and urged "friendliness as the code of our community."[1]

The Good Neighbors Council stands out as one of a very few voices calling for harmonious integration in West Garfield Park during the 1950s. Their activities, however, anticipated an upsurge in controversial interracial community-organizing efforts in Austin during the middle and late 1960s. National and international developments during the 1960s provided a new cultural context that encouraged some white American urbanites to accept a vision of biracial communities. Most notably, of course, the moral and legislative triumphs of the civil rights movement in the first half of the decade persuaded at least a minority of white Americans that continuing discrimination against African Americans was abhorrent. As white northerners watched on their television sets as southern police set dogs on and aimed fire hoses at black children, at least a few considered the implications for the local racial structure. Additionally, the reforms enacted by the Roman Catholic Church during the Second Vatican Council prompted some white American Catholics to consider their attitudes toward race in a religious framework.[2] Interpreting these religious, legal, and social sea changes through the lenses of their individual experiences and local neighborhoods in the 1960s, some Austin residents promoted the idea that whites could comfortably live alongside African Americans.

Austinites who shared these views formed organizations that sought, in sociologist Harvey L. Molotch's useful phrase, "managed integration." Concluding that the arrival of African Americans in Austin was inevitable— and that blacks had a right to live there if they could afford it—they hoped to discover methods for persuading whites to stay as well. Like the members of the South Shore Commission whom Molotch studied, members of such organizations hoped above all that Austin would remain "a community in which many whites, *including themselves*, would always live." If they could stop the neglect and deterioration that appeared to accompany the arrival of African Americans, they might be able to persuade incumbent whites to remain in an integrated neighborhood. Offering a warm welcome to African Americans was not high on their agendas—their major purpose was to find a way to keep whites in the neighborhood, not to encourage African Americans to move in. Most often, they expressed this goal through the tepid language of "neighborhood stabilization." Only rarely did anyone mention the possibility that the West Side ought to serve as a model of integration for the rest of the city, or that racial diversity should be a community objective. These activists usually stopped far short of being "interracialists," as historian John McGreevy calls Catholic activists who understood improving race relations in the United States as the central religious and moral issue of the postwar period.[3]

Telling the groups that could tolerate integration apart from their segregationist opponents is not an easy task, since both employed similar rhetoric. The language of stabilization, for example, was by no means the exclusive property of racial moderates. Forthright segregationists, like the renegade South Side priest Father Francis X. Lawlor and his supporters, also described their efforts to keep the areas west of Ashland Avenue all-white as an effort to promote "stability."[4] The two approaches can be distinguished primarily by the extent of their willingness to welcome some African Americans into their organization and neighborhood.

Notably, women led many of the organizations that engaged in the debate about the future of integration in Austin, both formally and informally.[5] While women were members and officers in the other community groups that acted to influence the West Side's postwar landscape, men usually assumed formal leadership of the organizations. Women who participated as officers typically served as recording or corresponding secretaries. In Austin, however, a few women emerged from supportive roles in the organizations and took control of them. The Austin Tenants and Owners Association, for example, was created by Marcella Kane, who translated her skills in organizing block clubs into a broader neighborhood organization. The Organization for a Better Austin, which achieved great notoriety in the city for deploying noisy and obnoxious tactics against its opponents, twice elected women as president. Women's activism in Austin was not confined to those working for an interracial neighborhood, however. Eileen McCaffrey, a North Austin resident, was a vice president of the Town Hall Assembly. Although the president of the group was always a man, McCaffrey was consistently the most visible spokesperson for the organization.

Like their neighbors who desired racially homogeneous neighborhoods, Austin's racial moderates used a combination of private pressure tactics and manipulation of public policy to try to slow the arrival of African Americans and stem the departure of whites. Because the 1968 federal Fair Housing Act effectively ended the broad debate over whether Austinites had the legal right to exclude African Americans altogether, these activists focused primarily on curbing the practices that enabled blockbusters to work in Austin. They developed more systematic efforts to shut down the operations of successful panic peddlers, encouraged their neighbors to sign up for a new statewide anti-solicitation registry, and agitated to ban "For Sale" signs in Chicago. In the early 1970s, they turned to the Federal Housing Administration in an effort to stop the federal government from helping African Americans to purchase Austin homes that were riddled with code violations. These groups, although dedicated and inventive, proved no more successful than their anti-black rivals at breaking the block-by-block pattern of racial change on the West Side. Even exemplars of the feasibility of racial cooperation could not stave off the last stage of whites' postwar urban crisis, the arrival of African Americans. White West Siders—both those involved in community groups and those who did not participate—continued to leave their homes when the edges of the ghetto reached their block.

Austin Tenants and Owners Association

The Austin Tenants and Owners Association (ATOA), active during the mid-1960s, managed simultaneously to oppose blockbusting and welcome African Americans as neighbors and members. Like other small West Side neighborhood organizations, ATOA bloomed suddenly into existence when the first African American moved onto the 4800 block of West Monroe in 1965. In marked contrast to other such groups, however, ATOA intentionally embraced two overlapping categories of people usually excluded from membership in white-run community organizations: blacks and renters. ATOA was short-lived and operated on a small scale, with only a couple hundred members, but the group's activities demonstrated that some white Austin residents in the 1960s were receptive to finding alternatives to wholesale segregation.[6]

The seed for ATOA rested in Joseph and Marcella Kane's move to the 5000 block of Washington Street in 1954. Activities on the block suggested that it contained a nucleus of whites with relatively liberal attitudes regarding race relations. In March 1959 residents formed a block club. The club worked so well that other groups in surrounding blocks of Austin turned to it for help in organizing their own clubs. Renamed the Neighborhood Conservation Council (NCC), the club was active in encouraging local upkeep for several years. NCC members distinguished themselves from other Chicago neighborhood groups with the explanation they gave for the sources of neighborhood decline. As the early chapters of this book argue, white groups in Chicago often assumed that the presence of African Americans inevitably spurred local physical decline. In a remarkable reversal of this common perception, NCC argued that deterioration and neglect *preceded* African American in-migration, concluding that "a 'Changing Neighborhood' is the result, not the cause, of deterioration."[7]

Marcella Kane was an energetic neighborhood citizen, described by the *Garfieldian* as "a pert red-headed Irish lass whose appearance belies her years and eight children." Kane rejected the assumption that community organizing should be left to professionals. She was involved as an amateur in almost every major community group active in southeast Austin during the 1960s: the United Property Group, the Austin Community Organization, and the Organization for a Better Austin. Kane's enthusiasm for participating in community organizations did not reflect a strong ideological commitment to the tenets of those groups, but a belief in the value of an organized community in itself.[8]

During 1965 Kane garnered kudos for organizing under the auspices of the Austin Community Organization. Pragmatically acknowledging that

PORTION OF THE PERSONS who attended an Austin Tenants and Owners Association meeting of officers, board members and committee chairmen Friday night are shown after the meeting. In the front row from left are the Rev. Dean Overholser, Jesse Madison, Mrs. Catherine Hoder and Margaret Woolsey of the Mandell Project. In the middle row are Shiloh Gardner, George Zelek, ATOA treasurer, Mike Turano, secretary, Mrs. Marcella Kane, chairman, Mrs. John Cincotta of the May school PTA, and Mrs. Mike Turano. In the back row are Leroy Harkins, Ed Grovas, Fred Ruiz, Al Austin, ATOA co-chairman, an the Rev. Arthur Johnson of Austin Westminster Presbyterian church.

Fig. 19. Both whites and African Americans attended meetings of the Austin Tenants and Owners Association. Participants in this meeting included Gale Cincotta (*second from right, standing row*), Marcella Kane (*third from right, standing row*), and Jesse Madison (*second from left, seated*), who became president of ATOA after Kane's resignation. *Austinite*, December 14, 1966. Courtesy of the Special Collections and Preservation Division, Chicago Public Library.

homeowners' "main concern is in their own immediate area," Kane organized more than a dozen block clubs in southeast Austin. Block clubs, she argued, were critical to "stabilizing a community." Although she was deeply concerned about the practice and profits of real estate speculation, racial change in and of itself did not appear to disturb her. Kane welcomed the participation of her new African American neighbors in the block clubs she organized, noting that black residents on the 4700 block of Jackson quickly "demonstrated they have pride in their new neighborhood and want to help in making it one of the most eye appealing blocks in Austin."[9]

Kane's amateur organizing work took a new turn in October 1965, when Manny Flowers became the first African American to move onto the 4800 block of Monroe. Kane's block clubs learned of the presence of blockbusters in their area when residents began receiving repeated phone calls soliciting their homes.[10] In contrast to some other African Americans who moved to the West Side, Flowers was not harassed by his new neighbors. Instead, just two weeks after his arrival, he learned that they were willing to help him.

Flowers deserved sympathy. He believed that he had purchased the home at 4853 Monroe from Time Realty Company with a $400 down payment toward a contract sale totaling $24,500. Shortly after delivering Time Realty $400, Flowers received a notice that the Niles Savings and Loan Association was filing a foreclosure suit on the building. The notice treated him as a renter who could be easily evicted rather than a homeowner who had a financial investment in the property. Time Realty's representatives concurred with Niles Savings and Loan Association, explaining that Flowers had rented the home for $400 and was mistaken to think that he was a contract buyer. Convinced that he had been cheated, Flowers filed a complaint with the Chicago Commission on Human Relations. CCHR staff ultimately found "no evidence that Flowers ever had any agreement to purchase the building."[11]

Although Flowers's complaint did not represent a classic case of blockbusting, his new neighbors understood his plight within that framework. But instead of expressing outrage that blacks had entered the area, residents condemned the exploitation of Flowers. Marcella Kane organized a community meeting to give him an opportunity to air his troubles. About 150 whites and blacks attended and decided to host another meeting in order to question the representatives of Time Realty about the case. Participants appointed a biracial committee of residents to run the investigation. When Time Realty's representatives refused to attend a meeting scheduled for St. Thomas Aquinas Parish Hall, Kane took a group of thirty residents to their offices to ask questions about their "methods of buying and selling homes and soliciting listings in the community."[12]

Kane's interest in Time Realty quickly expanded to other local real estate firms and landlords. At a public meeting in November, before an audience of two hundred, Kane challenged Austin residents and leaders to fight panic peddling. She turned out an impressive gathering of prominent citizens, including 30th Ward alderman Edwin McMahon, the president of the West Side Real Estate Board, the president of the Austin Businessmen's Council, and Bishop Raymond Hillinger of St. Mel Holy Ghost Church. At the meeting organizers passed out a proposed code of ethics they wanted real estate operators working in Austin to sign. The code's provisions included agreements not to promote racial conflict or display "For Sale" and "Sold" signs, which might induce panic selling in the neighborhood.[13]

By December this temporary real estate practices committee organized formally, selecting a name, locating office space, and identifying goals, all in short order. All three reflected ATOA's effort to straddle racial dividing lines in Austin. A local attorney donated office space in a storefront at 29

South Cicero. The location was significant, for just at this time Cicero Avenue, the 4800 block west, "gained a reputation as a dangerous, vice-ridden street. . . . It was the first and one of the most sharply perceived of the series of racial dividing lines that rose and fell in Austin." Additionally, ATOA's inclusion of renters in its mission was unusual. ATOA's members thought that property owners and renters should make common cause against the landlords and real estate agents whose practices undermined neighborhood peace. Where UPG assumed that black people bore responsibility for disrupting neighborhoods they moved into, ATOA argued that irresponsible property managers were the main problem.[14]

ATOA also made racial tolerance an explicit aim. The group's goals included the injunction, "To pray that the people of Austin, under God, accept any person without regard to race, color or creed so that this community will grow with respect and dignity for every person." This statement made ATOA one of only a few intentionally interracial neighborhood organizations on the postwar West Side. Combining its concerns about racial tolerance and tenant exploitation, ATOA activity had two major thrusts. First, they proposed to stop blockbusters from taking advantage of black home buyers and white home sellers. Their second goal was to persuade owners of neglected properties to improve them in accordance with the terms of the city's housing code.[15]

ATOA's primary approach to blockbusting was to discourage transient real estate brokers from operating in Austin. Kane insisted that she was not interested in making established local real estate dealers a "whipping boy." Instead, she was simply identifying honest and ethical dealers. ATOA intended to post for public inspection the names of those who signed their proposed ethics code, so that Austin residents could know with whom they should do business. The effort to secure agreement with the proposed code was unsuccessful. ATOA twice sent representatives to five Realtors' offices around Cicero and Madison to press them to sign. The West Side Real Estate Board, however, instructed its members not to sign codes from "competing" organizations.[16]

Kane's organization also tried to push unethical brokers out of Austin. The group worked with attorneys and a few other civic groups to lobby for a city ordinance banning telephone and door-to-door real estate solicitations. Kane hoped that ATOA could serve as a clearinghouse for information, as the United Property Group did. She asked property owners who received unwanted solicitations from real estate dealers to notify ATOA. Upon receiving concrete information about solicitors using pressure tactics, ATOA planned to notify the city agencies authorized to investigate: the Chicago Commission on Human Relations and the license court.[17]

ATOA soon broadened the scope of its activities. The ATOA offices at 29 South Cicero served as a gathering place for block club meetings. The group sent a delegation of residents to Spencer School to talk to the principal about encouraging courteous behavior in children traveling to and from school. ATOA's leaders also supported the May School PTA's efforts to improve the school in order to attract African American as well as white parents. ATOA founded a youth club "to keep youngsters aware of their responsibilities to the community" and hosted an outlet of the city's Project Champ program for young people in the summer of 1966. The organization also ran a beautification project under the auspices of the local Urban Progress Center, an arm of the federal War on Poverty. The leadership hoped that demonstrating their abilities with these last two projects would give them an opportunity to run a Neighborhood Youth Corps program as well.[18]

ATOA's initial spurt of activity depended on Marcella Kane's extraordinary energies. But late in 1966, her enthusiasm began to wane. In October she questioned whether the organization had stretched itself too thinly and strayed too far from the original focus on blockbusting. Kane suggested that ATOA return to its roots in fighting panic peddlers and "that she needed a rest." Kane's disengagement, however, did not leave Austin without liberal activists. Both the Austin Community Organization and its successor, the Organization for a Better Austin, drew from ATOA's constituency, staff, and logistical support. ATOA continued to exist for several more years without Kane's leadership, but these two new organizations dominated the struggle to forge a biracial community in Austin.[19]

Austin Community Organization

The Austin Community Organization (ACO) arose directly out of the opposition of religious professionals to the purposes of the United Property Group. Over the course of several years, Protestant, Catholic, and Jewish clergy discussed their role in helping the Austin community address its future. In late 1963, as African Americans began to enter Austin, two of the city's religious leaders sought to ensure that their arrival was more peaceful than in other communities. Monsignor John Egan, of the Chicago Archdiocese's Office of Urban Affairs and a resident of Austin, and Kris Ronnow, of the Church Federation of Greater Chicago, decided to create a new organization to "supplant" UPG. Egan was a true interracialist, pushing for liberalism in race relations with an enthusiasm not all of his colleagues found palatable. With considerable attention to local personalities and temperaments, in early 1964 Egan and Ronnow spurred Austin area clergy to commit to sponsoring a new community organization. An inter-

faith clergy group recruited laypeople to join a temporary steering committee, identified a broad range of community concerns, and began seeking male staff and leadership for the new institution.[20]

These participants created ACO (initially named Austin Good Neighbors),
which immediately became UPG's primary rival in Austin. About a dozen
representatives of UPG attended ACO's initial organizing meeting and tried
to interject the in-migration of African Americans into the discussion. UPG
recognized that a major purpose of ACO was to undermine its own (increasingly tenuous) popular base. The antagonists spurned a reconciliation effort
by Austin business groups and frequently squabbled in the local press about
who better represented community interests. But by the time UPG disbanded in the fall of 1965, ACO had alienated so many of its potential followers that it was in no position to benefit from its rival's demise.[21]

From the start, ACO had trouble establishing its legitimacy in the community, winning the approbation of its clerical financial backers, and communicating a coherent program to the public. ACO's difficulties in winning
support had numerous interrelated sources. ACO members evinced a brash
style in public, pointedly challenging those with whom they disagreed,
sometimes to the point of rudeness. For example, participants in an ACO
rally protesting the planned Crosstown Expressway roundly booed and
heckled their opponents, including three city aldermen in attendance. ACO's
decision to hire an executive director who lived outside the neighborhood
also drew criticism. Beyond these objections, ACO aroused further suspi-
cion in Austin by refusing to stake out strong positions on key local issues.
In his first public appearance on behalf of ACO, William Kruse, the executive director, denied that ACO held any position on residential integration.
Kruse clarified, "The people who make up ACO will determine the policy to
be followed." While ACO refused at first to state an official position on integration, the organization aroused the skepticism of residents who suspected
that "they'd be in seventh heaven if every block in Austin went black." Rather
than wait for ACO to declare a position, other Austin residents and suspicious clergy assumed that ACO supported integration.[22]

Despite the hostility ACO faced throughout its brief existence and the
energy the leaders devoted to coping with their opponents, the group's
various committees ran a vigorous program. ACO frequently offered workshops and community forums on a broad range of topics. For example,
in May 1965 ACO sponsored a workshop on "Rearing Children of Good
Will," a well-attended event that led to the formation of the Austin Women
for Community Good Will, a separate organization for mothers devoted
to interracial cooperation. ACO fronted more than a dozen standing committees attentive to such subjects as Austin's representation in the city

council, community relations, education, home finance, code violations, city planning, senior citizens, and youths. And as one of its first activities—to provide itself with a policy agenda—ACO undertook a survey of thousands of Austin residents to determine their views on the local quality of life and their primary concerns.[23]

The survey found that the next several years were crucial to Austin's future. Of the survey's early respondents living in southeast Austin, 40 percent were considering moving within the next three years because of anticipated racial change. Moreover, few of these respondents were willing to live near African Americans; in southeast Austin 84 percent indicated that integration was undesirable. While these survey results were not scientifically valid, they were consistent with other formal studies that documented Austinites' unwillingness to share their turf.[24]

While ACO remained officially undecided on integration, the group was, in fact, in the process of investigating whether to endorse open occupancy legislation, which would prohibit racial discrimination in housing. Lorraine Greenhouse, a steering committee member who unsuccessfully prodded an infant ACO to send a delegation to the 1964 Illinois Civil Rights rally, proposed in June 1965 that the organization support open occupancy legislation "as a means of stabilizing our community." Most of the steering committee members expressed reluctance to endorse the proposition immediately. In keeping with ACO's policy of determining local opinion before taking a position, the steering committee voted to hold a series of community forums on the question. Committee chair David Kissane explained, "Whether the Austin community will or will not include Negro residents is no longer a valid question. The big question is *how*: one family at a time, or a whole block at a time." The phrase "a whole block at a time" implied the wholesale departure of whites, while "one family at a time" suggested a less traumatic process of neighborhood change. A flyer announcing the forums put the choice more baldly: "Integration or Inundation?"[25]

About fifteen hundred people attended a total of five community forums to hear speakers discuss racial change and open occupancy in Austin and Chicago. At each event, attendees voted in an advisory poll; results showed that participants opposed open occupancy 325 to 229. Despite this apparent rejection of open occupancy, the steering committee concluded, "This small vote may indicate a [c]hanging climate of opinion in the community and that many people are undecided and looking for leadership." Members voted to recommend "that ACO support the principle of Open Occupancy legislation as a means of stabilizing our community." Kissane told the *Chicago Defender*, "We feel open occupancy is the only PRACTICAL means of stabilizing the community. By opening housing to Negroes all over, open occupancy would relieve pressure on the 'fringe' areas, and prevent the present block-by-block change and the blight that usually follows it."[26]

While ACO was innovative in pushing Austin residents to accept the possibility of having some black neighbors scattered in their midst, the group also pursued anti-blockbusting activities familiar from UPG's precedent. For example, on the heels of the open occupancy forums, ACO sought to discover the extent of blockbusting in Austin. In November 1965 a group of fifty-five volunteers conducted a house-to-house survey in southeast Austin to quantify the amount of ongoing real estate solicitation. The findings, unsurprisingly, revealed little solicitation in areas already occupied by African Americans, but much occurring in adjacent blocks. Eight of the twelve firms operating in the area were based outside of Austin. Shortly after the survey, ACO aided a few residents in filing three complaints of panic peddling against real estate dealers in Austin.[27] ACO's activities in the realm of housing were not as vigorous as they might have been, given the wealth of programming the organization offered in other arenas. This shortfall might have been due to the ambiguity of the group's thinking on race and housing; or perhaps ACO's continuous trouble securing financing and staff accounted for its failure to take decisive action on housing.

ACO's difficulty in winning the wholehearted support of Austin residents extended to the clergy members who initially agreed to support the new organization financially. Sponsored by Monsignor Egan, ACO's first executive director was William Kruse, a former executive director of the Uptown Chicago Commission and Peace Corps administrator. Kruse's personal style rankled some in Austin, especially the local press. The *Garfieldian* wrote that ACO "never really recovered from the reputation he left with it as the result of his tactics." Kruse submitted his resignation from ACO after less than a year on the job. ACO's clergy committee asked him to reconsider, but Kruse refused, insisting that his resignation was "not conditional." Kruse's successor, Bernard Lyons, a steering committee member who usually worked in public relations, served as an interim executive director for only three months, quitting before a permanent successor was hired. Both Kruse and Lyons blamed their departures on the clergy's failure to support the organization. Kruse wrote, "The clergy act as if once the A.C.O. has an office and a professional staff their job is done except to write a check once in a while." Lyons, "intemperately and imprudently," made more direct accusations against the clergy in his resignation letter. He charged the clergy with failing to live up to their "financial and moral commitment" to ACO, reneging on pledges, and even concealing their involvement with ACO from their congregations.[28]

The dissent among Austin's clergy and parishioners about the future of ACO reflected the deep and contentious divides among American Catholics about race and the civil rights movement in the period around the Second Vatican Council.[29] Some of the clergy whom Monsignor Egan recruited were indeed unwilling to continue supporting ACO with their churches' money or their personal authority. In January 1966 Chicago's new arch-bishop, John Cardinal Cody, transferred Egan, a vital behind-the-scenes motivator for ACO, from his residence in Austin to a parish in Lawndale. Austin's remaining priests, interpreting his transfer as tacit permission from the archdiocese to distance themselves from Egan's program, took the opportunity to withdraw their support from a group that aroused much controversy in their parishes. With its bank accounts empty (because of out-standing pledges of $20,000 from local churches), ACO nearly disbanded. David Kissane, ACO's chairman, arrived at a January 20 meeting with a draft resolution to dissolve the organization. He left, instead, with pledges from the Austin Clergy Council and the seven local Roman Catholic parishes that they would provide for ACO's finances.[30]

By the spring, however, Austin's Catholic clergy understood that the new archbishop would permit ACO's dissolution. The priests who had reluc-tantly continued to fund ACO decided—without consulting their Protestant and Jewish colleagues—to withdraw from the group, create a new organi-zation for Austin, and hire Saul Alinsky's student Thomas J. Gaudette as executive director. The non-Catholic clergy in the Austin group, and some of the laypeople committed to working with ACO, objected vociferously to this unilateral decision. In June, after two weeks of delicate and compli-cated negotiations, Austin's Protestant clergy agreed to cooperate with their Catholic colleagues in building a new community organization. ACO's lay leadership tried to continue operations without financing from the churches. Following a resolution to remain in business, they continued at least through 1967 to promote the causes they held dear. Showing them-selves to be "interracialists"—as ACO's opponents suspected—these activists worked openly to assist African Americans in the area and aligned themselves with the efforts of the civil rights movement in Chicago. But without the financial support of Austin's churches, they could not maintain the organization.[31]

Organization for a Better Austin

The new organization, initially designated the "Committee for a Better Austin," enjoyed greater success and attention—but no less controversy—than its predecessor. In obedience to Saul Alinsky's famous edict to "rub raw the resentments," the Organization for a Better Austin (OBA) employed aggressive tactics without concern for their alienating effects. Like ACO, OBA pursued a broad range of policy goals, including trying to keep whites living in Austin alongside African Americans. Toward this end, OBA members harassed real estate dealers, removed "For Sale" signs from neighborhood lawns and fences, and offered advice to whites and blacks about where they should live in Austin. From time to time, OBA representatives professed indifference about their reputation—including whether the label "racist" applied to the group. OBA's combative style and willingness to share Austin with blacks vexed some residents who had retreated to the neighborhood from other parts of Chicago. One such group in 1967 formed the Town Hall Assembly (THA), whose positions echoed the United Property Group's and who frequently clashed with OBA. Almost uniquely among white West Side community organizations, OBA remained in existence well after most of Austin's residents were African Americans. For most of its history, in fact, OBA operated with a combination of black and white officers.[32]

Thomas Gaudette, a professional organizer with substantial experience elsewhere in Chicago, began meeting with Austin residents in July 1966. His efforts concentrated on the southeastern section of Austin, just beginning to see black residents, "because of a consensus that this area was most lacking in leadership and cohesiveness." With $11,000 in start-up money provided by six of the seven pledging Catholic churches, Gaudette hired staff, opened offices, and began holding meetings and organizing residents by the fall. In June 1967 OBA held its founding Congress, the first of the annual meetings that drew hundreds of members to decide the organization's policy agenda.[33]

As its first president, OBA elected Justin McCarthy, a vice president of the Austin Tenants and Owners Association, who was nominated for the position by the Austin Women for Community Good Will. Two years later, in 1969, delegates chose Gale Cincotta, whom they passed over in the 1967 election, as their first female president. Cincotta described her involvement with OBA as "a natural move forward" from her activism with the May School PTA and United Committee. After she left OBA's presidency in 1971, she launched a career in community activism that brought her national attention. Cincotta later became a leader of both the National Training and Information Center (NTIC) and National People's Action, which helped pass the National Neighborhood Policy Act of 1977. At NTIC she led the charge for the federal Community Reinvestment Act, which outlawed the redlining practices of banks that denied blacks mortgages and contributed to the enormous profits of blockbusters across urban America.[34]

Fig. 20. The storefront offices of the Organization for a Better Austin. Courtesy of Thomas A. Gaudette Papers (CSLA-18), Department of Archives and Special Collections, Charles Von der Ahe Library, Loyola Marymount University.

OBA's constitution structured the group as an organization of organizations. OBA's senate met monthly and member groups sent delegations proportionate to their size to the annual congresses. These policy-making bodies, however, did not represent the center of OBA's activism. Paid staff and community-organizing trainees were responsible for OBA's day-to-day administration. Issue-focused committees, populated by OBA's officers and energetic volunteers, carried out the activities that made OBA notorious in Chicago. As William Kruse had insisted that ACO's focus depended on community opinion, so, too, did Tom Gaudette explain that OBA's activities would be up to participants. OBA ran committees on housing code compliance, real estate practices, schools, security, youths, zoning, and other topics.[35] OBA's exploits around housing issues, specifically those connected

Fig. 21. Gale Cincotta addresses a meeting. Courtesy of Thomas A. Gaudette Papers (CSLA-18), Department of Archives and Special Collections, Charles Von der Ahe Library, Loyola Marymount University.

to real estate practices like blockbusting, garnered the organization much attention within and beyond the Austin community.

OBA's most noticeable protests demonstrated the depths of their vilification of blockbusting real estate dealers. Like ATOA, OBA members sought to induce real estate dealers to sign agreements that they would not solicit property owners on various blocks to list their homes for sale. If the brokers refused to cooperate, OBA did not hesitate to use tactics as disagreeable as the ones they criticized from blockbusters. OBA invited real estate dealers to meetings where they barraged them with questions about their practices and demands that they sign an agreement to desist. By April 1968 OBA's real estate practices committee claimed to have obtained nonsolicitation agreements from six "realtors" and driven "three panic peddlers" out of the area. In May the committee obtained a verbal agreement from another real estate dealer. An April 1970 meeting attended by representatives of ten different firms operating in Austin yielded signatures on four nonsolicitation agreements. One real estate dealer who felt that he was tricked into attending an OBA senate meeting under false pretenses complained that the members had yelled at and confused him. Protesting that he was tried in a "kangaroo court," he eventually signed the agreement pressed upon him.[36] More often than not, however, real estate dealers were unwilling to abide by any terms dictated by OBA.

OBA was not an organization that docilely accepted rejection. Following Saul Alinsky's precepts, OBA embarrassed and humiliated real estate dealers into ceasing their solicitation practices. For example, when the owner of Superior Realty amended the template of a nonsolicitation agreement before signing, OBA volunteers picketed outside his office. If neither the threat nor the picketing of the office yielded results, OBA took their admonitions to their targets' homes and neighbors. Throughout June 1971 OBA picketers traveled to the neighboring village of Oak Park to confront a father-and-son team of real estate dealers whom they accused of blockbusting in Austin. Before the father consented to talk with them, picketers passed out pamphlets to his neighbors detailing their allegations against him. In a similar action, OBA activists leafleted in Westchester, Illinois, urging Jerome Keefe's neighbors to call and visit him to protest the results of his real estate dealings in Austin. Keefe turned to the Illinois courts in search of an injunction to stop OBA from invading his privacy. He briefly won the injunction, but in May 1971 the U.S. Supreme Court ruled that Keefe had "not met the heavy burden of justifying the imposition of the prior restraint of petitioners' peaceful distribution of informational literature of the nature."[37]

The Keefe case was not the only anti-blockbusting activity in which actions of OBA members tested the limits of legality. In the late 1960s, Austin activists identified Sky Realty as an agency whose operations undermined the stability of Austin's population. In July 1969 Sky's offices were firebombed. Chicago police arrested Mary Wallace, a housewife, mother of five, and OBA vice president, on arson charges. Wallace was acquitted in May 1970, but a former OBA participant told a reporter that a different woman from the group had indeed thrown a bomb into the offices, having first "checked it out good, and there was no one living upstairs or anything." While Mary Wallace awaited her trial, OBA and several other Austin groups picketed Sky's offices and carefully watched the prosecutions of several Sky employees for violating various city and state real estate practice laws.[38]

The Organization for a Better Austin did not act alone in trying to stop solicitation and real estate speculation through direct action. OBA members also participated in several multigroup campaigns against blockbusting. While OBA was still called the Committee for a Better Austin, the nascent group cooperated with ATOA and the Tri-Parish Committee in an effort to create a "moratorium on panic peddlers" in Austin. While this effort seems to have produced only a few contentious meetings, in 1970 several groups created the West Side Coalition Against Panic Peddling, a more sustained arrangement whose practices reflected Saul Alinsky's dicta. The West

Fig. 22. An Organization for a Better Austin panel confronts a representative of Sky Realty, whose offices were firebombed. An OBA vice president was acquitted on related charges. Gale Cincotta is seated at the center of the table. Courtesy of Thomas A. Gaudette Papers (CSLA-18), Department of Archives and Special Collections, Charles Von der Ahe Library, Loyola Marymount University.

Side Coalition originated with just three member groups—OBA, the Our Lady of Angels Community Organization, and the Northwest Community Organization (another Alinsky group)—but eventually included several other church and community groups.[39]

Although many Chicagoans associated OBA with their attention-getting protest tactics, the group also offered local initiatives to control the racial composition of Austin. Rather than allow real estate dealers to determine who would live where in Austin, OBA established two programs to help potential residents locate homes. The Metropolitan Housing Committee, or "Metro office," embodied the assumption that it was necessary to intervene directly in the block-by-block pattern of ghetto expansion. If African Americans could readily find homes throughout the metropolitan region, even in all-white areas, then neighborhoods like Austin—on the "fringe" of the ghetto—would not experience the wholesale racial transformation like Lawndale and West Garfield Park. Thus, the Metro office located housing opportunities for African Americans not in Austin, but elsewhere in the Chicago region's suburbs.[40]

The Housing Referral Service complemented the Metro office. The purpose of the Housing Referral Service was "to attract, encourage, and assist whites to move to Austin." The service created publicity materials about Austin's attractions and circulated them among potential residents at hospitals, universities, and other sites. A Housing Referral Service pamphlet advertised Austin as offering "Suburban Comfort with City Conveniences" and proclaimed, "Every race, every creed, every color are represented within our neighborhood. And there's room for your family too." The office maintained a list of apartments and houses available in Austin and matched them with white people who expressed interest in moving to the neighborhood. Cumulative data on the Housing Referral Service's success in bringing whites into Austin are not available, but in 1969 the OBA annual Congress passed a resolution praising the Housing Referral Service, which had placed "over 750 families in homes and apartments in Austin and still is not able to keep up with the demand it has created."[41]

Like most of OBA's activities, both the Metro office and the Housing Referral Service engendered criticism. In 1969 an OBA member group from a northern section of Austin, where African Americans were directed to seek housing, pronounced themselves "tired of being subjected to practices of the Metro Office." They tried, but failed, to win support for an OBA resolution condemning the Housing Referral Service and directing it to "cease its activities in N. Austin and concentrate its activities in Oak Park." While the Metro office was rebuked for sending blacks to live in white neighborhoods, the Housing Referral Service was castigated for neglecting blacks' difficulties locating housing in segregated Chicago and for offering help only to whites. Father Jim Zeller, a priest active with OBA, dismissed such complaints, explaining that if they did not find a way to stabilize Austin's population, then African Americans who did try to buy homes there would end up paying exploitative prices. He said, "Call us racist, fine . . . but that doesn't even enter into the picture. This is an economic situation. If you're black and want to move into Austin, fine, too. There are 250 real estate men to move you in; you don't need us."[42]

Although OBA's aggressive public style earned it much and varied disapproval, the most consistent opposition emanated from the Town Hall Assembly, and particularly from THA's main spokesperson, Eileen McCaffrey. An OBA participant told a reporter, "T.H.A. says we only cause dissension in Austin, but if it weren't for our activism, T.H.A. wouldn't exist. They exist only to attack everything we do." In fact, THA ran a broad variety of programming for North Austin residents but also frequently clashed with OBA over who should decide Austin's future. On occasion, THA argued that OBA's anti-blockbusting protests themselves promoted fear and panic among Austin property owners. McCaffrey, a resident of Austin who pur-chased her home in 1970 after living there for fifteen years, received a "Dear Newcomer" letter from OBA welcoming her to the area and describing the group's housing services. Angered by the letter's references to local prob-lems with schools, streets, and city services, McCaffrey claimed that OBA was effectively engaged in panic peddling. She filed a complaint against OBA with CCHR and ultimately saw one charge upheld.[43] Community organizations like ATOA, ACO, and OBA did not, however, spend all their time wrangling with their neighbors.

New Legal Approaches to Managing Integration

Like their counterparts who tried to preserve the West Side's segregation, OBA, ACO, and ATOA also sought innovative ways of using the legal sys-tem to promote the racial "stabilization" of Austin. Segregationist groups working against blockbusting made a practice of helping residents who felt harassed by real estate dealers take their complaints to the Chicago Commission on Human Relations. This approach to fighting blockbusting was only sporadically effective and did little to deter determined specula-tors. As was the case with property owners who violated the housing code, real estate speculators found it relatively easy to avoid even the rare pun-ishments that city officials meted out. In response to the shortcomings of the case-by-case approach to stopping blockbusters, groups like OBA—which also opposed blockbusters—experimented in the late 1960s and early 1970s with implementing new tools. These efforts endeavored to regulate the underpinnings of housing sales rather than focusing on the tactics of real estate salespeople. Activists worked to use local, state, and federal tools to stop exploitative practices in a variety of ways.

OBA and its allied groups realized that their initial tactics rarely accom-plished more than antagonizing the real estate dealer in question. In January 1967 Austin activists expressed the opinion that the city needed to put "more teeth put into the [fair housing] statute." OBA tried to adjust the relationships among dealers, homeowners, and CCHR in order to rid their neighborhood of the most active speculators altogether. Targeting partic-ularly obnoxious blockbusters, publicly humiliating them, and encourag-ing CCHR to go after their licenses obviated the necessity of finding homeowners willing to see a complaint of blockbusting through to the end of a dissatisfying conciliation process. OBA learned to follow through with government agencies, pressuring them to revoke the licenses of such deal-ers. For example, between 1968 and 1971, OBA and other groups moni-tored the progress of complaints against the owners of Beltone Realty

Fig. 23. Austin residents picket Beltone Realty, a firm OBA accused of blockbusting. Activists also sometimes took their pickets to the homes of real estate dealers whose practices they denounced. *Austin News*, May 6, 1970. Courtesy of the Special Collections and Preservation Division, Chicago Public Library.

through several complicated quasi-judicial proceedings conducted by CCHR, the Illinois Department of Registration and Education, and the City Collector's office (which issued brokers' licenses for Chicago). At the same time, the concerned community organizations picketed outside Beltone's office. The outcome of the Beltone case revealed just how complicated and ineffective the existing measures were. The city of Chicago revoked the license of Beltone's owner twice. The second revocation was required because after the first revocation the owner simply applied for and received a new license. The state of Illinois, moreover, did not concur with the city's judgment and refused to revoke his state license, citing a lack of evidence.[44]

Because city and state administrative processes were laborious and the results ineffective, OBA also tried to amend and stretch existing legal remedies for blockbusting. In September 1970 CCHR examined several blocks on the West Side for evidence of blockbusting. After finding no evidence of panic peddling on the half-white, half-black block of 400 North Lockwood, CCHR announced that it would never again conduct such a "fruitless" study. Gale Cincotta of OBA dismissed these findings as a "whitewash." Nonetheless, just a month later, the West Side Coalition convinced CCHR to set up a special task force to investigate panic-peddling complaints in Austin. By the end of March 1971, the head of the task force announced that he was ready to bring charges against several panic peddlers working the area.[45]

Austin's activists realized that getting CCHR and the state Department of Registration and Education to revoke individual brokers' right to operate was insufficient to protect the West Side against the collective efforts of blockbusters. In 1970 the Illinois legislature passed a law, modeled on a Philadelphia ordinance, creating a statewide registry where homeowners who did not want to be solicited by real estate dealers could file notarized requests to be left alone. The state was responsible for distributing the list to real estate dealers. Under the new law, real estate brokers and salesmen who approached homeowners registered with the Illinois Commission on Human Relations (ICHR) were subject to imprisonment for up to five years. The law's sponsor was uncertain whether the registry would work but thought it might have the capacity to solve "a major problem in Chicago."[46]

Delighted with this new weapon against blockbusting, West Side groups swung into action to help property owners list their homes with the anti-solicitation registry. Groups based in North Austin, which remained largely white in the early 1970s, organized sustained campaigns of door-to-door canvassers and public meetings where they encouraged property owners to list their names on the state registry. Among the organizations promoting the use of the registry law were the Concerned Neighbors in Austin, the LaFollette Neighbors, the West Side Coalition, the North Austin Anti-Solicitation Council, and the Northwest Austin Council, as well as OBA.[47]

Despite this enthusiasm for the registry's potential, the sponsor's fears about the law's efficacy proved well founded. The new law did nothing to soothe the anxieties whites felt that prompted them to respond to block-busters in the first place, and many continued to leave the West Side. Some of the groups operating in North Austin had difficulty winning their neighbors' cooperation, for a variety of reasons. Some people who were never solicited did not consider it necessary to protect themselves by signing up for the registry. Others anticipated moving and did not want to do anything that might jeopardize their ability to sell their property in the future. A resident of St. Lucy's Parish expressed reluctance to cooperate with anything the controversial Organization for a Better Austin favored. Real estate brokers criticized the law for interfering in their ability to conduct their businesses. The owner of one firm complained that the law implied that his staff could not talk to people listed in the registry even when they sought out his services.[48]

The state also proved ineffective in administering the anti-solicitation law. An entire year passed before ICHR distributed the first booklet containing the names of people who did not wish to be solicited. Gale Cincotta criticized this slow method of publicizing registrants, suggesting that the state should instead publish an updated list in monthly newspaper advertisements. Furthermore, an assistant attorney general outlined difficulties in investigating alleged violations. Because ICHR sent the booklets out to firms, rather than individual salesmen, without requiring a certificate of

Fig. 24. Residents of St. Philomena Parish are invited to a meeting to learn about the state's new anti-solicitation registry. *Austin News*, August 5, 1970. Courtesy of the Special Collections and Preservation Division, Chicago Public Library.

receipt, the state could not prove that alleged violators knowingly ignored registered names. The Chicago director for ICHR also explained that the agency was required to administer the new law without any additional financial resources for maintaining or distributing the list. Finally, in 1972 an Illinois court found the law unconstitutional.[49]

Thwarted on the registry front, West Siders also tried to prevent real estate dealers from posting "For Sale" and "Sold" signs on local properties, a practice that they thought accelerated the process of racial change in their neighborhoods. Harvey Molotch used the concentrations of such signs as an index of racial change in the South Shore neighborhood. As early as 1961, a member of the United Property Group's board of directors urged CREB to declare the use of such signs unethical. He explained, "When a prospective buyer comes to look at the home and sees signs on five or ten other homes in the block, he gets scared and starts wondering what's wrong with the area that everyone is selling." A section of the nonsolicitation agreements that OBA demanded local real estate dealers sign committed the agent not to post "For Sale" signs. At the fifth annual OBA Congress, in May 1971, delegates debated a resolution that claimed, "Any reputable realtor can sell a home through other means of advertising and it is only the panic-peddlers who use 'FOR SALE' signs to help them make their quick money off of our Austin home buyers and sellers." An OBA member also acknowledged participating in a "housewife's commando corps" which tore "For Sale" signs from Austin lawns while startled property owners watched.[50]

Beginning in the fall of 1971, opponents of "For Sale" signs shifted their informal battle on to legal territory. The West Side Coalition Against Panic

Peddling won Mayor Richard J. Daley's support for an ordinance banning signs and other advertisements on buildings in residential neighborhoods. Proponents of the law so jammed city council committee hearings on the proposal that one advocate signed up on the opposition list just to get floor time. A few West Siders, like James Dionesotes, president of the Town Hall Assembly, expressed skepticism about whether the ordinance would work. Aldermen passed the ordinance handily in November. Early reports suggested that real estate dealers complied with the law, if only reluctantly. One broker, however, challenged the constitutionality of the law, launching a complicated multiyear battle between the Chicago City Council and the Illinois court system over whether the city could regulate real estate dealers' speech.[51]

In the spirit of building a physically pleasing neighborhood where whites would be willing to live among African Americans, the West Side Coalition spared some of its attention for the local environment. In the early 1970s, the West Side Coalition's concerns about the quality of housing African Americans purchased in Austin led the group to challenge the role of the Federal Housing Administration (FHA) in changing the racial composition of the neighborhood. Since the 1930s FHA had contributed to racial segregation in the United States by insuring loans to white property buyers and designating areas occupied by African Americans as bad risks for credit. During the 1960s, however, the agency shifted its emphasis to include aiding poorer Americans and African Americans in acquiring homes. In particular, section 235 of the federal Housing and Urban Development Act of 1968 provided a subsidy for interest on mortgages of low-income home buyers.[52] By the early 1970s, African Americans used these provisions to buy homes in the Austin area. The homes to which the FHA program gave them access, however, were often in very poor condition, filled with violations of the city's housing code.

Like their counterparts in urban areas around the country, Austin residents discovered that the section 235 program was full of administrative flaws. Critics of the program objected that "a poor person who had never before been able to buy a home became a potential home buyer; no counseling or community support was available to help him understand this new proposition." In some cities lazy and corrupt administrators ran the program. The problem, from the point of view of a subset of established white Austin residents, lay in the descriptions of properties that FHA appraisers provided. Property transactions did not automatically involve inspections of the buildings involved, but FHA did require an appraisal before the agency would insure a loan. According to the Northwest Austin Council and the West Side Coalition Against Panic Peddlers, however, those appraisals were deeply flawed. Although the inspectors visited properties, they reported only minor code violations, not major ones that were costly to remedy. Further, appraisers sent their reports only to mortgage companies, not to the purchasers. These practices left new Austin property owners with homes riddled with code violations that they could not afford to fix, and that might have dissuaded them from purchasing the property in the first place.[53]

Austin activists dealt directly with the FHA in a search for remedies to this problem and compensation for the losses associated with these purchases. The Northwest Austin Council and the West Side Coalition, in meetings with FHA officials during the autumn of 1971, demanded a moratorium on further FHA-insured loans in the area. They proposed both a two-year moratorium and an indefinite ban that would be lifted when the FHA fixed the current "abuses." John Waner, a failed Republican mayoral candidate and the new area director for the Department of Housing and Urban Development, politely declined to institute a moratorium or even to receive petitions purported to bear five thousand signatures demanding changes to the system, but he did agree to require tougher appraisals and inform purchasers of the examination's findings. This response was not satisfactory to the activists and other Austin residents, who continued to reprimand the FHA for contributing to the area's decline. In the meantime, these groups waged an active campaign with local banks and savings and loans to guarantee that there was some mortgage money available for conventional home buyers in the area.[54]

The anti-FHA campaign signaled a shift in local approaches to housing activism. Community organizers turned to the federal government as routinely as to local and state governments to solve the problems that concerned them. In January 1973 the Nixon administration acceded to the demands of anti-FHA activists from cities around the country that the section 235 program be suspended for eighteen months. In 1974 President Ford signed into law the Housing and Community Development Act, which created, among other things, the section 8 housing program and the block grant program. These new approaches to urban policy ushered in a corresponding new period of urban activism by residents continuing to seek ways of protecting American cities from physical and economic decline.[55] Gale Cincotta, whose professional career as an organizer and lobbyist extended until her death in August 2001, represented the new generation of citizens dedicated to improving urban life.

But the new activism, with its share of successes and failures, proved insufficient to stem the tide of white migration to the suburbs of Chicago and other American cities. Whites who lived in neighborhoods like West

Garfield Park and Austin resettled newly built communities throughout the metropolitan area. Magazines targeting people moving between metropolitan areas directed new Chicagoland residents to bypass the city altogether in favor of the suburbs. An exodus of commercial and industrial enterprises—and their accompanying employment opportunities—occurred simultaneously with the residential emigration from cities. These developments enabled the rise of a new form of urban space in the United States, variously called "Edge Cities" and "Technoburbs."[56] While historians have only recently begun to document and interpret life in the postwar suburbs of the United States, many residents of these places brought with them memories of their bitter recent experiences in urban America.

Reconsidering White Flight

In late April 1961, more than six hundred people attended a United Property Group rally in the parish hall of St. Thomas Aquinas Church in Austin. The high point of the evening was the performance of a short play written by neighborhood activist Marcella Kane. The skit recounted Kane's chance meeting with a former neighbor—now a suburbanite—who was returning to her old city stomping grounds in search of consumer goods unavailable near her new home. The former neighbor recited a litany of woes about life in the suburbs. Not only were suburban stores inferior to those she was accustomed to patronizing in the city, but she also had to cope with high taxes and poor transportation. The clincher for her discontent was that even in the suburbs she was faced with "the same dirty kids she thought she 'was going to get rid of when she left the city.'" Repeated throughout the skit was the refrain "I've moved to the suburbs and I'm so sorry now." The audience's warm reception of the play prompted Kane to present an encore at another community meeting the next month.[1]

The audience members listening to Kane's comparison of the merits of city and suburb were in the midst of evaluating their own ties to Chicago. Around the nation, cities like Chicago seemed to be in crisis. For white residents of Chicago's West Side, this urban crisis consisted of the local threats of environmental decay and black in-migration. In response to these problems, Kane's audience might choose from a range of options—to stay in their neighborhoods and work for their improvement; to move elsewhere within the city; or to head out to the suburbs. In the early postwar years, some white West Siders tried each of the first two options and disdained the third. As one wrote to school board member Cyrus Adams, "If I wanted to live in the suburbs that is where I would have bought my home but I chose to live here, this neighborhood and community."[2] For such people, moving to the suburbs represented a defeat, a reluctant retreat from the crisis in the city, not the achievement of a lifelong "American dream."[3]

African Americans who moved into the West Side neighborhoods that whites left in this period also encountered an urban crisis. In part, the urban crisis that whites and African Americans encountered overlapped. Blacks moving into West Side neighborhoods confronted the same physical conditions that dismayed white residents—unenforced housing codes, neglected parks, crowded schools, and decaying infrastructure. But African Americans' urban crisis also had distinctive elements. The departures of local business enterprises for suburban and overseas locations, a process that white West Siders largely ignored, left the area's new occupants with diminished employment opportunities. African Americans seeking industrial work on the West Side confronted both fewer job listings and also racial discrimination. In Detroit, as Thomas Sugrue has shown, the economic and social consequences of deindustrialization and racism manifested as destructive riots in the mid-1960s.[4]

Rioting on the West Side in the wake of the assassination of Martin Luther King in 1968 proved particularly devastating to the area's landscape. Similar riots broke out on Chicago's West Side, and many other cities around the nation, in this period. Although the riots in this period had discrete proximate causes, there is little reason to believe the underlying sources were different. The West Side riots both exacerbated long-standing urban problems and also created new ones. In the last decades of the twentieth century, the urban crisis on the West Side took on new aspects, as its infrastructure, economy, and population declined further, turning it into one of the most desolate urban landscapes in the United States.

Suburbs

The second half of the twentieth century witnessed a national transformation in the character of suburbs surrounding old industrial centers like Chicago. The classical American suburb, which embodied a broadly recognized "suburban ideal," consisted of mansions of the affluent surrounded by manicured open spaces.[5] From the nineteenth century, North American cities were also surrounded by suburbs housing working-class people, African Americans, and manufacturing districts, but such places received little publicity or scholarly attention.[6] In the years after World War II, a modern form of suburb, fostered by new tools, opened up around the country. Innovative financing techniques, subsidized by the federal government, enabled millions of white Americans to purchase property beyond city limits. Using mass-production building techniques, pioneered by the Levitt brothers in New York, New Jersey, and Pennsylvania, developers filled large tracts of land with small affordable single-family homes. Some of these places consisted of new subdivisions within existing municipalities, while other new towns were built from scratch. It was places like these where white West Siders reluctantly contemplated moving as the urban crisis undermined their attachment to Chicago proper. Their appeal increased considerably in the last decades of the twentieth century, as they also became places where a majority of residents worked and played without ever feeling called into the urban center. Scholars continue to debate which terms best describe this new kind of place—edge city, technoburb, dual metropolis, sprawl, dysurban—but whatever one chooses to call them, these new postwar suburbs were, in effect, new cities beyond the orbits of the urban centers to which they owed their origins.[7]

White West Siders considering their options in the early 1960s had little reason to look forward to life outside Chicago. Kane's skit captured several important dimensions of early postwar skepticism about the desirability of suburbs for the middle class. In contrast to elite nineteenth-century suburbs that aspired to ideals of beauty and planning, the emerging postwar suburbs were inaccessible, ill served, and expensive, but, paradoxically, not remote from undesirable urban populations. A pamphlet reprinted in the *Garfieldian* posed the dilemma by playing on the area's geography: "There is a saying: 'Go West, Young Man.' Yes, that is true BUT going west is not as easy as it sounds. Go west and pay higher rents, go west and pay more car fare or buy another car so the wife can get to the nearest shopping center about three or four miles away. Pay an inflated price for your new home. Something really worth about $5,000, you pay about $15,000." A larger national body of commentary disparaged suburbs for their promotion of conformity and tastelessness, while local newspapers made a point of publicizing the location of the few African Americans who found suburban homes.[8]

Within a few years of the skit's performance, however, changes in the metropolitan Chicago suburbs undermined the basis of Kane's critique. In the latter decades of the twentieth century, Chicago's suburbs increasingly offered new amenities that made them attractive as destinations in their own right, rather than merely as refuges from the urban crisis. The northern Illinois expressway system, built in the 1950s, provided automobile owners with easy means of moving between the city and the suburbs. The

Fig. 25. The *Garfieldian* encouraged readers to think the city superior to the suburbs. *Garfieldian*, July 15, 1964. Courtesy of the Special Collections and Preservation Division, Chicago Public Library.

Regional Transportation Authority, created in 1974, coordinated public transportation beyond Chicago's city limits. New suburban shopping malls with plenty of parking attracted car-driving consumers trying to avoid the increasing presence of African Americans in Chicago's downtown stores.[9] Significantly, however, the passage of state and federal fair housing laws did not ameliorate the racial homogeneity of Chicago's suburbs. Some black families moved to the suburbs, and a few suburbs enjoyed reputations for successful integration. As a whole, however, the Chicago region remained racially segregated throughout the twentieth century.[10]

Thus, the skepticism Marcella Kane expressed in 1961 about the suburbs seemed increasingly irrelevant in the last decades of the twentieth century. To white people with financial wherewithal, suburbs appeared increasingly desirable places to live. Suburbs and cities came to seem dichotomous, inevitably opposed alternatives, rather than complementary pieces of a single region. Changes within cities also encouraged this perception. During the 1960s riots devastated African American urban neighborhoods, often places where whites had only recently lived. An active northern civil rights campaign, which included an extended stay in Chicago by the Reverend Martin Luther King Jr., suggested that African Americans might seek housing throughout cities, instead of continuing to acquiesce in the long-standing block-by-block pattern of neighborhood change. The migration of manufacturing and white-collar jobs to suburban locations eroded the tax base of urban centers and (without adequate public transportation) made it difficult for black city dwellers to reach potential jobs. The cultural discourse about suburban ascent and urban decline became so powerful a part of American culture that people moving into the region skipped over Chicago altogether and headed directly into suburbs in their search for homes.[11] This complex of actions and ideas about postwar suburbanization is often captured in the phrase "white flight." The term conjures up a set of notions about the transfer of white urbanites from declining cities into suburban havens: seeing that African Americans were "invading" their urban turf, white city dwellers lit out for the suburbs, leaving behind them old neighborhoods about which they felt nostalgic, but in which they were no longer willing to reside.

The experiences of West Siders in the years after World War II, however, suggest that "white flight" only partially describes the process by which whites left their urban homes for suburban pastures. The word "white" reflects the shared racial sensibilities of the out-migrants. Whatever their ethnic origins, the West Siders who moved out in the 1950s and 1960s functioned in American culture as white, positioning themselves rhetorically and socially against blacks.[12] As chapter 7 shows, white West Siders had little desire to live amid African American neighbors; and when blacks started buying or renting property on their blocks, they moved out swiftly. Looked at on the cold figures of a statistical table, their departures were quick, taking less than a decade for each of the neighborhoods scrutinized in this book, and a few months for most individual blocks. But, reviewing the longer history of the West Side, the term "white flight" reduces residents' behavior to a single decision and omits the larger context in which they operated.

First, the word "flight" misleadingly implies that whites picked up and ran at the moment when African Americans appeared on the horizon of their neighborhoods. Other historians, most notably William Tuttle, Arnold Hirsch, and Thomas Sugrue, have demonstrated the fierceness with which urban whites resisted black settlement in their racially homogenous neighborhoods.[13] Sugrue has argued for the classification of neighborhoods as "defended" or "undefended," depending on whether or not whites mobbed and organized to intimidate black home buyers. White West Siders' actions reveal another dimension of the notion of "defended neighborhoods." West Siders' appeals to public policy mechanisms suggest that neighborhood defense did not consist only of the alternatives of intimidating violence or steely, hostile silence. Some white West Siders sought to keep African Americans out of the neighborhood with mobs and threats; others, rejecting violence, tried to use legal means to keep their white neighbors around while directing African Americans elsewhere in the region;[14] still others endeavored both to welcome African Americans and also encourage whites to stay.

Secondly, the phrase "white flight" is incomplete because it extracts white West Siders from the context of their other efforts to influence the shape of the postwar city. Their struggle to exclude African Americans was not the only battle that white West Siders lost in the postwar years. White West Siders engaged in a variety of efforts to shore up crumbling local infrastructure. They sought to attract projects, most notably the University of Illinois campus, to promote local economic development. Until they departed, West Siders imagined an urban future for themselves and accordingly sought to enhance their environment. Individual and institutional improvements, they hoped, would encourage their white neighbors to repair their properties and recommit to the local community. Their motives, however, were mixed. When they realized that potential projects might also deter African Americans from living in the neighborhood, they grafted that consequence onto the list of reasons for supporting a given proposal. Just as West Siders failed to persuade city officials to invest in local improvements, they also failed to dissuade African Americans from buying into their neighborhoods. When they did move out, white West Siders left a neighborhood not only filled with people near whom they did not want to reside, but they also abandoned a place that city officials systematically ignored.

Finally, the popular assumption that whites routinely left urban neighborhoods for suburban residences obscures the choices of the few who remained urbanites. Many West Siders did, of course, move to the suburbs, rejecting the city that refused to protect their perceived interests. Many Jewish residents of North Lawndale, for example, moved to Skokie, a northern suburb adjacent to the city. But others, especially those who actively sought to create an interracial West Side, remained within Chicago's boundaries. Marcella Kane and her family, for example, left Austin in 1970 but relocated to a modest middle-class neighborhood on Chicago's North Side. Gale Cincotta, who became a nationally known urban advocate, spent the rest of her life as a resident of Chicago.[15] Other West Siders probably continued the search for all-white neighborhoods elsewhere in the city, moving to newly built-up areas on the Northwest and Southwest sides. Thus, the term "white flight" suggests a much more monolithic process of urban abandonment than was actually the case for Chicago's West Side.

City

Just as whites' departures from the West Side were more variegated than is commonly understood, so, too, was the experience of neighborhood decline that followed. In popular accounts, rioting by African Americans has epitomized the urban crisis of the postwar years and become the causal explanation for the terrible state of inner-city neighborhoods in the late twentieth century.[16] Emphasizing riots and violence as the sources of neighborhood decline has intuitive appeal. In the immediate aftermath of riots on the West Side of Chicago, for example, significant elements of the local infrastructure indeed vanished. Portions of the commercial strips along Madison and Roosevelt burned to the ground. Vacant lots on residential blocks more than three decades later bear witness to the riots' long-term devastation.

But the riots were not episodes of atavism, destructive furies springing inexplicably ex nihilo.[17] The cracks on the West Side were already in evidence by the time rioting broke out in the 1960s; in fact, some of the rioting represented a response to the very problems that spurred whites' withdrawal. African Americans on the West Side inherited declining environmental conditions from their white predecessors. Sometimes they were penalized for those problems, as the housing code sweeps in North Lawndale showed. These worsening conditions constituted one major element of the urban crisis black West Siders faced. A second major factor—which white West Siders' efforts ignored altogether—was decreasing local employment opportunities. Both deindustrialization and the reluctance of local employers to hire African Americans contributed to unemployment on the black West Side. Where whites could signal their discontent with the state of the city by moving—however grudgingly—to suburbs where they might exercise better control over the environment, some African Americans—effectively restricted to ghettos—used riots to protest the circumstances to which they were confined.

The dramatic fires, looting, gunshots, and the presence of the National Guard associated with the 1960s riots threw the West Side into the spotlight. In contrast to the "era of hidden violence" of the 1950s, when white Chicagoans mobbed against the real or imagined presence of African Americans in their neighborhoods, the West Side riots and their aftermath were widely covered by the city and national press. On Chicago's West Side, four major riots in 1965, 1966, and 1968 temporarily disrupted life. Similar large-scale events did not mar the South Side, contributing to the West Side's ill repute within Chicago.[18]

1965

The first notable riot on Chicago's West Side occurred in August 1965, a day after the start of the major uprising in Los Angeles. Compared to the devastation of Watts, the riot in West Garfield Park was a small affair. The West Garfield Park riot stemmed from an accident that occurred outside the city fire department station at Wilcox and Pulaski, just a few blocks south of the Madison-Pulaski shopping district. On July 18 the civil rights group called "ACT" began picketing the fire station for its failure to employ African Americans. Police assigned to the rally were caught off guard when the demonstration's numbers swelled to a couple hundred teenagers who threw bricks and bottles at passing cars. Picketers were again present at the fire station on Thursday, August 12, when an out-of-control fire truck killed a young black woman. The picketers smashed windows at the firehouse and nearby stores.[19]

The next day West Side activists offered two kinds of responses to Thursday's events. Representatives of the AFSC Project House, perhaps mindful of the ongoing riot in Los Angeles, organized young men trained in nonviolent action into a "Peace Patrol" to keep the streets clear and escort to safety "women and children . . . [who] would only get hurt or arrested." Similarly, the West Side Federation coordinated clergy patrols of the area. On the other hand, ACT advertised a protest rally with a flyer headed "(allegedly) Drunken white fireman kills black woman!!" ACT demanded, "No more all white fire stations in all black communities. Black people must control their own community! Protect Black Women!"[20]

The flyer drew an inattentive audience to the rally. A Project House Peace Patroller, who urged people to stay around the rally site rather than spread out in the streets, observed members of the crowd with "their backs turned to the speaker. . . . [They] formed a disturbed crowd, carrying signs, milling around, tormenting police, and shouting obscenities." Small groups from the crowd scattered throughout the neighborhood, picking up debris that they used to break windows, causing an estimated $20,000 in damage. A few fires were set. Police officers made more than a hundred arrests on Friday night, and thirty people sought medical treatment. The Illinois National Guard was put on alert but not deployed to the scene.[21] Reports of similar incidents trickled in from the area through the weekend before calm returned.

In response to the August 1965 riot, a group of white and African American business and civic leaders formed a "Committee of 13" to advocate solutions to the problems that underlay the disturbance. The co-chairs of the Committee of 13 were Bruce Sagan, a white newspaper publisher who had recently purchased the *Garfieldian*, and James Walton, an African American attorney. The Committee of 13 presented Mayor Richard J. Daley with a list of requests for local improvement. Their demands reflected a broad range of concerns, including some that had engaged white West Siders in preceding years (urban renewal, recreation, education, and code enforcement) and some that continued to concern black residents over the next several decades (employment opportunities). In subsequent months the committee expanded its concerns to include the needs of youth.[22]

1966

Two separate riots occurred on the West Side in the summer of 1966, the year Martin Luther King Jr. went to Chicago to open a northern civil rights movement.[23] The first occurred along Division Street, between Damen and California, over three evenings in June 1966. After a police officer shot a young man in the largely Puerto Rican neighborhood, crowds broke windows and looted shops. The events on Division Street were far enough removed from the concerns of its audience in West Garfield Park and Austin that the *Garfieldian* did not report their occurrence, except in passing a month later.[24]

The second riot took place over several days in mid-July and proved more severe, covering a much larger swath of territory than the previous riots. The riot started on Tuesday, July 12, at the intersection of Roosevelt and Throop, on the Near West Side, when police turned off fire hydrants that black youth were using to keep cool in the oppressive summer heat. The ensuing altercation over whether to restart the flow of water attracted the attention of a crowd, whose members fought with the police officers on the scene. As rioters began breaking windows and attacking drivers in passing cars, local organizations mobilized to quell the outbreak. Among those who converged on the scene were Martin Luther King Jr. and Southern Christian Leadership Conference staff members. Over the next several evenings, AFSC again organized Peace Patrols; the staff of Neighbors at Work, a community service group run from Marillac House, dispatched a crisis control team to urge West Side residents to stay inside; and the West Side Organization held a mass meeting where King appealed for peace. Despite these efforts, rioting continued throughout the week, expanding from the Near West Side into East and West Garfield Park and North Lawndale. Looting and arson damaged more than $2 million worth of property. By the time the National Guard—deployed to the streets this time—restored order, two people were dead.[25]

As the summer of 1967 approached, observers girded for another outbreak of rioting, which was threatening to become an annual national phenomenon. Sister Mary William, the director of Marillac House, feared that "the Westside pulsebeat registers a decidedly greater proviolent feeling than last year." Nonetheless, only minor riots broke out in Chicago in 1967, accounting for the city's relatively low profile in the March 1968 Kerner Commission Report on Civil Disorders. Explanations for the local calm varied: the police department kept tabs on people it believed incited riots; the Chicago Commission on Human Relations cooperated with West Side agencies in areas where it anticipated trouble; the *Chicago's American* newspaper credited individual leaders; and Sister Mary William, declining a CCHR award offered to Marillac House, argued, "The PEOPLE are the ones who kept the Summer calm. . . . The kids were smart enough to know that the goodies were coming; that the police were ready; and that the people in Detroit were invaded by non-residents who didn't care if somebody else's neighborhood burned."[26]

1968

The relative calm of Chicago in 1967 was shattered there, and around the nation, in April 1968. A little over a month after the release of the Kerner Commission Report, on Thursday, April 4, Martin Luther King was assassinated in Memphis. In African American neighborhoods in cities around the country, a sizable minority of residents vented their anger with vandalism, looting, arson, and gunfire. Chicago was not spared; rioting was again concentrated on the West Side, although incidents of vandalism were also reported on the city's North and South sides.[27]

The morning after King's death, students from high schools around Chicago walked out of their classes. At the crowded majority-black Marshall High, a flyer admonished students, "Dr. Martin Luther King has been assassinated. Show your respect by staying out of school." As the students left the building, someone set fires in the bathrooms. Joined by Farragut High School students, the growing crowd marched toward Austin, in order to encourage attendance at a memorial rally in Garfield Park. Police officers turned the students back as they approached Austin High School, at which point the marchers' sporadic stone throwing escalated into window breaking and looting. When the Garfield Park rally ended in the early afternoon, participants began looting shops on Madison, and adults joined in the activity. As shops were emptied of goods, rioters set them afire. Observers noted the selectivity of looters, who targeted stores and buildings owned by whites but bypassed black-owned businesses. A riot participant later explained to an investigator that they were trying to hurt what whites "valued the most—[their] property." Fires, once set, were of course not selective and destroyed black residences alongside white businesses. A young woman's letter, written amidst the riot, described the breadth of the damage: "Right now my sister and I are watching West Madison burn down. Pulaski and Roosevelt have already gone. All we can do is sit and watch the smoke, clouds, and flames, and the troops move in."[28]

The Illinois National Guard responded to the riot on Friday, and on Saturday Governor Samuel Shapiro sent a telegram to President Lyndon B. Johnson requesting additional federal troops. The riot, particularly the demolishing fires, continued into the weekend. In contrast to the earlier riots, when activists organized patrols to keep the peace, during the 1968 riots volunteer assistance focused on providing emergency relief to displaced West Siders. This shift reflected the larger scale and greater dangers of the 1968 riot. With local stores closed through the weekend, religious activists organized to distribute material aid to affected residents. Quakers at the AFSC Project House coordinated information about shelter for people burned out of their homes; their downtown counterparts dispensed spontaneous donations of food and clothing. The women religious at Marillac House distributed bedding and small amounts of food to burned-out residents. The physical damage to the West Side totaled $14 million, while human casualties included nine dead, with forty-six civilians and ninety police officers injured.[29]

In the aftermath of the riot, Mayor Richard J. Daley made what journalist Mike Royko called "the most famous utterance of his career." A week after the riots ended, Daley explained to reporters at a press conference that he was disappointed with the restraint exercised by police officers. He told the police superintendent "very emphatically and very definitely that an order be issued by him immediately and under his signature to shoot to kill any arsonist or anyone with a Molotov cocktail in his hand in Chicago because they're potential murderers, and to issue a police order to shoot to maim or cripple anyone looting any stores in our city." Under severe public criticism for inflaming the smoldering ashes of the riot, Daley backed away from his statement. Skeptics who doubted the sincerity of Daley's retraction felt confirmed in August, when the spectacle of the Democratic Party's presidential nominating convention included nationally televised lakefront fights between Chicago police and protesters of the Vietnam War.[30]

The riots of 1968 did grievous damage to both Daley's reputation and the West Side's landscape. Many commercial enterprises destroyed in the flames never reopened. Blocks and blocks of residential property remained vacant lots—unoccupied and unkempt—into the twenty-first century. In the years following 1968, new evidences of the West Side's travail appeared. Over the next several decades, the populations of North Lawndale, East Garfield Park, and West Garfield Park halved. Black families with means moved elsewhere in the city, leaving only the poorest families behind and making the West Side the epitome of inner-city desolation. In 1986 the *Chicago Tribune* singled out North Lawndale as the "American Millstone," the living exemplar of the ills of black inner-city neighborhoods that dragged down the rest of the nation. Only Austin's population remained near its earlier levels. Black West Siders lacked the political clout of black South Siders. Even when populist Harold Washington was elected Chicago's first African American mayor in 1983, West Siders remained almost entirely outside the corridors of power. Only at the end of the twentieth century did hints of better prospects appear, as carefully nurtured tendrils of revitalization blossomed in the West Side's park system, housing stock, and local economy.[31]

But if the riots of the 1960s changed the course of the West Side's history, this transformation was not immediately apparent to its white or black residents. Perhaps surprisingly, white as well as African American West Siders appear to have treated the riots as a temporary interruption rather than a watershed in their lives. Residents got on with their lives, returning to work and school. Those who lost their homes found new shelter in the aftermath of the riot. Community groups that focused on local problems continued on as before, with little noticeable change in their agendas.

Rather than setting off a precipitous decline in the West Side's fortunes, the riots exacerbated existing problems and widened established cleavages in race relations, the local economy, and employment. In the wake of the riots, some whites hardened their hostility to African Americans. After the Madison-Pulaski riot of 1965, one of the *Garfieldian*'s readers asked, "Can we have open occupancy as long as a large section of our Negro population behaves as they did in Chicago? Would it not be more profitable if our Negro leaders would spend more time to urbanize and educate their followers to the civilized way of law and order, so they will be accepted in any neighborhood, like the Japanese, Chinese and other races?" A newcomer to the Far West Side hit a similar note in 1966 when she warned, "Homeowners must stick together to preserve what they have, through years of hard work. What happened to Division and Western will happen here. Take heed. I know."[32] Yet even these bitter comments suggest that the speakers anticipated their own continued residence within the city. The riots certainly embodied the urban crisis, but they were neither the beginning nor the end of postwar urban decline.

Instead of attributing whites' abandonment of Chicago's West Side to rioting, we should understand that the transformation of that neighborhood was part of a broader change in the postwar urban scene. Racism was a central component of West Siders' departure, but it was hardly the only factor in their decisions to leave Chicago. In the decades before they moved on, West Siders encountered local officials unresponsive to their pleas for infrastructure improvements. City officials' neglect undermined West Siders' commitment to the local neighborhood, making it psychologically easier for them to leave when blacks did move onto their blocks. This is not to say, however, that white West Siders were willing to live in an improved landscape alongside black neighbors; in urging that the campus of the University of Illinois be placed in Garfield Park, for example, West Siders assumed that the project would divert African Americans' impending arrival to other parts of Chicago. Rather, white West Siders experienced a twofold urban crisis: one rooted in the landscape's physical decline, the other in an unwelcome social transformation. The failure of Chicago officials to look out for the perceived self-interest of white West Side neighborhoods eroded their residents' relationships with the city, even before the arrival of African Americans—among whom most would not abide—broke them. Waiting beyond city limits were suburbs undergoing their own postwar transformations. When West Siders turned to them for housing, the suburbs had only limited appeal, as Marcella Kane's lament suggested. But, within a few years, the postwar suburbs offered them new enticements and enabled them to turn a blind eye to the gathering devastation of their old haunts.[33]

ACC	Austin Community Collection
ACLU	American Civil Liberties Union Illinois Division Papers
AFSC	American Friends Service Committee Archives (Philadelphia)
AFSC-UIC	American Friends Service Committee Records (Chicago)
AHS	Austin High School Collection
ANC	Austin Newspaper Collection
BNL	Bethel New Life Collection
CAP	Chicago Area Project Records
CCDBR	Chicago Committee to Defend the Bill of Rights Records
CFGC	Church Federation of Greater Chicago Collection
CHA	Cyrus Hall Adams III Papers
CHS	Chicago Historical Society
CJEG	Monsignor John J. Egan Papers
CSC	Citizens Schools Committee Records
CUL	Chicago Urban League Records
DJM	Daniel J. Mallette Papers
EA	Ely Aaron Papers
EGP	East Garfield Park Community Collection
FR	Faith Rich Papers
GLCC-CHS	Greater Lawndale Conservation Commission Records, Chicago Historical Society
GLCC-UIC	Greater Lawndale Conservation Commission Records, University of Illinois at Chicago
IAF	Saul Alinsky/Industrial Areas Foundation Records
ICHR	Illinois Commission on Human Relations Records
IJB	Ira J. Bach Papers
JMA	Jacob M. Arvey Papers
LCCC	Lawndale-Crawford Community Collection
LCHA	Papers of the Lawndale-Crawford Historical Association
LCMOC	Leadership Council for Metropolitan Open Communities Records
MBW	Mary Bolton Wirth Papers
MH	Marillac House Records
MN	Marcy-Newberry Records
MPC	Metropolitan Planning Council Records
NLCC	North Lawndale Community Collection
NWSCC	Near West Side Community Committee Records
OCD	Office of Civilian Defense Records
OSC	Off the Street Club Records
RM	Ruth Moore Papers

UA	University Archives, Chancellor's Office Records, University of Illinois at Chicago
WCMC	Welfare Council of Metropolitan Chicago Records
WGP	West Garfield Park Community Collection
WSNC	West Side Newspaper Collection

ARCHIVAL COLLECTIONS

ABRAHAM LINCOLN PRESIDENTIAL LIBRARY, SPRINGFIELD, ILLINOIS
Illinois Commission on Human Relations Records
Otto Kerner Papers
Samuel H. Shapiro Papers

AMERICAN FRIENDS SERVICE COMMITTEE ARCHIVES,
PHILADELPHIA, PENNSYLVANIA
Chicago Regional Office Files

ARCHIVES DIVISION, HESBURGH LIBRARY,
UNIVERSITY OF NOTRE DAME, INDIANA
Monsignor John J. Egan Papers

CHICAGO HISTORICAL SOCIETY, CHICAGO, ILLINOIS
Cyrus Hall Adams III Papers
Jacob M. Arvey Papers
Ira J. Bach Papers
Chicago Area Project Records
Chicago Committee to Defend the Bill of Rights Records
Church Federation of Greater Chicago Collection
Citizens Schools Committee Records
Leon Despres Papers
Greater Lawndale Conservation Commission Records
Leadership Council for Metropolitan Open Communities Records
Daniel J. Mallette Papers
Marillac House Records
Ruth Moore Papers
Welfare Council of Metropolitan Chicago Records

DEPARTMENT OF SPECIAL COLLECTIONS, REGENSTEIN LIBRARY,
UNIVERSITY OF CHICAGO
American Civil Liberties Union Illinois Division Papers
Mary Bolton Wirth Papers

SPECIAL COLLECTIONS AND PRESERVATION DIVISION,
HAROLD WASHINGTON LIBRARY CENTER, CHICAGO
Austin Community Collection
Austin High School Collection
Austin Newspaper Collection
Bethel New Life Collection
East Garfield Park Community Collection
Lawndale-Crawford Community Collection
North Lawndale Community Collection

225

Office of Civilian Defense Records
O'Quinn Family Collection
Papers of the Lawndale-Crawford Historical Association
Faith Rich Papers
West Garfield Park Community Collection
West Side Newspaper Collection

SPECIAL COLLECTIONS AND UNIVERSITY ARCHIVES, RICHARD J. DALEY LIBRARY,
UNIVERSITY OF ILLINOIS AT CHICAGO
Ely Aaron Papers
Saul Alinsky/Industrial Areas Foundation Records
American Friends Service Committee Records
Chicago Urban League Records
Greater Lawndale Conservation Commission Records
Marcy-Newberry Records
Metropolitan Planning Council Records
Near West Side Community Committee Records
Off the Street Club Records
University Archives, Chancellor's Office Records

INTRODUCTION

1. J. Frank Lindsey to editor, *Garfieldian*, March 9, 1966; "40-Year Resident" to editor, *Garfieldian*, April 27, 1966; Mrs. A. M. Kungie to editor, *Garfieldian*, May 11, 1966; Mrs. Stanley A. Plona to editor, *Garfieldian*, June 2, 1966.

2. "Homeowner" to editor, *Garfieldian*, May 18, 1966.

3. Ibid. "Homeowner's" first letter to the editor appeared in the *Garfieldian*, April 13, 1966.

4. On the first Great Migration, see Peter Gottlieb, *Making Their Own Way: Southern Blacks' Migration to Pittsburgh, 1916–30* (Urbana: University of Illinois Press, 1987); James R. Grossman, *Land of Hope: Chicago, Black Southerners, and the Great Migration* (Chicago: University of Chicago Press, 1989); Kenneth L. Kusmer, *A Ghetto Takes Shape: Black Cleveland, 1870–1930* (Urbana: University of Illinois Press, 1976); Earl Lewis, *In Their Own Interests: Race, Class, and Power in Twentieth-Century Norfolk, Virginia* (Berkeley: University of California Press, 1991); Gilbert Osofsky, *Harlem: The Making of a Ghetto: Negro New York, 1890–1930*, 2nd ed. (New York: Harper & Row, 1971); Kimberley L. Phillips, *AlabamaNorth: African-American Migrants, Community, and Working-Class Activism in Cleveland, 1915–45* (Urbana: University of Illinois Press, 1999); Allan H. Spear, *Black Chicago: The Making of a Negro Ghetto, 1890–1920* (Chicago: University of Chicago Press, 1967); Joe William Trotter Jr., *Black Milwaukee: The Making of an Industrial Proletariat, 1915–45* (Urbana: University of Illinois Press, 1985); and Joe William Trotter Jr., ed., *The Great Migration in Historical Perspective: New Dimensions of Race, Class, and Gender* (Bloomington: Indiana University Press, 1991). On the second Great Migration, see Nicholas Lemann, *The Promised Land: The Great Black Migration and How It Changed America* (New York: Alfred A. Knopf, 1991).

5. Chicago Tribune, *The American Millstone: An Examination of the Nation's Permanent Underclass* (Chicago: Contemporary Books, 1986). For a similar assumption, see David K. Fremon, *Chicago Politics Ward by Ward* (Bloomington: Indiana University Press, 1988), 157.

6. For example, much of the qualitative data in William Julius Wilson, *When Work Disappears: The World of the New Urban Poor* (New York: Alfred A. Knopf, 1996), is drawn from interviews with West Side residents.

7. Laura S. Washington and Curtis Lawrence, "West Side Loses in Clout City," *Chicago Reporter*, December 1990; clipping, "West Side Story: Flux, Poverty and Despair," *Chicago Sunday Sun-Times*, September 12, 1965, folder 12, box 5, Austin Community Collection, Special Collections and Preservation Division, Harold Washington Library Center, Chicago; Lawrence Otis Graham, *Our Kind of People: Inside America's Black Upper Class* (New York: Harper Perennial, 2000), 200; History of the Friendship Missionary Baptist Church, p. 13, folder 30, box 1, Bethel New Life Collection, Special Collections and Preservation Division, Harold Washington Library Center, Chicago; Lemann, *Promised Land*, 81, 83–84.

8. Gerald Gamm, *Urban Exodus: Why the Jews Left Boston and the Catholics Stayed* (Cambridge, MA: Harvard University Press, 1999); Stephen Grant Meyer, *As Long as They Don't Move Next Door: Segregation and Racial Conflict in American Neighborhoods* (Lanham, MD: Rowman & Littlefield, 2000); W. Edward Orser, *Blockbusting in Baltimore: The Edmondson Village Story* (Lexington: University Press of Kentucky, 1994), 108; Kevin M. Kruse, "White Flight: Resistance to Desegregation of Neighborhoods, Schools and Businesses in Atlanta, 1946–1966" (Ph.D. diss., Cornell University, 2000); Jon Teaford, *The Twentieth-Century*

American City, 2nd ed. (Baltimore: Johns Hopkins University Press, 1993), chaps. 5, 6. On the rhetoric of crisis, see Robert A. Beauregard, *Voices of Decline: The Postwar Fate of US Cities* (Cambridge, MA: Blackwell, 1993).

9. Orser, *Blockbusting in Baltimore*, ix; Louis Rosen, *The South Side: The Racial Transformation of an American Neighborhood* (Chicago: Ivan R. Dee, 1998), 27; Gamm, *Urban Exodus*, 16.

10. See, for example, Jennifer Halperin, "Here Comes the Neighborhood," *Illinois Issues*, January 1996, 12–13.

11. For examples of historians' recent use of the term "white flight," see Kruse, "White Flight"; Becky M. Nicolaides, *My Blue Heaven: Life and Politics in the Working-Class Suburbs of Los Angeles, 1920–1965* (Chicago: University of Chicago Press, 2002), 328; Orser, *Blockbusting in Baltimore*, ix; Joseph A. Rodriguez, *City against Suburb: The Culture Wars in an American Metropolis* (Westport, CT: Praeger, 1999), 40, 133; Mark Santow, "Saul Alinsky and the Dilemmas of Race in the Post-war City" (Ph.D. diss., University of Pennsylvania, 2000), 3; and Heather Ann Thompson, "Rethinking the Politics of White Flight in the Postwar City: Detroit, 1945–1980," *Journal of Urban History* 25 (1999): 163–98.

12. The *Oxford English Dictionary* online provides 1967 as the earliest date for the term "white flight" from an item in the *New Republic*, July 22, 1967.

13. "How Resigning ACO Administrator Views Austin, Its Problems," *Garfieldian*, August 25, 1965; Real Estate Research Corporation, "Projections of Population and School Enrollments by Community Area for the City of Chicago, 1970 and 1975," report prepared for the Board of Education, City of Chicago, April 1968, p. VI-3; Norris Vitchek as told to Alfred Balk, "Confessions of a Block-Buster," *Saturday Evening Post*, July 14–July 21, 1962, 16. The *Saturday Evening Post* article was a hoax, but there is no reason to mistrust this estimate. See chapter 6.

14. Robert O. Self, *American Babylon: Race and the Struggle for Postwar Oakland* (Princeton: Princeton University Press, 2003), makes a related but distinct argument: that urbanites did not flee the city so much as they were drawn to suburbs by particular incentives. See especially pages 16 and 96.

15. Thomas J. Sugrue, *The Origins of the Urban Crisis: Race and Inequality in Postwar Detroit* (Princeton: Princeton University Press, 1996), 234–39. Historians' conception of "defended neighborhoods" is drawn from Gerald D. Suttles, *The Social Construction of Communities* (Chicago: University of Chicago Press, 1972), chap. 2. See also Rosalyn Baxandall and Elizabeth Ewen, *Picture Windows: How the Suburbs Happened* (New York: Basic Books, 2000), 188.

16. John T. McGreevy, *Parish Boundaries: The Catholic Encounter with Race in the Twentieth-Century Urban North* (Chicago: University of Chicago Press, 1996), 102; Dominic A. Pacyga and Ellen Skerrett, *Chicago, City of Neighborhoods: Histories and Tours* (Chicago: Loyola University Press, 1986), 245–50.

17. Arnold R. Hirsch, *Making the Second Ghetto: Race and Housing in Chicago, 1940–1960* (Cambridge: Cambridge University Press, 1983), 74; "Release Partial Tab of ACO Survey," *Garfieldian*, November 4, 1964.

18. Sugrue, *Origins of the Urban Crisis*, 3. See also William Julius Wilson, *The Truly Disadvantaged: The Inner City, the Underclass, and Public Policy* (Chicago: University of Chicago Press, 1987); Joel Rast, *Remaking Chicago: The Political Origins of Urban Industrial Change* (DeKalb: Northern Illinois University Press, 1999).

19. The city government had formal evidence, as early as 1952, that industrial concerns were removing beyond city limits. See Chicago Plan Commission, *Chicago Industrial Study, Summary Report*, 1952. Officials were divided on the significance of this information. See comments of Oscar E. Hewitt in "Industry Loss Hurting City, Hewitt Warns," *Garfieldian*, September 4, 1952; and F. D. Aschman in "City Not 'Doomed' Says Plan Director," *Garfieldian*, November 27, 1952.

20. Gamm, *Urban Exodus*, 13, conceptualizes the urban crisis as "two stories: in one story

whites abandon cities, and in the other story whites refuse to relinquish their old neighborhoods." At the November 2003 meeting of the Society for American City and Regional Planning History, a panel consisting of Howard Gillette, Wendell E. Pritchett, Robert O. Self, and Heather Ann Thompson offered reflections on "Rethinking the Urban Crisis: New Visions for the City in the 1960s and Beyond." Pritchett in particular challenged the utility of the term "urban crisis."

21. Robert A. Slayton, *Back of the Yards: The Making of a Local Democracy* (Chicago: University of Chicago Press, 1986); John Hall Fish, *Black Power/White Control: The Struggle of The Woodlawn Organization in Chicago* (Princeton: Princeton University Press, 1973); Sanford D. Horwitt, *Let Them Call Me Rebel: Saul Alinsky—His Life and Legacy* (New York: Alfred A. Knopf, 1989). For the hostility that groups modeled after Alinsky's precepts could generate, see "Against Alinsky Community Organizations" to the editor, *Austinite*, September 8, 1971, box 10, Austin Newspaper Collection, Special Collections and Preservation Division, Harold Washington Library Center, Chicago.

22. The failure of all white West Siders to join such organizations ought not to be surprising, or be taken as prima facie evidence of the failure of organizing on the West Side. Alinsky wrote, "In the most powerful and deeply rooted People's Organizations known in this country the degree of popular participation reached a point varying between 5 and 7 per cent." Saul D. Alinsky, *Reveille for Radicals* (1946; reprint, New York: Vintage Books, 1969), 181.

23. For profiles of Cincotta, see Patrick Barry, "Gale Cincotta and Heather Booth," in *After Alinsky: Community Organizing in Illinois*, ed. Peg Knoepfle (Springfield, IL: Sangamon State University, 1990); Lynne Navin, "Gale Cincotta," in *American Community Organizations: A Historical Dictionary*, ed. Patricia Mooney Melvin (New York: Greenwood Press, 1986). Her obituary appeared in the *New York Times* on August 17, 2001. To my knowledge, no full-length scholarly study of Cincotta's life and work has yet been published.

24. Hugh Graham Davis, *The Civil Rights Era: Origins and Development of National Policy, 1960–1972* (New York: Oxford University Press, 1990), 5.

25. For a different analytic approach, see David M. P. Freund, "Making It Home: Race, Development, and the Politics of Place in Suburban Detroit, 1940–1967" (Ph.D. diss., University of Michigan, 1999), who argues that racism was inscribed into the laws that structured cities' racial geography. Jerald Podair argues that in New York City in this period, the Ocean Hill–Brownsville Crisis created the white middle class as an independent political force in New York City politics; white West Siders did not become the same kind of effective force. Jerald E. Podair, *The Strike that Changed New York: Blacks, Whites, and the Ocean Hill–Brownsville Crisis* (New Haven: Yale University Press, 2002), 132. On the failure to enforce the federal fair housing law, see Douglas S. Massey and Nancy A. Denton, *American Apartheid: Segregation and the Making of the Underclass* (Cambridge, MA: Harvard University Press, 1993), 223–29. Heather Ann Thompson, *Whose Detroit?: Politics, Labor, and Race in a Modern American City* (Ithaca: Cornell University Press, 2001), 6, makes the point that whites who left Detroit did so as "losers—not victors—of the intense war for urban control that had raged since World War II."

26. Roger Biles, *Richard J. Daley: Politics, Race, and the Governing of Chicago* (DeKalb: Northern Illinois University Press, 1995), 69–74; Adam Cohen and Elizabeth Taylor, *American Pharaoh: Mayor Richard J. Daley, His Battle for Chicago and the Nation* (Boston: Little, Brown, 2000), 12, 258; Robert G. Spinney, *City of Big Shoulders: A History of Chicago* (DeKalb: Northern Illinois University, 2000), 213; Hirsch, *Making the Second Ghetto*, 257.

27. Observers noted Daley's capacity to sit "Buddha-like," without revealing his intentions. Cohen and Taylor, *American Pharaoh*, 406. The papers of Richard J. Daley, which his family promised to the library of the University of Illinois at Chicago too late to be available for this project, hold enormous potential for clarifying Daley's underlying motives and goals.

28. Daniel H. Burnham and Edward H. Bennett, *Plan of Chicago* (Chicago: Commercial Club, 1909; reprint, New York: Da Capo Press, 1970); Cohen and Taylor, *American Pharaoh*, 216; Carl W. Condit, *Chicago, 1910–29: Building, Planning and Urban Technology* (Chicago: University of Chicago Press, 1973), 80, chap. 3. On changes in downtown redevelopment

strategies over time, see Carl Abbott, "Five Downtown Strategies: Policy Discourse and Downtown Planning since 1945," *Journal of Policy History* 5 (1993): 5–27.

29. Wendell Pritchett, *Brownsville, Brooklyn: Blacks, Jews, and the Changing Face of the Ghetto* (Chicago: University of Chicago Press, 2002).

30. Opinions about the continuing utility of the word "ghetto" in scholarly discourse vary. For some, the word is so tainted by unsympathetic popular assumptions about the cultural practices of the residents of segregated areas that it cannot be used politely. I believe, however, that the word "ghetto" continues to convey what no other word in English does: the existence of deep racial or ethnic residential segregation. Robert C. Weaver's book *The Negro Ghetto* (New York: Harcourt, Brace, 1948) borrowed the term from the experience of Jews in Europe and applied it to African Americans. Thomas Lee Philpott's *The Slum and the Ghetto: Immigrants, Blacks, and Reformers in Chicago, 1880–1930* (Belmont, CA: Wadsworth, 1991; originally published as *The Slum and the Ghetto: Neighborhood Deterioration and Middle-Class Reform, 1880–1930* [New York: Oxford University Press, 1978]), xiv, explains, "The difference between the slum and the ghetto was that poverty alone defined the slum, whereas poverty combined with racism to create the ghetto." In this book, I use the word "ghetto" in a narrow sense, to mean a portion of a city that is racially segregated, against the wishes of its inhabitants, without any implications about the cultural characteristics of life there.

31. For an extended discussion of the meaning of Hirsch's term "second ghetto," see Amanda I. Seligman, "What Is the Second Ghetto?" *Journal of Urban History* 29 (March 2003): 272–80.

32. George M. Fredrickson, *Racism: A Short History* (Princeton: Princeton University Press, 2002), 158; Gamm, *Urban Exodus*, 15; McGreevy, *Parish Boundaries*, passim.

33. See, for example, "Chinatown Gentrifies, and Evicts," *New York Times*, August 23, 2002; and "Elgin Settles Complaints of Housing Discrimination," *Chicago Tribune*, August 20, 2002.

34. On changes in the rhetoric against affirmative action, see Thomas J. Sugrue, "The Tangled Roots of Affirmative Action," *American Behavioral Scientist*, 41(April 1998): 886–97. For a concise overview of how racism changed over time in Europe and the United States, see Fredrickson, *Racism*.

35. For an exception, see the article by Gordon L. Mattson, "Property Group Organizer Gives Appraisal of Racial Problem," *Garfieldian*, October 7, 1959.

36. See Brenetta M. Howell to editor, *Garfieldian*, November 24, 1966. For the concept of "microinsults" and the related idea of "microaggression," see Alex Kotlowitz and Suzanne Alexander, "The Gulf: Tacit Code of Silence on Matters of Race Perpetuates Divisions," *Wall Street Journal*, May 28, 1992, sec. A, p. 1; Carl C. Bell, "Finding a Way through the Maze of Racism," *Emerge*, September 30, 1994; and Chester M. Pierce, "Contemporary Psychiatry: Racial Perspectives on the Past and Future," in *The Mosaic of Contemporary Psychiatry in Perspective*, ed. Anthony Kales, Chester M. Pierce, and Milton Greenblatt (New York: Springer-Verlag, 1992), 106. For historians of racism, see, for example, Winthrop D. Jordan, *White over Black: American Attitudes toward the Negro, 1550–1812* (Durham: University of North Carolina Press, 1968; reprint, New York: W. W. Norton, 1977); David R. Roediger, *The Wages of Whiteness: Race and the Making of the American Working Class* (New York: Verso, 1991); and Nancy MacLean, *Behind the Mask of Chivalry: The Making of the Second Ku Klux Klan* (New York: Oxford University Press, 1994).

CHAPTER ONE

1. "600 Jam City Council Chamber to Protest Housing Site Here," *Community Reporter*, March 1, 1950. For popular resistance to public housing, see Arnold R. Hirsch, *Making the Second Ghetto: Race and Housing in Chicago, 1940–1960* (Cambridge: Cambridge University Press, 1983), esp. chap. 7, and also his "Massive Resistance in the Urban North: Trumbull Park, Chicago, 1953–1966," *Journal of American History* 82 (September 1995): 522–50.

2. Clipping, "What to Do about the West Side?" *West Town Herald*, March 9, 1950, folder 22, Off the Street Club Records, Special Collections and University Archives, Richard J. Daley

Library, University of Illinois at Chicago (hereafter OSC); see also clipping, "The Viaducts Come," *Austinite*, May 8, 1940, folder 17, box 12, Austin Community Collection, Special Collections and Preservation Division, Harold Washington Library Center, Chicago (hereafter ACC).

3. In this study, the term "West Side" refers primarily to the three neighborhoods of North Lawndale, West Garfield Park, and Austin, which were sites of African American in-migration and white out-migration in the years after World War II. The book occasionally touches on events that occurred in East Garfield Park, which contains both family public housing and private homes. The East Garfield Park area is largely excluded, in part because this book focuses on events surrounding the changing incumbents of *private* housing, and in part because East Garfield Park residents appear to have offered little collective response to the impending urban crisis. Similarly, this book has little to say about the Near West Side, an area of rich ethnic diversity most famous as the home of Jane Addams' Hull-House and later the University of Illinois at Chicago campus. As early as the nineteenth century, the Near West Side's population included a small cluster of African Americans. See Christopher Robert Reed, "Beyond Chicago's Black Metropolis: a History of the West Side's First Century, 1837–1940," *Journal of the Illinois State Historical Society* 92 (1999): 119–49.

4. In this way, the history of the West Side of Chicago is different from that of Brownsville, New York, as examined in Wendell Pritchett, *Brownsville, Brooklyn: Blacks, Jews, and the Changing Face of the Ghetto* (Chicago: University of Chicago Press, 2002).

5. On the history of Chicago in the nineteenth century, see Donald L. Miller, *City of the Century: The Epic of Chicago and the Making of America* (New York: Simon & Schuster, 1996); Harold M. Mayer and Richard C. Wade, *Chicago: Growth of a Metropolis* (Chicago: University of Chicago Press, 1969); and Bessie Louise Pierce, *A History of Chicago*, 3 vols. (Chicago: University of Chicago Press, 1937–57).

6. Mayer and Wade, *Chicago*, 46; William Cronon, *Nature's Metropolis: Chicago and the Great West* (New York: W. W. Norton, 1991).

7. Mayer and Wade, *Chicago*, 56.

8. After most census years, the community area data have been gathered into a *Local Community Fact Book*. On the creation of the community area map, see Albert Hunter, *Symbolic Communities: The Persistence and Change of Chicago's Local Communities* (Chicago: University of Chicago Press, 1974); Sudhir Alladi Venkatesh, "Chicago's Pragmatic Planners: American Sociology and the Myth of Community," *Social Science History* 25 (2001): 275–317; and Amanda Seligman, "Community Areas," in *The Encyclopedia of Chicago*, ed. James Grossman, Ann Durkin Keating, and Jan Reiff (Chicago: University of Chicago Press, 2004). Catholic Chicagoans often used parish boundaries rather than communities areas in drawing their mental maps of the city. See John T. McGreevy, *Parish Boundaries: The Catholic Encounter with Race in the Twentieth-Century Urban North* (Chicago: University of Chicago Press, 1996); and Eileen M. McMahon, *What Parish Are You From?: A Chicago Irish Community and Race Relations* (Lexington: University Press of Kentucky, 1995).

9. Dominic A. Pacyga and Ellen Skerrett, *Chicago, City of Neighborhoods: Histories and Tours* (Chicago: Loyola University Press, 1986), 277. On the changes in suburban residents' cognitive maps of their neighborhoods as the spaces between them filled in, see Henry C. Binford, *The First Suburbs: Residential Communities on the Boston Periphery, 1815–1860* (Chicago: University of Chicago Press, 1985), 170–78.

10. Clipping, Harold M. Mayer, "North Lawndale—A Crowded City within a City," *Real Estate*, December 20, 1941, folder 18a, box 1, North Lawndale Community Collection, Special Collections and Preservation Division, Harold Washington Library Center, Chicago (hereafter NLCC). On the process by which Chicago grew through annexation in the nineteenth century, see Ann Durkin Keating, *Building Chicago: Suburban Developers and the Creation of a Divided Metropolis* (Columbus: Ohio State University Press, 1988); Chicago Fact Book Consortium, *Local Community Fact Book, Chicago Metropolitan Area, Based on the 1970 and 1980 Censuses* (Chicago: Chicago Review Press, 1984), 79 (hereafter *1980 Fact Book*); unidentified clipping,

"Our Community Once Sold at $15 An Acre," and unidentified clipping, "Westward Came Industry Founders after Fire of '71," both in scrapbook, "Newspaper publicity reports & letters, Lawndale-Crawford Historical, 1939–1948," box 5, Papers of the Lawndale-Crawford Historical Association, Special Collections and Preservation Division, Harold Washington Library Center, Chicago (hereafter LCHA).

11. Card for "Lawndale," box 3, LCHA; "Lawndale. Property for Sale in this beautiful suburb by Millard & Decker Owners of the Lawndale Sub-Division" (Chicago: Lakeside Publishing, 1875), Chicago Historical Society; card for 1874, folder 8, box 1, LCHA; Larned E. Meacham, "Lawndale—A Half Century Reminiscence," November 25, 1934, folder 41, box 2, Lawndale-Crawford Community Collection, Special Collections and Preservation Division, Harold Washington Library Center, Chicago (hereafter LCCC); unpaginated manuscript, "History of Lawndale-Crawford," folder 14, box 4, LCCC; "Churches," folder 27, box 2, LCCC; unidentified clipping, "Our Community Once Sold at $15 an Acre," scrapbook, "Newspaper publicity reports & letters, Lawndale-Crawford Historical, 1939–1948," box 5, LCHA.

12. "Abstract of Title in collection of Lawndale-Crawford Historical Society," folder 33, box 5, LCCC; card for "Crawford District," box 3, LCHA; "Peter Crawford," folder 4, box 1, West Garfield Park Community Collection, Special Collections and Preservation Division, Harold Washington Library Center, Chicago (hereafter WGP); unpaginated manuscript, "History of Lawndale-Crawford," folder 14, box 4, LCCC; unidentified clipping, "Historical Group Fetes Crawford," October 31, 1951, folder 4, box 1, WGP; *1980 Fact Book*, 80.

13. Minutes of Lawndale-Crawford Historical Association, September 30, 1937, p. 3, scrapbook, "Newspaper publicity reports & letters, Lawndale-Crawford Historical, 1939–1948," box 5, LCHA; meeting of Crawford Lawndale Historical Society, September 25, 1936, folder 1, box 1, LCHA.

14. "Lawndale, Crawford Once Separate, Grew Together," *Community Reporter*, September 27, 1950; card for "International Harvester Co.," box 3, LCHA; clipping, Harold M. Mayer, "North Lawndale—A Crowded City within a City," *Real Estate*, December 20, 1941, folder 18a, box 1, NLCC; Nomenee B. Robinson, "Lawndale, Chicago—Replanned" (MS thesis, Illinois Institute of Technology, 1961), Faith Rich Papers, Special Collections and Preservation Division, Harold Washington Library Center, Chicago; offprint, Erich Rosenthal, "This Was North Lawndale," *Jewish Social Studies*, p. 69, folder 18b, box 1, NLCC; *1980 Fact Book*, 82.

15. "History of Garfield Park Community," *Garfieldian*, June 27, 1946; Alfred D. Chandler Jr., *Strategy and Structure: Chapters in the History of the American Industrial Enterprise* (Cambridge, MA: MIT Press, 1962), 227, 233–35; Gordon L. Weil, *Sears, Roebuck, U.S.A.: The Great American Catalog Store and How It Grew* (New York: Stein and Day, 1977), 18; Mayer and Wade, *Chicago*, 231; *Sears Yesterday and Today: A Brief History of the Origins and Development of Sears, Roebuck and Co.* ([Chicago?]: Sears, Roebuck and Co., 1982); Boris Emmet and John E. Jeuck, *Catalogues and Counters: A History of Sears, Roebuck and Company* (Chicago: University of Chicago Press, 1950), 117, 126, 132, 145, 146, 341; James C. Worthy, *Shaping an American Institution: Robert E. Wood and Sears, Roebuck* (Urbana: University of Illinois Press, 1984), 29; "Sears Tower Store Marks 25th Anniversary Today," *Community Reporter*, February 1, 1950.

16. *1980 Fact Book*, 80; "Extract from an Article in the *Chicago Daily News* of April 8, 1922," p. 2, folder 17, box 5, LCCC; Irving Cutler, *The Jews of Chicago: From Shtetl to Suburb* (Urbana: University of Illinois Press, 1996), 211, 213–14; Evelyn M. Kitagawa and Karl E. Taeuber, eds., *Local Community Fact Book, Chicago Metropolitan Area, 1960* (Chicago: Chicago Community Inventory, 1963), 72–73 (hereafter *1960 Fact Book*); offprint, Erich Rosenthal, "This Was North Lawndale," *Jewish Social Studies*, p. 67, folder 18b, box 1, NLCC; "JPI Quits Center after 28 Years," *Garfieldian*, October 5, 1955.

17. Chicago Plan Commission, *Report of the Chicago Land Use Survey*, vol. 1, *Residential Chicago* (Chicago: Chicago Plan Commission, 1942), 204, and appendix, pp. 4–5, 16, 25 (here-

after *Residential Chicago*); Philip M. Hauser and Evelyn M. Kitagawa, eds., *Local Community Fact Book for Chicago, 1950* (Chicago: Chicago Community Inventory, 1953), 125 (hereafter *1950 Fact Book*); *1960 Fact Book*, 73.

18. "History of Garfield Park Community," *Garfieldian*, May 16, 1946; *1960 Fact Book*, xi; clipping, *Garfieldian*, October 18, 1934, folder 2, box 1, East Garfield Park Community Collection, Special Collections and Preservation Division, Harold Washington Library Center, Chicago (hereafter EGP); unlabeled sheet, "History of Garfield Park," folder 4, box 4, EGP; "History of Garfield Park Community," *Garfieldian*, June 20, 1946; "Historical Sketch of Ward 29," December 6, 1935, folder 11, box 3, EGP.

19. Unlabeled six-page manuscript, p. 2, folder 10, box 5, WGP; Keating, *Building Chicago*, 67 and table 18; "History of Garfield Park Community," *Garfieldian*, May 16, 1946; unidentified clipping, "55 Years of Steady Growth Reflected in Store's Anniversary Celebration," October 1, 1936, folder 12, box 2, WGP; "History of Garfield Park Community," *Garfieldian*, May 23, 1946; "Central Park," folder 9, box 5, WGP; "History of Garfield Park Community," *Garfieldian*, June 13, 1946.

20. Clipping, "Announce Plans, Lease for Goldblatt $2,250,000 Store," *Garfield News*, February 12, 1947, folder 7, box 2, WGP; West Side Historical Society, "Garfield Park Race Track," folder 8, box 1, EGP; Murphy to Field, June 8, 1931, folder 4, box 2, WGP; "History of Garfield Park Community," *Garfieldian*, June 6, 1946; John Kelley, "Forty Years of Newspaper Nights," folder 8, box 1, EGP; "History of Garfield Park Community," *Garfieldian*, June 13, 1946; "Garfield Park Race Track," June 11, 1937, folder 5, box 2, WGP; sketch and map, folder 4, box 2, WGP; "History of Garfield Park Community," *Garfieldian*, June 20, 1946; "Historical Sketch of Ward 29," p. 3, December 6, 1935, folder 11, box 3, EGP.

21. "Historical Sketch of Ward 29," p. 2, December 6, 1935, folder 11, box 3, EGP; "History of Garfield Park Community," *Garfieldian*, June 20, 1946; newsletter, *Good Neighbor News*, folder 1, box 5, WGP; *1980 Fact Book*, 70; "History of Garfield Park Community," *Garfieldian*, May 23, 1946; clipping, "St. Mel's, Largest Parish in the World," *Garfield News*, March 20, 1948, folder 6, box 4, WGP. In 1941 St. Mel's and Holy Ghost parishes, which had served German Catholics, merged. Harry C. Koenig, ed., *A History of the Parishes of the Archdiocese of Chicago* (Chicago: Archdiocese of Chicago, 1980), 629.

22. "History of Garfield Park Community," *Garfieldian*, June 13, 1946; "History of Garfield Park Community," *Garfieldian*, June 20, 1946; "History of Garfield Park Community," *Garfieldian*, June 27, 1946; typescript headed "Presented in *Garfieldian* March 16th issue, 1933, 14th anniversary of 'Garfieldian,'" folder 12, box 5, WGP; clipping, "55 Years of Steady Growth Reflected in Store's Anniversary Celebration," October 1, 1936, folder 12, box 2, WGP; unidentified clipping, "Work on Midwest Athletic Club to Be Started at Once; Monument to Citizens of Community Says Alden," October 16, 1925, folder 6, box 2, WGP; clipping, "Protest Change of Crawford Av. to Pulaski Road," *Chicago Daily News*, October 30, 1933, folder 9, box 6, WGP; clipping, "Announce Plans, Lease for Goldblatt $2,250,000 Store," *Garfield News*, February 12, 1947, folder 7, box 2, WGP; clipping, "Reader Recalls History of Lambert Tree Corner," [*Garfieldian and Austin News*], March 23, 1950, folder 11, box 5, WGP.

23. On the assembly of this coalition, see John M. Allswang, *A House for All Peoples: Ethnic Politics in Chicago, 1890–1936* (Lexington: University Press of Kentucky, 1971).

24. See Amanda Irene Seligman, "The Street Formerly Known as Crawford," *Chicago History* (Spring 2001): 36–51.

25. "'Jobless' Cars Jam Parking," *Garfieldian*, June 25, 1952; "Cheaper to Build," *Garfieldian*, July 16, 1952; "Unemployment Office to be Moved by July 1," *Garfieldian*, February 11, 1953; "Employment Paradox Invades Area," *Garfield News*, May 4, 1949, West Side Newspaper Collection, Special Collections and Preservation Division, Harold Washington Library Center, Chicago.

26. *Residential Chicago*, appendix, table I, pp. 4, 5; table II, p. 16; and table VI, p. 25; *1950 Fact Book*, 113.

27. Clipping, Robert C. Klove, "Austin—A compact residential settlement of long standing," *Real Estate*, October 11, 1941, folder 1a, box 12, ACC. On the Austin area generally, see Pacyga and Skerrett, *City of Neighborhoods*, 268–97.

28. Anne N. Danegger, "Early Austin: From Its Beginnings until the Time of Annexation to the City of Chicago, 1899" (Chicago: Austin Friends of the Library, 1944), pp. 1, 3, 10, folder 6, box 5, ACC; "Austin's Early Days," *Austinite*, March 24, 1916, folder 5, box 4, ACC; clipping, "Austin Founded in 1866 with Five Families Here," *Austinite*, December 30, 1936, folder 11, box 11, ACC; clipping, "Early Austin History," *Austinite*, December 26, 1924, folder 12, box 4, ACC; Mrs. M. M. Harrisman, "Up from Pioneers," April 27, 1907, folder 6, box 4, ACC.

29. Danegger, "Early Austin," 8, 10, 11, 15, 23–28; clipping, "Early Austin History," *Austinite*, December 26, 1924, folder 12, box 4, ACC; clipping, "Austin Founded in 1866 with Five Families Here," *Austinite*, December 30, 1936, folder 11, box 11, ACC; W. H. Baker, *Picturesque Austin* (1888), folder 1, box 13, ACC; clipping, "Austin Town Hall," *Austinite*, August 31, 1923, folder 6, box 4, ACC; "Austin's Early Days," *Austinite*, March 24, 1916, folder 5, box 4, ACC; clipping, "History of Key School," *Austinite*, March 21, 1924, folder 7, box 4, ACC.

30. *1980 Fact Book*, 66; W. H. Baker, *Picturesque Austin* (1888), folder 1, box 13, ACC; "They Traveled by 'Dummy Line,'" *Austinite*, March 20, 1946, box 6, Austin Newspaper Collection, Special Collections and Preservation Division, Harold Washington Library Center, Chicago (hereafter ANC); clipping, "Oldtimers View Relics of Early Days in Austin," *Chicago Tribune*, March 12, 1933, folder 21, box 3, ACC; Pacyga and Skerrett, *City of Neighborhoods*, 272, 285, 294–95. The Austin-Schock district was entered on the National Register of Historic Places in 1985 and hosts an annual house tour.

31. Unidentified clipping, "Old Settlers of Austin Meet in Library Here," March 8, 1933, folder 21, box 3, ACC; "History of Garfield Park Community," *Garfieldian*, June 13, 1946; "History of Garfield Park Community," *Garfieldian*, June 20, 1946; unidentified clipping, "Austin in 1890's: 'Chicago's Most Desirable Suburb,'" March 14, 1945, scrapbook, box 8, ACC; clipping, *Chicago Daily News*, January 18, 1941, "Austin" clipping file, Chicago Historical Society.

32. Pacyga and Skerrett, *City of Neighborhoods*, 275; Danegger, "Early Austin," 13. On tensions between commuters from Oak Park and Austin, see unidentified clipping, "Austin in the Seventies," folder 10, box 4, ACC; and Keating, *Building Chicago*, 95, 111.

33. "Beautiful Austin Illustrated" (Chicago: F. A. Hill, 1905), Chicago Historical Society; *1980 Fact Book*, 69. Austin was not the only neighborhood in Chicago that promoted its suburban identity long past annexation. See Barbara M. Posadas, "Suburb into Neighborhood: The Transformation of Urban Identity on Chicago's Periphery—Irving Park as a Case Study, 1870–1910," *Journal of the Illinois State Historical Society* 76 (1983): 162–76.

34. Unidentified 1926 clipping, "Population Is 140,755," folder 10, box 4, ACC; clipping, "Suburb in City, Austin Has Charm," *Austinite*, June 19, 1940, folder 11, box 11, ACC; "Austin, 'City within a City,' Is a Model Community," *Austinite*, March 20, 1946, p. 50, box 6, ANC.

35. Glorida Gumbinger, "Austin: The City within the City," September 26, 1961, folder 90-1, box, 90, Welfare Council of Metropolitan Chicago Records, Chicago Historical Society (hereafter WCMC). For an example of a nineteenth-century Austin resident who emphasized his connection to the city, see Keating, *Building Chicago*, 106.

36. On the mistaken assumption that "suburban" must mean "residential," see Richard Harris and Robert Lewis, "The Geography of North America Cities and Suburbs, 1900–1950: A New Synthesis," *Journal of Urban History* 27 (March 2001): 262–92.

37. Clipping, Robert C. Klove, "Austin—A compact residential settlement of long standing," *Real Estate*, October 11, 1941, folder 1a, box 12, ACC; Lizabeth Cohen, *Making a New Deal: Industrial Workers in Chicago, 1919–1939* (1990; reprint, Cambridge: Cambridge University Press, 1991), 31–33 and passim; *Austinite*, May 6, 1959, box 6, ANC.

38. Pacyga and Skerrett, *City of Neighborhoods*, 277. According to a survey conducted in 1967, Austin's population was 58.4 percent Roman Catholic and 32.6 percent Protestant. Richard McKinlay and Ethyl Shanas, "Austin: Civil Rights and Integration in a Chicago

Community," (Chicago: Community and Family Study Center, University of Chicago, 1968), 4; Danegger, "Early Austin," 24; on specific churches in Austin, see folders 1–30, box 2, ACC, especially Dorothy S. Watts, "Austin" [typescript on green paper], June 1962, folder 2, box 2, ACC; clipping, "N. Austin Homeowners Battling to Balance Community," *Chicago Daily News*, September 27, 1974, folder 12, box 5, ACC.

39. *Residential Chicago*, appendix, pp. 4, 16, 25.

40. Carl W. Condit, *Chicago, 1930–70: Building, Planning, and Urban Technology* (Chicago: University of Chicago Press, 1974), 236–37; "Map Aid for Highway DP's," *Garfieldian*, May 11, 1950; "Occupy Public Housing Units by End of Week," *Garfieldian*, November 23, 1950; "1,056 Families Still to Move," *Garfieldian*, November 27, 1952; "Vandals Loot Highway Homes," *Garfieldian*, October 17, 1951; clipping, "Superhighway Creates Hazard," *West Town Herald*, May 4, 1950, folder 54, OSC; "One-Minute Interviews," *Garfieldian*, December 14, 1955; Houser to Smykal, October 8, 1956, folder "Oct. 1956," box 3, Greater Lawndale Conservation Commission Records, Chicago Historical Society (hereafter GLCC-CHS).

41. Daniel H. Burnham and Edward H. Bennett, *Plan of Chicago* (Chicago: Commercial Club, 1909; reprint, New York: Da Capo Press, 1970).

42. Edward R. Kantowicz, "Carter H. Harrison II: The Politics of Balance," in *The Mayors: The Chicago Political Tradition*, rev. ed., ed. Paul M. Green and Melvin G. Holli (Carbondale: Southern Illinois University Press, 1995), 17; Paul Green, "Anton J. Cermak: The Man and His Machine," in Green and Holli, *The Mayors*, 99–110; clipping, "'Big, Little' Assemble at Nash's Wake," *Chicago Daily News*, October 8, 1943, folder 5, box 1, EGP; Roger Biles, *Big City Boss in Depression and War: Mayor Edward J. Kelly of Chicago* (DeKalb: Northern Illinois University Press, 1984), 13–15; unidentified clipping, "Arvey, No. 3 Man of Kelly Machine, Goes to Camp," folder 1, box 1, NLCC. For evidence of the use of patronage, see Jacob M. Arvey Papers, box 4, Chicago Historical Society; Glorida Gumbinger, "Austin: The City within the City," September 26, 1961, folder 90-1, WCMC.

43. *1960 Fact Book*; *1980 Fact Book*; Department of Development and Planning, City of Chicago, *Chicago Statistical Abstract, Part I: 1970 Census, Community Area Summary Tables* (July 1973) (hereafter *Chicago Statistical Abstract*).

44. Interview with Mrs. H. A. Sanders, July 2, 1986, tape T2, Bethel New Life Collection, Special Collections and Preservation Division, Harold Washington Library Center, Chicago (hereafter BNL); interview with John Huston, July 16, 1986, videotape 1, BNL; clipping, *Chicago Defender*, March 22, 1913, images box, BNL; interview with Mrs. Margery Jones, videotape 7, BNL; interview with Mrs. Mabel Chrismon, videotape 4, BNL; interview with Dora Glasco, videotape 5, BNL; Archie Brown interview with Mrs. Elizabeth Tatum, November 21, 1984, audiotape T11, BNL; interview with Rosetta Taylor Caldwell, January 29, 1985, audiotape T2, BNL; comments of Mrs. Annabelle Smith Holmes, program, "Looking Backward to Move Forward," February 9, 1985, tape T20, BNL; interview with Mrs. Lorraine Heflin, videotape 3, BNL. Cf. interview with Mrs. Margery Jones, videotape 7, BNL, who denied that Western Avenue was a boundary during the 1930s, because a Dr. Haward had an office at Campbell and Lake Street; Reed, "Beyond Chicago's Black Metropolis," 124–25.

45. St. Clair Drake and Horace R. Cayton, *Black Metropolis: A Study of Negro Life in a Northern City*, 2 vols. (New York: Harcourt, Brace, 1945; rev. and enlarged ed., New York: Harcourt, Brace & World, 1962); Chicago Commission on Race Relations, *The Negro in Chicago: A Study of Race Relations and a Race Riot* (Chicago: University of Chicago Press, 1922), 108, 111–12; James R. Grossman, *Land of Hope: Chicago, Black Southerners, and the Great Migration* (Chicago: University of Chicago Press, 1989).

46. "Two Negro Stars Return to Help," *Garfieldian*, October 13, 1965; "Good Neighbor Policy Unknown," *Austinite*, March 20, 1946; "Talking It Over," *Garfieldian*, March 25, 1964; "Early Resident, Obern Jackson, Dies at 82," *Austinite*, January 5, 1972, box 10, ANC; clipping, "Simon Jackson—93 years in Austin," *Austinite*, August 2, 1972, scrapbook, box 8, ACC.

47. Grossman, *Land of Hope*, 113–16; Frank T. Cherry, "Southern In-Migrant Negroes in North Lawndale, Chicago, 1949–59: A Study of Internal Migration and Adjustment" (Ph.D.

diss., University of Chicago, 1965), 4; "A Summary of Work of the Migration Services Department, Mayor's Committee on New Residents, January 1957–1959," March 1959, folder "Dec. 26–31, 1959," box 12, GLCC-CHS; Chicago Commission on Human Relations, "A Six Month Report of the Migration Services Department, Mayor's Committee on New Residents, January–June 1958," October 1958, folder "Oct. 20–31, 1958," box 7, GLCC-CHS; Chicago Commission on Human Relations, "A Six Month Report of the Migration Services Department, Mayor's Committee on New Residents, January–June 1959," October 1959, folder "Oct. 23–31, 1959," box 11, GLCC-CHS; Chicago Commission on Human Relations, "A Six Month Report of the Migration Services Department, Mayor's Committee on New Residents, July–December 1957," January 1958, folder "Jan. 21–31, 1958," box 5, GLCC-CHS; Chicago Commission on Human Relations, "A Six Month Report of the Migration Services Department, Mayor's Committee on New Residents, July–December 1958," April 1959, folder "April 18–30, 1959," box 10, GLCC-CHS. On the postwar African American migration to Chicago, see Nicholas Lemann, *The Promised Land: The Great Black Migration and How It Changed America* (New York: Alfred A. Knopf, 1991); E. Marvin Goodwin, *Black Migration in America from 1915 to 1960: An Uneasy Exodus* (Lewiston, NY: Edwin Mellen Press, 1991).

48. Hirsch, *Making the Second Ghetto*, 121; flyer, Greater Lawndale Association of Block Clubs and Organizations, for meeting July 23, 1957, folder "June–July 1957," box 4, GLCC-CHS; Greater Lawndale Association of Block Clubs and Organizations, flyer, "Stay Awake," folder "June–July 1957," box 4, GLCC-CHS; Audley to GLCC Board of Directors, folder "1957 Undated Items," box 5, GLCC-CHS; statement of Jeanette Lamar, September 26, 1960, folder "September 1960," box 14, GLCC-CHS; *1960 Fact Book*, 220, table III-7.

49. Tables 2–5 compiled from the *1960 Fact Book*; *Chicago Statistical Abstract, 1970*; and *1980 Fact Book*.

50. Devereux Bowly Jr., *The Poorhouse: Subsidized Housing in Chicago, 1895–1976* (Carbondale: Southern Illinois University Press, 1978), 68, 70–71, 79, 112–13, 119–21. To trace the early history of residents of Rockwell Gardens, see the Marillac House Records, Chicago Historical Society. For the history of the Chicago Housing Authority, see D. Bradford Hunt, "What Went Wrong with Public Housing in Chicago?: A History of the Chicago Housing Authority, 1933–1982" (Ph.D. diss., University of California, Berkeley, 2000).

51. "GLCC at Work for Better Schools, 1955–1959," p. 2, folder 6, Greater Lawndale Conservation Commission Records, Special Collections and University Archives, Richard J. Daley Library, University of Illinois at Chicago; Lemann, *Promised Land*, 83.

52. David A. Wallace, "Residential Concentration of Negroes in Chicago" (Ph.D. diss., Harvard University, 1953), 167; Robert C. Weaver, *The Negro Ghetto* (New York: Harcourt, Brace, 1948), 106; Otis Dudley Duncan and Beverly Duncan, *The Negro Population of Chicago: A Study of Residential Succession* (Chicago: University of Chicago Press, 1957), 29, chap. 6; Karl E. Taeuber and Alma Taeuber, *Negroes in Cities: Residential Segregation and Neighborhood Change* (Chicago: Aldine, 1965), 100.

53. Louise Año Nuevo de Kerr, "Chicano Settlements in Chicago: A Brief History," *Journal of Ethnic Studies* 2, no. 4 (1975): 22–32; Louise Año Nuevo Kerr, "Mexican Chicago: Chicano Assimilation Aborted, 1939–1954," in *The Ethnic Frontier: Essays in the History of Group Survival in Chicago and the Midwest*, ed. Melvin G. Holli and Peter d'Alroy Jones (Grand Rapids, MI: William B. Eerdmans, 1977), 293–328; Felix M. Padilla, *Latino Ethnic Consciousness: The Case of Mexican Americans and Puerto Ricans in Chicago* (Notre Dame, IN: University of Notre Dame Press, 1985), chap. 1.

54. The name Little Village emerged the 1960s, when the leaders of the 26th Street Chamber of Commerce sought to distance their neighborhood's identity from the increasingly African American population of North Lawndale: unidentified clipping, "'Little Village' Offered to Give 'Old World' Atmosphere to Area," folder 25, box 3, LCCC; Lawndale Clergymen in Christian Action, minutes, April 10, 1964, folder "Lawndale Clergymen in Christian Action," box 34, Monsignor John J. Egan papers, Archives Division, Hesburgh Library, University of Notre Dame.

55. In addition to Padilla, *Latino Ethnic Consciousness*, chap. 1, see Gina Perez, "An Upbeat West Side Story: Puerto Ricans and Postwar Racial Politics in Chicago," *Centro Journal* 13, no. 2 (2001): 47–71; *1980 Fact Book*, 61.

56. Mike Royko, *Boss: Richard J. Daley of Chicago* (New York: Signet, 1971), 130; Roger Biles, *Richard J. Daley: Politics, Race, and the Governing of Chicago* (DeKalb: Northern Illinois University Press, 1995), 79.

57. Clipping, Mike Royko, "Fight City Hall? It Is Profitable Enough Just to Call," *Chicago Daily News*, February 25, 1965, folder 47, box 2, ACC; *Austin Community Organization Newsletter* 1, no. 3, June 14, 1965, folder 47, box 2, ACC; minutes, ACO Workshops and Steering Committee meeting, February 18, 1965, folder 48, box 2, ACC; Mrs. Stanley Plona to editor, *Garfieldian*, March 17, 1965. Barbara Plona is the same person as Mrs. Stanley Plona, whose comments appear in the opening paragraphs of this book. Letter, Amanda I. Seligman to Barbara J. Plona, May 24, 2003, in possession of the author.

58. "Daley Vow to Revive 'Neighborhood Spirit,'" *Garfieldian*, December 29, 1954.

CHAPTER TWO

1. "40–50 Families Crowd into 18-Flat on S. Hamlin Ave.," *Garfieldian*, March 1, 1961; Willing Willie column, *Garfieldian*, March 22, 1961. See Grady Clay, *Close-Up: How to Read the American City* (Chicago: University of Chicago Press, 1973), 39, for a description of this technique. Cf. Roger Sanjek, *The Future of Us All: Race and Neighborhood Politics in New York City* (Ithaca: Cornell University Press, 1998), 285, for a description of illegal conversions in which building owners were too sophisticated to allow such external evidence of overcrowding.

2. Harold M. Mayer and Richard C. Wade, *Chicago: Growth of a Metropolis* (Chicago: University of Chicago Press, 1969), 448–65; Roger Biles, *Richard J. Daley: Politics, Race, and the Governing of Chicago* (DeKalb: Northern Illinois University Press, 1995), 46–53; Adam Cohen and Elizabeth Taylor, *American Pharaoh: Mayor Richard J. Daley, His Battle for Chicago and the Nation* (Boston: Little, Brown, 2000), 167–68; "Put Teeth in Cleanup Law and Enforce It," *Garfieldian*, August 17, 1955. On Mayor Kennelly's clean-up drives, see "Use a Broom; It's Healthy!" *Community Reporter*, April 21, 1948; and "Area Named 'Model Community,'" *Community Reporter*, September 5, 1951.

3. Bryan D. Jones, "Party and Bureaucracy: The Influence of Intermediary Groups on Urban Public Service Delivery," *American Political Science Review* 75 (1981): 693, found fifty-two organizations in Chicago working on housing code and conservation activities in the 1975–79 period.

4. Robert A. Beauregard, *Voices of Decline: The Postwar Fate of US Cities* (Cambridge, MA: Blackwell, 1993), chap. 7.

5. Jared N. Day, *Urban Castles: Tenement Housing and Landlord Activism in New York City, 1890–1943* (New York: Columbia University Press, 1999), 158; Roy Lubove, *The Progressives and the Slums: Tenement Reform in New York City, 1890–1917* (Pittsburgh: University of Pittsburgh Press, 1962), chap. 6; Elizabeth Blackmar, *Manhattan for Rent, 1785–1850* (Ithaca: Cornell University Press, 1989), 265; Edith Abbott, *The Tenements of Chicago, 1908–1935* (Chicago: University of Chicago Press, 1936), 72–73; Bryan D. Jones, *Governing Buildings and Building Government: A New Perspective on the Old Party* (Alabama: University of Alabama Press, 1985), 3; Hugh Graham Davis, *The Civil Rights Era: Origins and Development of National Policy, 1960–1972* (New York: Oxford University Press, 1990); Karen Sawislak, *Smoldering City: Chicagoans and the Great Fire, 1871–1874* (Chicago: University of Chicago Press, 1995), 237.

6. Jones, *Governing Buildings*, xiv, 51–53; von Hoffman to Alinsky, "Re: What the city of Chicago Does in Housing, April 8, 1958," p. 23, folder 82, Saul Alinsky/Industrial Areas Foundation Records, Special Collections and University Archives, Richard J. Daley Library, University of Illinois at Chicago (hereafter IAF); Monday, May 29, 1961, Daily Reports: Jan.–Aug. 4, 1961, box 66, Monsignor John J. Egan Papers, Archives Division, Hesburgh Library, University of Notre Dame (hereafter CJEG).

7. "Municipal Housing Codes in the Courts, Report from Action (American Council to Improve Our Neighborhoods), 1956, p. 5, folder 27, box 7, Metropolitan Planning Council

Records, accession 80-59, Special Collections and University Archives, Richard J. Daley Library, University of Illinois at Chicago (hereafter MPC). See in general Andrew J. King, "Law and Land Use in Chicago: A Prehistory of Modern Zoning" (Ph.D. diss., University of Wisconsin–Madison, 1976), esp. 182; Charles E. Rosenberg, *The Cholera Years: The United States in 1832, 1849, and 1866* (Chicago: University of Chicago Press, 1962), 191, chap. 11; Richard Harris, "Building Regulations," in *Encyclopedia of Urban America: The Cities and Suburbs*, ed. Neil Larry Shumsky (Santa Barbara, CA: ABC-CLIO, 1998), vol. 1, p. 104; and Blackmar, *Manhattan for Rent*, conclusion, esp. 254, 260, 262–64. Fires in public buildings prompted specific building code changes believed to prevent future recurrences. See, for example, Anthony P. Hatch, "Inferno at the Iroquois," *Chicago History* 32 (Fall 2003): 4–31.

8. Lubove, *The Progressives and the Slums*, 25–33, regulation quoted on 26. On the distinction between apartments and tenements, see Day, *Urban Castles*, 192. Jacob A. Riis, *How the Other Half Lives* (New York: Charles Scribner's Sons, 1890; reprint, New York: Dover, 1971).

9. Lubove, *The Progressives and the Slums*, 134–35, 140–41, 144–46, 171; Richard Harris, "The Impact of Building Controls on Residential Development in Toronto, 1900–1940," *Planning Perspectives* 6 (1991): 269–96, argues that suburban housing remained largely unregulated until after World War II.

10. Lubove, *The Progressives and the Slums*, 141; Abbott, *Tenements of Chicago*, 37–43, 45, 53, 55–56; King, "Law and Land Use," chap. 6; Jones, *Governing Buildings*, 22–24.

11. Robin L. Einhorn, *Property Rules: Political Economy in Chicago, 1833–1872* (Chicago: University of Chicago Press, 1991), 129, 235–241; Abbott, *Tenements of Chicago*, 54, 184; Homer Hoyt, *One Hundred Years of Land Values in Chicago: The Relationship of the Growth of Chicago to the Rise in Its Land Values, 1830–1933* (Chicago: University of Chicago Press, 1933), 104–7; Christine Meisner Rosen, *The Limits of Power: Great Fires and the Process of City Growth in America* (New York: Cambridge University Press, 1986), chap. 6; Sawislak, *Smoldering City*, chap. 3, esp. 159–61. Abbott's *The Tenements of Chicago*, 184–85, enumerated several exceptions that appeared after the 1880s. See also Harris, "The Impact of Building Controls," 271.

12. Abbott, *Tenements of Chicago*, 58–59, 72–73; King, "Law and Land Use," 161; Robert Hunter, *Tenement Conditions in Chicago* (Chicago: City Homes Association, 1901). As Abbott, *Tenements of Chicago*, 164, noted, the Tenement House Act was written to include "fashionable apartment building[s]" in its purview. For changes in the building code, see Hatch, "Inferno at the Iroquois," 29.

13. Thomas Lee Philpott, *The Slum and the Ghetto: Neighborhood Deterioration and Middle-Class Reform, 1880–1930* (New York: Oxford University Press, 1978), 102–4; King, "Law and Land Use," 216–18; Joseph A. Spencer, "Tenant Organization and Housing Reform in New York City: The Citywide Tenants' Council, 1936–1943," in *Community Organization for Urban Social Change: A Historical Perspective*, ed. Robert Fisher and Peter Romanofsky (Westport, CT: Greenwood Press, 1981), 128. The sections of Chicago's West Side included in this book were generally well-off enough that they were not included in Abbott's study of tenement districts. See Abbott, *Tenements of Chicago*, 179.

14. Harris, "Building Regulation," 104–5; Harris, "The Impact of Building Controls," 272. For an overview of housing legislation in the mid-1920s, see James Ford, "The Enforcement of Housing Legislation," *Political Science Quarterly* 42, no. 4 (December 1927): 549–60. Address by Sidney D. Smith, to Chicago Kiwanis Club, August 6, 1964, p. 3, folder "Department of Buildings City of Chicago," box 20, CJEG; Board of Directors meeting, March 20, 1956, folder "Feb.–Mar. 1956," box 2, Greater Lawndale Conservation Commission Records, Chicago Historical Society (hereafter GLCC-CHS); Arnold R. Hirsch, *Making the Second Ghetto: Race and Housing in Chicago, 1940–1960* (Cambridge: Cambridge University Press, 1983), 22, 25. For illustrations of the kind of equipment that made kitchenettes possible, see *Landlord's Guide* (Chicago: Landlord's Bureau of Chicago, November 1948), 11, and *Landlord's Guide* (Chicago: Landlord's Bureau of Chicago, January 1948), 9. Ed Marciniak, *Reversing Urban Decline: The Winthrop-Kenmore Corridor in the Edgewater and Uptown Communities of Chicago* ([Chicago]: National Center for Urban Ethnic Affairs, 1981), 19; clipping, "Owners to Appeal Housing Code

Rules," *Chicago Daily News*, February 16, 1963, folder 9, box 4, MPC accession 76-102; "'Glass Panel' Fight Opens," *Garfieldian*, April 26, 1961. For examples of veterans' demand for housing, see "Help Vets Find Homes!" *West Side News*, November 25, 1945; and "Free 'Home Wanted' Ads Help 206 Garfield Park Vets," *Garfield News*, March 12, 1947. "Legislative Program of the Mayor's Emergency Housing Committee," folder 181, box 16, MPC accession 74-20; Citizens Building Code Committee, "History of Building Code," folder 9, box 7, MPC accession 75-104. See MHPC pamphlet, "Minimum Housing Standards in Chicago, May 1946," folder 120, box 11, MPC accession 74-20, for a list of the provisions of the building code that MHPC concluded applied to housing in 1946.

15. Note, "Municipal Housing Codes," *Harvard Law Review* 69 (April 1956): 1115–16; William L. Slayton, "Urban Redevelopment Short of Clearance: Rehabilitation, Reconditioning, Conservation, and Code Enforcement in Local Programs," in *Urban Redevelopment Problems and Practices*, ed. Coleman Woodbury (Chicago: University of Chicago Press, 1953), 358–70. On MHPC, see Kristin Serum McGrath, "American Values and the Slums: A Chicago Case Study" (Ph.D. diss., University of Minnesota, 1977); and Hirsch, *Making the Second Ghetto*, passim.

16. McGrath, "American Values and the Slums," 93, 214; First Conference on Chicago's New Housing Code, January 17, 1957, LaSalle Hotel, Chicago, p. 6, folder 64, box 6, MPC accession 74-20; "The Chicago Association of Commerce and the Metropolitan Housing Council Presents [*sic*] a Modern Building Code for Chicago," January 8, 1947, folder 57, box 5, MPC accession 74-20. Cf. Harris, "The Impact of Building Controls," 275, 278, for the existence of such a law in Toronto.

17. "Proposed Building Code Makes Way for Prefabs," *Tomorrow's Chicago* 2, no. 10 (June 25, 1948), folder 2, box 8, MPC accession 75-104. Richard Harris and Robert Lewis, "The Geography of North American Cities and Suburbs, 1900–1950: A New Synthesis," *Journal of Urban History* 27 (March 2001): 279; clipping, "Outmoded City Code Bars $6,300 Prefabs," *Chicago Daily Sun and Times*, September 12, 1949, uncataloged box 59, MPC accession 74-20; clipping, "Council O.K.s Building Code," *Chicago Daily News*, December 30, 1949, uncataloged box 59, MPC accession 74-20; Chicago Metropolitan Home Builders Association, press release, "No Immediate Small Home Boom to Result from Amended Code," January 8, 1950, folder 9, box 7, MPC accession 75-104.

18. Metropolitan Housing and Planning Council, "Needed! A Housing Code for Chicago, a Yardstick for Better Living," unprocessed box "Old Planning Materials," Faith Rich Papers, Special Collections and Preservation Division, Harold Washington Library Center, Chicago (hereafter FR); Report of the Committee on Enforcement of Minimum Housing Standards of the Metropolitan Housing Council, "Outline of Recommended Programs and Techniques for the Newly Created Bureau of Housing Inspection of the Building Department," March 31, 1946, p. 8, folder 66, box 6, MPC accession 74-20; McGrath, "American Values and the Slums," 236.

19. "An Analysis of Chicago Departmental Procedure for the Protection of Existing Buildings and Housing," October 19, 1948, folder 5, box 4, MPC accession 75-104; Address by Sidney D. Smith, to Chicago Kiwanis Club, August 6, 1964, p. 5, folder "Department of Buildings City of Chicago," box 20, CJEG; undated letter, MHPC to Kennelly, folder 5, uncataloged box 20, MPC accession 74-20; von Hoffman to Alinsky, "Re: What the City of Chicago Does in Housing," April 8, 1958, p. 23, folder 82, IAF; Committee to Reorganize the Building Department, "Memo of Meeting with General Smykal," October 15, [1953?], folder 5, uncataloged box 20, MPC accession 74-20; Jones, *Governing Buildings*, xiv, 51–53, 69, 133; clipping, "Union Boss Says He Rules 65 on City Building Staff," *Chicago Tribune*, December 8, 1954, folder 9, box 3, MPC accession 75-104.

20. Abbott, *Tenements of Chicago*, 179; "Standards of Housing and Sanitation in Chicago as given in the Building Ordinances and Sanitary Code," folder 4, box 3, MPC accession 75-104; Board of Directors meeting, March 20, 1956, folder "Feb.–Mar. 1956," box 2, GLCC-CHS; Citizens Committee to Fight Slums, "Housing Action Report of 1954," p. 12, folder 81, IAF; "Zoning Conversions," *Garfieldian*, May 23, 1951.

21. Clipping, "Views Cutting Up of Flats as Step to Slums," *Chicago Tribune*, November 8, 1951, folder 4, box 3, MPC accession 75-104; First Conference on Chicago's New Housing Code, January 17, 1957, LaSalle Hotel, Chicago, p. 6, folder 64, box 6, MPC accession 74-20; Sharpe to Mackelmann, October 31, 1952, folder 124, box 12, MPC accession 74-20; Kribben to Kennelly and Members of the City Council Joint Committee on Conservation Legislation, August 17, 1953, folder 66, box 6, MPC accession 74-20.

22. Hirsch, *Making the Second Ghetto*, 24–26; Report of the Committee on Enforcement of Minimum Housing Standards of the Metropolitan Housing Council, "Outline of Recommended Programs and Techniques for the Newly Created Bureau of Housing Inspection of the Building Department," March 31, 1946, folder 66, box 6, MPC accession 74-20; Hobbs to How and Greenwood, April 14–27, 1955, folder "Work and Study—Interns in Community Ser. Winter 54–55 Leaders' reports, Feb.–May, Chicago RO 1955," box "Chicago R.O. Files, 1955 (Peace Ed)," American Friends Service Committee Archives, Philadelphia, PA (hereafter AFSC); clipping, "City Moves in on S. Side Firetraps," *Chicago Daily News*, January 28, 1958, folder 9, box 4, MPC accession 76-102; "'Glass Panel' Fight Opens," *Garfieldian*, April 26, 1961; clipping, "Fight 'No Crash Door' Law," *Sunday Star*, March 5, 1961, folder 1, box 4, MPC accession 80-49; "Deaths by Fire in Chicago Tenements," six-page typescript manuscript, folder 1, box 49, Leon Despres Papers, Chicago Historical Society; "An Analysis of Chicago Departmental Procedure for the Protection of Existing Buildings and Housing," October 19, 1948, folder 5, box 4, MPC accession 75-104; *Chicago Daily News*, June 10, 11, 12, 13, 15, 16, 17, 18, 19, and 20, 1953; First Conference on Chicago's New Housing Code, January 17, 1957, LaSalle Hotel, Chicago, p. 6, folder 64, box 6, MPC accession 74-20; McGrath, "American Values and the Slums," 8–12.

23. First Conference on Chicago's New Housing Code, January 17, 1957, LaSalle Hotel, Chicago, p. 6, folder 64, box 6, MPC accession 74-20; Citizens Committee to Fight Slums, "Housing Action Report of 1954," folder 81, IAF; minutes of the Committee on Housing Code Modernization, July 20, 1966, folder 3, box 2, MPC accession 76-102; Sharpe to All Members of the Housing Code Committee, April 13, 1954, folder 124, box 12, MPC accession 74-20; memo to Mr. Nicholas von Hoffman, June 14, 1956, folder 104, IAF; Byron C. Sharpe, memo on conference with General Smykal, folder 121, box 11, MPC accession 74-20.

24. Hirsch, *Making the Second Ghetto*, 268–73, notes that the federal act was based on previous Illinois legislation. MHPC, "Proposed Housing Code for Chicago," folder 5-41, Chicago Urban League Records, Special Collections and University Archives, Richard J. Daley Library, University of Illinois at Chicago, CUL accession 82-4 (hereafter CUL); Kramer to Dear Alderman, July 7, 1955, folder 12-122, MPC accession 74-20; First Conference on Chicago's New Housing Code, January 17, 1957, LaSalle Hotel, Chicago, pp. 6, 19, folder 64, box 6, MPC accession 74-20; "Municipal Housing Codes," 1116.

25. Minutes of the Committee on Housing Code Modernization, July 20, 1966, folder 3, box 2, MPC accession 76-102; Kramer to All Cooperating Organizations, December 29, 1955, folder 12-122, MPC accession 74-20; memo to Mr. Nicholas von Hoffman, June 14, 1956, folder 104, IAF; First Conference on Chicago's New Housing Code, January 17, 1957, LaSalle Hotel, Chicago, p. 7, folder 64, box 6, MPC accession 74-20; clipping, "City Forges Powerful Weapon in Its War against Blight," *Chicago Daily News*, June 25, 1956, and clipping, "Council Group Approves New Housing Code," *Chicago Tribune*, June 16, 1956, both in folder 105, IAF.

26. MHPC, "Proposed Housing Code for Chicago," p. 2, folder 5-41, CUL accession 82-4; MHPC to Egan, June 28, 1956, folder 104, IAF; clipping, "City Forges Powerful Weapon in Its War against Blight," *Chicago Daily News*, June 25, 1956, folder 105, IAF.

27. First Conference on Chicago's New Housing Code, January 17, 1957, LaSalle Hotel, Chicago, pp. 13, 18, folder 64, box 6, MPC accession 74-20 (emphasis in the original); George L. Ramsey, "Housing Code Enforcement," January 17, 1957, folder 13, box 14, MPC accession 80-49; "W. Side May Be Next in City Housing War," *Garfieldian*, March 6, 1957; "Building Inspection Team Sent Here," *Garfieldian*, March 27, 1957.

28. MHPC, "Chicago's New Zoning Ordinance," June 1957, folder 5, box 30, MPC accession 75-104; "Broadcast No. 6; Subject: Rebuilding Chicago's Blighted Areas," August 14, 1939,

Station WJJD, Chicago, CHS; "Blight Can Be Stopped, Chaddick Tells 165 at $100 Plate Dinner," *Garfieldian*, October 31, 1956; Alderman P. J. Cullerton (38th), "Plan of Procedure to Activate City of Chicago Ordinance of Re-Zoning," March 26, 1952, folder 13, box 6, MPC accession 80-59.

29. *The Voice of the Midwest Community Council* 11, no. 7 (October 1958), folder 524, Near West Side Community Committee Records, Special Collections and University Archives, Richard J. Daley Library, University of Illinois at Chicago; "Dwelling Registration Ordinance a Must," *Garfieldian*, January 8, 1958; clipping, "City Council Backs the Slumlords," *Chicago Tribune*, January 1, 1958, folder 87, IAF; Association of Community Councils of Chicago, "Subject: Registration of Ownership Ordinance," folder 4, box 32, MPC accession 75-104. For more on blind trusts, see chapter 6, page 158.

30. Abbott, *Tenements of Chicago*, 168; "It All Boils Down to Enforcement," *Garfieldian*, July 18, 1956; Spencer, "Tenant Organization," 127–56; Wendell Pritchett, *Brownsville, Brooklyn: Blacks, Jews, and the Changing Face of the Ghetto* (Chicago: University of Chicago Press, 2002), 55.

31. Clipping, Robert C. Klove, "Austin—A compact residential settlement of long standing," *Real Estate*, October 11, 1941, folder 1a, box 12, Austin Community Collection, Special Collections and Preservation Division, Harold Washington Library Center, Chicago (hereafter ACC); clipping, *West Side News*, September 29, 1943, folder 3, box 2, Office of Civilian Defense Records; "Dirty Alleys," *Garfieldian*, June 20, 1946; "Slum Prevention Plan," *Garfieldian*, May 19, 1949.

32. "Legislative Program of the Mayor's Emergency Housing Committee," folder 181, box 16, MPC accession 74-20; "Help Vets Find Homes!" *West Side News*, November 25, 1945; "Free 'Home Wanted' Ads Help 206 Garfield Park Vets," *Garfield News*, March 12, 1947; *Tomorrow's Chicago* 2, no. 8 (April 30, 1948), folder 2, box 8, MPC accession 75-104. See Carl W. Condit, *Chicago, 1930–70: Building, Planning, and Urban Technology* (Chicago: University of Chicago Press, 1974), table 3 (pp. 286–87).

33. "First Hand Account of Apartment, Housing Conditions," *Garfieldian*, July 29, 1953.

34. "Blight Can Be Stopped, Chaddick Tells 165 at $100 Plate Dinner," *Garfieldian*, October 31, 1956; "Start Action to Eliminate Pocket of Blight in Austin," *Garfieldian*, June 3, 1959; "McGloon Ponders 'Old Town' Plan as Solution for Central Austin," *Garfieldian*, March 9, 1966; "Estimate 1,100 Building Conversions Here," *Garfieldian*, March 21, 1956; "A Weary Disgusted Tenant" to the editor, *Garfieldian*, August 12, 1953.

35. Alice Young to editor, *Garfieldian*, July 25, 1956.

36. Henry C. Binford, "Tenements, Slums, and Blight: The Figurative Landscape of Urban Poverty, 1880–1915," photocopy; Beauregard, *Voices of Decline*, 84–87; Mark I. Gelfand, *A Nation of Cities: The Federal Government and Urban America, 1933–1965* (New York: Oxford University Press, 1975), 109; Wendell Pritchett, "The 'Public Menace' of Blight: Urban Renewal and the Private Uses of Eminent Domain," *Yale Law and Policy Review* 21 (2003): 1–52. See also comments of Ferd Kramer, "Broadcast No. 6; Subject: Rebuilding Chicago's Blighted Areas," p. 4, August 14, 1939, Station WJJD, Chicago, CHS.

37. "Just a Little Elbow Grease Needed," *Garfieldian*, August 5, 1953; "Facts for Action, Data for Lawndale Leaders: Housing Is for People," folder "May–June 1956," box 2, GLCC-CHS; statement of Dominick J. Galli, October 9, 1956, folder "Oct. 1956," box 3, GLCC-CHS; "Rent Control and Conversions," *Garfieldian*, June 20, 1951; Rich to Hauser, March 6, 1960, folder with illustrated card, "The Christmas Story," box 1, FR; Report of Planning and Development Committee to Kaczmarek, September 18, 1962, p. 4, folder "September 1962," box 19, GLCC-CHS; Youngs to Smykal, October 9, 1956, folder "Oct. 1956," box 3, GLCC-CHS.

38. Joe Tsuchiyama to editor, *Garfieldian*, May 17, 1961; J. Frank Lindsey to editor, *Garfieldian*, February 23, 1966; "Estimate 1,100 Building Conversions Here," *Garfieldian*, March 21, 1956; "Seek to Settle Zoning Problem," *Garfieldian*, January 19, 1957; "Landlords Here Plagued by Irresponsible Tenants," *Garfieldian*, March 5, 1958; "Housing Not Just a Landlord Problem," *Garfieldian*, March 12, 1958. For a more sanguine view of boarding and

lodging, see Richard Harris, "The End Justified the Means: Boarding and Rooming in a City of Homes, 1890–1951," *Journal of Social History* 26 (Winter 1992): 331–58.

39. "The Baltimore Plan," *Garfieldian*, December 1, 1949; Mrs. C. R. Rennison to editor, *Garfieldian*, March 9, 1950; Burgh to editor, *Garfieldian*, December 9, 1953; "A Necessary First Step," *Garfieldian*, February 17, 1954.

40. Memo for file—Mr. Henry Collins, Austin, June 2, 1962, folder "Austin Community Organization, Correspondence," box 24, CJEG; "Tell Appalling Bldg. Problem," *Garfieldian*, February 3, 1960; "Inspectors Find 273 Violations in Bldg.," *Garfieldian*, February 10, 1960; "Mayor Acts in Building Case," *Garfieldian*, February 17, 1960; "City May Ask Demolition Order for 4400 Jackson," *Garfieldian*, July 15, 1960; "Mona Building Fixed after 3 Year Fight," *Garfieldian*, May 1, 1963. Jones, *Governing Buildings*, 162–64, describes the process through the court system.

41. "Crack Down on Eyesores," *Garfieldian*, January 1, 1953; "How to Stop the Blight," *Garfieldian*, October 14, 1953; *NLCC Newsletter* 4, no. 1 (January 1954), folder "Jan.–Nov. 1954," box 1, GLCC; "Council Acts to Cause Pool Room Move," *Garfieldian*, August 4, 1954; Mildred Berman, Community Contacts Report, week ending August 1, 1958, p. 2, folder "August 1–19, 1958," box 7, GLCC-CHS.

42. James McCawley to editor, *Garfieldian*, August 25, 1965; "Estimate 1,100 Building Conversions Here," *Garfieldian*, March 21, 1956; "Is Overcrowding Rampant in Area?" *Garfieldian*, November 9, 1960; "Speculator Tactics Bared by 2 Victims," *Garfieldian*, October 11, 1961; Greater Lawndale Conservation Commission, excerpts from weekly log of George Klein, folder 9, box 234, Welfare Council of Metropolitan Chicago Records, Chicago Historical Society; *GLCC News Notes* 4, no. 9 (November 1960), folder with letter from Julio Vivas to Faith Rich, FR; "List Residential Building," *Garfieldian*, March 9, 1955.

43. "Join Forces to Fight Apartment Conversion," *Garfieldian*, June 24, 1953; "Owner to Rehabilitate Homan–Van Buren Bldg.," *Garfieldian*, July 22, 1953; "Now Let's Enforce Building Regulations," *Garfieldian*, July 29, 1953. It is impossible to tell from these articles whether the ten families were African American or not. In the period when they appeared, the *Garfieldian* inconsistently identified African Americans by race. Certainly the subsequent activities of the Garfield Park Improvement Association suggested their hostility to blacks in the neighborhood. See, for example, Bob and Liza Hobbs, to Thelma How, John Willard, and Bob Greenwood, May 24, 1955, folder "Work and Study—Interns in Community Ser. Winter 54–55 Leaders' reports, Feb.–May, Chicago RO 1955," box "Chicago R.O. Files, 1955 (Peace Ed)," AFSC. On improvement associations, see Zorita Mikva, "The Neighborhood Improvement Association: A Counter-Force to the Expansion of Chicago's Negro Population" (M.A. thesis, University of Chicago, 1951).

44. "Central Civic Improvement Association," folder "1957 Undated Items," box 5, GLCC-CHS. On class tensions among black Chicagoans, see St. Clair Drake and Horace R. Cayton, *Black Metropolis: A Study of Negro Life in a Northern City*, 2 vols. (New York: Harcourt, Brace, 1945; rev. and enlarged ed., New York: Harcourt, Brace & World, 1962), vol. 2, 525; and James R. Grossman, *Land of Hope: Chicago, Black Southerners, and the Great Migration* (Chicago: University of Chicago Press, 1989), 146.

45. Cohen and Taylor, *American Pharaoh*, 168; Association of Community Councils of Metropolitan Chicago, "A Guide to Housing and Zoning Code Enforcement," May 1960, folder 17, box 6, MPC accession 80–59; *GLCC News Notes* 4, no. 9 (November 1960), folder with letter from Julio Vivas to Faith Rich, box 1, FR. Jones, "Party and Bureaucracy," 691, notes that groups and aldermen had a special service desk. See also Jones, *Governing Buildings*, 74.

46. *LPCA Newsletter*, May–June 1962, CHS; *GLCC News Notes* 3, no. 41 (August 1959), folder "August 1959," box 11, GLCC-CHS; *GLCC News Notes* 3, no. 36 (February 22, 1959), folder "Feb. 19–28, 1959," box 9, GLCC-CHS; "'Carpetbaggers' Flooding Back," *Garfieldian*, August 3, 1966.

47. "Citizens Group to Hear How Area Checked Blight," *Garfieldian*, November 23, 1950;

"Crack Down on Eyesores," *Garfieldian*, January 1, 1953; "Neighborhood Responsibility," *Garfieldian*, October 1, 1958.

48. *Garfield Park Business Men's Association Bulletin* 2, no. 1 (April 1941), folder 3, box 5, West Garfield Park Community Collection, Special Collections and Preservation Division, Harold Washington Library Center, Chicago; minutes of the special meeting of the Midwest Community Council, March 6, 1950, p. 2, folder 30, Off the Street Club Records, Special Collections and University Archives, Richard J. Daley Library, University of Illinois at Chicago (hereafter OSC); "Improvement Association Plans Clean Alley Drive," *Garfieldian*, January 5, 1955; unidentified clipping, "Hundreds March in Cleanup Parade," April 26, 1951, folder 54, OSC; Johnson to Mathien [*sic*], May 26, 1952, folder 33, OSC; "Area in Fine Shape, Says Cleanup Head," *Garfieldian*, May 1, 1957; "4 Community Groups Help Solicit Cleanup Pledges," *Garfieldian*, August 17, 1955; "Cut Weeds, Pick Up Litter Block Committees Urge," *Garfieldian*, September 10, 1959; "Boulevard Residents Sign Vow to Beautify Homes," *Garfieldian*, July 29, 1959; "Neighborhood Plans Repeat of Plantup Drive Saturday," *Garfieldian*, April 16, 1958; GLCC Women's Auxiliary, list of entries in contest, folder "1957 Undated Items," box 5, GLCC-CHS; clipping, *Lawndale Booster*, January 8, 1960, folder "1959 undated," box 12, GLCC-CHS; minutes of the Holiday Lighting Committee, December 14, 1964, folder 22, GLCC-UIC; "Join in the Spirit," *Garfieldian*, December 14, 1966; "Christmas Lighting Contest Announced," *Garfieldian*, November 11, 1959.

49. "Voluntary Efforts Urged to Save City," *Garfieldian*, November 20, 1957; staff meeting minutes, August 3, 1959, folder "August 1959," box 11, GLCC-CHS.

50. Clipping, "Owners to Appeal Housing Code Rules," *Chicago Daily News*, February 16, 1963, folder 9, box 4, MPC accession 76-102; clipping, "High Court Ruling Seen as Turning Point in Slum Housing," *Chicago Sun-Times*, March 3, 1963, folder "Urban Renewal, Ruth Moore By-Lines 1959–1964," box 7, Ruth Moore Papers, Chicago Historical Society (hereafter RM); clipping, "Daley Meets with Property Owners; Agrees to Public Hearings on Code," *Chicago Daily News*, March 25, 1964, folder 4, box 2, MPC accession 75-104; Docket No. 37293-Agenda 46—November 1962, *Adolph Kaukas et al., Appellees, v. The City of Chicago Appellant*, folder 2, box 4, MPC accession 80-49; "Proposed Amendments and Revisions to the Municipal Code of Chicago," folder 57, box 5, MPC accession 74-20; clipping, "Building Code Defended and Hit at Hearing," *Chicago Tribune*, May 6, 1964, folder 9, box 4, MPC accession 76-102; "Testimony Given by Frank J. Schneider, Before a Joint Meeting of the Building and Zoning Committee and the Planning and Housing Committee of the Chicago City Council," May 5, 1965, folder 3, box 2, MPC accession 75-104; MHPC press release, "Interpretation of the Proposed Amendments to the Housing Code," April 1, 1964, folder 5, box 2, MPC accession 75-104; Robert Lucas statement to the Committee of Building and Zoning, May 6, 1964, folder 3, box 2, MPC accession 75-104.

51. "Congratulations for Action on Overcrowding," *Garfieldian*, September 11, 1957.

52. Testimony of William Busch, District 8 budget hearing, September 29, 1960, folder "September 1960," box 14, GLCC-CHS; Board of Directors, May 26, 1959, p. 5, folder "May 20–31, 1959," box 10, GLCC-CHS; Lubove, *The Progressives and the Slums*, 97; minutes of the meeting of the Committee on Codes and Enforcement, March 17, 1958, folder 72, box 7, MPC accession 74-20; meeting of the Committee on Codes and Enforcement, March 24, 1958, p. 4, folder 72, box 7, MPC accession 74-20; James Borchert, *Alley Life in Washington: Family, Community, Religion, and Folklife in the City, 1850–1970* (Urbana: University of Illinois Press, 1980), 82, 304–8; *GLCC News Notes* 4, no. 9 (November 1960), folder with letter from Julio Vivas to Faith Rich, box 1, FR; Executive Committee meeting, September 12, 1961, p. 2, folder "September 1961," box 17, GLCC-CHS; Jones, *Governing Buildings*, 140–41; "Two Good Causes," *Garfieldian*, September 6, 1962. On the failure to enforce similar provisions of New York City's housing code in the 1980s, see Sanjek, *Future of Us All*, 189–91.

53. Lubove, *The Progressives and the Slums*, 97; von Hoffman to Alinsky, "Re: What the City of Chicago Does in Housing," April 8, 1958, pp. 24–25, folder 82, IAF.

54. Minutes of the meeting of the Committee on Codes and Enforcement, March 17, 1958, p. 3, box 7, folder 72, MPC accession 74-20.

55. Clipping, "City Spares the Rod in Handling Tenants," *Chicago Daily News*, October 18, 1961, folder 9, box 4, MPC accession 76-102; "Include Tenants in Housing Code Enforcement," *Garfieldian*, December 17, 1958; clipping, "City Forges Powerful Weapon in Its War against Blight," *Chicago Daily News*, June 25, 1956, folder 105, IAF; "Realtor, Civic Crusader Differ on Slum Cause," *Garfieldian*, June 26, 1963.

56. Report on meeting with Building Commissioner Ramsey, October 3, 1957, folder "Oct. 1–24, 1957," box 4, GLCC-CHS; clipping, "City Court Fails to Collect Half of the Fines from Building Code Violators," *Chicago Sun-Times*, May 18, 1959; clipping, "Push Action on Building Fines," *Chicago Sun-Times*, May 19, 1959, both in folder "Code Enforcement—Newspaper clippings," box 29, CJEG; unidentified clipping, "Huge Fine KOs Slum Owner," folder 12, box 4, Mary Bolton Wirth Papers, Department of Special Collections, Regenstein Library, University of Chicago (hereafter MBW); Hirsch, *Making the Second Ghetto*, 34.

57. It was reportedly also possible to bribe court clerks to remove cases from a judge's docket, for as little as $25 per violation: one page typescript sheet, dated July 15, 1965, folder 2, box 33, MPC accession 80-49; Jones, *Governing Buildings*, 48; address by Sidney D. Smith to Chicago Kiwanis Club, August 6, 1964, p. 6, folder "Department of Buildings City of Chicago," box 20, CJEG; Mary B. Wirth, "Chapter I: The Housing Court—Obstacle to Housing Progress?" folder 8, box 1, MBW; Rubel to Drevs, March 1, 1962, folder 73, box 7, MPC accession 74-20; clipping, "Slum Landlords Can Play Waiting Game with Court," *Chicago Daily News*, June 19, 1959, folder 12, box 4, MBW.

58. Clipping, "How Slum Fines Fail: Ownership Quickly Changes," *Chicago's American*, June 19, 1959, folder 12, box 4, MBW; Mary B. Wirth, "Chapter I: The Housing Court—Obstacle to Housing Progress?" p. 2, folder 8, box 1, MBW.

59. Press releases, Chicago Building Department, July 17, 1962, August 17, 1962, and October 15, 1964, all in folder 8, box 3, MPC accession 75-104; address by Sidney D. Smith to Chicago Kiwanis Club, August 6, 1964, p. 10, folder "Department of Buildings City of Chicago," box 20, CJEG; clipping, "75,000 Dwellings Razed in 10 Years," *Chicago Daily News*, April 6, 1962, folder 418, IAF; minutes of the meeting of the Housing Code Modernization Committee, October 7, 1970, folder 19, box 32, MPC accession 80-49.

60. Minutes of the meeting of the Housing Code Modernization Committee, August 3, 1966, folder 3, box 2, MPC accession 76-102; minutes of the meeting of the Housing Code Modernization Committee, November 15, 1967, p. 2, folder 2, box 2, MPC accession 76-102; Rothschild to Board of Governors, December 18, 1970, folder 3, box 32, MPC accession 80-49; Jones, *Governing Buildings*, 36–37. During the rest of Mayor Daley's administration, the city council continued to make small changes in the building code, but it was not until 1982 that another major round of reform occurred. See Joel Rast, *Remaking Chicago: The Political Origins of Urban Industrial Change* (DeKalb: Northern Illinois University Press, 1999), 42–44; and Jones, *Governing Buildings*, 27–31.

61. This observation is consistent with Jones's conclusion in "Party and Bureaucracy," 696, that community organizations in the late 1970s did not stimulate significant additional levels of enforcement.

62. "ACO Queries Building Owner for Converting 2 Flats to 8," *Garfieldian*, August 26, 1964; OBA News Brief, folder 24, box 3, ACC; "OBA Slates Housing Compliance Meeting," *Austin News*, August 5, 1970, box 2, Austin Newspaper Collection, Special Collections and Preservation Division, Harold Washington Library Center, Chicago.

63. "'Carpetbaggers' Flooding Back," *Garfieldian*, August 3, 1966; "ATOA Marchers Protest West End Slum Building," *Garfieldian*, August 17, 1966; "ATOA Block Club News," *Garfieldian*, September 8, 1966; clipping, "Landlord Rebuffs Marchers," *Garfieldian*, January 25, 1967, folder 98-18, CUL accession 76-116; clipping, "West End Tenants Win Concessions," *Garfieldian*, February 22, 1967, folder 33-1, box 33, Cyrus Hall Adams III Papers, Chicago Historical Society.

64. Flyer, for conference on February 5, folder "Jan.–Feb. 1966," box 3, Marillac House Records, Chicago Historical Society.

65. Urban Affairs Weekly Report, for week ending October 2, 1966, and Urban Affairs Report, for week ending October 23, 1966, both in folder "Urban Affairs Program, Reports, Weekly, Chicago Regional Office, 1966," box "Chicago R.O. 1966 (Pre-Adolescent Enrichment Prog. to Urban Affairs Prog.)," AFSC; James R. Ralph Jr., *Northern Protest: Martin Luther King, Jr., Chicago, and the Civil Rights Movement* (Cambridge, MA: Harvard University Press, 1993); David J. Garrow, ed., *Chicago 1966: Open Housing Marches, Summit Negotiations and Operation Breadbasket* (Brooklyn: Carlson, 1989).

66. Clipping, "What Building Inspectors Found in Study of 3 W. Side Neighborhoods," *Chicago Sun-Times*, July 25, 1966, folder "West Side Areas, 1959–1967," box 7, RM; clipping, "City to Begin Slum Search," *Chicago Tribune*, March 2, 1966, folder 3, box 5, MPC accession 76-102; "Reporter Tours West Garfield with City Building Inspectors," *Garfieldian*, March 9, 1966; Harris, "The Impact of Building Controls," 274; Christopher MacGregor Scribner, *Renewing Birmingham: Federal Funding and the Promise of Change, 1929–1979* (Athens: University of Georgia Press, 2002), 68. See also Andrew Wiese, "The Other Suburbanites: African American Suburbanization in the North before 1950," *Journal of American History* 85 (March 1999): 1521–22.

67. See chapter 6, pages 158–59. Day, *Urban Castles*, 49.

68. "Problems in Lawndale," folder "Greater Lawndale Conservation Commission," box 2, CJEG; Lubove, *The Progressives and the Slums*, 96–97; Harris, "The End Justified the Means," esp. 350; Abbott, *Tenements of Chicago*, 363; address by Sidney D. Smith to Chicago Kiwanis Club, August 6, 1964, p. 9, folder "Department of Buildings City of Chicago," box 20, CJEG; clipping, "Hearing Monday on Bill to Curb Slum Gypping," *American*, June 19, 1963, folder 7, box 3, MPC accession 75-104; Williams to Moffett and Lafayette, June 24, 1966, folder "Housing Opportunities Program, General, Chicago Regional Office, 1966," box "Chicago R.O. 1966 (High School Program—Teachers Workshops to Peace Ed)," AFSC; clipping, "Home Buying Soars into New Slum Problem," *Chicago Sun-Times*, August 6, 1967, folder "West Side Areas, 1959–1967," box 7, RM; *GLCC News Notes* 5, no. 6 (July 1961), folder "July 1961," box 16, GLCC-CHS; "Charge Building Inspectors Plague 'Contract' Buyers," *Garfieldian*, July 13, 1966; comments of Julia Fairfax, "Program . . . Looking Backward to Move Forward," meeting, Midwest Complex, February 9, 1985, tape T21, Bethel New Life Collection, Special Collections and Preservation Division, Harold Washington Library Center, Chicago. On the use of zoning code enforcement as a tool of racial harassment, see Raymond A. Mohl, "Making the Second Ghetto in Metropolitan Miami, 1940–1960," *Journal of Urban History* 21 (March 1995): 405.

69. Clipping, "Housing Code Battle Brings Sharp Words," *Chicago Defender*, May 7, 1964, folder 4, box 2, MPC accession 75-104; Robert Lucas statement to the Committee of Building and Zoning, May 6, 1964, folder 3, box 2, MPC accession 75-104.

70. *GLCC News Notes* 5, no. 6 (July 1961), folder "July 1961," box 16, GLCC-CHS; *GLCC News Notes* 3, no. 46 (December 1959), folder "Dec. 26–31, 1959," box 12, GLCC-CHS.

CHAPTER THREE

1. Clipping, *Chicago Sun-Times*, April 10, 1959, folder "Urban Renewal, Ruth Moore By-Lines 1959–1964," box 7, Ruth Moore Papers, Chicago Historical Society (hereafter RM).

2. Cf. June Manning Thomas's observations about the ineffectiveness of conservation in keeping whites in Detroit: "Yet many people were leaving because of demographic changes . . . upward mobility . . . or racial change. Federal policies encouraged this exodus outward. Conservation could not make even a dent in these trends." June Manning Thomas, *Redevelopment and Race: Planning a Finer City in Postwar Detroit* (Baltimore: Johns Hopkins University Press, 1997), 90.

3. "Why Urban Renewal Delay," *Austin News*, June 24, 1970, box 2, Austin Newspaper Collection, Special Collections and Preservation Division, Harold Washington Library Center, Chicago. For an example of the difficulty that ordinary Chicagoans had inferring Daley's specific

intent, see Rich to Vivas, April 20, 1965, folder with letter from Julio Vivas to Faith Rich, FR. It is possible that the Richard J. Daley Papers promised to the University of Illinois at Chicago library will provide insight into Daley's vision for the city; these papers were not available to the public in time to be of use in this project.

4. It was not until the 1970s that community-based organizations began to focus on industrial retention as a strategy for neighborhood revitalization. See Joel Rast, *Remaking Chicago: The Political Origins of Urban Industrial Change* (DeKalb: Northern Illinois University Press, 1999), 17, chap. 4.

5. For an overview of contemporary criticism of urban renewal, see A. Scott Henderson, *Housing and the Democratic Ideal: The Life and Thought of Charles Abrams* (New York: Columbia University Press, 2000), 193–203; and Martin Anderson, *The Federal Bulldozer; a Critical Analysis of Urban Renewal, 1949–1962* (Cambridge: MIT Press, 1964). For the classic statement on the destructiveness of urban renewal to vital urban communities, see Herbert J. Gans, *The Urban Villagers: Group and Class in the Life of Italian-Americans* (New York: Free Press, 1962). Nonetheless, West Siders were not unique in the nation in calling for local urban renewal. See Wendell E. Pritchett, "Race and Community in Postwar Brooklyn: The Brownsville Neighborhood Council and the Politics of Urban Renewal," *Journal of Urban History* 27 (May 2001): 445–70, and his *Brownsville, Brooklyn: Blacks, Jews, and the Changing Face of the Ghetto* (Chicago: University of Chicago Press, 2002), 62, for New York residents who sought to introduce not only urban renewal, but also public housing, into their neighborhoods. William D. Jenkins, "Before Downtown: Cleveland, Ohio, and Urban Renewal, 1949–1958," *Journal of Urban History* 27 (May 2001): 471–96, argues that in Cleveland, benign social concerns motivated early urban renewal efforts.

6. Memo to the Legislative Committee, December 26, 1963, folder 11, box 32, Metropolitan Planning Council Records, accession 75-104, Special Collections and University Archives, Richard J. Daley Library, University of Illinois at Chicago (hereafter MPC); Pritchett, *Brownsville, Brooklyn*, 144; John H. Mollenkopf, *The Contested City* (Princeton: Princeton University Press, 1983), chap. 5, "Consequences of the Neighborhood Revolt against Renewal."

7. For an overview of various cities' approaches to urban renewal, see Jon C. Teaford, *The Rough Road to Renaissance: Urban Revitalization in America, 1940–1985* (Baltimore: Johns Hopkins University Press, 1980), 105–20. See also Carl Abbott, "Five Downtown Strategies: Policy Discourse and Downtown Planning since 1945," *Journal of Policy History* 5 (1993): 5–27.

8. For the idea of such a "pro-growth coalition" between business and government, see Mollenkopf, *Contested City*. For a nice summary of the growth coalition's actions in Chicago, see Barbara Ferman, *Challenging the Growth Machine: Neighborhood Politics in Chicago and Pittsburgh* (Lawrence: University Press of Kansas, 1996), 58–63; Carl W. Condit, *Chicago, 1910–29: Building, Planning and Urban Technology* (Chicago: University of Chicago Press, 1973), chap. 4, "Buildings of the Commercial City," and table 4, 306–8; "Broadcast No. 6; Subject: Rebuilding Chicago's Blighted Areas," August 14, 1939, Station WJJD, Chicago, Chicago Historical Society; and Loomis Mayfield, "The Reorganization of Urban Politics: The Chicago Growth Machine after World War II" (Ph.D. diss., University of Pittsburgh, 1996), 34–40.

9. Chicago's master plan is often referred to as the "1909 Plan." See Daniel H. Burnham and Edward H. Bennett, *Plan of Chicago* (Chicago: Commercial Club, 1909; reprint, New York: Da Capo Press, 1970). Barbara Page Fiske, ed., *Key to Government in Chicago and Suburban Cook County* (Chicago: University of Chicago Press, 1989), 109, 174–175; Carl W. Condit, *Chicago, 1930–70: Building, Planning, and Urban Technology* (Chicago: University of Chicago Press, 1974), 270; Arnold R. Hirsch, *Making the Second Ghetto: Race and Housing in Chicago, 1940–1960* (Cambridge: Cambridge University Press, 1983), 102–5, 151. Hirsch's critique of MHPC stems from the overlap between members and downtown real estate interests. For a more sympathetic account of MHPC's purposes, see Kristin Serum McGrath, "American Values and the Slums: A Chicago Case Study" (Ph.D. diss., University of Minnesota, 1977).

10. Chicago Plan Commission, *Master Plan of Residential Land Use of Chicago* (Chicago:

Chicago Plan Commission, 1943) (hereafter *Master Plan*); Chicago Plan Commission, *Report of the Chicago Land Use Survey*, vol. 1, *Residential Chicago* (Chicago: Chicago Plan Commission, 1942) (hereafter *Residential Chicago*), and vol. 2, *Land Use in Chicago* (Chicago: Chicago Plan Commission, 1943) (hereafter *Land Use*).

11. These 22.62 square miles contained 241,692 dwelling units and 839,445 people in 1939. Figures derived by aggregating blighted and near-blighted figures from table 18, p. 73, *Master Plan*. On p. 131 of the 1943 *Master Plan*, the figure is rounded to 23 square miles. The *Master Plan*, table 17, p. 72, provides the following statistical definitions: "Blighted": "*Age*: 50% or more of the residential structures built before 1895, and *Condition*: 50% or more of the dwelling units substandard, and 20% or more of the dwelling units in structures in need of major repairs or unfit for use, and *Per cent of land in residential use*: 50% or more." "Near-Blighted": "EITHER: *Age*: 50% or more of the residential structures built before 1895, or *Condition*: 50% or more of the dwelling units substandard, and *Rent*: 50% or more of the dwelling units renting for less than $25 per month and *Per cent of land in residential use*: 50% or more."

12. *Master Plan*, 119, 124.

13. Edith Elmer Wood, *Slums and Blighted Areas in the United States* (Washington, DC: Federal Emergency Administration of Public Works, 1935), 3, 77.

14. *Residential Chicago*, 211; *Master Plan*, 71. Another 45 percent, however, needed minor repairs. In the areas designated "blighted," almost 35 percent of the structures were classified as needing major repairs or unfit for use, while in the "near-blighted areas" those figures were 10.6 percent and 0.63 percent, respectively.

15. Wood, *Slums and Blighted Areas*, 80–81, counting "in bad condition" as comparable to the categories "needing major repair" and "unfit for use."

16. Ibid., 80–81.

17. Ibid., 34–36.

18. Harold M. Mayer and Richard C. Wade, *Chicago: Growth of a Metropolis* (Chicago: University of Chicago Press, 1969), 108. On Chicago housing conditions in the early twentieth century, see Edith Abbott, *The Tenements of Chicago, 1908–1935* (Chicago: University of Chicago Press, 1936).

19. Thomas H. O'Connor, *Building a New Boston: Politics and Urban Renewal, 1950–1970* (Boston: Northeastern University Press, 1993); Janet R. Daly-Bednarek, *The Changing Image of the City: Planning for Downtown Omaha, 1945–1973* (Lincoln: University of Nebraska Press, 1992); Thomas, *Redevelopment and Race*, 66ff.; Hirsch, *Making the Second Ghetto*, 107.

20. Mayer and Wade, *Chicago*, 380–84; Hirsch, *Making the Second Ghetto*, 116–19.

21. Wendell Pritchett, "The 'Public Menace' of Blight: Urban Renewal and the Private Uses of Eminent Domain," *Yale Law and Policy Review* 21 (2003): 1–52; unlabeled clipping, November 29, 1953, folder "Urban Renewal: 1949–1960," box 7, RM; newsletter, Metropolitan Center for Neighborhood Renewal of the Metropolitan Housing and Planning Council, June 1960, folder "Urban Renewal: 1949–1960," box 7, RM; Hirsch, *Making the Second Ghetto*, 150–51; Neighborhood Redevelopment Commission of the City of Chicago, "What You Should Know about Neighborhood Redevelopment Corporations," folder "Urban Renewal, 1964–1968," box 7, RM. Hirsch, *Making the Second Ghetto*, 151, explains that the original 1941 Neighborhood Redevelopment Corporation Act was enacted "to keep blacks out of the 63rd and Halsted area" but was never used. See also Peter H. Rossi and Robert A. Dentler, *The Politics of Urban Renewal: The Chicago Findings* (New York: Free Press of Glencoe, 1961), 85.

22. Metropolitan Housing and Planning Council of Chicago, *Conservation: A Report to the Conservation Committee by Its Conservation Study Staff*, 3 vols. (Chicago: Metropolitan Housing and Planning Council, 1953). In addition to Hirsch, *Making the Second Ghetto*, chap. 5, "A Neighborhood on a Hill: Hyde Park and the University of Chicago," particularly 149–50, 151, and 152–70, see Julia Abrahamson, *A Neighborhood Finds Itself* (New York: Harper & Brothers, 1959); and Rossi and Dentler, *Politics of Urban Renewal*, 242–48. For Levi's reasoning, see undated memo of discussion with Julian Levi, folder 8, box 4, MPC accession 77-29. Mayer and Wade, *Chicago*, 394.

23. Condit, *Chicago, 1930–70*, 129–41. For a similar approach to redevelopment in Detroit, see Thomas, *Redevelopment and Race*, 66–71.

24. Harvey Warren Zorbaugh, *The Gold Coast and the Slum: A Sociological Study of Chicago's Near North Side* (1929; reprint, Chicago: University of Chicago Press, 1983). Rubloff was interested in shifting the economic and political center of the city north of the river. The Sandburg Village residential project complemented his promotion of the shopping district on North Michigan Avenue as the "Magnificent Mile." On Rubloff, see the clipping files of the Chicago Historical Society, s.v. "Arthur Rubloff" including (Chicago) *Reader*, January 20, 1978, and Iris Krasnow, "Arthur the Magnificent," *Chicago*, April 1981; see also Miles L. Berger, *They Built Chicago: Entrepreneurs Who Shaped a Great City's Architecture* (Chicago: Bonus Books, 1992), 271–82. On the Magnificent Mile's history, see John W. Stamper, *Chicago's North Michigan Avenue: Planning and Development* (Chicago: University of Chicago Press, 1991), epilogue.

25. Howard Melvin Rieger, "Redeveloping Chicago's Lincoln Park Area" (Ph.D. diss., Southern Illinois University, 1970), 60. The Lincoln Park Conservation Association was adamantly opposed to clearance in the wealthier eastern district of Lincoln Park, where the majority of its members lived. In a piece of doggerel written to the meter of "The Night Before Christmas," Dorothy McNally had Santa urging LPCA members to write to Mayor Daley and Conservation Commissioner Smykal that "Conservation is good, to the end we will fight / To prevent slum clearance and eliminate blight." *LPCA Newsletter* 2, no. 12 (December 1956), Chicago Historical Society. See also Larry Bennett, *Fragments of Cities: The New American Downtowns and Neighborhoods* (Columbus: Ohio State University Press, 1990), 56–64; Margaret Stockton Warner, "The Renovation of Lincoln Park: An Ecological Study of Neighborhood Change" (Ph.D. diss., University of Chicago, 1979); and A. Rod Paolini, "Lincoln Park Conservation Association: The Politics of a Community Organization" (M.A. thesis, Northwestern University, 1970).

26. Condit, *Chicago, 1930–70*, 127–29, 141–43; Mayer and Wade, *Chicago*, 406; Miles L. Colean, *Renewing Our Cities* (New York: Twentieth Century Fund, 1953), 130. See also the League of Women Voters, *The Key to Our Local Government*, 3rd ed. (Chicago: Citizens Information Service of Illinois, 1972), 178–79.

27. John F. Bauman, *Public Housing, Race, and Renewal: Urban Planning in Philadelphia, 1920–1974* (Philadelphia: Temple University Press, 1987), analyzes the interdependence of clearance and public housing in Philadelphia. On the shifting purposes of housing reform in Cincinnati, see Robert B. Fairbanks, *Making Better Citizens: Housing Reform and the Community Development Strategy in Cincinnati, 1890–1960* (Urbana: University of Illinois Press, 1988). For the argument that this center-out strategy also had differential effects on various kinds of enterprises, see Rast, *Remaking Chicago*, chaps. 2, 3. For accounts of the difficulty in removing residents of clearance areas, see the Mary Bolton Wirth Papers, Department of Special Collections, Regenstein Library, University of Chicago.

28. Hirsch, *Making the Second Ghetto*, 112, 121; Tenants Relocation Bureau of Chicago, "Number of Residential and Non-Residential Occupants in Chicago Relocated from Clearance Sites, 1948–1961," folder "1961, undated," box 17, Greater Lawndale Conservation Commission Records, Chicago Historical Society (hereafter GLCC-CHS). David A. Wallace, "Residential Concentration of Negroes in Chicago" (Ph.D. diss., Harvard University 1953), 296, calculated in 1953 that the clearance projects planned for non-white areas of Chicago would replace 22,831 housing units with only 14,000 new ones.

29. In 1969 Judge Richard Austin condemned this practice as illegal discrimination in the celebrated *Gatreaux* case. Hirsch, *Making the Second Ghetto*, 265.

30. The Frances Cabrini Homes were an existing federal housing project planned before World War II. Its population was initially interracial. Devereux Bowly Jr., *The Poorhouse: Subsidized Housing in Chicago, 1895–1976* (Carbondale: Southern Illinois University Press, 1978), 35. No family public housing projects were built in white areas after 1950. Memo, William Moyer to the Agenda Committee of the Chicago Freedom Movement, March 1, 1967,

p. 13, folder "Housing Opportunities Program Activities—January 1967," box, "Chicago Regional Office, 1967, High School Prog. to Housing Opportunities Prog.," Chicago Regional Office Files, American Friends Service Committee Archives, Philadelphia, Pennsylvania (hereafter AFSC).

31. Hirsch, *Making the Second Ghetto*, 2nd ed. (Chicago: University of Chicago Press, 1998), xi. See also chapters 2 and 3, and Hirsch's article "Massive Resistance in the Urban North: Trumbull Park, Chicago, 1953–1966," *Journal of American History* 82 (September 1995): 522–50; and Wallace, "Residential Concentration of Negroes in Chicago," chaps. 7, 8. The building of the Dan Ryan Expressway on the city's South Side further reinforced the displacement and containment of African Americans. On the use of highway construction to shore up segregation, see Ronald H. Bayor, *Race and the Shaping of Twentieth-Century Atlanta* (Chapel Hill: University of North Carolina Press, 1996).

32. Mayor Daley's commitment to the traditional Loop was underscored by his reaction to developer Arthur Rubloff's proposal for a "Fort Dearborn Project," which would have shifted Chicago's money and government north of the Chicago River: Daley quietly tabled the plan. Condit, *Chicago, 1930–70*, 271–72; Mayfield, "Reorganization of Urban Politics," 250, 256–57; Ross Miller, *Here's the Deal: The Buying and Selling of a Great American City* (New York: Alfred A. Knopf, 1996), 61–62; Department of City Planning, *Development Plan for the Central Area of Chicago, a Definitive Text for Use with Graphic Presentation* (August 1958), 42, recommended approving the Fort Dearborn proposal's residential portion, which called for five thousand new dwelling units.

33. Hyman to Gold, June 26, 1951, folder "1951–1952," box 1, GLCC-CHS; Alphine Wade Jefferson, "Housing Discrimination and Community Response in North Lawndale (Chicago), Illinois 1948–1978" (Ph.D. diss., Duke University, 1979), 6. In at least one case in postwar redevelopment, an urban renewal project ended up racially integrated. Guian A. McKee, "Liberal Ends through Illiberal Means: Race, Urban Renewal, and Community in the Eastwick Section of Philadelphia, 1949–1990," *Journal of Urban History* 27 (July 2001): 547–83; *North Lawndale Citizens' Council Newsletter*, no. 5 (May 1951), folder "1951–1952," box 1, GLCC-CHS; *North Lawndale Citizens' Council Newsletter* 2, no. 1 (July 1952), folder "1951–1952," GLCC-CHS; Rieser to Peterson, May 5, 1952, folder "1951–1952," box 1, GLCC-CHS; "Introducing the Executive Board of the North Lawndale Citizens' Council," November 24, 1953, folder "1953," box 1, GLCC-CHS. For the Back of the Yards Neighborhood Council, see Robert A. Slayton, *Back of the Yards: The Making of a Local Democracy* (Chicago: University of Chicago Press, 1986); and Thomas J. Jablonsky, *Pride in the Jungle: Community and Everyday Life in Back of the Yards Chicago* (Baltimore: Johns Hopkins University Press, 1993).

34. *Lawndale Times*, October 31, 1951, folder "1951–1952," box 1, GLCC-CHS; Steinberg to Norlander, June 25, 1953, folder "1953," box 1, GLCC-CHS; Dunn to Myers, November 3, 1953, folder "1953," box 1, GLCC-CHS.

35. Summary notes of meetings on Community Conservation Sponsored by the North Lawndale Citizen's Council, November 25, 1953, folder "1953," box 1, GLCC-CHS. Indeed, the Near West Side did attract more clearance and urban renewal than other West Side communities. See Anthony Chukwuemeka Ijomah, "The Role of Major Institutions in the Redevelopment of Chicago's Near West Side, 1940–1990" (Ph.D. diss., University of Wisconsin–Milwaukee, 1991), esp. 83–107, for a description of the Medical Center area. Downs to Sternberg, November 12, 1953, folder "1953," box 1, GLCC-CHS; agenda, "'Greater Lawndale Conservation Commission' (tentative title) members, and interested community leaders," January 26, 1954, folder "Jan.–Nov. 1954," box 1, GLCC-CHS.

36. Although NLCC continued publishing its newsletter and pursuing its housing inspection work for several months, its financial support and staff energies shifted to GLCC. The Jewish People's Institute, which paid the salary of NLCC's staff member, Maida Steinberg, transferred her to the new organization. The men involved in NLCC also moved over to GLCC, leaving an assortment of mothers busy with their young children to sustain the old group. Queries about the status of NLCC made in the late 1950s suggested that it had dissolved. Blyth

to Walton, March 11, 1958, folder 382-7, Welfare Council of Metropolitan Chicago Records, Chicago Historical Society (hereafter WCMC); "GLCC at Work for Better Schools, 1955–1959," folder 6, Greater Lawndale Conservation Commission Records, Special Collections and University Archives, Richard J. Daley Library, University of Illinois at Chicago (hereafter GLCC-UIC).

37. James C. Worthy, "I Believe in Chicago's West Side," November 21, 1957, folder "Nov. 16–30, 1957," box 4, GLCC-CHS; "Report of Status and Plans to Be Submitted to Philadelphia," folder "Job Opportunities Program, 1954, Reports on Work of Program," box "Chicago R.O. Files, 1954 (Peace Ed)," AFSC.

38. Offprint, Daniel Seligman, "The Battle for Chicago," *Fortune*, June 1955, folder "April–June 1955," box 1, GLCC-CHS; James C. Worthy, "I Believe in Chicago's West Side," November 21, 1957, folder "Nov. 16–30, 1957," box 4, GLCC-CHS; Houser to Smykal, October 8, 1956, folder "Oct. 1956," box 3, GLCC-CHS; Donald R. Katz, *The Big Store: Inside the Crisis and Revolution at Sears* (New York: Viking, 1987), 257; "Report of Status and Plans to Be Submitted to Philadelphia," folder "Job Opportunities Program, 1954, Reports on Work of Program," box "Chicago R.O. Files, 1954 (Peace Ed)," AFSC; Yoshino to file, April 14, 1955, folder "Job Opportunities Program, 1955, Visits to Firms (Stores)," box "Chicago R.O. Files, 1954 (Social-Industrial) to 1955 (Job Opportunities)," AFSC; "Robert E. Wood," in *American National Biography*, ed. John A. Garraty and Mark C. Carnes (New York: Oxford University Press, 1999), 776; Yoshino to file, July 13, 1954, folder "Job Opportunities Program—Visits to Firms (Stores) 1954," box "Chicago R.O. Files, 1954 (Peace Ed)," AFSC; James C. Worthy, *Shaping an American Institution: Robert E. Wood and Sears, Roebuck* (Urbana: University of Illinois Press, 1984), 179; Gordon L. Weil, *Sears, Roebuck, U.S.A.: The Great American Catalog Store and How It Grew* (New York: Stein and Day, 1977), 105. On Wood's broader political significance, see Justus D. Doenecke, "General Robert E. Wood: The Evolution of a Conservative," *Journal of the Illinois State Historical Society* 71 (1978): 162–75. The efforts of the American Friends Service Committee to persuade Sears to hire African Americans can be traced through the following boxes in their archives in Philadelphia: "Chicago R.O. Files, 1947–1950," "Chicago R.O. Files, 1951 & 1952 (Peace Ed)," "Chicago R.O. Files, 1954 (Peace Ed)," and "Chicago R.O. Files, 1954 (Social-Industrial) to 1955 (Job Opportunities)."

39. Houser to Smykal, October 8, 1956, folder "Oct. 1956," box 3, GLCC-CHS. As late as 1964, Sears reiterated its intention to stay in Lawndale: Griffin to McCurine, November 6, 1964, folder 79, GLCC-UIC; Worthy, *Shaping an American Institution*, 173. For an overview of Sears' activities in this philanthropy, see Boris Emmet and John E. Jeuck, *Catalogues and Counters: A History of Sears, Roebuck and Company* (Chicago: University of Chicago Press, 1950) chap. 31, "Public Relations: Scholarships and Special Services." Osgood to Worthy, "Urban Renewal Program," September 29, 1955, folder "July–Sept. 1955," box 2, GLCC-CHS; Worthy to Store Managers, October 11, 1955, folder "Oct.–Dec. 1955," box 2, GLCC-CHS; *ABC's of Urban Renewal* (Chicago: Urban Renewal Division of Sears, Roebuck and Co., 1957); *ABC's of Community Planning* (Chicago: Community Planning Division of Sears, Roebuck and Co., 1962); *ABCitizens in Urban Renewal* (Chicago: Urban Renewal Division of Sears, Roebuck and Co., 1959), all in "Unprocessed Box: Planning Materials," Faith Rich Papers, Special Collections and Preservation Division, Harold Washington Library Center, Chicago (hereafter FR); Weil, *Sears*, 231–32; Theodore V. Houser, *Big Business and Human Values* (New York: McGraw-Hill, 1957), 52; James C. Worthy, "I Believe in Chicago's West Side," November 21, 1957, folder "Nov. 16–30, 1957," box 4, GLCC-CHS; Jefferson, "Housing Discrimination," 97; GLCC minutes, July 15, 1954, folder "Jan.–Nov. 1954," box 1, GLCC-CHS; membership list, December 30, 1954, folder "Dec. 1954, 1954 Undated Items," box 1, GLCC-CHS; Board of Directors meeting, December 20, 1955, folder "Oct.–Dec. 1955," box 2, GLCC-CHS. For evidence that Sears required GLCC's accounting, see Osgood to Vivas, September 11, 1957, folder "Sept. 1957," box 4, GLCC-CHS; and "The Greater Lawndale Conservation Commission," p. 4, folder "Greater Lawndale Conservation Commission," box 2, Monsignor John J. Egan Papers, Archives Division, Hesburgh Library, University of Notre Dame (hereafter CJEG).

40. Contributions, January 1955, folder "Jan.–March 1955," box 1, GLCC-CHS; Vivas to Schwartz, June 6, 1958, folder "June 1–16, 1958," box 6, GLCC; *GLCC News Notes* 3, no. 35 (January 17, 1959), folder "Jan. 1–18, 1959," box 9, GLCC-CHS; Hirsch, *Making the Second Ghetto*, 1st ed., 153; Summary notes of meetings on Community Conservation Sponsored by the North Lawndale Citizen's Council, November 25, 1953, p. 2, folder "1953," box 1, GLCC-CHS. For a sample of GLCC stationery, see folder "Jan. 1956," box 1, GLCC-CHS.

41. Mildred Berman, staff report, October 7, 1958, folder "Oct. 1–19, 1958," box 7, GLCC-CHS; minutes, staff meeting, October 6, 1958, folder "Oct. 1–19, 1958," box 7, GLCC-CHS; Steinberg to Myers, December 17, 1954, folder "Dec. 1954, 1954 Undated Items," box 1, GLCC-CHS; Douglas Park Federation of Neighborhood Clubs and Churches, folder "Jan.–Nov. 1954," box 1, GLCC-CHS; notes from the meeting of the Greater Lawndale Conservation Commission, June 24, 1954, folder "Jan.–Nov. 1954," box 1, GLCC-CHS; flyer, "TENANTS AND PROPERTY OWNERS UNITE AGAINST THIS HOAX!" folder "Jan.–March 1955," box 1, GLCC-CHS. The flyer listed the NAACP as a sponsor of the meeting. The NAACP responded with a telegram denying it had any involvement in the meeting. Western Union Telegram, Executive Committee, NAACP, to L. C. Branch, July 13, 1954, folder "Jan.–Nov. 1954," box 1, GLCC-CHS. See Hirsch, *Making the Second Ghetto*, 1st ed., 126, for a reproduction of a similar flyer. "Basis for Proposition Re: Activation of Planning and Development Committee of GLCC," October 4, 1957, folder 324-9, "Greater Lawndale Conservation Commission, 1955–61," box 324, WCMC.

42. Jefferson, "Housing Discrimination," 135; clipping, *Guidepost* 1, no. 32 (September 9, 1956), folder "Sept. 1956," box 3, GLCC-CHS. Despite these criticisms, both Branch and his wife, Dr. Dorothy Branch, remained involved in GLCC. In 1969 Mr. Branch became the organization's president. Jefferson, "Housing Discrimination," 135–39, details this conflict. Board of Directors meeting, October 16, 1956, folder "Oct. 1956," box 3, GLCC-CHS; Greater Lawndale Association of Block Clubs, folder 324-8, box 324, WCMC; clipping, *Chicago Courier*, February 10, 1962, folder "February 1962," box 18, GLCC-CHS; Board of Directors meeting, September 25, 1956, folder "Sept. 1956," box 3, GLCC-CHS.

43. Dooley to Downs, September 15, 1954, folder "Jan.–Nov., 1954," box 1, GLCC-CHS; Mackelmann to Dooley, September 23, 1954, folder "Jan.–Nov. 1954," box 1, GLCC-CHS; list of "Lawndale Leaders," March 13, 1956, and Williams to Smykal, March 12, 1956, both in folder "Feb.–Mar. 1956," box 2, GLCC-CHS; Board of Directors meeting, July 22, 1958, folder "July 1–24, 1958," box 7, GLCC-CHS.

44. Press release, September 13, 1956, folder "July–Aug. 1956," box 3, GLCC-CHS; Board of Directors meeting, September 25, 1956, folder "Sept. 1956," box 3, GLCC-CHS; Thomas A. Guglielmo, *White on Arrival: Italians, Race, Color, and Power in Chicago, 1890–1945* (New York: Oxford University Press, 2003), 152; Board of Directors meeting, October 16, 1956, folder "Oct. 1956," box 3, GLCC-CHS.

45. Williams to Osgood, October 4, 1956, folder "Oct. 1956," box 3, GLCC-CHS; see also the other statements in this folder; Board of Directors meeting, October 16, 1956, and clipping, "Salesman Dies while Giving Talk at Civic Hearing," *Chicago Sun-Times*, October 11, 1956, both in folder "Oct. 1956," box 3, GLCC-CHS; Board of Directors meeting, December 18, 1956, and clipping, *Austin News*, December 19, 1956, both in folder "Dec. 13–31, 1956," box 3, GLCC-CHS.

46. Board of Directors meeting, October 16, 1956, folder "Oct. 1956," box 3, GLCC-CHS; for details on opposition to urban renewal in Lincoln Park, see Rieger, "Redeveloping Chicago's Lincoln Park Area," 91; Paolini, "Lincoln Park Conservation Association," 57; Warner, "Renovation of Lincoln Park," 52–57; and Michael H. Ducey, *Sunday Morning: Aspects of Urban Ritual* (New York: Free Press, 1977), 27. On the relationship between the University of Chicago and the local residentially based group, see Hirsch, *Making the Second Ghetto*, 1st ed., chap. 5, especially 139.

47. Audley to Board of Directors, GLCC, "re: Housing Problems in Lawndale," folder "1957 Undated Items," box 5, GLCC-CHS; Board of Directors meeting, June 18, 1957, folder "June–July 1957," box 4, GLCC-CHS.

48. Board of Directors meeting, September 17, 1957, folder "Sept. 1957," box 4, GLCC-CHS; Board of Directors meeting, December 18, 1956, folder "Dec. 13–31, 1956," box 3, GLCC-CHS; *GLCC News Notes* 3, no. 17 (July 1957), folder "June–July 1957," box 4, GLCC-CHS; Directory of the Ladies Auxiliary, fiscal year September 1963–July 1964, folder 25, "Ladies' Auxiliary, May, 1959–January, 1966," GLCC-UIC. The motives of the members of the Ladies Auxiliary for cooperating with GLCC remain obscure. For the argument that some African American professionals in Greensboro, North Carolina, supported urban renewal despite the damage it did to the local black business district, see Sigmund G. Shipp, "Winning Some Battles but Losing the War?: Blacks and Urban Renewal in Greensboro, NC, 1953–1965," in *Urban Planning and the African American Community: In the Shadows*, ed. June Manning Thomas and Marsha Ritzdorf (Thousand Oaks, CA: Sage, 1997), 187–200.

49. Report of Executive Director to the Executive Committee of the Board, October 9, 1962, p. 3, folder "October 1962," box 19, GLCC-CHS. See also pamphlet, "Greater Lawndale Conservation Commission and What It Means to You," folder "Dec. 13–31, 1956," box 3, GLCC-CHS; Report of Executive Director, GLCC general meeting, November 18, 1957, folder "Nov. 16–30, 1957," box 4, GLCC-CHS; minutes, staff meeting, January 5, 1959, folder "Jan. 1–18, 1959," box 9, GLCC-CHS; Confidential, IRCUA, July 20, 1966, folder "Community Organizations and Officers, 1966," box 24, CJEG.

50. Statement by George H. Dovenmuehle, December 3, 1957, folder "Urban Renewal: 1949–1960," box 7, RM; clipping, *Guidepost*, November 16, 1957, scrapbook, box 31, GLCC-CHS; GLCC Board of Directors meeting, December 17, 1957, folder "Dec. 11–31, 1957," box 5, GLCC-CHS; press release, Community Conservation Board of Chicago, December 12, 1957, folder "Urban Renewal: 1949–1960," box 7, RM; GLCC Board of Directors meeting, July 22, 1958, folder "July 1–24, 1958," box 7, GLCC-CHS; list, "Names of individuals recommended as candidates to serve as members of the Lawndale Conservation Community Council," folder "August 1–19, 1958," box 7, GLCC-CHS.

51. Clipping, "Chicago Needs Renewal Cash, Doyle Says," *Chicago Sun-Times*, November 12, 1961; clipping, "New Merged Agency Will Now Direct City's $205-Million Project Face-Lift," *Chicago Sun-Times*, July 1, 1962; clipping, "Slum Eradication in Reach, Planning Council Director Says," *Chicago Sun-Times*, July 9, 1961; clipping, "Bach Sees a Doubled Attack on Blight," *Chicago Sun-Times*, July 20, 1961, all in folder "Urban Renewal, Ruth Moore By-Lines 1959–1964," box 7, RM.

52. Clipping, "Chicago Needs Renewal Cash, Doyle Says," *Chicago Sun-Times*, November 12, 1961, and clipping, "Ask $42 Million Renewal Funds," *Chicago Sun-Times*, September 4, 1964, both in folder "Urban Renewal, Ruth Moore By-Lines 1959–1964," box 7, RM; "Building Chicago," January 1960, folder 52-5, box 52, WCMC; report, Monday, March 25, 1963, folder "Daily Reports: Jan. 1963–May 1963," box 66, CJEG. On the defeat of the bond issue, see Roger Biles, *Richard J. Daley: Politics, Race, and the Governing of Chicago* (DeKalb: Northern Illinois University Press, 1995), 78–79; John G. Duba, "Urban Renewal Bond Issue Case Study," folder "Urban Renewal, 1961–1963," box 7, RM; John McMullen Ducey, "Who Killed the Urban Renewal Bond Issue?" (Center for Research in Urban Government, Loyola University, Chicago, Illinois, March 1966); and Keith McClellan, "Citizen Participation and the Role of a Civic Organization in a Large City," address before the Milwaukee County League of Women Voters, annual meeting, April 17, 1968, Chicago Historical Society.

53. Msgr. John Egan, memo for file, July 25, 1962, folder "Department of Urban Renewal," box 20 CJEG; clipping, "Chicago's Urban Renewal Clearance Almost at an End," *Chicago Sun-Times*, December 30, 1962, folder "Urban Renewal, Ruth Moore By-Lines 1959–1964," box 7, RM; memo to the Legislative Committee, Metropolitan Housing and Planning Council, December 26, 1963, folder 11, box 32, MPC accession 75-104.

54. Pritchett, "The 'Public Menace' of Blight," 16, 17; John T. McGreevy, *Parish Boundaries: The Catholic Encounter with Race in the Twentieth-Century Urban North* (Chicago: University of Chicago Press, 1996), 113; Abrahamson, *A Neighborhood Finds Itself*, 16; Mitchell to Kramer, February 1, 1945, folder 181, box 16, MPC accession 74-20.

55. "No Fair Pushing," *Garfieldian*, September 30, 1959; Brinegar to editor, *Garfieldian*, January 20, 1965; "Property Group Organizer Gives Appraisal of Racial Problem," *Garfieldian*, October 7, 1959; Tuomey to Cole, January 15, 1959, folder "Garfield Park–Austin Community Council," box 30, CJEG; Thomas, *Redevelopment and Race*, 89–98.

56. "The Baltimore Plan," *Garfieldian*, December 1, 1949; "Removing a Blight," *Garfieldian*, October 27, 1949; "A Necessary First Step," *Garfieldian*, February 17, 1954.

57. "History of Garfield Park Community," *Garfieldian*, June 27, 1946; Young to editor, *Garfieldian*, July 25, 1956; "Austin Property Owner" to editor, *Garfieldian*, July 25, 1956.

58. "Seek Name for Improvement Group," *Garfieldian*, March 17, 1954; "Ring Door Bells Today in Membership Drive," *Garfieldian*, July 14, 1954; "Civic Group Sets Meeting," *Garfieldian*, March 24, 1954. The group was initially called the "Garfield Park West Community Council," but after a year changed its name to reflect the fact that its boundaries incorporated portions of Austin. "Garfield Park Council Adds Austin to Name," *Garfieldian*, November 30, 1955. On improvement associations, see Zorita Mikva, "The Neighborhood Improvement Association: A Counter-Force to the Expansion of Chicago's Negro Population" (M.A. thesis, University of Chicago, 1951).

59. "Over 2,000 Enrolled in New Council," *Garfieldian*, September 9, 1954; "Council Acts to Cause Pool Room Move," *Garfieldian*, August 4, 1954; "4 Community Groups Help Solicit Cleanup Pledges," *Garfieldian*, August 17, 1955.

60. "Smykal Vows Aid in War on Blight," *Garfieldian*, March 14, 1956; "Estimate 1,100 Building Conversions Here," *Garfieldian*, March 21, 1956; typescript document by Tim Tuomey Jr. for "presentation to Bishop's Conference in Washington, D.C.," folder "Garfield Park–Austin Community Council," box 30, CJEG. For a comparable act of initiative by a very different residential neighborhood, see Joel Schwartz, *The New York Approach: Robert Moses, Urban Liberals, and Redevelopment of the Inner City* (Columbus: Ohio State University Press, 1993), 146–51. "Conversion Fight Gets Added Push," *Garfieldian*, April 11, 1956; "Pre-Conservation Study to Be Made by Board," *Garfieldian*, August 15, 1956.

61. GLCC Board of Directors meeting, September 25 1956, folder "Sept. 1956," box 3, GLCC-CHS; "Conservation Hearing Set," *Garfieldian*, September 19, 1956; "Ask Expansion of Conservation Area," *Garfieldian*, October 17, 1956; Janice L. Reiff, "Rethinking Pullman: Urban Space and Working-Class Activism," *Social Science History* 24 (2000): 20–21.

62. Statement of Hyman Mizruchy, October 8, 1956, folder "Oct. 1956," box 3, GLCC-CHS; "Smykal Dashes Hopes for Making Area a Conservation District," *Garfieldian*, December 19, 1956; "Council Head Rips Zoning Proposals," *Garfieldian*, December 27, 1956.

63. Tuomey, an employee of US Gypsum, may have been an enthusiastic activist because of that company's involvement in innovative rehabilitation projects; on US Gypsum's efforts, see John Thackeray, "The S.O.B.s Get Religion," *Interplay*, August–September 1968, 36–38. "Council Head Rips Zoning Proposals," *Garfieldian*, December 27, 1956; "Protest Smykal Conservation Plan," *Garfieldian*, July 24, 1957; "Area Still Fuming over Smykal Plan," *Garfieldian*, July 31, 1957; "City Planner Asked Why Garfield Park Slighted," *Garfieldian*, August 7, 1957.

64. "A Bureaucrat's Dream," *Garfieldian*, April 18, 1956; "Map Public Meeting on '220' Project," *Garfieldian*, May 14, 1958; "Conservation Board Starts Plans for Garfield Pk. Renewal Project," *Garfieldian*, July 19, 1958; "Await Federal Ruling on Conservation Plea," *Garfieldian*, April 8, 1959. For more information on section 220, see Mara Sidney, "Section 220: Mortgage and Major Home Improvement Loan Insurance for Urban Renewal Areas," 512, and Roger W. Caves, "Housing Act of 1954," 252, both in *The Encyclopedia of Housing*, ed. Willem van Vliet (Thousand Oaks, CA: Sage, 1998); "Act to Upgrade District," *Garfieldian*, May 7, 1958.

65. "Act to Upgrade District," *Garfieldian*, May 7, 1958; unidentified clipping, "55 Years of Steady Growth Reflected in Store's Anniversary Celebration," October 1, 1936, folder 12, box 2, West Garfield Park Community Collection, Special Collections and Preservation Division, Harold Washington Library Center, Chicago (hereafter WGP); "History of Garfield Park Community," *Garfieldian*, May 23, 1946; typescript, "Central Park," folder 9, box 5, WGP; *Land*

Use, 164; "Act Tomorrow on Conservation Area," *Garfieldian*, July 9, 1958; "Map Public Meeting on '220' Project," *Garfieldian*, May 14, 1958; "Conservation Hearing Tuesday," *Garfieldian*, June 25, 1958; "Conservation Board Starts Plans for Garfield Pk. Renewal Project," *Garfieldian*, July 19, 1958. The originally proposed boundaries, enclosing twelve city blocks, were Maypole, Kenton, Washington, and Pulaski. The expanded boundaries were Madison, Pulaski, Lake, and the Belt Line Railroad, an area roughly doubled in size.

66. "Now Let's Get on with Conservation," *Garfieldian*, November 19, 1958; "Time for New Push," *Garfieldian*, March 16, 1960; "Illustration," *Garfieldian*, September 14, 1960; "Community Conservation Vital Factor in City's Economic Growth," *Garfieldian*, May 24, 1961; *The Voice of St. Mel Holy Ghost Parish*, August 21, 1960, folder "West Garfield Park," box 44, CJEG; "Await Federal Ruling on Conservation Plea," *Garfieldian*, April 8, 1959; "Fr. Kelly President of Family Council," *Garfieldian*, May 15, 1963. Sociologist Pierre de Vise explained that loans made under the 220 provision "have been confined almost exclusively to structures of 50 or more units located on or close to the lake front." Buildings financed in part with 220 money included the South Shore Apartments, the Crandon Towers, Sixty-seventh and Crandon, the Oglesby Towers, and the South Shore Towers. Pierre de Vise, *Chicago's Widening Color Gap* (Chicago: Community and Family Study Center, University of Chicago, December 1967), 117–19.

67. Tuomey to Cole, January 15, 1959, folder "Garfield Park–Austin Community Council," box 30, CJEG; "Comments on the Gold Dome Dinner," *Garfieldian*, November 20, 1957; [Egan] to Coggins, May 24, 1961, folder "Midwest Community Council: Correspondence & Printed Matter," box 35, CJEG.

68. Austin Community Organization, Steering Committee, May 19, 1966, folder 48, box 2, Austin Community Collection, Special Collections and Preservation Division, Harold Washington Library Center, Chicago. For African American resistance to urban renewal, see Christopher Silver, *Twentieth-Century Richmond: Planning, Politics, and Race* (Knoxville: University of Tennessee Press, 1984), part 4, especially chap. 10, "The Era of Massive Renewal: The Battle over Fulton." On the long history of redevelopment projects in New York City neighborhoods, see Schwartz, *New York Approach*. Clipping, Jack Mabley, "Erasing Slums? Renewal Just Moving Them!" *Chicago's American*, May 29, 1962, folder 418, Saul Alinsky/Industrial Areas Foundation Records, Special Collections and University Archives, Richard J. Daley Library, University of Illinois at Chicago; Mrs. Magnolia P. Ivery to "Dear Sir," November 23, 1965, folder 4, box 50, Marcy-Newberry Records, Special Collections and University Archives, Richard J. Daley Library, University of Illinois at Chicago (hereafter MN); memo to the Legislative Committee, December 26, 1963, folder 11, box 32, MPC accession 75-104; Mollenkopf, *Contested City*, chap. 5.

69. Community Renewal Program, "Lawndale: Background for Planning," part 1, reprint Dec. 1964, and Community Renewal Program, "Lawndale . . . Proposals and Recommendations for planning," part 2, both in folder 54-3, box 54, MN; clipping, "New Plan Shows Lawndale Community as It Might Be," December 3, 1964, folder "West Side Areas, 1959–1967," box 7, RM; minutes of the Lawndale Executives meeting, November 19, 1964, folder "November 1964," box 25, GLCC-CHS; de Vise, *Chicago's Widening Color Gap*, 145.

70. Minutes, Lawndale Executives, January 21, 1965, folder 91-3, box 91, WCMC; Rich to Vivas, April 20, 1965, FR; GLCC Board of Directors meeting, January 26, 1965, folder "February–March 15, 1965," box 25, GLCC-CHS; "Recent Activities and Accomplishments, Greater Lawndale Conservation Commission," February 4, 1965, folder "Greater Lawndale Conservation Commission: Meetings, Notices, Reports," box 31, CJEG; Parks to Lawndale Executives, August 9, 1966, folder 87-6, box 87, Chicago Area Project Records, Chicago Historical Society (hereafter CAP); program, Herzl School Auditorium, November 17, 1965, folder "October–November 1965," box 27, GLCC-CHS; Parks to Council members, June 30, 1965, folder 50-4, box 50, MN.

71. Memo, Molloy to Smith, July 11, 1966, folder 8, box 5, CJEG; Lawndale Conservation

Community Council, "North Lawndale: Proposals for Conservation," August 11, 1966, folder "July 1966–March 1967," box 27, GLCC-CHS (emphasis in the original).

72. Clipping, "Lawndale Offers to Serve as a Renewal Test Area," *Chicago Sun-Times*, September 18, 1966, folder "West Side Areas, 1959–1967," box 7, RM; "Resolution on the Urban Renewal Policy for Chicago," folder "East Garfield Park Organizations, 1966–March 1969," box 7, Marillac House Records, Chicago Historical Society (hereafter MH); David L. Protess, "Community Power and Social Policy: Citizen Participation in the Chicago Model Cities Program" (Ph.D. diss., University of Chicago, 1974), 57. For the Model Cities program in Chicago, see also Richard A. Hoehn, "Model Cities and Community Organizations in Chicago: A Study in Social Ethics" (Ph.D. diss., University of Chicago, 1972). GLCC was less active in this phase of the urban renewal process than it might have been. Evidence suggests it experienced an organizational crisis in early 1967: Kellman to Egan, January 23, 1967, folder "Greater Lawndale Conservation Commission," box 2, CJEG.

73. Clipping, "Plan Threatens Lawndale, Council Candidate Charges," *Chicago Sun-Times*, February 15, 1967, folder 98–18, Chicago Urban League Records, accession 76-116, Special Collections and University Archives, Richard J. Daley Library, University of Illinois at Chicago (hereafter CUL); GLCC Board of Directors meeting, February 23, 1967, folder "Greater Lawndale Conservation Commission," box 2, CJEG. Sears denied knowledge of this plan. See water-damaged document, possibly West Side Federation minutes, folder 73-3, CUL accession 76–116. Flyer, for election of Luster H. Jackson as alderman of 29th Ward, folder "CCDBR–Lawndale, Elections 1966–1969," box 30, Chicago Committee to Defend the Bill of Rights Records, Chicago Historical Society. For more information about Draper and Kramer, see Hirsch, *Making the Second Ghetto*, 1st ed., 102; and Lois Wille, *At Home in the Loop: How Clout and Community Built Chicago's Dearborn Park* (Carbondale: Southern Illinois University Press, 1997), 61–63. See also clipping, "Luster Jackson Fights 'Puppets,'" *Garfieldian*, February 22, 1967, folder 33-1, box 33, Cyrus Hall Adams III Papers, Chicago Historical Society (hereafter CHA); clipping, "Candidate Hits Lawndale Project," *Chicago Daily News*, February 14, 1967, folder 91-7, box 91, WCMC; "A MODEL CITY IS BEING BUILT BEHIND CLOSED DOORS—AT CITY HALL," February 20, 1967, folder 93-4, box 93, WCMC; preliminary draft, Analysis of Lawndale Urban Renewal Prospects, folder 73-4, CUL accession 76-116; Charles Bowden and Lew Kreinberg, *Street Signs Chicago: Neighborhood and Other Illusions of Big-City Life* (Chicago: Chicago Review Press, 1981), 175; "Urban Affairs Weekly Report, for week ending April 30, 1967," folder "Urban Affairs Program, Reports, Weekly, Chicago Regional Office, 1966," box "Chicago R.O. 1966 (Pre-Adolescent Enrichment Prog. to Urban Affairs Prog.)," AFSC. Thirty-seventh Ward aldermanic candidate John J. Brett also raised the question, from the other side, suggesting that if the project went through, then all those displaced African Americans would no doubt bring about "total racial change of all areas of Austin!" in clipping, "Plan Would Doom Austin Brett Warns," *Garfieldian*, February 22, 1967, folder 33-1, box 33, CHA; West Side Federation, Common Council minutes, July 25, 1967, folder 73-4, CUL accession 76-116.

74. Undated press release, City-Wide Committee on Urban Renewal, folder "1967 undated," box 5, MH; Department of Urban Renewal, "Community Improvement Program Study Area: Lawndale," March 1967, folder 73-3, CUL accession 76-116. On the Chicago Freedom Movement, see James R. Ralph Jr., *Northern Protest: Martin Luther King, Jr., Chicago, and the Civil Rights Movement* (Cambridge, MA: Harvard University Press, 1993); Alan B. Anderson and George W. Pickering, *Confronting the Color Line: The Broken Promise of the Civil Rights Movement in Chicago* (Athens: University of Georgia Press, 1986); and David J. Garrow, ed., *Chicago 1966: Open Housing Marches, Summit Negotiations and Operation Breadbasket* (Brooklyn: Carlson, 1989). "Urban Affairs Weekly Report, for week ending March 12, 1967," folder "Urban Affairs Program, Reports, Weekly, Chicago Regional Office, 1966," box "Chicago R.O. 1966 (Pre-Adolescent Enrichment Prog. to Urban Affairs Prog.)," AFSC; "Urban Affairs Weekly Report, for week ending June 4, 1967," folder "Urban Affairs Program, Reports, Weekly, Chicago Regional Office, 1967," box "Chicago Regional Office 1967 Madison Area Com. to

1968 Admin. (Convention Demonstrations)," AFSC; "Recommendation to the West Side Federation," March 18, 1965, folder "West Side Federation 1965–68, Undated," box 7, MH. In Pullman, residents obtained historic landmark status in order to stave off an urban renewal effort. Reiff, "Rethinking Pullman," 27–28.

75. Background fact sheet, June 6, 1967, folder "East Garfield Park Organizations, 1966–March 1969," box 7, MH; undated press release, City-Wide Committee on Urban Renewal, folder "1967 undated," box 5, MH; "Urban Affairs Weekly Report, for week ending June 4, 1967," folder "Urban Affairs Program, Reports, Weekly, Chicago Regional Office, 1967," box "Chicago Regional Office 1967 Madison Area Com. to 1968 Admin. (Convention Demonstrations)," AFSC; "Evaluation of Pre-Conference Activity," p. 2, folder 73-3, CUL accession 76-116; "Lawndale, City Council Differ on Plans," folder 1, box 1, Daniel J. Mallette Papers, Chicago Historical Society. For similar actions in other city councils, see Mollenkopf, *Contested City*, 185, 188.

76. Jefferson, "Housing Discrimination," 134; "Urban Affairs Weekly Report, for week ending June 4, 1967, folder "Urban Affairs Program, Reports, Weekly, Chicago Regional Office, 1967," box "Chicago Regional Office 1967 Madison Area Com. to 1968 Admin. (Convention Demonstrations)," AFSC. On Abrams's experience of the conference, see Henderson, *Housing and the Democratic Ideal*, 216–17. West Side Federation, Lawndale Peoples' Planning Conference, June 6 & 7, 1967, folder 7, box 3, MPC accession 80-49; contents of folder 73-3, CUL accession 76-116; Sean Zielenbach, *The Art of Revitalization: Improving Conditions in Distressed Inner-City Neighborhoods* (New York: Garland, 2000), 153–58.

77. Department of Urban Renewal, City of Chicago, *Lawndale Conservation Plan*, March 1968, folder 50–1, MN; City of Chicago Department of Urban Renewal, *[Revised] Lawndale Conservation Plan*, January 1970, Chicago Historical Society; clipping, "Community Cancer—Can Lawndale Live?" *Chicago Today*, December 7, 1971, folder 87-4, CAP. On *Gatreaux*, see Hirsch, *Making the Second Ghetto*, 1st ed., 265. "Review at the Ending of the Year by Mrs. Pearlie Mae Robinson," folder "UN and Vista PMG," unprocessed box, top folder labeled "Westside," FR. See also Zielenbach, *Art of Revitalization*, 149–51.

78. Miller, *Here's the Deal*, 4; O'Connor, *Building a New Boston*, 137–39; Biles, *Richard J. Daley*, 48; Zielenbach, *Art of Revitalization*, 153–54; Adam Cohen and Elizabeth Taylor, *American Pharaoh: Mayor Richard J. Daley, His Battle for Chicago and the Nation* (Boston: Little, Brown, 2000), 504–5; Weil, *Sears*, 2; Jay Pridmore, *Sears Tower: A Building Book from the Chicago Architecture Foundation* (San Francisco: Pomegranate, 2002), 15–20. Sears completed its pullout from Lawndale in the 1980s: Zielenbach, *Art of Revitalization*, 159–60; Katz, *Big Store*, 259, 506; Weil, *Sears*, 121. Sears sold the Loop tower in the early 1990s, for more than five times the cost of its construction, and transferred its workers to suburban Hoffman Estates: Pridmore, *Sears Tower*, 60. Chicago Tribune, *The American Millstone: An Examination of the Nation's Permanent Underclass* (Chicago: Contemporary Books, 1986). On Lawndale's late twentieth-century turn toward revitalization, see Zielenbach, *Art of Revitalization*, 147–70.

CHAPTER FOUR

1. For one of the most important contemporary statements of how universities in urban settings should operate in the context of the "urban crisis," see the Carnegie Commission on Higher Education, *The Campus and the City: Maximizing Assets and Reducing Liabilities* (New York: McGraw-Hill, 1972). On the history of urban universities in the United States, see Thomas Arthur Kaluzynski, "An Historical View of the Concept of the Urban University" (Ph.D. diss., University of Illinois at Urbana–Champaign, 1975); and Sheldon Hackney, "The University and Its Community: Past and Present," *Annals of the American Academy of Political and Social Science* 488 (1986): 135–47. See also Gene D. Lewis and Zane L. Miller, "Charles W. Dabney and the Urban University: An Institution in Search of a Mission, 1904–1914," *Cincinnati Historical Society Bulletin* 1980 (38): 150–79.

2. George Rosen, "The Siting of the University of Illinois at Chicago Circle: A Struggle of the 1950s and 1960s," *Chicago History* 9 (Winter 1980–81): 219–33; Douglas Bukowski, *Navy*

Pier: A Chicago Landmark (Chicago: Metropolitan Pier and Exposition Authority, 1996), 42–45; Gene Arnold Burd, "The Role of the Chicago Daily Newspapers in the Selection of the Chicago Campus for the University of Illinois" (Ph.D. diss., Northwestern University, 1964), 19; Mrs. Edward S. Schneider to Mayor Daley, July 24, 1959, folder "Expansion—Sites—Garfield Park, June, 1957–March, 1961," box 8, University Archives, Chancellor's Office Records, Special Collections and University Archives, Richard J. Daley Library, University of Illinois at Chicago (hereafter UA). For an extended photo-essay on the history of the university, see Fred W. Beuttler et al., *The University of Illinois at Chicago* (Charleston, SC: Arcadia Tempus, 2000).

3. Clipping, Wolfram to *Austin News*, April 22, 1959, folder 67, box 8, UA.

4. James W. Ford Jr., "Open Land Politics in Chicago" (MA thesis, University of Chicago 1964), 54. As Barbara Ferman, *Challenging the Growth Machine: Neighborhood Politics in Chicago and Pittsburgh* (Lawrence: University Press of Kansas, 1996), 68, writes of the site-selection process, "It was not about the 'little guy' after all but about a top-down decision-making process in which powerful elites rode roughshod over neighborhood residents because it was politically possible to do so."

5. Ford, "Open Land Politics in Chicago," 51–52.

6. See M. Gordon Seyffert, "The University as an Urban Neighbor," in *Universities in the Urban Crisis*, ed. Thomas P. Murphy (New York: Dunellen, 1975), 139, on the reasons urban residents resisted nearby universities in this period. "Group Plans Bus Tour of Proposed U of I Site," *Garfieldian*, June 19, 1957.

7. "Lake-Hamlin Site Proposed for UI," *Garfieldian*, April 17, 1957; Riggs to editor, *Garfieldian*, May 27, 1959.

8. "Chicago's Opportunity: An Editorial," *Garfieldian*, October 29, 1958; "Don't Try to Con Us Out of University," *Garfieldian*, September 10, 1959; "City Planners Refuted," *Garfieldian*, June 2, 1960; Tsuchiyama to editor, *Garfieldian*, May 17, 1961. The *Garfieldian* continued to link the campus with urban renewal as the campaign proceeded: "Thousands Eagerly Sign U.I. Petitions," *Garfieldian*, September 14, 1960. See also Austin Citizens Council to editor, *Chicago Tribune*, March 27, 1959, folder 44, box 2, Austin Community Collection, Special Collections and Preservation Division, Harold Washington Library Center, Chicago; clipping, "Campus Hopes Rise," *Austin News*, April 29, 1959, folder 67, UA; "The Test of Sincerity," *Garfieldian*, March 8, 1961. The authors of a recent biography of Mayor Daley accept the arguments of the Far West Side activists, observing that "the truth was, Garfield Park was in many ways an ideal site." Adam Cohen and Elizabeth Taylor, *American Pharaoh: Mayor Richard J. Daley: His Battle for Chicago and the Nation* (Boston: Little, Brown, 2000), 227.

9. Memo, Ace and Kathy Backus to Roether, May 7, 1957, folder "Work and Study Program—Internes in Community Service Summer Project, Chicago RO 1957," box "Chicago R.O. Files 1957 #2," Chicago Regional Office Files, American Friends Service Committee Archives, Philadelphia, Pennsylvania (hereafter AFSC); Chicago ICS Report, January 22, 1958, folder "Work and Study—Internes in Community Service Winter Proj. 57–58—Staff Reports Jan.–June Chicago RO 1958," box "Chicago R.O. Files 1958," AFSC; McCawley to editor, *Garfieldian*, November 10, 1965; McCawley to editor, *Garfieldian*, August 25, 1965; Drake and Douty to Daley, April 19, 1957, folder 11, box 9, American Civil Liberties Union Illinois Division Papers, Department of Special Collections, Regenstein Library, University of Chicago; Hobbs to How and Ross, February 16, 1956, folder "Work and Study Prog.—Internes in Community Service Winter Proj. Staff Reports, Feb.–June. Chicago RO 1956," box "Chicago R.O. Files 1956 (Work & Study Prog.) to 1957 (Job Opportunities Prog.)," AFSC. For comment on the rarity of residents' awareness of the "non-physical effects of campus development," see Seyffert, "University as an Urban Neighbor," 150.

10. Ford, "Open Land Politics in Chicago," 51; "Public Support for U. of I. Campus in Park Grows," *Garfieldian*, May 28, 1958; "Chicago's Opportunity: An Editorial," *Garfieldian*, October 29, 1958; Sarafin to editor, *Garfieldian*, October 5, 1960; "80% Polled Willing to Give Up Land," *Garfieldian*, December 11, 1957; Rasky to editor, *Garfieldian*, March 25, 1959.

11. "Lake-Hamlin Site Proposed for UI," *Garfieldian*, April 17, 1957. The car barns were

still in use, but the Chicago Transit Authority indicated that it expected to vacate them within the year: "CTA to Quit Shops Here by This Fall; Could Tie-in with UI Plan," *Garfieldian*, June 3, 1959; "Outlines Boundaries of Proposed U.I. Site," *Garfieldian*, May 8, 1957; "Give Up All of Park to UI, Say Many W. Side Leaders," *Garfieldian*, December 4, 1957; "80% Polled Willing to Give Up Land," *Garfieldian*, December 11, 1957.

12. Galen Cranz, *The Politics of Park Design: A History of Urban Parks in America* (Cambridge, MA: MIT Press, 1982), 37; Everett Chamberlin, *Chicago and Its Suburbs* (Chicago: T. A. Hungerford, 1874), 326; Bessie Louise Pierce, *A History of Chicago*, 3 vols. (Chicago: University of Chicago Press, 1940), 2:341; unlabeled manuscript, folder 10, box 5, West Garfield Park Community Collection, Special Collections and Preservation Division, Harold Washington Library Center, Chicago (hereafter WGP); Julia Sniderman, "Bringing the Prairie Vision into Focus," in Chicago Historical Society, *Prairie in the City: Naturalism in Chicago's Parks, 1870–1940* ([Chicago]: Chicago Historical Society, in cooperation with the Chicago Park District and the Morton Arboretum, 1991), 21; unlabeled sheet of paper on Garfield Park history, folder 4, box 4, East Garfield Park Community Collection, Special Collections and Preservation Division, Harold Washington Library Center, Chicago (hereafter EGP).

13. Leonard K. Eaton, *Landscape Artist in America: The Life and Work of Jens Jensen* (Chicago: University of Chicago Press, 1964), 18, 33; Sniderman, "Bringing the Prairie Vision into Focus," 22; Wim de Wit and William W. Tippens, "Prairie School in the Parks," in Chicago Historical Society, *Prairie in the City*, 37; Steven A. Riess, *City Games: The Evolution of American Urban Society and the Rise of Sports* (Urbana: University of Illinois Press, 1989), 184; Robert E. Grese, *Jens Jensen: Maker of Natural Parks and Gardens* (Baltimore: Johns Hopkins University Press, 1992), 34, 69.

14. Sniderman, "Bringing the Prairie Vision into Focus," 21; de Wit and Tippens, "Prairie School in the Parks," 36; "History of Garfield Park Community," *Garfieldian*, June 6, 1946; "The West Parks and Boulevards of Chicago," folder 1, box 4, EGP; Grese, *Jens Jensen*, 71; "Historical Facts about the Garfield Park District," compiled by Martha Seewer, folder 10, box 5, WGP; Eaton, *Landscape Artist*, 33.

15. Jim Bowman, "The Way We Were," *Chicago Tribune Magazine*, October 17, 1982; "History of Garfield Park Community," *Garfieldian*, June 6, 1946; invitation, "Official Opening of Jackson Boulevard Extension through Garfield Park," Wednesday, June 9, 1937, box 15, EGP; unlabeled typescript manuscript, folder 10, box 5, WGP; "Historical Sketch of Ward 29," December 6, 1935, folder 11, box 3, EGP; interview with Mrs. Mabel Chrismon, videotape 4, Bethel New Life Collection, Special Collections and Preservation Division, Harold Washington Library Center, Chicago; clipping, *Garfieldian*, October 18, 1934, folder 2, box 1, EGP.

16. "Let's Make It a Real Park Again," *Garfieldian*, June 21, 1961; Ford, "Open Land Politics in Chicago," 41; "Lagoon Gets Cleaned Up," *Garfieldian*, July 6, 1961.

17. "Caution Bums, Keep Moving," *Garfieldian*, September 8, 1949; "W. Siders Complain Jobless Clutter Park," *Garfieldian*, July 23, 1952.

18. Clipping, "How Safe Are Our Parks?" *Chicago's American*, May 17, 1964, folder "Parks. 1950–," clipping files, Chicago Historical Society; "Public Parks—or Urban Jungles?" *Chicago Sun-Times*, June 24, 1960; "Admit 'Big Park' Police Problem," *Garfieldian*, June 28, 1960; "Teens Attack Couples, Youth in Lincoln Park," *Chicago Sun-Times*, July 27, 1960; "Daylight Attack on Woman in Grant Pk.," *Chicago Sun-Times*, August 24, 1960. For the significance of Grant Park in the city's history, see Dennis H. Cremin, "Chicago's Front Yard," *Chicago History* 27 (Spring 1998): 22–43. A few exceptional episodes drew power from a sense of implicit danger lingering in the parks over the next quarter century. In 1968, for example, the Chicago Tenants Union (CTU) staged a "tent-in" of families evicted from urban renewal land in Garfield Park. CTU intended to dramatize the shortage of housing for African Americans by sleeping in the park; their point was that the dangerous parks were safer than the housing available for blacks in Chicago. It was not until 1997, a few years into the reform of the park system under Mayor Richard M. Daley, that children again camped out in the large parks as a way of getting back to nature. In 2002 an exhibit of glass sculpture by the artist Dale Chihuly drew thousands of

Chicagoans, including whites, to Garfield Park for the first time in decades. Williams and Weston to Executive Committee, Metropolitan Program Committee, and Friends Meetings in Chicago area, September 27, 1968, folder "Metropolitan Program, Housing Program, Chicago Tenants Union Proposals, Chicago Regional Office, 1968," box "Chicago Regional Office 1968, Admin. to Metropolitan Prog. (Peace/War Issues)," AFSC; "City Kids Get a Taste of the Wild," *Chicago Tribune*, July 14, 1997; "Westward, Hope," *Chicago Tribune*, January 24, 2002. See also "East, West Garfield Magnets for Change," *Chicago Tribune*, May 18, 2003.

19. Clipping, Jack Mabley, "Erasing Slums? Renewal Just Moving Them!" *Chicago's American*, May 29, 1962, folder 418, Saul Alinsky/Industrial Areas Foundation Records, Special Collections and University Archives, Richard J. Daley Library, University of Illinois at Chicago; "W. Siders Complain Jobless Clutter Park," *Garfieldian*, July 23, 1952; McNeill to editor, *Garfieldian*, July 30, 1952; "80% Polled Willing to Give Up Land," *Garfieldian*, December 11, 1957; "20,000 Petition Park Board for U.I. Here," *Garfieldian*, June 10, 1959; Goldberg to editor, *Garfieldian*, July 27, 1960; newsletter, *Good Neighbor News*, folder 1, box 5, WGP; Cranz, *Politics of Park Design*, 137. For tension over the use of New York's Central Park by racial minorities and criminals, see Roy Rosenzweig and Elizabeth Blackmar, *The Park and the People: A History of Central Park* (Ithaca: Cornell University Press, 1992), 471–81.

20. Eaker to editor, *Garfieldian*, June 8, 1960; "Stones Tossed at Woman, Youngsters in Garf. Pk.," *Garfieldian*, August 31, 1960; Tsuchiyama to editor, *Garfieldian*, May 17, 1961; "Gang Chases Hotel Owner Out of Park," *Garfieldian*, July 6, 1961. Hotel owner Wolf sold the hotel that December: "Graemere 'Writing' New 'W. Side Story,'" *Garfieldian*, February 21, 1962. For the Graemere hotel, see folder 8, box 2, WGP.

21. Arnold R. Hirsch, *Making the Second Ghetto: Race and Housing in Chicago, 1940–1960* (New York: Cambridge University Press, 1983), 63, 89; Vincent J. Giese, *Revolution in the City* (Notre Dame, IN: Fides, 1961), 30; Cranz, *Politics of Park Design*, 199; Arnold R. Hirsch, "Massive Resistance in the Urban North: Trumbull Park, Chicago, 1953–1966," *Journal of American History* 82 (September 1995): 533; James R. Ralph Jr., *Northern Protest: Martin Luther King, Jr., Chicago, and the Civil Rights Movement* (Cambridge, MA: Harvard University Press, 1993), 13.

22. For an overview of the creation of community areas, see R. D. McKenzie, "The Ecological Approach to the Study of the Human Community," in *The City*, ed. Robert E. Park, Ernest W. Burgess, and Roderick D. McKenzie (1925; reprint, with an introduction by Morris Janowitz, Chicago: University of Chicago Press, 1967); Louis Wirth and Margaret Furez, eds., *Local Community Fact Book, 1938* (Chicago: Chicago Recreation Commission, 1938); Harvey Warren Zorbaugh, *The Gold Coast and the Slum: A Sociological Study of Chicago's Near North Side* (1929; reprint, Chicago: University of Chicago Press, 1983); Albert Hunter, *Symbolic Communities: The Persistence and Change of Chicago's Local Communities* (Chicago: University of Chicago Press, 1974); and Sudhir Alladi Venkatesh, "Chicago's Pragmatic Planners: American Sociology and the Myth of Community," *Social Science History* 25 (2001): 275–317. Venkatesh, 302, points out that once both East and West Garfield Park were occupied by African Americans, residents of both tended to refer to their neighborhood simply as "Garfield Park."

23. "Miller Meadow Best Site," *Garfieldian*, July 11, 1956; "High Housing Official Backs U.I. Site Here," *Garfieldian*, September 11, 1957; clipping, *Chicago Daily News*, May 2, 1959, folder 67, box 6, UA; Carl W. Condit, *Chicago, 1930–70: Building, Planning, and Urban Technology* (Chicago: University of Chicago Press, 1974), 229; Burd, "Role of the Chicago Daily Newspapers," 44. George Rosen, *Decision-Making Chicago-Style: The Genesis of a University of Illinois Campus* (Urbana: University of Illinois Press, 1980), chap. 4, provides a detailed overview of the steps taken by the trustees and legislators. Edward C. Banfield, *Political Influence: A New Theory of Urban Politics* (New York: Free Press, 1961), chap. 6, details the internal politics involving the proposal and rejection of the Miller Meadows site.

24. "Hint Decision Near on U. of I. Site," *Garfieldian*, September 25, 1957; Rosen, *Decision-Making*, 50–52; Edwards to Kennelly, June 16, 1953, folder 279, Chicago Urban League Records, initial accession, Special Collections and University Archives, Richard J. Daley Library,

University of Illinois at Chicago; "Support for Selling Slice of Park Grows," *Garfieldian*, May 14, 1958. On fears of displacement around the Berkeley campus, see Warren M. Campbell, *Campus Expansion and the City of Berkeley* (Syracuse, NY: Inter-University Case Program, 1973), 4–5, 52–55.

25. "Hint Decision Near on U. of I. Site," *Garfieldian*, September 25, 1957; "Support for Selling Slice of Park Grows," *Garfieldian*, May 14, 1958; "Mayor Says Site Decision Up to UI," *Garfieldian*, December 22, 1959. Rosen, *Decision-Making*, 69, notes that the motives for Daley's preference were "obscure." On the involvement of American universities in urban renewal in the postwar era, see Carnegie Commission, *Campus and the City*, 81. Department of City Planning, *Development Plan for the Central Area of Chicago, a Definitive Text for Use with Graphic Presentation* (August 1958), 19–21; Burd, "Role of the Chicago Daily Newspapers," 73–78.

26. "Council Urges U. of I. Campus in W. Garfield," *Garfieldian*, April 3, 1957; "Lake-Hamlin Site Proposed for UI," *Garfieldian*, April 17, 1957; Ford, "Open Land Politics in Chicago," 50–51; "The Case for a Four Year Branch of the University of Illinois in West Garfield Park," folder "Expansion—Sites—Garfield Park, June, 1957–March, 1961," box 8, UA.

27. "Lake-Hamlin Site Proposed for UI," *Garfieldian*, April 17, 1957.

28. Ibid. See also "Group Plans Bus Tour of Proposed U of I Site," *Garfieldian*, June 19, 1957.

29. "80% Polled Willing to Give Up Land," *Garfieldian*, December 11, 1957. Ford, "Open Land Politics in Chicago," 51, writes that it was in the context of a discussion of the possibility of putting an elementary school on another piece of parkland that locating the campus entirely within the park emerged. Mildred Berman, staff report, July 20, 1959, folder "July 1–28, 1959," box 10, Greater Lawndale Conservation Commission Records, Chicago Historical Society (hereafter GLCC-CHS); clipping, "Marillac Nuns Protest U. of I. Park Site," *Chicago Sun-Times*, May 11, 1960, folder 73, box 7, UA; Ford, "Open Land Politics in Chicago," 56. The Midwest Community Council, a Near West Side institution with little local credibility in this period, did eventually come out in favor of the park campus. Midwest Community Council, 14th Annual Dinner Meeting, May 23, 1960, Program and Annual Report, unpaginated, folder 38, Off the Street Club Records, Special Collections and University Archives, Richard J. Daley Library, University of Illinois at Chicago.

30. The editor of the *Garfieldian* wrote to the University of Illinois trustees, suggesting the Garfield Park site. Arthur H. Rotstein, "The Circle Campus—The Site *Was* the Ball Game" (Center for Policy Study, University of Chicago, 1971), 29.

31. "Give Up All of Park to UI, Say Many W. Side Leaders," *Garfieldian*, December 4, 1957; "80% Polled Willing to Give Up Land," *Garfieldian*, December 11, 1957; "Chicago's Opportunity: An Editorial," *Garfieldian*, October 29, 1958; "Survey Reveals 90% OK U. of I. in Park," *Garfieldian*, May 27, 1959.

32. The *Garfieldian*'s polls were almost certainly not reliable in any scientific sense. In the context of the controversial change of the name of Crawford Avenue to Pulaski Road, an outraged high school teacher lambasted the *Garfieldian*'s polling practices as so flawed that he would use it with his students as an example of the abuse of statistics: clipping, Czech to *Garfieldian*, January 1, 1953, folder 7, box 6, WGP. Burd, "Role of the Chicago Daily Newspapers," 82, notes that the *Garfieldian* did not feel compelled to present sides of issues that were contrary to its own opinion, so it is possible that it covered up some local opposition. Wolfram to editor, *Garfieldian*, April 22, 1959; Goldberg to editor, *Garfieldian*, July 27, 1960; Sarafin to editor, *Garfieldian*, October 5, 1960; Sarafin to editor, *Garfieldian*, February 28, 1962; Rosen, *Decision-Making*, 67. Cf. Columbia University's failed attempt, a few years later, to remove unwanted users of Morningside Park by clearing the land and building a new gymnasium, with services for Harlem residents and university students segregated. See Robert E. Price, "Columbia: Turning the University Around," in *The University and the City*, ed. George Nash (New York: McGraw-Hill, 1973), 99–101; and Roger Starr, "The Case of the Columbia Gym," *Public Interest* 13 (1968): 102–21.

33. Ford, "Open Land Politics in Chicago," 54–55; "Enthusiastic Rally Spurs Park Hopes," *Garfieldian*, April 15, 1959. It is also possible that Tuomey's long illness in 1959 prevented coop-

eration among the various West Garfield Park organizations. Garfield Park–Austin Community Council, Inc., newsletter, Autumn 1959, folder "Garfield Park–Austin Community Council," box 30, Monsignor John J. Egan Papers, Archives Division, Hesburgh Library, University of Notre Dame (hereafter CJEG); "Strong Support for UI in Park, Survey Shows," *Garfieldian*, December 11, 1957; "Block Group Considering Membership Pledge Card," *Garfieldian*, August 26, 1959; "Common Sense Arguments All Favor Park for UI Campus, Says UPG Chairman," *Garfieldian*, February 3, 1960; "University More Important to Area than Park, Says Council President," *Garfieldian*, May 25, 1960; clipping, *Chicago Tribune*, November 22, 1957, scrapbook, box 31, GLCC-CHS; Rosen, *Decision-Making*, 67; press release, March 19, 1959, folder "March 18–31, 1959," box 9, GLCC-CHS; report from committee on whether to recommend Garfield Park for UIC site, March 14, 1960, folder "March 1–16, 1960," box 13, GLCC-CHS; clipping, *Irving Park News*, March 26, 1959, folder 66, box 6, UA; clipping, "Support Mounts for Park Campus," *Austin News*, March 26, 1959, folder 66, box 6, UA; minutes, Austin YWCA Kiwanis Board, March 2, 1959, folder 5, Greater Lawndale Conservation Commission Records, Special Collections and University Archives, Richard J. Daley Library, University of Illinois at Chicago. For more on the Midwest Community Council's position, see clipping, Robson to *Chicago Daily News*, June 9, 1959, folder 71, box 6, UA; memo, July 12, 1960, "Subject: University of Illinois," box 25, folder 4, Metropolitan Planning Council Records, accession 75-104, Special Collections and University Archives, Richard J. Daley Library, University of Illinois at Chicago (hereafter MPC).

34. Rosen, *Decision-Making*, 58–59, 65; Ferman, *Challenging the Growth Machine*, 68. Mayor Richard M. Daley, the son of Richard J. Daley, waged an extended campaign during the 1990s and 2000s to close Meigs Field and convert it to parkland. Saltiel to Boemi, November 25, 1959, uncataloged box 21, folder 2, MPC accession 74-20. In the 1980s and 1990s, housing geared toward professionals working in the Loop was built on the railroad site. See Lois Wille, *At Home in the Loop: How Clout and Community Built Chicago's Dearborn Park* (Carbondale: Southern Illinois University Press, 1997). Daniel H. Burnham and Edward H. Bennett, *Plan of Chicago* (Chicago: Commercial Club, 1909), chap. 5; Condit, *Chicago, 1930–70*, 182; "Park OK Only Hurdle to U.I. Campus Site," *Garfieldian*, May 20, 1959; "Showdown Looms on Campus Site," *Garfieldian*, September 16, 1959; "Lawyers File Appeal Note in Park Suit," *Garfieldian*, September 28, 1960.

35. "Group Plans Bus Tour of Proposed U of I Site," *Garfieldian*, June 19, 1957; "Garfield Park U. of I. Site in Top 4," *Garfieldian*, October 29, 1958; Rosen, *Decision-Making*, 58; "Trustees Flunk," *Garfieldian*, March 11, 1959.

36. Clipping, "Mayor, Trustees to Confer Today on Site Problem," *Garfieldian*, May 6, 1959, folder 68, UA; "Call Mass Meeting to Boost U.I. Drive," *Garfieldian*, April 8, 1959; "Springfield Caravan Wins Support for Park Site," *Garfieldian*, April 22, 1959; Ford, "Open Land Politics in Chicago," 66.

37. "2 Civic Groups Issue Brochure Proclaiming Area's Advantages," *Garfieldian*, September 30, 1959; Garfield Park Improvement Association, "The Garfield Park Area: 'Where the City and the Suburbs Meet'" (Illinois: Westlake Press, [1959]), foreword and 15, Chicago Historical Society.

38. Ford, "Open Land Politics in Chicago," 47, notes that this parcel was different from the recommendation in the Real Estate Research Corporation report, a change whose source was obscure. Clipping, "They're Loyal to 'New' Illinois," *Chicago Daily News*, April 10, 1959, folder 67, box 6, UA; Rosen, *Decision-Making*, 65–66; clipping, "U. of I. Picks Garfield Park," *Chicago Tribune*, May 17, 1959, folder 68, box 6, UA; "Enthusiastic Rally Spurs Park Hopes," *Garfieldian*, April 15, 1959; "Springfield Caravan Wins Support for Park Site," *Garfieldian*, April 22, 1959; "Mayor, Trustees to Confer Today on Site Problem," *Garfieldian*, May 6, 1959; "Park OK Only Hurdle to U.I. Campus Site," *Garfieldian*, May 20, 1959; "20,000 Petition Park Board for U.I. Here," *Garfieldian*, June 10, 1959; "U. of I. Trustees 'Won't Back Down' on Park Site," *Garfieldian*, July 22, 1959; Garfield Park–Austin Community Council, Inc., newsletter, Autumn 1959, folder "Garfield Park–Austin Community Council," box 30, CJEG.

39. Rosen, *Decision-Making*, 68; clipping, "Garfield Pk. U. of I. Site Faces Fight," *Chicago Daily News*, May 18, 1959, folder 68, box 6, UA; "Park Land Poses Big 'If' in Drive to Get U. of I.," *Garfieldian*, December 4, 1957; "Park Availability Still Top Obstacle in Campus Drive," *Garfieldian*, March 5, 1958; "CTA to Quit Shops Here by This Fall; Could Tie-in with UI Plan," *Garfieldian*, June 3, 1959; "'Assume' Campus Set for Garf. Pk.," *Garfieldian*, June 17, 1959; "U. of I. Trustees 'Won't Back Down' on Park Site," *Garfieldian*, July 29, 1959; clipping, "Park Site Sales OKD by House," *Chicago Daily News*, June 11, 1959, folder 71, box 6, UA.

40. Condit, *Chicago, 1930–70*, 182; Mostek to Jenner, December 30, 1959, uncataloged box 20-3, MPC accession 74-20; Carter to Livingston, December 22, 1958, folder "Expansion—Sites—Garfield Park, June, 1957–March, 1961," box 8, UA; clipping, Mostek to *Chicago Daily News*, January 27, 1961, folder 74, box 7, UA; Rosen, *Decision-Making*, 68; Santogrossi to editor, *Garfieldian*, December 3, 1958; "Admit 'Big Park' Police Problem," *Garfieldian*, June 28, 1960; "Now Maybe They'll Listen," *Garfieldian*, October 26, 1960. On the debate over whom park spaces are for, see Alexander von Hoffman, *Local Attachments: The Making of an American Urban Neighborhood, 1850–1920* (Baltimore: Johns Hopkins University Press, 1994), chap. 3, "The Paradox of Parks."

41. Clipping, *Chicago Tribune*, May 11, 1960, folder "Parks. Garfield Park," clipping files, Chicago Historical Society; clipping, "Marillac Nuns Protest U. of I. Park Site," *Chicago Sun-Times*, May 11, 1960, folder 73, box 7, UA; Burd, "Role of the Chicago Daily Newspapers," 333; Mildred Berman, staff report, July 20, 1959, folder "July 1–28, 1959," box 10, GLCC-CHS.

42. Minutes, Joint Action Committee of Civic Organizations to Facilitate Selection of the South Loop Rail Terminal Site for the Chicago Campus of the University of Illinois, May 22, 1959, uncataloged box 20, folder 2, MPC accession 74-20; memo, meeting of the Central Area Action Committee, Friday, March 27, 1959, uncataloged box 21, folder 8, MPC accession 74-20; minutes of the Executive Committee meeting, May 19, 1959, uncataloged box 21, folder 2, MPC accession 74-20 (emphasis in the original); memo, July 12, 1960, "Subject: University of Illinois," box 25, folder 4, MPC accession 75-104.

43. Ford, "Open Land Politics in Chicago," 79; minutes of the Joint Action Committee of Civic Organizations, March 23, 1960, uncataloged box 21, folder 1, MPC accession 74-20; "It's Definite Now—U. of I. Wants Park," *Garfieldian*, March 23, 1960; minutes of the meeting of the Joint Action Committee, January 5, [1960?], uncataloged box 20, folder 2, MPC accession 74-20; Director, Metropolitan Housing and Planning Council, to Cooper, March 24, 1960, folder 9, box 3, MPC accession 80-49; Johnson to Boemi, May 5, 1960, folder 9, box 3, MPC accession 80-49; "Resolution of the Joint Action Committee of Civic Organizations," February 22, 1961, uncataloged box 21, folder 3, MPC accession 74-20.

44. "File Test Case for Park Campus," *Garfieldian*, March 2, 1960; "Park to Cooperate on UI Site," *Garfieldian*, March 9, 1960; "It's Definite Now—U. of I. Wants Park," *Garfieldian*, March 23, 1960; letter to Gately, April 5, 1960, folder 10, box 7, Jacob M. Arvey Papers, Chicago Historical Society (hereafter JMA). The offer for $3 million was far less than an estimate for replacement facilities scattered through the area. A confidential study produced in June 1959 estimated replacement costs at almost $37 million. Memo, Donghue and Black, to the Honorable Board of Commissioners, Chicago Park District, June 9, 1959, folder 7, box 10, JMA; clipping, "Park Board Takes No Action on U. of I. Garfield Site Plea," *Chicago Sun-Times*, March 23, 1960, folder 72, box 6, UA; "U.I. Not Giving Up on Site Here," *Garfieldian*, April 6, 1960.

45. It is possible that JAC, which was doing research into the provenance of the property in Garfield Park, had a hand in identifying suitable plaintiffs for this phase of the case. Minutes of the meeting of the Joint Action Committee, January 5, [1960?], uncataloged box 20, folder 2, MPC accession 74-20.

46. Cohen and Taylor, *American Pharaoh*, 229, point out that the judge in the case was indebted to the Cook County Democratic machine.

47. The park commissioners also allowed the board of education to lease enough land in Douglas Park to house twenty-six mobile classrooms in 1962. See attachment to letter, Flaherty, to Arvey, May 2, 1962, folder 8, box 6, JMA. In addition, the board opened the Ericson school

in Garfield Park in December 1962. "Grammar School Built in Park Opens Monday," *Garfieldian*, November 28, 1962.

48. Clipping, "Park Board Takes No Action on U. of I. Garfield Site Plea," *Chicago Sun-Times*, March 23, 1960, folder 72, box 6, UA; Rosen, *Decision-Making*, 72, 77; clipping, "U. of I. Garfield Park Bid Still Faces Many a Snag," *Chicago Daily News*, March 23, 1960, folder 72, box 6, UA; "Park to Cooperate on UI Site," *Garfieldian*, March 9, 1960; "Garfield P. Campus 'Virtually Assured,'" *Garfieldian*, April 13, 1960; "Await Ruling in Park Suit," *Garfieldian*, June 15, 1960; "To Appeal Harrington's Decision in Garf. Pk. Suit," *Garfieldian*, August 31, 1960; "Cite Cases of Park Land Sale," *Garfieldian*, November 30, 1960; "Supreme Court Rules Park Can Be Used for Campus," *Garfieldian*, January 18, 1961. See also attachment to letter, Kerwin to Arvey, January 23, 1961, folder 10, box 7, JMA.

49. "'Assume' Campus Set for Garf. Pk.," *Garfieldian*, June 17, 1959; Ford, "Open Land Politics in Chicago," 57; clipping, "Clouter with Conscience," *Time*, March 15, 1963, 24, folder 19-5, box 19, Citizens Schools Committee Records, Chicago Historical Society; Rosen, *Decision-Making*, 45.

50. Rosen, *Decision-Making*, 73, 77; "Not a Serious Threat," *Garfieldian*, July 15, 1960; "Start New Petition to Boost U.I. Here," *Garfieldian*, September 8, 1960; Ford, "Open Land Politics in Chicago," 82; Daily Report entries, August 1, 5, 21, and September 12, folder "Daily Reports: July–December 1960," box 55, CJEG; press release, Department of City Planning, September 27, 1960, folder 7, box 21, MPC accession 74-20; "Lawyers File Appeal Note in Park Suit," *Garfieldian*, September 28, 1960; "'Assume' Campus Set for Garf. Pk.," *Garfieldian*, June 17, 1959; multiple articles, *Garfieldian*, February 15, 1961; Burd, "Role of the Chicago Daily Newspapers," 312, 341, 361, 509, 511; unidentified clipping, "Board Listens, Ignores Pleas," folder "University of Illinois Chicago Campus, Newspaper clippings," box 35, CJEG. On learning of the decision, JAC disbanded: clipping, "Committee OK's Site, Disbands," *Chicago's American*, February 22, 1961, folder 68, box 6, MPC accession 74-20.

51. "Residents Shocked, Angry at U. of I. Site Decision," *Garfieldian*, February 15, 1961.

52. "Reverse Site, 2 Areas Ask," *Garfieldian*, February 15, 1961; "Harrison-Halsted Groups Organize to Fight U.I.," *Garfieldian*, February 22, 1961; "Near Riot after Vote on UI Site," *Garfieldian*, April 19, 1961; Studs Terkel, *Division Street, America* (New York: Pantheon, 1967), 7; Rosen, *Decision-Making*, 116–18; Cohen and Taylor, *American Pharaoh*, 229–31; Harold M. Mayer and Richard C. Wade, *Chicago: Growth of a Metropolis* (Chicago: University of Chicago Press, 1969), 442, note that the university was the only one in the world known to be named for a traffic interchange. The campus is now called the University of Illinois at Chicago. For an example of conflicts between a university and the city of Berkeley, California, see Campbell, *Campus Expansion*; and Carroll Brentano, "The Two Berkeleys: City and University through 125 Years," *Minerva* 33 (1995): 361–71. On the "acrimonious" construction of University City to serve Wayne State University, see June Manning Thomas, *Redevelopment and Race: Planning a Finer City in Postwar Detroit* (Baltimore: Johns Hopkins University Press, 1997), 108–11.

53. For early postwar acknowledgments of this shortage, see "No Vacant Lots," *Garfieldian*, March 15, 1945; "Play's the Thing," *Garfieldian*, July 12, 1945; and "The Playground Problem," *Garfieldian*, May 14, 1947. Condit, *Chicago, 1930–70*, 228–29, notes that in 1967 Chicago had only 1.9 acres of parkland per 1,000 residents, well below the 10 acres recommended by the National Recreation Association.

54. Burd, "Role of the Chicago Daily Newspapers," 90, notes this development but does not elaborate on it. For overviews of the creation of small parks in Chicago, see Michael Patrick McCarthy, "Politics and the Parks: Chicago Businessmen and the Recreation Movement," *Journal of the Illinois State Historical Society* 65 (1972): 158–172, and his "Businessmen and Professionals in Municipal Reform: The Chicago Experience, 1887–1920" (Ph.D. diss., Northwestern University, 1970); Special Collections Department, the Chicago Public Library, and the Chicago Park District, *A Breath of Fresh Air: Chicago's Neighborhood Parks of the Progressive Reform Era, 1900–1925* (n.p., 1989) (hereafter *A Breath of Fresh Air*); Benjamin McArthur, "The Chicago Playground Movement: A Neglected Feature of Social Justice," *Social*

Science Review 49 (September 1975): 379; and Joan E. Draper, "The Art and Science of Park Planning in the United States: Chicago's Small Parks, 1902 to 1905," in *Planning the Twentieth Century American City*, ed. Mary Corbin Sies and Christopher Silver (Baltimore: Johns Hopkins University Press, 1996).

55. "Chicago's Opportunity: An Editorial," *Garfieldian*, October 29, 1958; Santogrossi to editor, *Garfieldian*, December 3, 1958; "Thousands Eagerly Sign U.I. Petitions," *Garfieldian*, September 14, 1960; "West Side Small Park Plan Presented to Park Head," *Garfieldian*, December 7, 1960.

56. Cranz, *Politics of Park Design*, 199; Thomas J. Jablonsky, *Pride in the Jungle: Community and Everyday Life in Back of the Yards Chicago* (Baltimore: Johns Hopkins University Press, 1993), 109–14. By contrast, David Nasaw, *Children of the City: At Work and at Play* (Garden City, NY: Anchor Press/Doubleday, 1985), 35–38, argues that children at the turn of the century did not use small parks extensively.

57. "The Mayor's Belated Admission," *Garfieldian*, October 6, 1965; Daphne Christensen, ed., *Chicago Public Works: A History* (Chicago: Rand McNally, 1973), 218–21; Benjamin McArthur, "Parks, Playgrounds, and Progressivism," in *A Breath of Fresh Air*, 11; Dominic Pacyga, "Parks for the People," in *A Breath of Fresh Air*, 19; McArthur, "The Chicago Playground Movement," 388; Cranz, *Politics of Park Design*, viii, 135–37.

58. Memo, Dunagan to Sister Mary William, February 11, 1964, folder "Jan.–May, 1964," box 2, Marillac House Records, Chicago Historical Society; Carlyle to Mrs. Marie Clayton, March 21, 1958, folder "March 18–31, 1958," box 6, GLCC-CHS; "OK Youth Office for West Garfield Park," *Garfieldian*, November 3, 1965; "WACA Tells Urban Improvement Plan," *Garfieldian*, July 28, 1965; "West Garfield Community News and Comment," *Garfieldian*, August 10, 1966; memo, Martin to Cash, August 5, 1965, folder "August 1965," box 26, GLCC-CHS.

CHAPTER FIVE

1. Dewsberry to Adams, January 5, 1965, folder 8-5, box 8, Cyrus Hall Adams III Papers, Chicago Historical Society (hereafter CHA); clipping, "Controversy Revolves around Principal," *Chicago Tribune*, April 5, 1970, folder 14, box 1, Austin High School Collection, Special Collections and Preservation Division, Harold Washington Library Center, Chicago (hereafter AHS); "McKeag Reveals 'Loophole' Precedent," *Austinite*, January 28, 1970, box 7, Austin Newspaper Collection, Special Collections and Preservation Division, Harold Washington Library Center, Chicago (hereafter ANC).

2. For an overview of school desegregation in the United States, see Richard Kluger, *Simple Justice: The History of Brown v. Board of Education and Black America's Struggle for Equality* (New York: Vintage Books, 1975); and James T. Patterson, *Brown v. Board of Education: A Civil Rights Milestone and Its Troubled Legacy* (Oxford: Oxford University Press, 2001). Liva Baker, *The Second Battle of New Orleans: The Hundred-Year Struggle to Integrate the Schools* (New York: HarperCollins, 1996), 395–401, 411–21, 431–33; Matthew D. Lassiter and Andrew B. Lewis, eds., *The Moderates' Dilemma: Massive Resistance to School Desegregation in Virginia* (Charlottesville: University Press of Virginia, 1998); James McGrath Morris, "A Chink in the Armor: The Black-Led Struggle for School Desegregation in Arlington, Virginia, and the End of Massive Resistance," *Journal of Policy History* 13 (2001): 329–66.

3. Vincent P. Franklin, "The Persistence of School Segregation in the Urban North: An Historical Perspective," *Journal of Ethnic Studies* 1 (Winter 1974): 51–68; Ronald P. Formisano, *Boston against Busing: Race, Class, and Ethnicity in the 1960s and 1970s* (Chapel Hill: University of North Carolina Press, 1991); J. Anthony Lukas, *Common Ground: A Turbulent Decade in the Lives of Three American Families* (New York: Vintage Books, 1986).

4. Michael W. Homel, *Down from Equality: Black Chicagoans and the Public Schools, 1920–41* (Urbana: University of Illinois Press, 1984), 172–73.

5. On moderates, see Formisano, *Boston against Busing*, chap. 8; and Andrew B. Lewis, "Emergency Mothers: Basement Schools and the Preservation of Public Education in Charlottesville," in Lassiter and Lewis, *Moderates' Dilemma*, 72–103.

6. Clipping, "Chicago: Legacy of an Ice Age," *SR*, May 20, 1967, folder 28-2, box 28, CHA; John L. Rury, "Race, Space, and the Politics of Chicago's Public Schools: Benjamin Willis and the Tragedy of Urban Education," *History of Education Quarterly* 39 (1999): 134; Jennifer L. Hochschild, *The New American Dilemma: Liberal Democracy and School Desegregation* (New Haven: Yale University Press, 1984), chap. 5.

7. John M. Wozniak, "Oral History and Collective Biography: Three Selected Board Veterans of the Chicago Public Schools," *Vitae Scholasticae* 2 (Fall 1983): 433; Rury, "Race, Space," 125; Mary J. Herrick, *The Chicago Schools: A Social and Political History* (Beverly Hills: Sage, 1971), 43, 75, 83, 113, 114, 134, 149, 179, 223, chap. 15; Homel, *Down from Equality*, chap. 5, "Black Activism," esp. 152–57.

8. Paul E. Peterson, *School Politics, Chicago Style* (Chicago: University of Chicago Press, 1976), 83. The opinion of Mary Herrick, the historian of the Chicago Public Schools, about their administration between the 1930s and the 1950s is clearly expressed in the titles of the chapters about this period in *Chicago Schools*. Chapter 12, about the effects of the Great Depression on the school system, is entitled "The Axe Falls on Instruction—Not on Patronage"; Rury, "Race, Space," 125; Roger Biles, *Big City Boss in Depression and War: Mayor Edward J. Kelly of Chicago* (DeKalb: Northern Illinois University Press, 1984), 137–42; Peterson, *School Politics, Chicago Style*, 85, attributes Kelly's downfall to the scandal over his unwillingness to participate in school reform; Herrick, *Chicago Schools*, chap. 15, 306, 311; Benjamin Coppage Willis, "A Mid-Century View of Staffing a City School System" (Ed.D. diss., Teachers College, Columbia University, 1950). Faith Rich, a persistent critic of Willis's administration of the schools, said that the thesis "boiled down to promoting the ones you wanted to. Naturally, the results do not correlate with scholarship, ability, or the welfare of the community. But they do correlate with system control or keeping the lid on." Faith to Meyer, June 22, 1967, "1967 Correspondence," Faith Rich Papers, Special Collections and Preservation Division, Harold Washington Library Center, Chicago (hereafter FR). For an overview of Willis's career, see "Benjamin Coppage Willis," in *Biographical Dictionary of Modern American Educators*, ed. Frederick Ohles, Shirley M. Ohles, and John G. Ramsay (Westport, CT: Greenwood Press, 1997), 333. For Willis's tenure in Chicago, see Rury, "Race, Space." Neil E. Lloyd, "The Decision-Making Process and the Chicago Board of Education: The 1968 Busing Decision" (Ph.D. diss., Loyola University, 1974), 97; and Dionne Danns, *Something Better for Our Children: Black Organizing in Chicago Public Schools, 1963–1971* (New York: Routledge, 2003), chap. 3. Cf. Formisano, *Boston against Busing*, 41, who points out that the elected members of the Boston School Committee treated their positions as stepping-stones to higher political office.

9. Hauser to Berry, January 15, 1965, folder 22–2, box 22, Citizens Schools Committee Records, Chicago Historical Society (hereafter CSC). Only New York governor Nelson Rockefeller, New York City mayor Robert Wagner, and President Kennedy earned more than Willis. Clipping, "Retains Chicago Position," *Chicago Daily News*, January 11, 1963, clipping file "Biography. Willis, Benjamin C.," Chicago Historical Society; clipping, "Stormy School Era Will End with Willis," May 29, 1966, *Chicago Sun-Times*, folder 20-1, box 20, CHA.

10. Clipping, "Willis' Resignation," October 5, 1963, *Chicago's American*, folder 1-4, box 1, CHA; Katz to Adams, April 19, 1965, folder 10-4, box 10, CHA; Thomas Foster Koerner, "Benjamin C. Willis and the Chicago Press" (Ph.D. diss., Northwestern University, 1968), 5–9, 180. Herrick, *Chicago Schools*, 306, 311; "Willis' Resignation," *Garfieldian*, October 9, 1963; "Few Seek Transfers," *Garfieldian*, December 26, 1963; clipping, James Yuenger, *Chicago Tribune*, October 2, 1966, Benjamin C. Willis clipping file, Chicago Historical Society.

11. Adam Cohen and Elizabeth Taylor, *American Pharaoh: Mayor Richard J. Daley, His Battle for Chicago and the Nation* (Boston: Little, Brown, 2000), 307, 350; clipping, James Yuenger, *Chicago Tribune*, October 2, 1966, Benjamin C. Willis clipping file, Chicago Historical Society; Robert J. Havighurst, *The Public Schools of Chicago: A Survey for the Board of Education for the City of Chicago* (Chicago: Board of Education of the City of Chicago, 1964), 17, 335; Roger Biles, *Richard J. Daley: Politics, Race, and the Governing of Chicago* (DeKalb: Northern Illinois University Press, 1995), 115; Mrs. Junerous Cook, "Public School Segregation: City of

Chicago, 1963–1964 and 1964–1965," May 12, 1965, folder 11-1, box 11, CHA; Leonard Nathaniel Moore, "The School Desegregation Crisis of Cleveland, Ohio, 1963–1964: The Catalyst for Black Political Power in a Northern City," *Journal of Urban History* 28 (2002): 149; Adams to Spacek, June 5, 1967, folder 28–3, box 28, CHA; typescript, Jan.–Feb. of 1967, brown scrapbook, "Cyrus H. Adams III, Carson Pirie Scott & Company, 1932–1968," CHA.

12. Herrick, *Chicago Schools*, 286; Brian J. L. Berry et al., *Chicago: Transformations of an Urban System* (Cambridge, MA: Ballinger, 1976), 60–61; Kelly to editor, *Garfieldian*, September 10, 1959; "It Looks Like Overcrowding," *Garfieldian*, November 17, 1965; minutes, Orientation Committee for new and old neighbors, August 28, 1959, folder "Rendu House, 1954–1961," box 7, Marillac House Records, Chicago Historical Society; clipping, Edward R. F. Sheehan, "Not Peace, but the Sword: The New Anguish of American Catholicism," *Saturday Evening Post*, November 28, 1964, p. 28, box 6, Daniel J. Mallette Papers, Chicago Historical Society.

13. Willis statement to the Board of Education, October 10, 1962, folder 19-4, box 19, CSC; Rury, "Race, Space," 126; "More on Speculators," *Garfieldian*, August 21, 1963; "Paradox," *Garfieldian*, November 8, 1961.

14. "Ask Relief of Bryant School Overcrowding," *Garfieldian*, January 5, 1956; report of Schools Committee meeting, June 10, 1960, folder 10, Greater Lawndale Conservation Commission Records, Special Collections and University Archives, Richard J. Daley Library, University of Illinois at Chicago (hereafter GLCC-UIC). On the fire at Our Lady of the Angels, see David Cowan and John Kuenster, *To Sleep with the Angels: The Story of a Fire* (Chicago: Ivan R. Dee, 1996); and Daniel Greene, "Tragedy in the Parish," *Chicago History* (Spring 2001): 4–19. Moore, "School Desegregation Crisis," 136; Wendell Pritchett, *Brownsville, Brooklyn: Blacks, Jews, and the Changing Face of the Ghetto* (Chicago: University of Chicago Press, 2002), 221.

15. Statements of Rev. Warren Kelly, James King, and Lillian Bickham, September 26, 1960, all in folder "September 1960," box 14, Greater Lawndale Conservation Commission Records, Chicago Historical Society (hereafter GLCC-CHS); statement of James King, December 20, 1960, folder "December 1960," box 15, GLCC-CHS. For objections to the use of double shifts in the 1930s, see Danns, *Something Better*, 14–15.

16. "Urge Action in Lawndale School Crisis," *Garfieldian*, July 11, 1956; "Lawndale Eyes Empty School Seats," *Garfieldian*, July 7, 1960; "GLCC at Work for Better Schools, 1955–1959," p. 3, folder 6, GLCC-UIC; Williams to Rogers, July 12, 1955, folder 1, GLCC-UIC; Thomas to Willis, August 5, 1957, folder 3, GLCC-UIC; Peck to Shriver, June 14, 1960, folder "June 1–20, 1960," box 13, GLCC-CHS; "Lawndale Group Renews School Bus Plan Fight," *Garfieldian*, October 5, 1960; statement of Franklin Park Community Council, December 26, 1956, folder 2, GLCC-UIC; minutes, Board of Directors, July 26, 1960, folder "July 1960," box 14, GLCC-CHS; statement of James King, December 20, 1960, folder 12, GLCC-UIC; statement of Claude Peck, December 16, 1959, folder "Dec. 1–25, 1959," box 11, GLCC-CHS.

17. "Lawndale Eyes Empty School Seats," *Garfieldian*, July 7, 1960; John E. Coons, *Chicago: Civil Rights U.S.A., Public Schools: Cities in the North and West, 1962: A Report to the United States Commission on Civil Rights* ([Washington, DC]: The Commission, 1962), 223, explained that elementary schools running on a normal schedule conducted just under of five hours of classes and recess, while a double shift lasted three hours and fifty-five minutes. Mrs. Lauri Wynn, "A Statement concerning Community Problems in the Greater Lawndale Area," April 10–12, 1959, folder "Lawndale (Greater, Conserv. Area): Proposals, Printed Matter," box 34, Monsignor John J. Egan Papers, Archives Division, Hesburgh Library, University of Notre Dame (hereafter CJEG); *GLCC News Notes* 4, no. 8 (October 1960), folder "October, 1960," box 14, GLCC-CHS; Shriver to Jones, July 24, 1957, folder 3, GLCC-UIC; Greater Lawndale Conservation Commission, Board of Directors meeting of January 31, 1961, folder "Jan. 20–31, 1961," box 15, GLCC-CHS; Pritchett, *Brownsville, Brooklyn*, 226; Formisano, *Boston against Busing*, 37.

18. Willis to Peck, April 25, 1960, folder 9, GLCC-UIC; "Lawndale Group Renews School Bus Plan Fight," *Garfieldian*, October 5, 1960; clipping, *Chicago Sun-Times*, December 27, 1957,

scrapbook, box 31, GLCC-CHS; "2 Garfield Park Sites Sought for Schools," *Garfieldian*, June 17, 1959; meeting of Greater Lawndale Conservation Commission Committee with Dr. Benjamin Willis, folder 2, GLCC-UIC; "Another first born" to "J," June 17, 1960, folder "June 21–30, 1960," box 14, GLCC-CHS; clipping, "Your Community Newspaper," January 25, 1961, folder "Jan. 20–31, 1961," box 15, GLCC-CHS.

19. Coons, *Civil Rights U.S.A.*, 188; "Consider New Boundaries for 8 West Side Schools," *Garfieldian*, June 24, 1959; Lloyd, "Decision-Making Process," 79; Tommy to Faith, October 2, 1961, FR. For a similar policy in Louisiana, justified by the "Parker Doctrine," see Baker, *Second Battle of New Orleans*, 246–48.

20. "Lawndale Eyes Empty School Seats," *Garfieldian*, July 7, 1960; "West Side Hearings Thursday September 29: *End Double Shift Now*," folder 11, GLCC-UIC; "Austin Group Fights School Transport Plan," *Garfieldian*, August 31, 1960. On the practice of using geography as a mask for racial descriptions in Chicago, see Joleen Kirschenman and Kathryn M. Neckerman, "'We'd Love to Hire Them, But . . .': The Meaning of Race for Employers," in *The Urban Underclass*, ed. Christopher Jencks and Paul E. Peterson (Washington, DC: Brookings Institution, 1991): 203–32.

21. "Alderman to Probe Gregory Transfers," *Garfieldian*, October 16, 1957; "The Gregory Problem," *Garfieldian*, October 23, 1957; "Horan Raps Transfer of Gregory Students," *Garfieldian*, November 20, 1957. The Ladies Auxiliary of the Greater Lawndale Conservation Commission, which consisted of African American professional women, responded by gathering six hundred signatures requesting that the school board keep Gregory integrated. *GLCC News Notes* 3, no. 20 (October 15, 1957), folder "Oct. 1–24, 1957," box 4, GLCC-CHS.

22. "Blocks Organize South of Highway," *Garfieldian*, September 10, 1959; "End Sumner Terror, Appeal of Parents," *Garfieldian*, September 16, 1959; "Look to Meeting with District Head to Solve Sumner 'Terror,'" *Garfieldian*, September 23, 1959; "Meet on Sumner Problems Friday," *Garfieldian*, September 30, 1959. The use of the Catholic schools as an alternative to public schools beginning to include black students was not an uncommon practice. See William Anton Vrame, "A History of School Desegregation in Chicago since 1954" (Ph.D. diss., University of Wisconsin, 1970), 119n9, 134.

23. "District 8" in "A long range school facilities program, 1967–71," folder 34-1, box 34, CHA; "2 Garfield Park Sites Sought for Schools," *Garfieldian*, June 17, 1959; "Enroll 1,700 at Hefferan Grade School," *Garfieldian*, December 13, 1961; "Zig-Zag Boundaries in 4 School Areas Hit by UPG," *Garfieldian*, August 22, 1962; "School Aid [*sic*] Says There's 'Pattern' in Attacks on Marconi Girls," *Garfieldian*, May 15, 1963. For the history of the United Property Group, see chapter 7.

24. "Zig-Zag Boundaries in 4 School Areas Hit by UPG," *Garfieldian*, August 22, 1962; Becky M. Nicolaides, *My Blue Heaven: Life and Politics in the Working-Class Suburbs of Los Angeles, 1920–1965* (Chicago: University of Chicago Press, 2002), 301–2; "Block Club News and Comment," *Garfieldian*, October 20, 1965.

25. "UPG Circulating School Petitions," *Garfieldian*, August 29, 1962; "Schools, UPG Confer in Boundary Dispute," *Garfieldian*, September 6, 1962; "Willis Ignores Boundary Fight," *Garfieldian*, September 12, 1962; "Mayor Aide Meets UPG on Protests," *Garfieldian*, September 19, 1962; "Again, Perseverance Pays," *Garfieldian*, November 7, 1962.

26. "Lawndale Group Renews School Bus Plan Fight," *Garfieldian*, October 5, 1960; "Gregory Club Urges School 'Bus' Plan," *Garfieldian*, December 29, 1960; Faith to Mama, January 28, 1961, FR; statement of Rev. Warren Kelly, September 26, 1960, folder "September 1960," box 14, GLCC-CHS; Chicago Branch NAACP, "Membership Meeting on Public Schools, Draft of Summary and Recommendations," March 28, 1958, folder 15-4, box 15, CSC; Homel, *Down from Equality*, chap. 5.

27. Rich to Cruse, May 9, 1969, FR; clipping, "Faith," *Chicago Reader*, August 5, 1983, FR; report of the GLCC Schools Committee meeting, July 14, 1961, folder "July 1961," box 16, GLCC-CHS.

28. Rich to Rose, April 28, 1959, FR papers; Faith [Rich] to Jay [Vivas], August 14, 1960,

folder 11, "Citizens School Committee, 1960, August–September, 1960," GLCC-UIC; "Facts Show Double Shift and Crowded Schools No Longer Necessary," folder "August 1960," box 14, GLCC-CHS; "Lawndale Eyes Empty School Seats," *Garfieldian*, July 7, 1960; Report of Schools Committee meeting, June 10, 1960, folder 10, "Citizen School Committee 1960, June–July 1960," GLCC-UIC; statement of Claude Peck, December 16, 1959, folder "Dec. 1–25, 1959," box 11, GLCC-CHS (emphasis in the original); "De Facto Segregation in the Chicago Public Schools," *Crisis* (February 1958): 87–93, 126–27; statement of Edwin C. Berry, February 1, 1962, folder "February 1962," box 18, GLCC-CHS; "Willis Refutes Urban League Room Count," *Garfieldian*, January 17, 1962; Lloyd, "Decision-Making Process," 70; Vrame, "History of School Desegregation," 39.

29. Clipping, *Chicago Sun-Times*, February 9, 1962, folder "February 1962," box 18, GLCC-CHS; "Double Shift Ends at Delano School!" *Garfieldian*, March 7, 1962; clipping, *Chicago Sun-Times*, March 1, 1962, folder "March 1–20, 1962," box 18, GLCC-CHS; Rury, "Race, Space," 131; James R. Ralph Jr., *Northern Protest: Martin Luther King, Jr., Chicago, and the Civil Rights Movement* (Cambridge, MA: Harvard University Press, 1993).17; on The Woodlawn Organization, see John Hall Fish, *Black Power/White Control: The Struggle of The Woodlawn Organization in Chicago* (Princeton: Princeton University Press, 1973). *Lawndale Journal*, March 1962, folder "March 21–30, 1962," box 18, GLCC-CHS; for an example of Willis's denials, see clipping, *Chicago Defender*, January 11–17, 1961, folder "Jan. 1–19, 1961," box 15, GLCC-CHS.

30. Herrick, *Chicago Schools*, 329.

31. Alan B. Anderson and George W. Pickering, *Confronting the Color Line: The Broken Promise of the Civil Rights Movement in Chicago* (Athens: University of Georgia Press, 1986), 348; Danns, *Something Better*, 44–49. For more detailed narratives, see Catherine Sardo Weidner, "Debating the Future of Chicago's Black Youth: Black Professionals, Black Labor and Educational Politics during the Civil Rights Era, 1950–1965" (Ph.D. diss., Northwestern University, 1989), chap. 4, "The Board of Education and De Facto Segregation, 1950–1965"; and Coons, *Civil Rights U.S.A.*, 209–15. The cases were *Webb v. the Board of Education* (Civ. No. 61C1569 D.C., N.D. Ill.) and *Burroughs v. the Board of Education* (Civ. No. 62C206, D.C., N.D. Ill.). Baron to Berry, July 23, 1964, folder 1-2, Chicago Urban League Records, accession 81-12, Special Collections and University Archives, Richard J. Daley Library, University of Illinois at Chicago (hereafter CUL); Benjamin C. Willis, statement to the Board of Education, August 28, 1963, folder 20-1, box 20, CSC; Weidner, "Debating the Future," 270–71. Advisory Panel on Integration in the Public Schools, *Report to the Board of Education of the City of Chicago* (Chicago Board of Education, March 31, 1964), 14–15, 26–29; Herrick, *Chicago Schools*, 324; Lloyd, "Decision-Making Process," 88. The *Chicago Tribune* noted that the term "cluster," used to describe this plan, did not appear in the Hauser Report itself: clipping, "1964 Was the Year of Surveys in City's Schools," *Chicago Tribune*, January 3, 1965, Information folder, box 1, CHA; Havighurst, *Public Schools of Chicago*, 370, 380, 383.

32. Rury, "Race, Space," 133; clippings from all the major daily newspapers, October 5, 1963, folder 1-4, box 1, CHA; Herrick, *Chicago Schools*, 316–18; Anderson and Pickering, *Confronting the Color Line*, 117–18.

33. Baker, *Second Battle of New Orleans*, 401; see Lewis, "Emergency Mothers"; and Amy E. Murrel, "The 'Impossible' Prince Edward Case: The Endurance of Resistance in a Southside County, 1959–1964," in Lassiter and Lewis, *Moderates' Dilemma*, 134–67. Jerald E. Podair, *The Strike that Changed New York: Blacks, Whites, and the Ocean Hill–Brownsville Crisis* (New Haven: Yale University Press, 2002), 29, notes that a group of white parents in New York City opened a private school for their children rather than cooperate in desegregating the public schools in 1964. List of CCCO demands, October 21, 1963, folder 1-5, box 1, CHA; Anderson and Pickering, *Confronting the Color Line*, 118–21, 128–33.

34. Raby to Keppel, July 4, 1965, folder 12-2, box 12, CHA.

35. Baron to Berry, June 4, 1964, folder 3-3, box 3, CHA; clipping, "Whiston to Head School Board," *Chicago Tribune*, May 27, 1964, folder 8-4, box 8, CHA; clipping, "School Bd. Told of

Transfer Plan, Elects Whiston," *Chicago Sun-Times*, May 28, 1964, folder 8-4, box 8, CHA; transcript of minutes of the meeting of the Special Committee on the Hauser Report, Wednesday, May 26, 1964, p. 29, folder 3-2, box 3, CHA; unidentified clipping, "28 of 1,653 Pupils Seek to Transfer," folder 8-4, box 8, CHA.

36. Clipping, "'Cluster' Plan Rescued," *Chicago Daily News*, June 19, 1964, folder 8-4, box 8, CHA; verbatim transcript of the minutes of the meeting of the Special Committee on the Hauser Report, Wednesday, June 17, 1964, folder 3-3, box 3, CHA; report, Citizens Schools Committee, December 1964, folder 22-1, box 22, CSC; "No Definite Plan for Clusters Here," *Garfieldian*, November 26, 1964. The student bodies at Marshall and Sumner were 97 percent and 99 percent African American, respectively; at May and Austin they were 76 percent and 97 percent white. "Board to Take Up Cluster Plan Today," *Garfieldian*, December 9, 1964; "To Seek Community View on Clustering," *Garfieldian*, December 16, 1964.

37. "Few Attend Marshall, Sumner Cluster Talks," *Garfieldian*, December 22, 1964. It is possible that the low turnout at the meetings resulted from their timing in the middle of the workday. Undated letter, Malone to parents, folder 7-2, box 7, CHA; Cyrus H. Adams III, "Cluster Letter," folder 16-5, box 16, CHA; Nicolaides, *My Blue Heaven*, 298; Larsen to editor, *Garfieldian*, December 30, 1964; Shirriff to Dear Sir, folder 8-5, box 8, CHA; letter, Mr. and Mrs. T. Angelos, January 8, 1965, folder 8-5, box 8, CHA; Littman to Willis, January 7, 1965, folder 8-5, box 8, CHA; Hagemen to Dear Sir, December 29, 1964, folder 7-4, box 7, CHA; Burgess to Adams, January 2, 1965, folder 8-5, box 8, CHA.

38. George J. Kuesis and Jean E. Kuesis to Dear Sir, folder 8-5, box 8, CHA; Hagemen to Dear Sir, December 29, 1964, folder 7-4, box 7, CHA; Board of Education of the City of Chicago, Special Committee on the Hauser Report, January 6, 1965, p. 5, folder 8-5, box 8, CHA; unidentified clipping, "Proposed Cluster Plan Blasted at UPG Rally," folder 16-3, box 16, CHA; "To Seek Community View on Clustering," *Garfieldian*, December 16, 1964.

39. Greenhouse to editor, *Garfieldian*, December 30, 1964; Greenhouse to Whiston, December 24, 1964, folder 7-4, box 7, CHA; clipping, "Here's ACO Resolution Opposing Clustering," *Community Publications*, January 13, 1965, folder "Austin Community Organization—Newspaper Clippings," box 24, CJEG; Board of Education of the City of Chicago, Special Committee on the Hauser Report, January 6, 1965, p. 4, folder 8-5, box 8, CHA.

40. "Drop Plan for School Clusters," *Garfieldian*, January 20, 1965; "Details of High School Changes," *Garfieldian*, May 27, 1964; clipping, "Boundary Change Is Opposed," *Community Publications*, August 23, 1967, folder 14, box 1, AHS; "New High School Lines," *Garfieldian*, June 17, 1964; Dorothy S. Watts, "Austin" [typescript on green paper], June 1962, folder 2, box 2, Austin Community Collection, Special Collections and Preservation Division, Harold Washington Library Center, Chicago (hereafter ACC); Vrame, "History of School Desegregation," 117; "Full Text of ABC Boundary Change Request," *Austinite*, December 14, 1966, box 7, ANC; Bacigalupo to property owners of the Austin area, December 2, 1963, folder "Austin Community Organization, Correspondence," box 24, CJEG; "Proud West Sider" to editor, *Garfieldian*, September 25, 1963; "79 Transfer to Austin High School," *Garfieldian*, November 11, 1964; Bacigalupo to editor, *Garfieldian*, December 11, 1963.

41. "Arrest 45 at Austin High for Mobbing," *Garfieldian*, November 4, 1964; "79 Transfer to Austin High School," *Garfieldian*, November 11, 1964; "17 Arrested in Racial Incident," *Garfieldian*, May 19, 1965.

42. West Side Federation, Common Council minutes, October 14, 1965, folder "October–November 1965," box 27, GLCC-CHS; "Austin High to Get 93 Transfers," *Garfieldian*, May 12, 1965, estimated that more than half the students receiving the transfers were African American. "Lay Incidents to 'Boisterousness,'" *Garfieldian*, September 15, 1965; "Return to Normal at Austin High," *Garfieldian*, September 29, 1965.

43. "Map Parent Meeting to Maintain Order," *Garfieldian*, October 13, 1965; West Side Federation, Common Council minutes, October 14, 1965, folder "October–November 1965," box 27, GLCC-CHS.

44. "Map Parent Meeting to Maintain Order," *Garfieldian*, October 13, 1965; "School

Officials Study Proposals," *Garfieldian*, October 27, 1965; West Side Federation, Common Council minutes, October 14, 1965, folder "October–November 1965," box 27, GLCC-CHS. See Rosalyn Baxandall and Elizabeth Ewen, *Picture Windows: How the Suburbs Happened* (New York: Basic Books, 2000), 191–200, for community response to a riot in a recently integrated high school on Long Island.

45. Clipping, "Hunt Willis Successor," *Chicago's American*, June 1, 1965, folder 11-4, box 11, CHA; clipping, "Red Carpet for Willis—on Way Out," *Chicago Daily News*, May 24, 1966, folder 24-4, box 24, CHA; clipping, "Supt. Willis Resigns Early," *Chicago Sun-Times*, May 24, 1966, and clipping, "Willis Stuns Board with Resignation," *Chicago Tribune*, May 24, 1966, both in clipping files "Biography. Willis, Benjamin C.," Chicago Historical Society; Willis to Whiston and Members of the Board of Education, May 23, 1966, folder 20-1, box 20, CHA; clipping, "Protests by Segregationists Nothing New for Redmond," *Chicago Daily News*, January 10, [1968], folder 36-4, box 36, CHA; Baker, *Second Battle of New Orleans*, 458; "Austin High a Year Later—No Friction, High Standards," *Garfieldian*, November 16, 1966.

46. "Austin High a Year Later—No Friction, High Standards," *Garfieldian*, November 16, 1966; "ABC to Mayor: Restore Old Austin Boundaries," *Garfieldian*, December 14, 1966; clipping, "The 'Whys' of Boundary Change Proposal," *Austinite*, April 5, 1967, folder 98-16, CUL accession 76-116; "Full Text of ABC Boundary Change Request," *Austinite*, December 14, 1966, box 7, ANC; Byford School Committee, Report to the Chicago Board of Education, folder 27-3, box 27, CHA; "Return High School Boundaries to Belt Line, ABC Recommends," *Austinite*, December 14, 1966, box 7, ANC.

47. "New Austin Group Picks Name," *Garfieldian*, April 14, 1965; clipping, "Form Business Group," *Austinite*, February 18, 1965, folder, "Austin Community Organization—Newspaper Clippings," box 24, CJEG; "ABC to Mayor: Restore Old Austin Boundaries," *Garfieldian*, December 14, 1966. For an insider account of conditions at Marshall, see Susan Gregory, *Hey, White Girl!* (New York: W. W. Norton, 1970). "Return High School Boundaries to Belt Line, ABC Recommends," *Austinite*, December 14, 1966, box 7, ANC; letter, corresponding secretary, Austin Unit No. 52, American Legion Auxiliary, to Grant, March 13, 1967, folder 27-1, box 27, CHA; "Full Text of ABC Boundary Change Request," *Austinite*, December 14, 1966, box 7, ANC; Vrame, "History of School Desegregation," 165.

48. For examples, see folder 23-2, box 23, and folder 27-1, box 27, CHA.

49. Members of the John Hay PTA to Redmond and Grant, January 20, 1967, folder 25-1, box 25, CHA; Jordan to Redmond, January 26, 1967, folder 25-2, box 25, CHA; Truppo and Oliver, Policy Hearing Statement, March 30, 1967, folder 27-1, box 27, CHA; Vrame, "History of School Desegregation," 178n54; clipping, "'Give Us More Time,' School Aide Urges THA Delegation," *Austin News*, August 9, 1967, folder 26, box 2, ACC; clipping, "Renew Pleas for School Line Change; CAM Opposed," *Garfieldian*, April 19, 1967, folder 98-16, CUL accession 76-116; clipping, "School Complaint Temporarily Off," *Chicago Tribune*, August 31, 1967, folder 33-1, box 33, CHA.

50. Austin High School Boundary change issue, CAM position, folder 27-3, box 27, CHA; clipping, "Redmond Proposes to Close Hay Branch of Austin High," *Garfieldian*, March 15, 1967, folder 98-15, CUL accession 76-116; clipping, "Renew Pleas for School Line Change; CAM Opposed," *Garfieldian*, April 19, 1967, folder 98-16, CUL accession 76-116; clipping, "Seek Enrollment Projections for Austin High," *Garfieldian*, March 22, 1967, folder 98-15, CUL accession 76-116; clipping, "Redmond Plan for Stabilization," *Garfieldian*, March 1, 1967, folder 98-15, CUL accession 76-116; clipping, "See Little Hope in Boundary Issue," *Austin News*, August 23, 1967, folder 14, box 1, AHS.

51. "McKeag Reveals 'Loophole' Precedent," *Austinite*, January 28, 1970, box 7, ANC; "Parents Probe Attendance Option Plan," *Austinite*, March 4, 1970, box 8, ANC; "Board Refuses AHS Option," *Austinite*, September 15, 1971, box 10, ANC; "THA Proposes Program—Asks for Assistance," *Austin News*, August 18, 1971, box 4, ANC; "Four Enrollment Plans Proposed for Austin High," *Austin News*, September 8, 1971, box 4, ANC; Baker, *Second Battle of New Orleans*, 466. Formisano, *Boston against Busing*, 138, observes that the anti-busing activists in Boston

were "in profound ways . . . heirs of the protesters of 1960s, even as they reacted against them and their values"; Thomas J. Sugrue, "The Tangled Roots of Affirmative Action," *American Behavioral Scientist* 41 (April 1998): 886–97. Nicolaides, *My Blue Heaven*, 299; "Board to Give Reply on Option Request," *Austinite*, September 8, 1971, box 10, ANC; "School Proposal Made," *Austinite*, June 17, 1970, box 8, ANC; Taylor and Reichel to editor, *Austin News*, March 3, 1971, box 3, ANC; "Austin Girls Gird for Male Harassment," *Austinite*, September 8, 1971, box 10, ANC; clipping, "Controversy Revolves around Principal," *Chicago Tribune*, April 5, 1970, folder 14, box 1, AHS; James C. Moses, "Desegregation in Catholic Schools in the Archdiocese of Chicago, 1964–1974, Including a Case Study of a Catholic High School" (Ph.D. diss., Loyola University of Chicago, 1977), 72; "Board Refuses AHS Option," *Austinite*, September 15, 1971, box 10, ANC.

52. "'End Violence,' Demand 40 at May School Meeting," *Garfieldian*, November 30, 1966.

53. "School Hearings Achieve 'Instant Results' at May," *Garfieldian*, April 20, 1966; "Austin Groups to Speak Piece at School Board Public Hearing," *Austinite*, December 7, 1966, box 7, ANC; clipping, "Renew Pleas for School Line Change; CAM Opposed," *Garfieldian*, April 19, 1967, folder 98-16, CUL accession 76-116; statement of Mrs. John E. Cincotta to the Board of Education Policy Hearing, March 1967, folder 27-1, box 27, CHA.

54. Undated letter, Kuesis to Dear Sir, folder 27-1, box 27, CHA; "Pick Up Reporter Roaming Halls," *Garfieldian*, December 14, 1966; Lukazewski to Adams, March 5, 1967, folder 27-1, box 27, CHA; clipping, "Boundary Proposal Strikes Sparks at May Meeting," *Garfieldian*, February 22, 1967, folder 33-1, box 33, CHA.

55. Clipping, "Stormy Meeting as May Group 'Visits' McKeag," *Garfieldian & Austin News*, March 1, 1967, folder 33-1, box 33, CHA; Peg Knoepfle, ed., *After Alinsky: Community Organizing in Illinois* (Springfield, IL: Sangamon State University, 1990), 56.

56. Kuesis to Adams, March 3, 1967, folder 27-1, box 27, CHA; clipping, "No Change in School Lines without Hearing May Group," *Community Publications*, March 8, 1967, folder 33-1, box 33, CHA; clipping, "No Change in School Lines without Hearing May Group," *Garfieldian*, March 8, 1967, folder 98-15, CUL accession 76-116; clipping, "Prepare May Boundary Change Objections," *Austinite*, March 8, 1967, folder 33-1, box 33, CHA; Cincotta to Adams, March 18, 1967, folder 27-1, box 27, CHA.

57. Clipping, "May Boundary Change 'Out'; Spencer Problem Lingers," *Austinite*, May 15, 1967, folder 33-1, box 33, CHA; Adams to Cincotta, November 14, 1967, folder 31-4, box 31, CHA; statement of Mrs. George Kuesis to the Board of Education Budget Hearing, December 8, 1967, folder 32-2, box 32, CHA.

58. Clipping, "Racial Count to Start Integration Program," *Chicago Daily News*, August 25, 1967, folder 33-1, box 33, CHA; unlabeled clipping, "Redmond Offer Plan for Racial Stability," oversize 1.2, ACC. See also Vrame, "History of School Desegregation"; Lloyd, "Decision-Making Process," 187, 192; Danns, *Something Better*, 66–69; and Nicolaides, *My Blue Heaven*, 304.

59. Skonie to Adams, January 8, 1968, folder 34-4, box 34, CHA; Jahnke to Dear Sir, January 6, 1968, folder 34-4, box 34, CHA; deGroh to Adams, January 12, 1968, folder 34-5, box 34, CHA; Mendelson to Redmond, January 5, 1968, folder 34-4, box 34, CHA; Vrame, "History of School Desegregation," 267; Adams to King, February 27, 1968, folder 36-1, box 36, CHA. On whites' protests of busing in New York, see Jerald E. Podair, "The Strikes that Changed New York: Race, Culture, and Ocean Hill–Brownsville, 1960–1975," *Afro-Americans in New York Life and History* 26 (January 2002): 11.

60. "68-17-1, Approve Plan to Implement the Non-Contiguous Attendance Area Recommendations of the Desegregation Report in the Austin Area and District 4," folder 34-4, box 34, CHA; Vrame, "History of School Desegregation," 186, 215; clipping, "South Shore Unit Calls Proposal Inadequate," *Chicago Tribune*, January 9, [1968], folder 34-4, box 34, CHA.

61. Vrame, "History of School Desegregation," 238; clipping, "Violence at Anti-Bus Meeting," *Chicago's American*, February 1, 1968, folder 36-4, box 36, CHA; clipping, "Right-Wingers Support Foes of School Busing," *Chicago's American*, February 7, [1968], folder 36-4, box 36, CHA; clipping, "Busing Foes Picket City Hall, Cardinal," *Chicago Tribune*, January 31,

[1968], folder 36-4, box 36, CHA; statement of Roman C. Pucinski, February 15, 1968, pp. 3, 13, folder 35-5, box 35, CHA; Nicolaides, *My Blue Heaven*, 300.

62. Board of Education, City of Chicago, Committee on Transferring of Students, February 19, 1968, p. 16, folder 35-6, box 35, CHA.

63. Clipping, "School Bd. Warned to Yield," *Chicago Daily News*, January 11, 1968, folder 36-4, box 36, CHA. For the kinds of pressures Louisiana legislators brought to bear on education officials, see Baker, *Second Battle of New Orleans*, 420, 430.

64. Undated letter, Cordo to Adams, folder 35-3, box 35, CHA.

65. Smerko to Adams, February 26, 1968, folder 36-1, box 36, CHA.

66. Irene Mazurek and Stanley Mazurek to Redmond, January 7, 1968, folder 34-4, box 34, CHA. Nicolaides, *My Blue Heaven*, 294, observes that in South Gate, California, men provided leadership and women the social networks through which such protests were generated and sustained.

67. Cincotta to Redmond, January 17, 1968, folder 34-5, box 34, CHA; "68-327-10, Voluntary Transfer Program, an Amendment to Board Report #68-17-1," April 10, 1968, folder 36-2, box 36, CHA; clipping, "Board Defers Plan to Bus Negro Pupils," *Chicago Tribune*, January 11, 1968, folder 36-4, box 36, CHA.

68. Clipping, "Furor Has Killed It, Says Member Adams," *Chicago Tribune*, January 15, [1968], folder 34-5, box 34, CHA; untitled clipping, *Chicago Sun-Times*, January 12, [1968], folder 36-4, box 36, CHA; clipping, "300 Jeer Transfer Students," *Chicago Daily [News]*, January 29, 1968, folder 36-4, box 36, CHA; clipping, "Never," *Chicago Daily News*, February 2, 1968, folder 36-4, box 36, CHA; clipping, "Police Guard against New School Clash," *Chicago's American*, February 2, [1968], folder 36-4, box 36, CHA; Adams to Sajowitz, January 16, 1968, folder 34-5, box 34, CHA; Nicolaides, *My Blue Heaven*, 297; clipping, "Overflow Crowd Moves In," *[Chicago Daily] News*, February 28, 1968, folder 36-1, box 36, CHA; "68-327-10, Voluntary Transfer Program, an Amendment to Board Report #68-17-1," April 10, 1968, folder 36-2, box 36, CHA; clipping, "Push to Start Busing Austin Pupils Monday," *Chicago's American*, March 5, 1968, folder 36-3, box 36, CHA; clipping, "Program for 573 Pupils to Begin in Next 2 Weeks," *Chicago Tribune*, March 5, [1968], scrapbook, CHA.

69. Clipping, "Why Parents Aren't Busing," *[Chicago Daily] News*, March 8, [1968]; clipping, "NW Side Plans Won't Be Affected," *Chicago Daily News*, March 11, [1968]; clipping, "Busing Backers Act to Calm Neighbors," *Chicago Tribune*, March 10, [1968]; clipping, "Propose Jam-in to Sabotage Plan for Pupil Shift," *Chicago's American*, March 5, [1968]; clipping, "Busing Sabotage Plan on NW Side Fizzles," *[Chicago Daily] News*, March 8, [1968]; clipping, "N.W. Side School Boycott Cancelled," *[Chicago Sun-]Times*, March 6, [1968]; clipping, "Anti-Busing Boycott Loses Steam," *Chicago Daily News*, March 5, [1968]; and clipping, *Chicago Daily News*, March 5, 1968, all in folder 36-3, box 36, CHA; Formisano, *Boston against Busing*, 140–41; Lewis, "Emergency Mothers," 72–103; clipping, "Fire Bomb Brings Heavy Police Guard," *Chicago's American*, March 11, [1968], folder 36-3, box 36, CHA; unidentified clipping, "Fire-Bomb Only Incident: Busing Start Is Peaceful," March 11, 1968, scrapbook, CHA; clipping, "Bus Foes, Backers to March on Board," *Chicago Sun-Times*, January 10, [1968], folder 36-4, box 36, CHA; clipping, "Report 25 Pct. of Parents Quit Busing Project," *[Chicago Sun-]Times*, March 7, 1968, folder 36-3, box 36, CHA.

70. Clipping, "Fire Bomb Brings Heavy Police Guard," *Chicago's American*, March 11, [1968], folder 36-3, box 36, CHA; clipping, "249 Pupils Bused on 1st Day of Plan," *Chicago Tribune*, March 13, [1968]; and clipping, "First Day of Pupil Busing Quiet; 249 Enter 8 N.W. Side Schools," *[Chicago Sun-]Times*, March 12, [1968], all in folder 36-3, box 36, CHA; unidentified clipping, "Fire-Bomb Only Incident: Busing Start Is Peaceful," March 11, 1968, scrapbook, CHA; Vrame, "History of School Desegregation," 283, 290; Lloyd, "Decision-Making Process," 285.

71. "Approval Expected on Bids to Build Modulars," *Austinite*, June 2, 1971, box 10, ANC; "Lane, Prosser Coed? Not by Fall: Connelly," *Austinite*, July 15, 1970, box 9, ANC; "Expect Class Units by Mid-April," *Austinite*, April 1, 1970, box 8, ANC; "$51,510 Payment Asked for Emmet

Demountable Construction Site," *Austinite*, February 3, 1971, box 10, ANC; "Emmet Grade School Division Is Approved," *Austin News*, June 3, 1970, box 2, ANC; "Board Appoints 3 Emmet Principals," *Austinite*, October 21, 1970, box 9, ANC; "A Key Decision," *Austinite*, January 14, 1970, box 7, ANC.

72. "Board of Ed. 'Never Gets Ahead,'" *Austin News*, May 20, 1970, box 2, ANC.

73. "Overcrowding Joins List of Problems at Emmet," *Austinite*, September 23, 1970, box 9, ANC; "Expect Class Units by Mid-April," *Austinite*, April 1, 1970, box 8, ANC; "Emmet Unit Seeks Solutions," *Austinite*, December 2, 1970, box 9, ANC; "School Groups Tell Board Budget Needs," *Austinite*, December 23, 1970, box 9, ANC; "Board One Step 'Ahead,'" *Austinite*, October 6, 1971, box 10, ANC; "Approval Expected on Bids to Build Modulars," *Austinite*, June 2, 1971, box 10, ANC; "3 Key School Classes to Use Town Hall Space," *Austin News*, November 3, 1971, box 4, ANC.

74. Clipping, "A Dream Turns to Bitterness in Austin," *Chicago Tribune*, October 14, 1973, folder 14, box 6, ACC; G. Alfred Hess, "Renegotiating a Multicultural Society: Participation in Desegregation Planning in Chicago," *Journal of Negro Education* 53 (1984): 132–46; G. Alfred Hess and Christina A. Warden, "Who Benefits from Desegregation Now?" *Journal of Negro Education* 57 (1988): 536–51.

CHAPTER SIX

1. The *Oxford English Dictionary*, 2nd ed., vol. 2, 298, dates the first appearance of the phrase "block-busting," in the sense described here, to the January 31, 1959, issue of the *Economist*. During World War II, the word "block-buster" referred to "an aerial bomb capable of destroying a whole block of buildings." *Webster's Ninth New Collegiate Dictionary*, 160, dates the use of "blockbusting," in the sense of real estate profiteering, to 1954. John F. Bauman, *Public Housing, Race, and Renewal: Urban Planning in Philadelphia, 1920–1974* (Philadelphia: Temple University Press, 1987), 129, cites the use of the term "blockbuster" in Philadelphia as early as 1952. Other early printed uses of the term include clipping, editorial, "Job Well Done," *Southtown Economist*, October 21[?], 1959; and reprint, "New Weapon in the War against Slums," *House & Home*, May 1959, both in folder 80, Saul Alinsky/Industrial Areas Foundation Records, Special Collections and University Archives, Richard J. Daley Library, University of Illinois at Chicago (hereafter IAF). The block-by-block pattern of change was not universal. In Atlanta black real estate dealers arranged for the simultaneous arrival of African American home buyers in an entire neighborhood, on January 2, 1952. Kevin M. Kruse, "White Flight: Resistance to Desegregation of Neighborhoods, Schools and Businesses in Atlanta, 1946–1966" (Ph.D. diss., Cornell University, 2000), 99. Gilbert Osofsky, *Harlem: The Making of a Ghetto: Negro New York, 1890–1930*, 2nd ed. (New York: Harper & Row, 1971), 92, notes examples of blockbusting practices in Harlem in the early twentieth century.

2. Norris Vitchek as told to Alfred Balk, "Confessions of a Block-Buster," *Saturday Evening Post*, July 14–21, 1962, 15–19. Vitchek's reference to annual earnings of $100,000 made a lasting impression on livid white West Siders; the comment appeared almost a decade later on a picket sign photographed in Robert Bailey Jr., *Radicals in Urban Politics: The Alinsky Approach* (Chicago: University of Chicago Press, 1972).

3. *Saturday Evening Post*, August 25–September 1, 1962, 4.

4. *Chicago Daily News*, July 10, 1962, 5; *Chicago Defender*, week of July 14–20, 1962, 6; "'I Wrote Post Article, but I'm No Blockbuster,' Declares Satter," *Garfieldian*, August 1, 1962; Weekly Report, Raymond J. Carlyle, director, April 16–21, 1958, folder "April 1–17, 1958," box 6, Greater Lawndale Conservation Commission Records, Chicago Historical Society (hereafter GLCC-CHS); "Negroes File Suit Alleging Gouge, Bought Homes on Contract," folder "April 1–17, 1958," box 6, GLCC-CHS; clipping, *Chicago Daily News*, February 2, 1961, folder, "Feb. 1–15, 1961," box 15, GLCC-CHS; columns entitled "So You're Buying a Home" in *GLCC News Notes*, GLCC-CHS, passim; Mark J. Satter, "Land Contract Sales in Chicago: Security Turned Exploitation," *Chicago Bar Record* 39 (March 1958): 262–64; "Satter 'Worked with' Post Story Author," *Garfieldian*, July 25, 1962.

5. "Satter 'Worked with' Post Story Author," *Garfieldian*, July 25, 1962; "'I Wrote Post Article, but I'm No Blockbuster,' Declares Satter," *Garfieldian*, August 1, 1962; Vincent J. Giese, *Revolution in the City* (Notre Dame, IN: Fides, 1961), 17; clipping, *Chicago Tribune*, February 16, 1961[?], folder "Feb. 16–28, 1961," box 15, GLCC-CHS. Beryl Satter, the daughter of Mark J. Satter and a professional historian, is writing a book about the history of her father's work and the practice of contract selling in Chicago.

6. "St. Mel Maps 5-Year Plan to Boost Area," *Garfieldian*, February 24, 1960.

7. St. Clair Drake and Horace R. Cayton, *Black Metropolis: A Study of Negro Life in a Northern City*, 2 vols. (New York: Harcourt, Brace, 1945; rev. and enlarged ed., New York: Harcourt, Brace & World, 1962); James R. Grossman, *Land of Hope: Chicago, Black Southerners, and the Great Migration* (Chicago: University of Chicago Press, 1989); Allan H. Spear, *Black Chicago: The Making of a Negro Ghetto, 1890–1920* (Chicago: University of Chicago Press, 1967); David A. Wallace, "Residential Concentration of Negroes in Chicago" (Ph.D. diss., Harvard University, 1953). This resistance was sometimes violent. See William M. Tuttle Jr., *Race Riot: Chicago in the Red Summer of 1919* (New York: Atheneum, 1970); E. Franklin Frazier, *The Negro Family in Chicago* (Chicago: University of Chicago Press, 1932); and Otis Dudley Duncan and Beverly Duncan, *The Negro Population of Chicago: A Study of Residential Succession* (Chicago: University of Chicago Press, 1957), 88–99.

8. Rose Helper, *Racial Policies and Practices of Real Estate Brokers* (Minneapolis: University of Minnesota Press, 1969), 3, 26; Stephen Grant Meyer, *As Long as They Don't Move Next Door: Segregation and Racial Conflict in American Neighborhoods* (Lanham, MD: Rowman & Littlefield, 2000), 7; Thomas Lee Philpott, *The Slum and the Ghetto: Immigrants, Blacks, and Reformers in Chicago, 1880–1930* (Belmont, CA: Wadsworth, 1991; originally published as *The Slum and the Ghetto: Neighborhood Deterioration and Middle-Class Reform, 1880–1930* [New York: Oxford University Press, 1978]), 163–65.

9. For examples, see Duncan and Duncan, *Negro Population of Chicago*; Frazier, *Negro Family in Chicago*; and Egbert F. Schietinger, "Racial Succession and Changing Property Values in Residential Chicago" (Ph.D. diss., University of Chicago, 1953). For an effective summary of the views underpinning such policies as the ones promulgated by NAREB, see Raymond A. Mohl, "The Second Ghetto and the 'Infiltration Theory' in Urban Real Estate, 1940–1960," in *Urban Planning and the African American Community: In the Shadows*, ed. June Manning Thomas and Marsha Ritzdorf (Thousand Oaks, CA: Sage, 1997), 58–74.

10. In 1945 the National Association of Real Estate Boards, to which CREB belonged, acknowledged that one of its responsibilities was to supply housing to nonwhites: Helper, *Racial Policies*, 199, 236–37; Kevin Fox Gotham, *Race, Real Estate, and Uneven Development: The Kansas City Experience, 1900–2000* (Albany: State University of New York Press, 2002), 107. Thomas J. Sugrue, *The Origins of the Urban Crisis: Race and Inequality in Postwar Detroit* (Princeton: Princeton University Press, 1996), 195, notes the alternative term "realtist" used by black real estate dealers in Detroit. See also Andrew Wiese, *Places of Their Own: African American Suburbanization in the Twentieth Century* (Chicago: University of Chicago Press, 2004), 133–34.

11. Helper's study, *Racial Policies*, 348n16, finds that in June 1964 CREB had 1,669 members; in 1963 there were 11,403 real estate brokers licensed in Cook County, which was only slightly larger than the city of Chicago. These figures suggest that 85 percent of the people brokering real estate deals in Chicago were not Realtors bound by CREB's rules.

12. For the practice of blockbusting in Buffalo, see Neil Kraus, *Race, Neighborhoods, and Community Power: Buffalo Politics, 1934–1997* (Albany: State University of New York Press, 2000), 102–4. For Baltimore, see W. Edward Orser, *Blockbusting in Baltimore: The Edmondson Village Story* (Lexington: University Press of Kentucky, 1994).

13. "How Do Blockbusters Operate? Southeast Sider Tells Story," *Garfieldian*, May 10, 1961.

14. Jeffrey Eugenides, *Middlesex* (New York: Picador, 2003), 201.

15. *Chicago Daily News*, October 13, 14, 15, 16, 17, 19, 20, 21, and 22, 1959. "'Panic Peddlers'

Exposed on a Wide Scale," *Garfieldian*, October 21, 1959. The *Garfieldian* credited the *Chicago Daily News* series with coining the term "panic peddlers." "New Tactic," *Garfieldian*, October 7, 1959; Giese, *Revolution in the City*, 16.

16. "'Panic' Tactics Charged in Letter Sent Out by Real Estate Firm," *Garfieldian*, December 2, 1959; "Speculators Active Again in Garf. Pk.," *Garfieldian*, February 10, 1960; "UPG Chairman Blasts Real Estate Firm's Scare Letter," *Garfieldian*, March 16, 1960; "Blockbuster Run Out of Neighborhood," *Garfieldian*, April 6, 1960; "It's Spring Already for Blockbusters," *Garfieldian*, March 14, 1962; "South Sider" to editor, *Garfieldian*, September 6, 1962; Walsh to editor, *Garfieldian*, September 15, 1965; James Alan McPherson, "In My Father's House There Are Many Mansions—and I'm Going to Get Me Some of Them Too: The Story of the Contract Buyers League," *Atlantic Monthly*, April 1972, 51–82; *Chicago Daily News*, October 15, 1959.

17. "'Panic' Tactics Charged in Letter Sent Out by Real Estate Firm," *Garfieldian*, December 2, 1959. Louis Rosen said that when he interviewed Calumet Heights residents for *The South Side: The Racial Transformation of an American Neighborhood* (Chicago: Ivan R. Dee, 1998), none of them discussed the content of solicitation letters. Louis Rosen, interview on *848*, radio station WBEZ, Chicago, July 27, 1998.

18. "Central Austin Reacts to Real Estate Canvass," *Austin News*, July 1, 1970, box 2, Austin Newspaper Collection, Special Collections and Preservation Division, Harold Washington Library Center, Chicago (hereafter ANC); Gotham, *Race, Real Estate*, 115.

19. "Talking It Over," *Garfieldian*, August 15, 1962. See also *Chicago Daily News*, October 15, 1959; "Nip Speculator's Bid to Incite Panic," *Garfieldian*, May 8, 1963.

20. Clipping, "Blockbusters, Block Clubs Near Showdown in Austin," *Chicago Sun-Times*, November 16, 1965, folder "Austin Community Organization—Newspaper Clippings," box 24, Monsignor John J. Egan Papers, Archives Division, Hesburgh Library, University of Notre Dame (hereafter CJEG); Gotham, *Race, Real Estate*, 105; "South Sider" to editor, *Garfieldian*, September 6, 1962; "Warns against Blockbusters," *Garfieldian*, May 6, 1964; *Chicago Daily News*, October 15, 1959; McPherson, "In My Father's House"; John Fish et al., *The Edge of the Ghetto: A Study of Church Involvement in Community Organization* (New York: Seabury Press, 1966), xiii–xvi; undated letter, Strugar to editor, [*Chicago Daily News*], folder 80, IAF; McPherson, "In My Father's House," 53; "Seek to Help Widow, Victim of Blockbuster," *Garfieldian*, May 2, 1962.

21. Newsletter, Block Steering Committee for Mayor's Campaign for a Cleaner Chicago, November 1, 1955, folder "Oct.–Dec. 1955," box 2, GLCC-CHS; Board of Directors meeting, June 23, 1964, folder "June 1964," box 24, GLCC-CHS; Jean Wehrheim, "Report on Housing and Zoning," July 19, 1964, folder "July 17–31, 1964," box 24, GLCC-CHS; Johnston to Vivas, "re: 3857 W. Polk street," folder "Undated Items [2]," box 28, GLCC-CHS; "This Is Integration?" *Garfieldian*, November 23, 1961; "Talking It Over," *Garfieldian*, July 4, 1962; reprint from St. Thomas Aquinas Parish bulletin, *Garfieldian*, July 21, 1965; McCawley to editor, *Garfieldian*, November 10, 1965; "Politicians, Businessmen Pledge to Fight 'Peddlers,'" *Garfieldian*, November 25, 1965; McCawley to editor, *Garfieldian*, December 22, 1965; clipping, "Blockbusters, Block Clubs Near Showdown in Austin," *Chicago Sun-Times*, November 16, 1965, folder "Austin Community Organization—Newspaper Clippings," box 24, CJEG. For comparable details in the South Shore area a few years later, see Harvey Luskin Molotch, *Managed Integration: Dilemmas of Doing Good in the City* (Berkeley: University of California Press, 1972), 25–32.

22. "Satter 'Worked with' Post Story Author," *Garfieldian*, July 25, 1962; "'I Wrote Post Article, but I'm No Blockbuster,' Declares Satter," *Garfieldian*, August 1, 1962; McCawley to editor, *Garfieldian*, December 22, 1965.

23. "'Blockbusters,' 'Education,' 'Fear' Key Words in Integration Issue," *Garfieldian*, August 11, 1965; Walton to editor, *Garfieldian*, January 5, 1966. Calvin Bradford, "Financing Home Ownership: The Federal Role in Neighborhood Decline," *Urban Affairs Quarterly* 14, no. 3 (March 1979): 325, observes that what blockbusting real estate dealers were selling was a model of property values created by appraisers, based on standards first articulated by Homer Hoyt.

24. Undated, notes on a speech by Mark J. Satter given to the members of the Dearborn Real Estate Board, folder 163, IAF; clipping, "Self-Help Program Works in Lawndale," *New World*, February 9, 1968, folder "1–1, Biographical Materials," box 1, Daniel J. Mallette Papers, Chicago Historical Society; Satter, "Land Contract Sales in Chicago"; Chicago Commission on Human Relations, City of Chicago, *Selling and Buying Real Estate in a Racially Changing Neighborhood: A Survey* (June 1962). A dissertation on the Contract Buyers League cited a case in which an agreed-upon property value of $14,500 resulted in $39,125 of financial obligations, of which $15,125 was interest. Jeffrey Michael FitzGerald, "The Contract Buyers League: A Case Study of the Interaction between a Social Movement and the Legal System" (Ph.D. diss., Northwestern University, 1972), 15, 36, 87. See John R. MacNamara, "The Contract Buyers League: A View from the Inside," *Yale Review of Law and Social Action* 1 (1971): 73, for a table of such purchases.

25. In his fascinating study of commercial real estate deals, Ross Miller, *Here's the Deal: The Buying and Selling of a Great American City* (New York: Alfred A. Knopf, 1996), 291n13, treats blind trusts as if they were sanctified by Illinois legislation. According to legal scholars, however, the legislative branch did not create the blind trust mechanism. Rather, Illinois courts established their validity. Comment, "Some Aspects of Illinois Land Trusts," *De Paul Law Review* (Autumn/Winter 1958): 385–93; Mary Conrad, "Trusts—Illinois Land Trusts—A Beneficial Interest Is a 'General Intangible' under U.C.C. Article 9," *De Paul Law Review* 18 (1969): 875–85; Edward Contorer, "Illinois Land Trusts in Theory and Practice," *Decalogue Journal* (September 1957): 5–7; Michael R. Lewis, "The Illinois Land Trust—Shroud with a Silver Lining?" *Loyola University Law Journal* 5 (1974): 412–27. According to FitzGerald, "Contract Buyers League," 466n2, pressure brought by the Contract Buyers League prompted changes in state law in 1969, requiring the disclosure of the identities of trustees of residential property sold on contract.

26. Draft article for *GLCC News Notes*, "Preliminaries in Buying a Property in Lawndale," folder "August 20–31, 1958," box 7, GLCC-CHS.

27. For redlining practices, see Kenneth T. Jackson, *Crabgrass Frontier: The Suburbanization of the United States* (New York: Oxford University Press, 1985), 197–218; Helper, *Racial Policies*, 166–72; FitzGerald, "Contract Buyers League," 2, 16; and *Garfieldian*, October 28, 1964. Mark Santow, "Saul Alinsky and the Dilemmas of Race in the Post-war City" (Ph.D. diss., University of Pennsylvania, 2000), 106, claims that the restrictions on mortgages for African Americans eased in the early 1960s.

28. For discussion of installment land contracts, see Thomas J. Boodell, "Hope for the Future: The Contract Buyers' League," Adlai Stevenson Institute Working Paper 1, 1972; Lisa A. Danielson, "Installment Land Contracts: The Illinois Experience and the Difficulties of Incremental Judicial Reform," *University of Illinois Law Review* 1 (1986): 91–125; Ray D. Henson, "Installment Land Contracts in Illinois: A Suggested Approach to Forfeiture," *De Paul Law Review* 7 (Autumn/Winter 1957): 1–15; Robert Kratovil, "Forfeiture of Installment Land Contracts in Illinois," *Illinois Bar Journal* 53 (November 1964): 188–97; Grant S. Nelson and Dale A. Whitman, "The Installment Land Contract—A National Viewpoint," *Brigham Young University Law Review* (1977): 541–76; and Michael L. Stone, "Relief from Forfeitures of Installment Land Contracts," *Chicago Bar Record* 46 (October 1964): 40–46.

29. "The Management of Neighborhood Change," abridged proceedings, citywide workshop, sponsored by the Chicago Commission on Human Relations, College Camp, Lake Geneva, Wisconsin, April 10–12, 1959, folder 127, Greater Lawndale Conservation Commission Records, Special Collections and University Archives, Richard J. Daley Library, University of Illinois at Chicago; McPherson, "In My Father's House," 53; Staff of the Chicago Commission on Human Relations, "Questions and Answers on Housing (preliminary draft)," January 1958, folder "Jan. 21–31, 1958," box 5, GLCC-CHS; "Evicted for Being Month Late, They Ruin Building," *Garfieldian*, March 27, 1963; *Chicago Daily News*, October 14, 1959; Chicago Commission on Human Relations, *Selling and Buying Real Estate*, 9; Lendol Calder, *Financing the American Dream: A Cultural History of Consumer Credit* (Princeton: Princeton University

Press, 1999), 165–66. In the late 1960s, two groups of contract buyers challenged the legality of these transactions. See Jeffrey M. FitzGerald, "The Contract Buyers League and the Courts: A Case Study of Poverty Litigation," *Law and Society Review* 9 (1975): 165–95; MacNamara, "Contract Buyers League"; and note, "Discriminatory Housing Markets, Racial Unconscionability, and Section 1988: The *Contract Buyers League* Case," *Yale Law Journal* 80 (1971): 516–66. Arnold R. Hirsch, *Making the Second Ghetto: Race and Housing in Chicago, 1940–1960* (Cambridge: Cambridge University Press, 1983), 32.

30. Samuel Eberly Gross, one of the Chicago area's most successful late nineteenth-century real estate developers, used a form of installment land contract. According to Ann Durkin Keating, *Building Chicago: Suburban Developers and the Creation of a Divided Metropolis* (Columbus: Ohio State University Press, 1988), 71, by the last decade of the nineteenth century, Gross's customers could purchase their homes "on installment terms, one-tenth down and the rest in monthly payments, which went as low as ten dollars." See also Edith Abbott, *The Tenements of Chicago, 1908–1935* (Chicago: University of Chicago Press, 1936), 392. On the broader history of installment buying, see Calder, *Financing the American Dream*, chap. 4.

31. Upton Sinclair, *The Jungle* (1905; reprint, New York: Bantam Books, 1981), 49–52, 65–70, 175–78. Calder, *Financing the American Dream*, 171–73, discusses the credit practices in *The Jungle*.

32. FitzGerald, "Contract Buyers League" (1972), 60; Rosen interview on *848*; Rosen, *The South Side*, 24; Orser, *Blockbusting in Baltimore*, 108, describes residential racial change as a "trauma" for both whites and blacks. *Garfieldian*, August 11, 1965. Eileen M. McMahon, *What Parish Are You From?: A Chicago Irish Community and Race Relations* (Lexington: University Press of Kentucky, 1995), 121.

33. Helper, *Racial Policies*, 25; Rosen, *The South Side*, 26; "Just a Little Elbow Grease Needed," *Garfieldian*, August 5, 1953; "Speculators at Work on Monroe St.: UPG Warns Residents to Beware of Sharks," *Garfieldian*, February 24, 1960; "How United Property Group Helps," *Garfieldian*, April 27, 1960; Belden Morgan, "Values in Transition Areas," *Review of the Society of Residential Appraisers* 18 (March 1952): 5–10. On the complexity of precisely calculating the effects of race on housing prices, see Luigi Laurenti, "Effects of Nonwhite Purchases on Market Prices of Residences," *Appraisal Journal* 20 (July 1952): 314–29; *GLCC News Notes* 3, no. 41 (August 1959), folder "August 1959," box 11, GLCC-CHS.

34. "'Open Occupancy,'" *Garfieldian*, February 19, 1958; "Oppose Open Housing," *Garfieldian*, August 7, 1963. See also Sugrue, *Origins of the Urban Crisis*, 226; and Donald Craig Parson, "Urban Politics during the Cold War: Public Housing, Urban Renewal, and Suburbanization in Los Angeles" (Ph.D. diss., University of California at Los Angeles, 1985), esp. chap. 4, "Public Housing and McCarthyism." John T. McGreevy, *Parish Boundaries: The Catholic Encounter with Race in the Twentieth-Century Urban North* (Chicago: University of Chicago Press, 1996), 105–6; Becky M. Nicolaides, *My Blue Heaven: Life and Politics in the Working-Class Suburbs of Los Angeles, 1920–1965* (Chicago: University of Chicago Press, 2002), 311–12.

35. "Beware This . . ." *Garfieldian*, September 10, 1959; "No Fair Pushing," *Garfieldian*, September 30, 1959; "UPG Chairman Blasts Real Estate Firm's Scare Letter," *Garfieldian*, March 16, 1960; Sarafin to editor, *Garfieldian*, October 4, 1961; "Eliminate Speculator and Integration Will Be Successful, Say Whites," *Garfieldian*, July 14, 1965; Orser, *Blockbusting in Baltimore*, 87; 5th Annual OBA Convention resolutions, May 19, 1917, p. 5, folder 23, box 3, Austin Community Collection, Special Collections and Preservation Division, Harold Washington Library Center, Chicago (hereafter ACC); "Takes Blockbuster Complaint to City," *Garfieldian*, October 14, 1964.

36. Wallace, "Residential Concentration of Negroes in Chicago," 136, reports the claim of a black-owned real estate firm to have "opened up" Lawndale for African American settlement.

37. Oscar C. Brown to editor, *Chicago Daily News*, October 26, 1959, folder 80, IAF. For the autobiography of Brown, the father of entertainer Oscar Brown Jr., see Oscar C. Brown Sr., *By a Thread* (New York: Vantage Press, 1983). In the middle decades of the twentieth

century, there were probably never more than a hundred licensed African American real estate dealers in Chicago at any one time. Directories of African American businesses in Chicago listed both firms and individual brokers, so it is difficult to suggest precisely how many black brokers there were. In 1923 *Simms' Blue Book and National Negro Business and Professional Directory* (Chicago, 1923) listed a total of fifty firms in Chicago. *Scott's Blue Book Business and Service Directory* had listings for fifty-four, thirty-one, and thirty-two firms and individual brokers in 1947, 1956, and 1965, respectively. The 1970 *Black Book Directory* counted thirty-eight firms. The 1947 *Scott's Blue Book*, 269, carried a half-page advertisement for the Dearborn Real Estate Board, Chicago's professional organization for African American real estate dealers. This advertisement listed the names of thirty members and associates. For the experiences of one African American real estate dealer, see Dempsey Travis, *Autobiography of Black Chicago* (Chicago: Urban Research Institute, 1981). Wendy Plotkin's dissertation looks briefly at conflicting views of playwright Lorraine Hansberry's father, Carl Hansberry, a successful real estate dealer in Chicago in the interwar years. See Wendy Plotkin, "Deeds of Mistrust: Race, Housing, and Restrictive Covenants in Chicago, 1900–1953" (Ph.D. diss., University of Illinois at Chicago, 1999), 141, 187n9.

38. "Can't Do Much to Control Blockbusters: State Official," *Garfieldian*, August 22, 1962.

39. Raymond A. Mohl, "Making the Second Ghetto in Metropolitan Miami, 1940–1960," *Journal of Urban History* 21 (March 1995): 419; "Program . . . Looking Backward to Move Forward," meeting, Midwest Complex, February 9, 1985, tape T21, Bethel New Life Collection, Special Collections and Preservation Division, Harold Washington Library Center, Chicago. See also "Sky Disclaims Wrongdoing on Ethics, License Charges," *Austinite*, March 25, 1970, box 8, ANC, for the defense of accused blockbusters by African Americans; Gotham, *Race, Real Estate*, 112.

40. For the history of the Contract Buyers League, an organization that sought to modify the exorbitant rates of the installment land contracts, see Boodell, "Hope for the Future"; FitzGerald, "Contract Buyers League" (1972); Alphine Wade Jefferson. "Housing Discrimination and Community Response in North Lawndale (Chicago), Illinois 1948–1978" (Ph.D. diss., Duke University, 1979); and McPherson, "In My Father's House."

41. Clipping, "A Dream Turns to Bitterness in Austin," *Chicago Tribune*, October 14, 1973, folder 14, box 6, ACC.

CHAPTER SEVEN

1. Lorraine Hansberry, *A Raisin in the Sun* (New York: Random House, 1959), 103–4, emphasis in the original. For the Hansberry family's experience with discrimination in Chicago, see Wendy Plotkin, "Deeds of Mistrust: Race, Housing, and Restrictive Covenants in Chicago, 1900–1953" (Ph.D. diss., University of Illinois at Chicago, 1999), 140–47.

2. Bob and Liza Hobbs to How, Willard, and Greenwood, May 24, 1955, folder "Work and Study—Interns in Community Ser. Winter 54–55 Leaders' reports, Feb.–May, Chicago RO 1955," box "Chicago R.O. Files, 1955 (Peace Ed)," Chicago Regional Office Files, American Friends Service Committee Archives, Philadelphia, Pennsylvania (hereafter AFSC); Vincent J. Giese, *Revolution in the City* (Notre Dame, IN: Fides, 1961), 10; John T. McGreevy, *Parish Boundaries: The Catholic Encounter with Race in the Twentieth-Century Urban North* (Chicago: University of Chicago Press, 1996), 96; Arnold R. Hirsch, *Making the Second Ghetto: Race and Housing in Chicago, 1940–1960* (Cambridge: Cambridge University Press, 1983), 55. Whites in Atlanta appear to have been more successful at raising funds for repurchasing properties bought by blacks. See Kevin M. Kruse, "White Flight: Resistance to Desegregation of Neighborhoods, Schools and Businesses in Atlanta, 1946–1966" (Ph.D. diss., Cornell University, 2000), 62, 77, 156, 197, 382–83.

3. On neighborhood defense, see Thomas J. Sugrue, *The Origins of the Urban Crisis: Race and Inequality in Postwar Detroit* (Princeton: Princeton University Press, 1996), 235–46, and his article "Crabgrass-Roots Politics: Race, Rights, and the Reaction against Liberalism in the Urban North, 1940–1964," *Journal of American History* 82 (1995): 551–78.

4. On black migration to Chicago and white reaction, see William M. Tuttle Jr., *Race Riot: Chicago in the Red Summer of 1919* (New York: Atheneum, 1970), 176; James R. Grossman, *Land of Hope: Chicago, Black Southerners, and the Great Migration* (Chicago: University of Chicago Press, 1989); St. Clair Drake and Horace R. Cayton, *Black Metropolis: A Study of Negro Life in a Northern City*, 2 vols. (New York: Harcourt, Brace, 1945; rev. and enlarged ed., New York: Harcourt, Brace & World, 1962); Allan H. Spear, *Black Chicago: The Making of a Negro Ghetto, 1890–1920* (Chicago: University of Chicago Press, 1967), 211; and Hirsch, *Making the Second Ghetto*, 63.

5. Zorita Mikva, "The Neighborhood Improvement Association: A Counter-Force to the Expansion of Chicago's Negro Population" (M.A. thesis, University of Chicago, 1951), 26; clipping, *Sun-Times Midwest Magazine*, March 9, 1969, Francis X. Lawlor clipping file, Chicago Historical Society.

6. For an extended discussion of the differences in the histories of the racial composition of public and private housing, see Amanda I. Seligman, "What Is the Second Ghetto?" *Journal of Urban History* 29 (March 2003): 272–80.

7. Louis Rosen, *The South Side: The Racial Transformation of an American Neighborhood* (Chicago: Ivan R. Dee, 1998), 27–28; Otis Dudley Duncan and Beverly Duncan, *The Negro Population of Chicago: A Study of Residential Succession* (Chicago: University of Chicago Press, 1957). For a concise summary of African American movement in Chicago in the postwar period, see Mark Santow, "Saul Alinsky and the Dilemmas of Race in the Post-war City" (Ph.D. diss., University of Pennsylvania, 2000), 100–107.

8. Becky M. Nicolaides, *My Blue Heaven: Life and Politics in the Working-Class Suburbs of Los Angeles, 1920–1965* (Chicago: University of Chicago Press, 2002), 275.

9. Hirsch, *Making the Second Ghetto*, 52, maps seven large-scale disturbances conducted by whites in the Chicago area during the postwar period: Airport Homes, Fernwood Park, Park Manor, Englewood, Cicero, Trumbull Park, and Calumet Park. Four of the seven riots took place during the 1940s, and none of them occurred on the West Side. Hirsch also discovered a total of 485 racial "incidents" between 1945 and 1950.

10. Ibid., 41, 97; Arnold R. Hirsch, "Massive Resistance in the Urban North: Trumbull Park, Chicago, 1953–1966," *Journal of American History* 82 (September 1995): 529. See also Thomas A. Guglielmo, *White on Arrival: Italians, Race, Color, and Power in Chicago, 1890–1945* (New York: Oxford University Press, 2003), 161.

11. For similar criticisms during the 1919 riot on the South Side, see Tuttle, *Race Riot*, 51. "An Alarming Situation," *Garfieldian*, September 2, 1953; Clancy to editor, *Garfieldian*, October 28, 1953; "School Walks Unprotected," *Garfieldian*, November 4, 1953; "Assault of Woman Shocks Austin," *Garfieldian*, August 11, 1954; "Some Plain Talk on Crime Problem," *Garfieldian*, September 5, 1957.

12. Hirsch, *Making the Second Ghetto*, 57, 63; Chicago Council against Racial and Religious Discrimination, "To Secure These Rights: The Right to Safety and Security of the Person in Chicago," folder "Chicago, 1948–1950," box 7, Illinois Commission on Human Relations Records, Abraham Lincoln Presidential Library, Springfield, Illinois (hereafter ICHR). See also Homer A. Jack, *Homer's Odyssey: My Quest for Peace and Justice* (Becket, MA: One Peaceful World Press, 1996), 128.

13. Hirsch, *Making the Second Ghetto*, 65–66.

14. AFSC Interne Reports, 7/29/57–8/4/57, folder "Work and Study Program—Internes in Community Service Summer Project, Chicago RO 1957," box "Chicago R.O. Files 1957 #2," AFSC. This building was located just west of Independence Boulevard, which connected Douglas Park and Garfield Park, explaining the presence of Park District police. Vivas to Wilson, August 5, 1957, folder "August 1957," box 4, Greater Lawndale Conservation Commission Records, Chicago Historical Society (hereafter GLCC-CHS); undated, handwritten ms., folder "1957 Undated Items," box 5, GLCC-CHS; Greater Lawndale Association of Block Clubs and Organizations, flyer, "Important Events in Chicago—1957," folder "June–July 1957," box 4, GLCC-CHS (emphasis in the original); Chicago Commission on Human Relations, "A

Preliminary Report on Racial Disturbances in Chicago for the Period July 21 to August 4, 1957," folder 6, box 94, American Friends Service Committee Records, accession 67-87, Special Collections and University Archives, Richard J. Daley Library, University of Illinois at Chicago (hereafter AFSC-UIC).

15. Clipping, *Chicago Defender*, October 21, 1957, folder "Oct. 1–24, 1957," box 4, GLCC-CHS; Chicago ICS Report, January 22, 1958, folder "Work and Study—Internes in Community Service Winter Proj. 57–58—Staff Reports Jan.–June Chicago RO 1958," box "Chicago R.O. Files 1958," AFSC.

16. Chicago Title and Trust Company, tract index search for 4107 W. Cullerton Street, folder "Oct. 1–24, 1957," box 4, GLCC-CHS; handwritten chronology, folder "Oct. 1–24, 1957," box 4, GLCC-CHS.

17. Clipping, *Chicago Daily News*, February 15, 1958, folder "Feb. 1–29, 1958," box 5, GLCC-CHS; clipping, *Chicago Tribune*, February 28, 1958, folder "Feb. 1–29, 1958," box 5, GLCC-CHS; Human Relations Committee meeting, March 10, 1958, folder "March 1–17, 1958," box 6, GLCC-CHS.

18. GLCC staff meeting, minutes, August 17, 1959, folder "August 1959," box 11, GLCC-CHS; report, Hobbs to How and Ross, October 7–20, 1955, folder "Work and Study—Interns in Community Ser. Winter 55–56 Leaders' Reports Sept.–Dec. Chicago RO 1955," box "Chicago R.O. Files, 1955 (Peace Ed)," AFSC; Beittel to How, August 18, 1959, folder "Work and Study—Interns in Community Ser. Summer Project, Chicago RO 1959," box "Chicago R.O. Files 1959 (Work & Study) to 1960 (Housing Opportunities Program)," AFSC; "The Management of Neighborhood Change," abridged proceedings, citywide workshop, sponsored by the Chicago Commission on Human Relations, College Camp, Lake Geneva, Wisconsin, April 10–12, 1959, p. 16, folder 127, Greater Lawndale Conservation Commission Records, Special Collections and University Archives, Richard J. Daley Library, University of Illinois at Chicago; clipping, *Chicago Defender*, September 4, 1957, folder "Sept. 1957," box 4, GLCC-CHS; Bob and Liza Hobbs to How, Willard, and Greenwood, May 24, 1955, folder "Work and Study—Interns in Community Ser. Winter 54–55 Leaders' reports, Feb.–May, Chicago RO 1955," box "Chicago R.O. Files, 1955 (Peace Ed)," AFSC; "1964—summer tensions bulletin—May 27," folder 20, Ely Aaron Papers, Special Collections and University Archives, Richard J. Daley Library, University of Illinois at Chicago (hereafter EA); Tensions Bulletin, April 2, 1965, folder 20, EA.

19. "Jap's New Home Stoned Twice," *Garfieldian*, November 21, 1946; Bob and Liza Hobbs to How, Willard, and Greenwood, May 24, 1955, folder "Work and Study—Interns in Community Ser. Winter 54–55 Leaders' reports, Feb.–May, Chicago RO 1955," box "Chicago R.O. Files, 1955 (Peace Ed)," AFSC; Hobbs to How and Ross, February 16, 1956, folder "Work and Study Prog.—Internes in Community Service Winter Proj. Staff Reports, Feb.–June. Chicago RO 1956," box "Chicago R.O. Files 1956 (Work & Study Prog.) to 1957 (Job Opportunities Prog.)," AFSC; Chicago ICS Report, January 22, 1958, folder "Work and Study—Internes in Community Service Summer Project, Chicago RO 1958," box "Chicago R.O. Files 1958," AFSC; Carol Honnold, Daily Report, September 26, 1963, folder "Youth Opportunities Program—Staff Reports (C. Honnold) Chicago RO 1963," box "Chicago R.O. 1963 (Peace Ed.—Newsletter to Youth Oppors. Program)," AFSC; Hobbs to How and Ross, December 2–29, 1955, folder "Work and Study—Interns in Community Ser. Winter 54–55 Leaders' reports, Feb.–May, Chicago RO 1955," box "Chicago R.O. Files, 1955 (Peace Ed)," AFSC; Chicago Commission on Human Relations, "Six Month Report, July 1, 1956–December 31, 1956," folder 6, box 94, AFSC-UIC; Chicago Commission on Human Relations, "Six Month Report, January 1, 1957–June 30, 1957," folder 6, box 94, AFSC-UIC.

20. Clipping, "Hunt Ended, Family Moves Quietly into W. Side Home," *Chicago Sun-Times*, August 13, 1959, folder "Garfield Park," box 31, Monsignor John J. Egan Papers, Archives Division, Hesburgh Library, University of Notre Dame (hereafter CJEG); clipping, *Chicago Sun-Times*, August 13, 1959, folder "Chicago 1959–1957," box 6, ICHR; "'Constructive Program Urged to Aid Community," *Garfieldian*, August 12, 1959; clipping, *Chicago Defender*, August 15, 1959, folder "August 1959," box 11, GLCC-CHS; GLCC Board of Directors meeting, August 25,

1959, folder "August 1959," box 11, GLCC-CHS. For formal descriptions of the industrial urban renewal areas in East Garfield Park, see Staff to the Commissioners, Chicago Land Clearance Commission, "Site Designation Redevelopment Project, Lake-California," September 12, 1956, and Staff to the Commissioners, Chicago Land Clearance Commission, "Site Designation Redevelopment Project, Lake-Maplewood," September 12, 1956, both in Chicago Historical Society.

21. Ace and Kathy Backus to Herman Roether, May 7, 1957, folder "Work and Study Program—Internes in Community Service Summer Project, Chicago RO 1957," box "Chicago R.O. Files 1957 #2," AFSC; Steinberg to Quilici, October 19, 1953, folder "1953," box 1, GLCC-CHS. Beryl Satter interview with Harry Gaynor, August 15, 2001, audiotape in possession of author, provided by Beryl Satter; Julia Fairfax, an African American hotel owner, explained that many blacks were able to buy property through friendly Jewish intermediaries. "Program . . . Looking Backward to Move Forward," meeting, Midwest Complex, February 9, 1985, tape T21, Bethel New Life Collection, Special Collections and Preservation Division, Harold Washington Library Center, Chicago. Harry Gaynor, the son of Ukrainian Jewish immigrants, joined the Third Unitarian Church in Austin in the 1960s, following the support the congregation and its minister offered him in the wake of the sale to the Hargraves. He later moved to Galewood, the northern section of Austin. *Third Unitarian* newsletter, September 8, 1998; program, 1998 People's Weekly World Banquet, Sunday, September 20, 1998, both in possession of author; clipping, "Urge Mayor to Act in Racial Flare-up," *Chicago Defender*, August 14, 1959, folder 11, box 9, American Civil Liberties Union Illinois Division Papers, Department of Special Collections, Regenstein Library, University of Chicago (hereafter ACLU).

22. Clipping, *Chicago Defender*, August 15, 1959, folder "August 1959," box 11, GLCC-CHS; GLCC Board of Directors meeting, August 25, 1959, folder "August 1959," box 11, GLCC-CHS; Danish to Vivas, October 18, 1959, folder "Oct. 1–22, 1959," box 11, GLCC-CHS. The Hargraves also defended their right to live unmolested in their home in an open letter disseminated throughout the city. "Property Group Organizer Gives Appraisal of Racial Problem," *Garfieldian*, October 7, 1959.

23. Drake and Douty to Daley, April 19, 1957, folder 11, box 9, ACLU; clipping, *Chicago Daily News*, August 7, 1959, folder "August 1959," box 11, GLCC-CHS; clipping, *Chicago Defender*, August 15, 1959, folder "August 1959," box 11, GLCC-CHS; "'Constructive' Program Urged to Aid Community," *Garfieldian*, August 12, 1959; "Block Group Considering Membership Pledge Card," *Garfieldian*, August 26, 1959; Chicago Urban League Resolution on "Racial Disturbances and Law Enforcement," adopted August 19, 1959, folder "August 1959," box 11, GLCC-CHS; Civil Rights Department, Chicago Commission on Human Relations, to Law and Order Committee members, August 26, 1959, folder 11, box 9, ACLU. Sugrue, *Origins of the Urban Crisis*, 252, notes that in Detroit "the gender dynamics of protest changed at night, when most demonstrations took place."

24. Clipping, *Chicago Defender*, August 15, 1959; clipping, *Chicago Defender*, August 15, 1959[?]; and GLCC Board of Directors meeting, August 25, 1959, all in folder "August 1959," box 11, GLCC-CHS. The Gaynors had experienced threats and violence in the past. In May 1958 an arsonist tried to burn down their apartment building. Lerners to Thelma, May 9, 1958, folder "Work and Study—Internes in Community Service Winter Proj. 57–58—Staff Reports Jan.–June Chicago RO 1958," box "Chicago R.O. Files 1958," AFSC; clipping, "Poison-Pen Letter Clue in Slaying of Lawyer," *Chicago Sun-Times*, August 14, 1959, folder 11, box 9, ACLU.

25. Clipping, *Defender*, August 15, 1959, folder "August 1959," box 11, GLCC-CHS; clipping, "Urge Mayor to Act in Racial Flare-up," *Chicago Defender*, August 14, 1959, folder 11, box 9, ACLU; GLCC Board of Directors meeting, August 25, 1959, folder "August 1959," box 11, GLCC-CHS; Danish to Vivas, October 18, 1959, folder "Oct. 1–22, 1959," box 11, GLCC-CHS.

26. Undated clipping, "Aid Family Move in House," *Chicago Defender*, folder 11, box 9, ACLU; "Talking It Over," *Garfieldian*, August 25, 1965.

27. "Calmness, Resistance to Speculators Stressed," *Garfieldian*, August 12, 1959; "Meet Gordon Mattson, Block Club Leader," *Garfieldian*, September 23, 1959. Bishop Hillinger of St.

Mel's, apparently unhappy with the direction UPG took, announced plans for a separate program to improve West Garfield Park without racial discrimination. Monday, August 22, 1960, folder "Daily Reports: July–December 1960," box 66, GJEG. Cf. Gerald Gamm, *Urban Exodus: Why the Jews Left Boston and the Catholics Stayed* (Cambridge, MA: Harvard University Press, 1999), 93.

28. "Calmness, Resistance to Speculators Stressed," *Garfieldian*, August 12, 1959; "Block Organizations Snowball," *Garfieldian*, August 19, 1959; "Block Group Considering Membership Pledge Card," *Garfieldian*, August 26, 1959; "Block Drive Still Gaining Steam Here," *Garfieldian*, September 2, 1959; "Mattson Selected Group's Chairman," *Garfieldian*, November 11, 1959.

29. "Property Group Organizer Gives Appraisal of Racial Problem," *Garfieldian*, October 7, 1959.

30. Ibid.

31. "Block Organizations Snowball," *Garfieldian*, August 19, 1959; "Block Group Considering Membership Pledge Card," *Garfieldian*, August 26, 1959; "'Not for Sale' Campaign Growing; 4,000 Signs Up," *Garfieldian*, September 30, 1959; "Mattson Selected Group's Chairman," *Garfieldian*, November 11, 1959; "Block Clubs Rapidly Organizing in Austin," *Garfieldian*, July 27, 1960.

32. Sugrue, *Origins of the Urban Crisis*, 247; W. Edward Orser, *Blockbusting in Baltimore: The Edmondson Village Story* (Lexington: University Press of Kentucky, 1994), 221n13, 222n18; Kevin Fox Gotham, *Race, Real Estate, and Uneven Development: The Kansas City Experience, 1900–2000* (Albany: State University of New York Press, 2002), 104; "Block Drive Still Gaining Steam Here," *Garfieldian*, September 2, 1959; "Blocks Organize South of Highway," *Garfieldian*, September 10, 1959; "'Not for Sale' Campaign Growing; 4,000 Signs Up," *Garfieldian*, September 30, 1959; "Speculators at Work on Monroe St.: UPG Warns Residents to Beware of Sharks," *Garfieldian*, February 24, 1960; Mildred Berman, staff report, September 14, 1959, folder "Sept. 1–22, 1959," box 11, GLCC-CHS; "Decal, UPG Weapon in Speculator War," *Garfieldian*, June 14, 1961; Eileen M. McMahon, *What Parish Are You From?: A Chicago Irish Community and Race Relations* (Lexington: University Press of Kentucky, 1995), 123; Kruse, "White Flight," 113.

33. "New Warning of Danger in Rumors," *Garfieldian*, September 16, 1959; "Speculators at Work on Monroe St.: UPG Warns Residents to Beware of Sharks," *Garfieldian*, February 24, 1960; "UPG Chairman Blasts Real Estate Firm's Scare Letter," *Garfieldian*, March 16, 1960; Bacigalupo to editor, *Garfieldian*, December 11, 1963.

34. "400 UPG Members in Spirited Rally,'" *Garfieldian*, October 18, 1961; "UPG to Oppose City Bond Issues," *Garfieldian*, February 21, 1962; "United Property Group Meeting Draws 750," *Garfieldian*, April 3, 1963; "What UPG Leader Intended to Say When Time Expired," *Garfieldian*, July 15, 1964; clipping, "UPG Gives Up the Fight," *Austinite*, August 12, 1965, folder "Austin Community Organization—Newspaper Clippings," box 24, CJEG. For more on the Town Hall Assembly, see chapter 8.

35. "Lies Trap Blockbuster; State Agency Notified," *Garfieldian*, April 4, 1962; "To File Slander Suit against Blockbusters," *Garfieldian*, April 11, 1962; "Blockbusting Drive Moves in Low Gear," *Garfieldian*, June 27, 1962.

36. Evelyn M. Kitagawa and Karl E. Taeuber, eds., *Local Community Fact Book, Chicago Metropolitan Area, 1960* (Chicago: Chicago Community Inventory, 1963), 67; "How Resigning ACO Administrator Views Austin, Its Problems," *Garfieldian*, August 25, 1965; Pierre de Vise, *Chicago's Widening Color Gap* (Chicago: Interuniversity Social Research Committee, December 1967), 66, 145; "Oppose Open Housing," *Garfieldian*, August 7, 1963; Bacigalupo to editor, *Garfieldian*, December 26, 1963; "UPG to Disband Effective Sept. 1," *Garfieldian*, August 11, 1965; clipping, "UPG Gives Up the Fight," *Austinite*, August 12, 1965, folder "Austin Community Organization—Newspaper Clippings," box 24, CJEG; memo for file—Mr. Henry Collins, Austin, June 2, 1962, folder "Austin Community Organization, Correspondence," box 24, CJEG.

37. Plotkin, "Deeds of Mistrust"; Mikva, "Neighborhood Improvement Association"; James R. Ralph Jr., *Northern Protest: Martin Luther King, Jr., Chicago, and the Civil Rights Movement*

(Cambridge, MA: Harvard University Press, 1993), chap. 3; David J. Garrow, *Bearing the Cross: Martin Luther King, Jr., and the Southern Christian Leadership Conference* (New York: Vintage Books, 1986), chap. 9.

38. "Anti-Block Busting Law under Study," *Garfieldian*, May 3, 1961. Orser, *Blockbusting in Baltimore*, 88, however, writes that it was not until 1966 that Baltimore passed an ordinance that outlawed door-to-door solicitation and distribution of mass circulars. "Blockbusting Law Argued," *Garfieldian*, May 10, 1961; Susan Spiegel Glassberg, "Legal Control of Blockbusting," *Urban Law Annual* 1972: 145–70. On related efforts in New York City in the 1980s, see Roger Sanjek, *The Future of Us All: Race and Neighborhood Politics in New York City* (Ithaca: Cornell University Press, 1998), 284–85.

39. Rose Helper, *Racial Policies and Practices of Real Estate Brokers* (Minneapolis: University of Minnesota Press, 1969), 244; Division of Housing and Community Services, Commission on Human Relations, City of Chicago, "Remedies for Panic Peddling," April 1965, Chicago Historical Society; "Human Relations Group Wars on Panic Peddlers," *Garfieldian*, October 25, 1961; "State Bureau Vows to Help Fight Panic Peddlers," *Garfieldian*, November 1, 1961; "UPG Gives State Realty Evidence," *Garfieldian*, November 8, 1961; "State Starts Probe of 2 Realty Firms," *Garfieldian*, December 13, 1961; "Lies Trap Blockbuster; State Agency Notified," *Garfieldian*, April 4, 1962; "'A Shameful Disclosure,'" *Garfieldian*, July 18, 1962; "State Should Wake Up," *Garfieldian*, August 22, 1962; "Encouragement, But . . ." *Garfieldian*, April 17, 1963.

40. Neil Kraus, *Race, Neighborhoods, and Community Power: Buffalo Politics, 1934–1997* (Albany: State University of New York Press, 2000), 85; Santow, "Saul Alinsky," 167–68; Preston H. Smith II, "The Quest for Racial Democracy: Black Civic Ideology and Housing Interests in Postwar Chicago," *Journal of Urban History* 26 (2000): 147–51; Hirsch, *Making the Second Ghetto*, 127–29; "Fight 'Open Occupancy,'" *Garfieldian*, March 15, 1961; Clifford J. Campbell and Ed Marciniak, "A Report to the Mayor and the City Council of Chicago on the Present Status and Effectiveness of Existing Fair Housing Practices Legislation in the United States as of April 1, 1963" (Chicago: Chicago Commission on Human Relations, 1963), Chicago Historical Society; Chicago Commission on Human Relations, "A Report to the Mayor and the City Council of Chicago on the Present Status and Effectiveness of Existing Fair Housing Practices Legislation in the United States as of August 31, 1967," Chicago Historical Society (hereafter CCHR 1967); Helper, *Racial Policies*, 278.

41. CCHR, "Selling and Buying Real Estate in a Racially Changing Neighborhood: A Survey," June 14, 1962, folder "June 1–15, 1962," box 19, GLCC-CHS; "Commission Studies Blockbuster Attack," *Garfieldian*, August 15, 1962; McMahon, *What Parish Are You From?*, 169.

42. McMahon, *What Parish Are You From?*, 169; Helper, *Racial Policies*, 277–78; "Oppose Open Housing," *Garfieldian*, August 7, 1963; "Drafts New Housing Bill," *Garfieldian*, August 21, 1963.

43. CCHR 1967, 1; Helper, *Racial Policies*, 268, 364n1; "Says City Fights Panic Peddlers," *Garfieldian*, June 3, 1964. CREB filed suit against this ordinance, but it was upheld in court. CCHR 1967, 37. Legislative Committee meeting, October 2, 1963, folder 11, box 32, Metropolitan Planning Council Records, accession 75-104, Special Collections and University Archives, Richard J. Daley Library, University of Illinois at Chicago.

44. Cf. Sugrue, *Origins of the Urban Crisis*, 197; "Two Complaints Signed against Panic Peddlers," *Garfieldian*, May 13, 1964, "Report of a Conference with Human Relations Aide," *Garfieldian*, May 20, 1964; "Seek Community Approval of Anti-Blockbuster Code," *Garfieldian*, December 8, 1965; "Fine Realty Peddler, No License," *Garfieldian*, April 13, 1966; untitled clipping October 10, 1963, *SW News Herald*, folder 6, box 11, ACLU; "Report of Complaints Received under the Chicago Fair Housing Ordinance for the Period Ending September 30, 1964," folder 20, EA.

45. Harvey Luskin Molotch, *Managed Integration: Dilemmas of Doing Good in the City* (Berkeley: University of California Press, 1972), 125; Helper, *Racial Policies*, 288. According to an AFSC member, there were six hundred complaints, resulting in three revoked licenses in

1969: James Reedy, "Open Housing Compliance Testing Program," February 1969, folder "Metropolitan Program, Open Communities, General, Chicago Regional Office, 1969," box "Chicago Regional Office 1969 Admin. to Metropolitan Prog. (Pre-Adolescent Enrichment Prog.)," AFSC. Figures for 1967 are reported in CCHR 1967, 12; undated reprint, "Fair Housing Report," *Chicago Sun-Times*, folder 19, EA; Division of Housing and Community Services, Commission on Human Relations, City of Chicago, "Remedies for Panic Peddling," April 1965, Chicago Historical Society, 66. The law was restructured in 1971 to allow hearings in the neighborhoods. "Commission to Hear Fair Housing Complaints in Field," *Austin News*, November 24, 1971, box 4, Austin Newspaper Collection, Special Collections and Preservation Division, Harold Washington Library Center, Chicago.

46. "Realtor Board Launches Property Owners Division," *Garfieldian*, December 11, 1963; unidentified clipping, "Realtor Board Launches New Division for Property Owners," folder 6, box 11, ACLU; clipping, "HOPE Organization Leads in Fund Raising for POCC," *Community Reporter*, February 12, 1964, folder "Home-Owners Protective Enterprise (H.O.P.E.)," box 31, CJEG; organization chart: The Property Owners Coordinating Committee, Members of the Board of Directors, folder "Property Owners Coordinating Committee—S.T. Sutton," box 47, CJEG; Helper, *Racial Policies*, 279; Ralph, *Northern Protest*, 154; "Start Petitions to Put Open Occupancy on Ballot," *Garfieldian*, February 5, 1964. Helper, *Racial Policies*, 365n10, cites *Chicagoland's Real Estate Advertiser*, "An Introduction to POCC" (February 7, 1964), 10; clipping, "HOPE Organization Leads in Fund Raising for POCC," *Community Reporter*, February 12, 1964, folder "Home-Owners Protective Enterprise (H.O.P.E.)," box 31, CJEG; statement by S. T. Sutton to members of the board of education of the city of Chicago, folder 2, box 6, Cyrus Hall Adams III Papers, Chicago Historical Society (hereafter CHA); Monsignor John J. Egan, "Common Sense, the Real Estate Market and Free Enterprise in 1965," speech to the West Side Real Estate Board, February 8, 1965, folder "West Side Real Estate Board," box 26, CJEG.

47. Whether the signature effort achieved its goal is unclear. Lindsey to editor, *Garfieldian*, September 16, 1964; Port to "Dear member," July 16, 1964, folder "Open Occupancy," box 36, ACLU 1970 addendum; unidentified clipping, "Proposed Cluster Plan Blasted at UPG Rally," folder 16-3, box 16, CHA; unidentified clipping, "Housing Vote Opponents Hunt Petitions," July 23, 1964, folder "Open Occupancy," box 36, ACLU 1970 addendum; Potts to editor, *Garfieldian*, September 9, 1965. See also Santow, "Saul Alinsky," 330–31. Cf. the contemporaneous passage of Proposition 14 in California, which repealed that state's fair housing law. Robert O. Self, *American Babylon: Race and the Struggle for Postwar Oakland* (Princeton: Princeton University Press, 2003), 167–69, 260–65.

48. Unidentified clipping, "Seek State Vote on Housing," October 10, 1963, folder 6, box 11, ACLU; "Participating Organizations," folder "Property Owners Coordinating Committee—S.T. Sutton," box 47, CJEG; pamphlet, Chicago Conference on Religion and Race, "WHY the Three Major Faiths Oppose the Proposed Referendum on Open Occupancy Legislation," folder "Open Occupancy," box 36, ACLU 1970 addendum; bulletin, Property Owners Coordinating Committee, 105 West Madison St., May 27, 1964, "Real Estate: Open Occupancy," box 47, CJEG; letter, S. T. Sutton, May 18, 1964, "Real Estate: Open Occupancy," box 47, CJEG; Callahan to Executive Committee, June 3, 1964, "Real Estate: Open Occupancy," box 47, CJEG; Helper, *Racial Policies*, 280; Legislative Reference Bureau, *No. 25 Final Legislative Synopsis and Digest of the Seventy-fifth General Assembly, State of Illinois, Action on All Bills and Resolutions Received through October 19, 1967*, 76, 769. On the floor fight in the Illinois legislature over open housing, see Taylor Pensoneau, *Governor Richard Ogilvie: In the Interest of the State* (Carbondale: Southern Illinois University Press, 1997), 88–90.

49. Box 526, "Urban Renewal," and box 1140, "Open Occupancy," Otto Kerner Records, Abraham Lincoln Presidential Library, Springfield, Illinois; "North Lawndale: Proposals for Conservation, Lawndale Conservation Community Council," folder "July 1966–March 1967," box 27, GLCC-CHS; "ACO Applauds Kerner on Open Occupancy," *Garfieldian*, August 3, 1966; clipping, "Rights Leaders Hail Ruling Upholding Open Housing," *News*, January 20, 1967,

folder 98-18, Chicago Urban League Records, accession 76-116, Special Collections and University Archives, Richard J. Daley Library, University of Illinois at Chicago; Report #7, September 1968, folder "Metropolitan Program, Open Communities Program, Reports, Numbered, Chicago Regional Office, 1968," box "Chicago Regional Office 1968, Admin. to Metropolitan Prog. (Peace/War Issues)," AFSC; CCHR 1967, 1; Douglas S. Massey and Nancy A. Denton, *American Apartheid: Segregation and the Making of the Underclass* (Cambridge, MA: Harvard University Press, 1993), 191–95; Orser, *Blockbusting in Baltimore*, 9; Illinois Constitution (1970), art. 1, sec. 17; Hugh Graham Davis, *The Civil Rights Era: Origins and Development of National Policy, 1960–1972* (New York: Oxford University Press, 1990), 271–73.

CHAPTER EIGHT

1. Lerners to How, July 17, 1958, folder "Work and Study—Internes in Community Service Summer Project, Chicago RO 1958," box "Chicago R.O. Files 1958," Chicago Regional Office Files, American Friends Service Committee Archives, Philadelphia, Pennsylvania; flyer announcing Emergency Membership meeting for Garfield Park Good Neighbors Council, for August 19, 1959, folder "August 1959," box "August 1–December 25, 1959," Greater Lawndale Conservation Commission Records, Chicago Historical Society; undated newsletter, *Good Neighbor News*, folder 1, box 5, West Garfield Park Community Collection, Special Collections and Preservation Division, Harold Washington Library Center, Chicago. On Brotherhood Week, see Sylvie Murray, "Suburban Citizens: Domesticity and Community Politics in Queens, New York, 1945–1960" (Ph.D. diss., Yale University, December 1994), 166–67.

2. John T. McGreevy, *Parish Boundaries: The Catholic Encounter with Race in the Twentieth-Century Urban North* (Chicago: University of Chicago Press, 1996).

3. Harvey Luskin Molotch, *Managed Integration: Dilemmas of Doing Good in the City* (Berkeley: University of California Press, 1972), 71, emphasis in the original; Vincent J. Giese, *Revolution in the City* (Notre Dame, IN: Fides, 1961), 75; "Leaders Stress 'Pride,'" *Garfieldian*, April 10, 1963; McGreevy, *Parish Boundaries*, 41; Heather Ann Thompson, *Whose Detroit?: Politics, Labor, and Race in a Modern American City* (Ithaca: Cornell University Press, 2001), 26, notes that not all whites in Detroit were working for segregation in this period.

4. Clipping, "'Holding the Line' at Ashland Av.," *Chicago Daily News*, April 18, 1968, and clipping, "Father Lawlor: His Kingdom and Power," *Chicago Tribune Magazine*, February 21, 1971, both in Francis X. Lawlor clipping file, Chicago Historical Society. On Lawlor, see McGreevy, *Parish Boundaries*, 231–34.

5. On women in twentieth-century organizing, see Jennifer Frost, *"An Interracial Movement of the Poor": Community Organizing and the New Left in the 1960s* (New York: New York University Press, 2001), 82.

6. "ATOA Group Wants 'Better Austin for All,'" *Austinite*, May 25, 1966, box 7, Austin Newspaper Collection, Special Collections and Preservation Division, Harold Washington Library Center, Chicago (hereafter ANC).

7. *Chicago Telephone Directory* (1953) and (1954); "Boulevard Residents Start Block Club," *Garfieldian*, March 18, 1959; "Block Club Idea Spreading," *Garfieldian*, April 22, 1959; "5000 Block Club Adopts Platform," *Garfieldian*, April 29, 1959; Hoffmeister to editor, *Garfieldian*, March 30, 1960; "Conservation Council Maps Community Rally," *Garfieldian*, April 12, 1961. NCC broke away from UPG: "Future of Block Club Movement Depends on Austin Residents," *Austinite*, May 25, 1966, box 7, ANC.

8. "An Energetic Civic Worker Tells Success in Forming Block Clubs," *Garfieldian*, August 4, 1965. Kane was criticized for working with both UPG and ACO, which UPG rules prohibited. "Says School Problem Rooted in Overcrowded Community," *Garfieldian*, September 30, 1964.

9. "An Energetic Civic Worker Tells Success in Forming Block Clubs," *Garfieldian*, August 4, 1965.

10. CCHR staff found that Flowers moved to the building in June, not in October.

Summary—65 FHO 86-163, folder 20, Ely Aaron Papers, Special Collections and University Archives, Richard J. Daley Library, University of Illinois at Chicago (hereafter EA); "Cicero Ave. Block Clubs Urge War on Speculators," *Garfieldian*, October 13, 1965.

11. "Seek to Question Realty Man in Blockbuster Fight," *Garfieldian*, October 27, 1965; Summary—65 FHO 86-163, folder 20, EA; "Not a Panic Peddler, Time Realty Man Tells Group," *Garfieldian*, November 10, 1965. Time Realty did receive a summons to appear in license court for failing to purchase a broker's license. The case was continued once because the representative had a mild heart attack ("Seek Community Approval of Anti-Blockbuster Code," *Garfieldian*, December 8, 1965) and then eventually dismissed because the complainants failed to attend court in April 1966 ("Time Realty Case Dismissed by Judge," *Garfieldian*, May 4, 1966).

12. "Seek to Question Realty Man in Blockbuster Fight," *Garfieldian*, October 27, 1965; "3 Firms 'Invited' to Rally," *Garfieldian*, November 3, 1965; "Not a Panic Peddler, Time Realty Man Tells Group," *Garfieldian*, November 10, 1965.

13. "Politicians, Businessmen Pledge to Fight 'Peddlers,'" *Garfieldian*, November 25, 1965. Cf. Eileen M. McMahon, *What Parish Are You From?: A Chicago Irish Community and Race Relations* (Lexington: University Press of Kentucky, 1995), 152, on the Organization of the Southwest Community's use of a similar tactic; "Anti-Panic Group Picks Name; to Submit Code," *Garfieldian*, December 1, 1965. For a detailed history of the Off the Street Club, see Mark Santow, "Saul Alinsky and the Dilemmas of Race in the Post-war City" (Ph.D. diss., University of Pennsylvania, 2000), esp. chaps. 2, 5.

14. "Anti-Blockbusting Group Opens Office on S. Cicero," *Garfieldian*, December 15, 1965; Carole Goodwin, *The Oak Park Strategy: Community Control of Racial Change* (Chicago: University of Chicago Press, 1979), 97.

15. "Anti-Panic Group Picks Name; to Submit Code," *Garfieldian*, December 1, 1965; see Molotch, *Managed Integration*, chap. 4, on the similar goals of the South Shore Commission, and Santow, "Saul Alinsky," 284, for the Organization of the Southwest Community.

16. The Organization for a Better Austin made more effective use of this approach: undated OBA News Brief, folder 24, box 3, Austin Community Collection, Special Collections and Preservation Division, Harold Washington Library Center, Chicago (hereafter ACC); "Seek Community Approval of Anti-Blockbuster Code," *Garfieldian*, December 8, 1965; "Anti-Blockbusting Group Opens Office on S. Cicero," *Garfieldian*, December 15, 1965; "5 Firms Visited by ATOA Refuse to Sign Code," *Garfieldian*, January 12, 1966; "ATOA Tells of Visits to Firms," *Garfieldian*, January 19, 1966.

17. "Anti-Blockbusting Group Opens Office on S. Cicero," *Garfieldian*, December 15, 1965; "'Carpetbaggers' Flooding Back," *Garfieldian*, August 3, 1966.

18. "Meet to Improve Cicero Ave. Area," *Garfieldian*, March 2, 1966; "ATOA Block Club News," *Garfieldian*, April 13, 1966; "Parents Don't Care What Children Do, ATOA Told," *Garfieldian*, April 20, 1966; "ATOA Forms Youth Club," *Garfieldian*, April 27, 1966; "ATOA to Operate Urban Project," *Garfieldian*, June 29, 1966; "ATOA Starts 'Project Champ,'" *Garfieldian*, July 13, 1966; "Work with Progress Center to Build Playgrounds," *Garfieldian*, July 27, 1966; "ATOA Backs May PTA Policy," *Garfieldian*, December 7, 1966.

19. "Gaudette Names Mrs. Kane, Mary Duffy to Staff," *Garfieldian*, August 10, 1966; "Gaudette Cleared by ATOA," *Garfieldian*, October 12, 1966; "Gaudette and ATOA Reach Accord after Week's Dispute," *Garfieldian*, October 19, 1966; Report of the GRA Nominating Committee, June 11, 1967, folder 23, box 3, ACC; agenda, Busing Rally, January 19, 1968, folder 25, box 3, ACC; press release, May-Spencer United Committee, January 20, 1968, folder 5, box 34, Cyrus Hall Adams III Papers, Chicago Historical Society.

20. "100 at First Meeting of Protestant Group," *Garfieldian*, October 5, 1960; memo for file, Mr. Henry Collins, June 2, 1962, folder "Austin Community Organization, Correspondence," box 24, Monsignor John J. Egan Papers, Archives Division, Hesburgh Library, University of Notre Dame (hereafter CJEG); Monday, July 3, 1961, folder "Daily Reports: July–December 1960," box 66, CJEG; Daily Report—Jan. 2, 1964, folder "Daily Reports: Dec. 1963–Jan. 1964," box 66, CJEG; memo for file, January 14, 1964, folder "Daily Reports: Dec. 1963–Jan. 1964,"

box 66, CJEG; clipping, "Austin Community Group Seeking 2 Men for Staff," *Chicago Tribune*, February 6, 1964, folder "Austin Community Organization—Newspaper Clippings," box 24, CJEG. The role of Chicago Archbishop Meyer in the founding of ACO is unclear; on the South Side, McGreevy, *Parish Boundaries*, 122, suggests, Meyer forced the local Catholic clergy to fund the Organization for a Southwest Community. On the Office of Urban Affairs, see Steven M. Avella, *This Confident Church: Catholic Leadership and Life in Chicago, 1940–1965* (Notre Dame: University of Notre Dame Press, 1992), 236–38. On Egan, see Margery Frisbie, *An Alley in Chicago: The Ministry of a City Priest* (Kansas City, MO: Sheed & Ward, 1991).

21. "A Tentative Statement Directed towards the Establishment of a Community Council in Austin," folder 47, box 2, ACC; memo for file, January 14, 1964, folder "Daily Reports: Dec. 1963–Jan. 1964," box 66, CJEG; Bacigalupo to editor, *Austinite*, folder "Austin Community Organization, Correspondence," box 24, CJEG; Egan to Doyle, January 21, 1964, folder "Austin Community Organization, Correspondence," box 24, CJEG; "We're Not Competing with UPG, Says ACO Director," *Garfieldian*, July 22, 1964; Proesser to Alinsky and Egan, March 19, 1964, folder "Austin Community Organization, Correspondence," box 24, CJEG; "Resume of Meeting at Belden Manufacturing Company, May 19th, 1964," folder "Archbishop Cody/Austin Community Organization," box 7, CJEG; "Talking It Over," *Garfieldian*, June 24, 1964. It is difficult to gauge the size of ACO's membership, for three reasons. First, ACO had a continuously troubled relationship with the local press. Second, documentation of ACO's history is scattered, not deposited in a single comprehensive archive. Third, perhaps because of difficulty attracting member organizations, ACO switched to individual memberships midway through its brief existence.

22. Memo, Egan to Cody, August 26, 1965, folder "Archbishop Cody/Austin Community Organization," box 7, CJEG; "Planned Hostility," *Garfieldian*, October 21, 1964. The Crosstown Expressway was proposed as a North–South highway to run through the western portion of Chicago. As a result of a freeway revolt in the 1970s, it was never built. Ald. Robert L. Massey to editor, *Garfieldian*, November 18, 1964; "Questions and Answers about ACO," folder 47, box 2, ACC; "ACO Aim Is to Represent All People, Says New Director," *Garfieldian*, May 13, 1964. See also Santow, "Saul Alinsky," 130. "Eliminate Speculator and Integration Will Be Successful, Say Whites," *Garfieldian*, July 14, 1965; McGreevy, *Parish Boundaries*, 170.

23. *Austin Community Organization Newsletter* 1, no. 9 (December 11, 1965), folder 47, box 2, ACC; *Austin Community Organization Newsletter* 1, no. 3 (June 14, 1965), folder 47, box 2, ACC; "ACO to Conduct Opinion Surveys," *Garfieldian*, June 24, 1964; "Release Partial Tab of ACO Survey," *Garfieldian*, November 4, 1964.

24. "Release Partial Tab of ACO Survey," *Garfieldian*, November 4, 1964; Richard McKinlay and Ethyl Shanas, "Austin: Civil Rights and Integration in a Chicago Community" (Chicago: Community and Family Study Center, University of Chicago, August 1, 1968). See esp. p. 22, table 3.14, "Index of Anticipatory Residential Stability."

25. "ACO to Conduct Opinion Surveys," *Garfieldian*, June 24, 1964; "Kissane Elected Chairman of Steering Committee," *Garfieldian*, June 23, 1965; Austin Community Organization, Steering Committee meeting, June 17, 1965, folder 48, box 2, ACC; Austin Community Organization, Steering Committee, minutes of June 17, 1965, folder "Austin Community Organization: meetings-agenda-notices," box 24, CJEG; "Plan Occupancy Forums," *Garfieldian*, July 8, 1965; clipping, "ACO Accepts Resignation of Lyons," *Community Publications*, August 25, 1965, folder "Austin Community Organization—Newspaper Clippings," box 24, CJEG; *Austin Community Organization Newsletter* 1, no. 5 (July 26, 1965), folder 47, box 2, ACC (emphasis in original); flyer, "Integration or Inundation?," folder 47, box 2, ACC.

26. "Open Occupancy" and "ACO Steering Committee Backs Open Occupancy," both in *Garfieldian*, October 27, 1965; Austin Community Organization, Steering Committee minutes, October 21, 1965, folder "Austin Community Organization: meetings-agenda-notices," box 24, CJEG; clipping, *Chicago Defender*, November 4, 1965, folder 58, Greater Lawndale Conservation Commission Records, Special Collections and University Archives, Richard J. Daley Library, University of Illinois at Chicago.

27. Austin Community Organization, Steering Committee meeting, July 15, 1965, folder "Austin Community Organization: meetings-agenda-notices," box 24, CJEG; "Find 'Heavy' Real Estate Soliciting," *Garfieldian*, November 17, 1965; "Politicians, Businessmen Pledge to Fight 'Peddlers,'" *Garfieldian*, November 25, 1965; "3 Charged with Panic Tactics," *Garfieldian*, December 22, 1965.

28. Clipping, "ACO Names Ex–Peace Corps Aide as Executive Director," *Austinite*, May 14, 1964, folder "Austin Community Organization—Newspaper Clippings," box 24, CJEG; memo for file, first meeting of interreligious clergy alliance, Austin, January 14, 1964, folder "Daily Reports: Dec. 1963–Jan. 1964," box 66 CJEG; "ACO Aim Is to Represent All People, Says New Director," *Garfieldian*, May 13, 1964; "Austin's New Civic Organization," *Garfieldian*, June 22, 1966; "Kruse Resigning as ACO Head," *Garfieldian*, April 14, 1965; Kruse to Lyons and Doyle, folder "Austin Community Organization, Correspondence," box 24, CJEG; *Austin Community Organization Newsletter* 1, no. 2 (May 3, 1965), folder 47, box 2, ACC; "Lyons Resigns as Director of ACO," *Garfieldian*, August 11, 1965; clipping, "Lyons Leaves ACO, Cites Lack of Funds," *Austinite*, August 12, 1965, folder "Austin Community Organization—Newspaper Clippings," box 24, CJEG; undated letter of resignation, folder "Austin Community Organization—Newspaper Clippings," box 24, CJEG; memo, Egan to Cody, August 26, 1965, folder "Archbishop Cody/Austin Community Organization," box 7, CJEG; Lyons to Kissane and Doyle, August 5, 1965, folder "Austin Community Organization, Correspondence," box 24, CJEG.

29. The existing scholarship about the Austin Community Organization usually cites a split between Catholic and Protestant clergy as the source of ACO's collapse in 1966: see Jerome Don Harris, "Grass-Roots Organizing in the City of Chicago" (Ph.D. diss., University of Illinois at Chicago Circle, 1980), 77. "Community Group OK's Bond Issue," *Garfieldian*, June 8, 1966. Robert Bailey Jr., *Radicals in Urban Politics: The Alinsky Approach* (Chicago: University of Chicago Press, 1972), 66, attributes the failure of ACO to its rivalry with UPG. The evidence presented here suggests that the split *among* Catholics about race was more important to the group's difficulties, although the Catholic clergy involved did not consistently consult their non-Catholic colleagues on the group's future. On the divisions among American Catholics around race and the civil rights movement, see McGreevy, *Parish Boundaries*, especially chaps. 4, 5, 6, and 8.

30. Egan to Mrs. Thomas Fitzgerald, December 9, 1966, folder "Office of Urban Affairs, Correspondence: To be sorted and filed," box 56, CJEG; Frisbie, *Alley in Chicago*, 176; Avella, *Confident Church*, 344; Charles W. Dahm, *Power and Authority in the Catholic Church: Cardinal Cody in Chicago* (Notre Dame: University of Notre Dame Press, 1981), 28; McGreevy, *Parish Boundaries*, 186–87; McGreevy explains that Cody's tenure in New Orleans had shown him clearly to be a racial liberal, but his early months in Chicago suggested he did not subscribe to the anti-authoritarian brand of Catholicism promoted by the Second Vatican Council; clipping, "Austin Community Group May Disband for Lack of Funds," *Chicago Sun-Times*, January 19, 1966, folder "Archbishop Cody/Austin Community Organization," box 7, CJEG; "Report of Clergy 'Switch' Denied," *Garfieldian*, February 2, 1966; clipping, "Austin Group Gets Pledges to Cover 1966 Budget," *Chicago Sun-Times*, January 21, 1966, folder "Austin Community Organization—Newspaper Clippings," box 24, CJEG.

31. Frisbie, *Alley in Chicago*, 178; "'The Week That Was' in Austin Civic Controversy," *Garfieldian*, June 8, 1966; "Question Where ACO Will Get Funds for Budget," *Austinite*, May 25, 1966, box 7, ANC. Gaudette lived on the city's Far South Side but had experience organizing the Northwest Community Organization. For more about Tom Gaudette, see Peg Knoepfle, "From Tom Gaudette: Good Stories and Hard Wisdom," in *After Alinsky: Community Organizing in Illinois*, ed. Peg Knoepfle (Springfield, IL: Sangamon State University, 1990). See also Gaudette's obituary, *Chicago Tribune*, September 23, 1998; "Gaudette Starts in Austin July 5," *Garfieldian*, June 22, 1966; minutes of special meeting called by Protestant clergy of the greater Austin area, June 13, 1966, folder "Austin Community Organization: meetings-agenda-notices," box 24, CJEG; Austin Community Organization, Steering Committee, May 19, 1966, folder 48, box 2, ACC; agenda for steering committee, June 16, 1966, folder 48, box 2, ACC; press release,

December 19, 1966, folder "Austin Community Organization 1967," box 4, Leadership Council for Metropolitan Open Communities Records, Chicago Historical Society (hereafter LCMOC); Austin Community Organization, "A Report on Discussions with Catholic Clergymen Regarding Implementation of the August 26, 1966 Summit Agreements on Fair Housing and Their Answers to the Question: 'Will You Help This Negro Catholic Family Move into Your Parish?,'" folder "Austin Community Organization 1967," box 4, LCMOC; "ACO Applauds Kerner on Open Occupancy," *Garfieldian*, August 3, 1966. On interracialist activities, see McGreevy, *Parish Boundaries*, passim.

32. "'The Week That Was' in Austin Civic Controversy," *Garfieldian*, June 8, 1966; Saul D. Alinsky, "From Citizen Apathy to Participation," Sixth Annual Fall conference, Association of Community Councils of Chicago, October 19, 1957, copy in author's possession. On Alinsky, see Sanford D. Horwitt, *Let Them Call Me Rebel: Saul Alinsky—His Life and Legacy* (New York: Alfred A. Knopf, 1989). On OBA, see Goodwin, *Oak Park Strategy*; Harris, "Grass-Roots Organizing"; Bailey, *Radicals in Urban Politics*; and Brian J. L. Berry, *The Open Housing Question: Race and Housing in Chicago, 1966–1976* (Cambridge, MA: Ballinger, 1979), chap. 11. Clipping, "Hi, I'm Your Outraged Neighborhood Citizen on the March," *Chicago Tribune Magazine*, December 5, 1971, oversize 1.9, ACC; Guian A. McKee, "Liberal Ends through Illiberal Means: Race, Urban Renewal, and Community in the Eastwick Section of Philadelphia, 1949–1990," *Journal of Urban History* 27 (July 2001): 547–83; Goodwin, *Oak Park Strategy*, 139–42; clipping, *Chicago Tribune*, September 9, 1971; clipping, "Chicago Profile: A Look at Austin," *Chicago Defender*, December 27, 1980, Organization for a Better Austin clipping file, Chicago Municipal Reference Library, Harold Washington Library Center, Chicago.

33. Clipping, "Austin Clergymen Hire Gaudette; to Form CBA," *Austinite*, June 22, 1966, folder 26, box 3, ACC; "Gaudette Starts in Austin July 5," *Garfieldian*, June 22, 1966; unidentified clipping, "Gaudette Starts Austin Job by 'Walking the Streets,'" folder "Austin Community Organization—Newspaper Clippings," box 24, CJEG; "Overholser to Assist Gaudette," *Garfieldian*, September 28, 1966; Gaudette to Egan, July 18, 1966, folder "Office of Urban Affairs, Correspondence: To be sorted and filed," box 56, CJEG; *The West Side Story*, Newsletter of AWCGW, June 1967, folder 8, box 3, ACC; Greater Austin Convention, June 11, 1967, folder 23, box 3, CJEG; agenda, Greater Austin Convention, June 11, 1967, folder 4, box 45, Church Federation of Greater Chicago Collection, Chicago Historical Society.

34. Clipping, "OBA Convention Elects McCarthy, Adopts Resolutions," *Austinite*, June 14, 1967, oversize 1.6, ACC; 3rd Annual All Austin Congress, OBA, April 27, 1969, folder 23, box 3, ACC; *Passage Publications, Salute to Our 200th Year*, June 23, 1976, box 10, ANC. On Cincotta, see Patrick Barry, "Gale Cincotta and Heather Booth," in *After Alinsky*, ed. Knoepfle, 53–61; Lynne Navin, "Gale Cincotta," in *American Community Organizations: A Historical Dictionary*, ed. Patricia Mooney Melvin (New York: Greenwood Press, 1986), 30.

35. *The West Side Story*, Newsletter of AWCGW, vol. 1, no. 10, folder 8, box 3 ACC; Constitution of the Organization for a Better Austin, folder 25, box 3, ACC; "Gaudette and ATOA Reach Accord after Week's Dispute," *Garfieldian*, October 19, 1966; Second Congress, Organization for a Better Austin, April 28, 1968, folder 27, box 3, ACC.

36. Second Congress, Organization for a Better Austin, April 28, 1968, folder 27, box 3, ACC; Organization for a Better Austin, Executive Board minutes, May 20, 1968, folder 27, box 3, ACC; "Four Agents Sign Agreements," *Austinite*, May 6, 1970, box 8, ANC; "Calls Senate Session 'Kangaroo Court,'" *Austinite*, August 5, 1970, box 9, ANC.

37. Clipping, *New World*, June 19, 1970, OBA clipping file, Chicago Historical Society; "OBA Pickets Ben Garth Realty Firm Again," *Austin News*, July 29, 1970, box 2, ANC; "Sky Faces 'Practices' Probe," *Austinite*, February 18, 1970, box 7, ANC; "155 Picket Realty Office," *Austin News*, February 18, 1970, box 1, ANC; "OBA Pickets Oak Park Home of Realty Dealer," *Austin News*, June 9, 1971, box 4, ANC; clipping, "Hi, I'm Your Outraged Neighborhood Citizen on the March," *Chicago Tribune Magazine*, December 5, 1971, oversize 1.9, ACC; "To Picket or Not to Picket Legally," *Austin News*, February 10, 1971, box 3, ANC; OBA newsletter, January 7, 1968, folder 24, box 3, ACC; *Organization for a Better Austin v. Keefe*, 402 U.S. 415 (1971).

38. "Court Dismisses Case, Acquits Mrs. Wallace," *Austinite*, May 20, 1970, box 8, ANC; "Woman Cleared in Arson Case," *Austin News*, May 20, 1970, box 2, ANC; clipping, "Hi, I'm Your Outraged Neighborhood Citizen on the March," *Chicago Tribune Magazine*, December 5, 1971, oversize 1.9, ACC; "Sky Faces 'Practices' Probe," *Austinite*, February 18, 1970, box 7, ANC; "Both Sides Await Ethics Hearing," *Austinite*, March 4, 1970, box 8, ANC; "Revoke, Suspend Sky Licenses," *Austinite*, May 20, 1970, box 8, ANC.

39. Clipping, "500 at Aquinas Rally Vow Blockbuster Fight," *Garfieldian*, February 1, 1967, folder 98-18, Chicago Urban League Records accession 76-116, Special Collections and University Archives, Richard J. Daley Library, University of Illinois at Chicago (hereafter CUL); clipping, "Group Opens Fight on Block Busters," *Garfieldian*, February 15, 1967, folder 98-18, CUL accession 76-116; clipping, "Hi, I'm Your Outraged Neighborhood Citizen on the March," *Chicago Tribune Magazine*, December 5, 1971, oversize 1.9, ACC; Avella, *Confident Church*, 241–42; 5th Annual OBA Convention resolutions, May 19, 1971, folder 23, box 3, ACC; "Call Meeting on 'Panic Peddling,'" *Austin News*, August 5, 1970, box 2, ANC; "Six Bills Aimed at Unfair Real Estate Dealings," *Austin News*, May 12, 1971, box 4, ANC.

40. On the failures of local initiatives, see Santow, "Saul Alinsky," 297. "Stability? Newcomers Hold Key," *Austin News*, November 18, 1970, box 3, ANC; "OBA, Austin Clergy Meeting," *Austin News*, January 20, 1971, box 3, ANC; "RESOLUTIONS: Richard Harris, William Roberts, Co-Chairmen," folder 23, box 3, ACC; "OBA Convention May 1; Housing Meet Tonight," *Austin News*, April 7, 1971, box 4, ANC.

41. "OBA Convention May 1; Housing Meet Tonight," *Austin News*, April 7, 1971, box 4, ANC. OBA did not invent the idea of the Housing Referral Service. The South Shore Commission, a less militant community organization from the South Side, had a similar operation; see Molotch, *Managed Integration*, chap. 6. Austin Branch Report 1967, section 6, Branch Annual Reports, Chicago Public Library Archives, Special Collections and Preservation Division, Harold Washington Library Center, Chicago; "Austin" Free Housing Referral Service Pamphlet, folder 24, box 3, ACC; "resolutions: Richard Harris, William Roberts, Co-Chairmen," folder 23, box 3, ACC; Second Congress, Organization for a Better Austin, April 28, 1968, folder 27, box 3, ACC; OBA Finance Committee to "Gentlemen," May 1968, folder 23, box 3, ACC.

42. "RESOLUTIONS: Richard Harris, William Roberts, Co-Chairmen," folder 23, box 3, ACC. The neighboring village of Oak Park used a similar tactic successfully; see Goodwin, *Oak Park Strategy*; clipping, "Hi, I'm Your Outraged Neighborhood Citizen on the March," *Chicago Tribune Magazine*, December 5, 1971, oversize 1.9, ACC.

43. Clipping, "Hi, I'm Your Outraged Neighborhood Citizen on the March," *Chicago Tribune Magazine*, December 5, 1971, oversize 1.9, ACC; "Church Closes, Looks for Occupant," *Austinite*, May 24, 1970 [June 24, 1970], box 8, ANC; "Confrontation Livens Meeting," *Austinite*, February 18, 1970, box 7, ANC; "THA Calls Police on 'Invaders,'" *Austinite*, March 25, 1970, box 8, ANC; "Realty Alliance Fights Back," *Austin News*, September 9, 1970, box 3, ANC; "HRC Calls OBA to Public Hearing," *Austinite*, April 28, 1971, box 10, ANC; "Panic Peddling? OBA Scoffs at the Charge," *Austin News*, February 3, 1971, box 3, ANC; "'Panic Peddling' Case Reslated," *Austin News*, September 8, 1971, box 4, ANC; "OBA VP Awaits Decision in Panic Peddling Charge," *Austin News*, November 17, 1971, box 4, ANC.

44. Clipping, "500 at Aquinas Rally Vow Blockbuster Fight," *Garfieldian*, February 1, 1967, folder 98-18, CUL accession 76-116; "Picket Beltone Realty Firm," *Austin News*, May 6, 1970, box 2, ANC; "Belltone's [*sic*] Dice Broker's License Again," *Austin News*, March 10, 1971, box 3, ANC; "Beltone City License Revoked; Start Appeal," *Austinite*, December 2, 1970, box 9, ANC; "Broker Is Refused City Realty License, OLA Told," *Austin News*, April 7, 1971, box 4, ANC; "State Drops Case against Realty Co.," *Austin News*, February 3, 1971, box 3, ANC.

45. "Human Relations Commission Test Block for Panic Peddling," *Austinite*, September 23, 1970, box 9, ANC; "CHR Finds No Violations," *Austinite*, December 2, 1970, box 2, ANC; "West Side Coalition Lists Gains, Goals," *Austin News*, December 30, 1970, box 3, ANC; "City Accuses Realty USA of Subterfuge; Hearing Set," *Austin News*, March 31, 1971, box 3, ANC.

46. "Legislator Tells How to Thwart Panic Peddlers," *Austin News*, March 25, 1970, box 2,

ANC; "'Anti-Solicitation' Workable?" *Austin News*, September 23, 1970, box 3, ANC; "Hear How to File Anti-Solicitation Suits," *Austinite*, November 4, 1970, box 9, ANC.

47. "'Anti-Solicitation' Workable?" *Austin News*, September 23, 1970, box 3, ANC; full-page advertisement, p. 7, *Austin News*, September 30, 1970, box 3, ANC; "CNA to Hear Gang Unit Detective," *Austinite*, March 25, 1970, box 8, ANC; "Legislator Tells How to Thwart Panic Peddlers," *Austin News*, March 25, 1970, box 2, ANC; *Austinite*, February 18, 1970, box 7, ANC. For a similar effort on Long Island, see Rosalyn Baxandall and Elizabeth Ewen, *Picture Windows: How the Suburbs Happened* (New York: Basic Books, 2000), 192, 202.

48. "'Anti-Solicitation' Workable?" *Austin News*, September 23, 1970, box 3, ANC; Central Austin Resident to editor, *Austin News*, September 30, 1970, box 3, ANC; "Thompson: REBO 'Not Secretive,'" *Austin News*, September 16, 1970, box 3, ANC; "State Law Passed to Prohibit Realtors from Solicitation," *Austin News*, June 9, 1971, box 4, ANC.

49. "State Law Passed to Prohibit Realtors from Solicitation," *Austin News*, June 9, 1971, box 4, ANC; "Anti-Solicitation Law Hits Snags," *Austin News*, September 16, 1970, box 3, ANC; "'Anti-Solicitation' Workable?" *Austin News*, September 23, 1970, box 3, ANC; "Real Estate Soliciting Law Illegal," *Chicago Tribune*, April 18, 1972; "Overturn Law on Soliciting," *Austin News*, April 26, 1972, box 4, ANC.

50. Molotch, *Managed Integration*, 13; "Urges 'Common Sense' in Use of 'For Sale' Signs," *Garfieldian*, June 1, 1961; "Intensify Drive against Unfair Realty Practices," *Austin News*, June 24, 1970, box 2, ANC; 5th Annual OBA Convention resolutions, p. 5, May 19, 1971, folder 23, box 3, ACC; clipping, "Hi, I'm Your Outraged Neighborhood Citizen on the March," *Chicago Tribune Magazine*, December 5, 1971, oversize 1.9, ACC. For residents elsewhere in Chicago vandalizing "For Sale" signs, see Santow, "Saul Alinsky," 282. Cf. Thomas J. Sugrue, *The Origins of the Urban Crisis: Race and Inequality in Postwar Detroit* (Princeton: Princeton University Press, 1996), 250, and Murray, "Suburban Citizens," 317–26, who discovered women pushing baby carriages and strollers as part of their public neighborhood defense activities.

51. "Hearing Slated on Prohibiting For Sale Signs," *Austin News*, September 22, 1971, box 4, ANC; Baraniak to editor, *Austinite*, October 6, 1971, box 10, ANC; "For Sale Sign Ordinance Now in Effect," *Austin News*, November 24, 1971, box 4, ANC; *Austin News*, October 20, 1971, box 4, ANC; "Sign Ban Violators Decrease," *Austin News*, May 17, 1972, box 4, ANC; Arnold Hirsch, "Blockbusting," in *The Encyclopedia of Chicago History*, ed. James Grossman, Ann Durkin Keating, and Janice L. Reiff (Chicago: University of Chicago Press, forthcoming). The intricacies of the "For Sale" sign laws can be traced in the clipping files of the Chicago Municipal Reference Library, Harold Washington Library Center, Chicago. See also Baxandall and Ewen, *Picture Windows*, 203.

52. Kenneth T. Jackson, *Crabgrass Frontier: The Suburbanization of the United States* (New York: Oxford University Press, 1985), 203–15; Alexander von Hoffmann, "Federal Housing Administration," in *Encyclopedia of Urban America: The Cities and Suburbs*, ed. Neil Larry Shumsky (Santa Barbara, CA: ABC-CLIO, 1998), vol. 1, 298; John McClaughry, "The Troubled Dream: The Life and Times of Section 235 of the National Housing Act," *Loyola University Law Journal* 6 (1975): 1–45; Michael S. Carliner, "Development of Federal Homeownership 'Policy,'" *Housing Policy Debate* 9 (1998): 307, 313–14; Beth J. Lief and Susan Goering, "The Implementation of the Federal Mandate for Fair Housing," in *Divided Neighborhoods: Changing Patterns of Racial Segregation*, ed. Gary A. Tobin (Newbury Park, CA: Sage, 1987), 243–44, 247–48; R. Allen Hayes, *The Federal Government and Urban Housing: Ideology and Change in Public Policy*, 2nd ed. (Albany: State University of New York Press, 1995), 89; Robert Schafer and Charles G. Field, "Section 235 of the National Housing Act," *Journal of Urban Law* 46 (1969): 667–85.

53. McClaughry, "Troubled Dream," 20–21; Hayes, *Federal Government and Urban Housing*, 113–21; "Seek Moratorium Waner-FHA Meeting Draws Crowd of 1,000 to OLHC Hall," *Austin News*, November 3, 1971, box 4, ANC; "Vavoulis Tells Coalition Little Aid for Past Victims," *Austin News*, November 3, 1971, box 4, ANC.

54. Hayes, *Federal Government and Urban Housing*, 149, 195, and passim; "Seek

Moratorium Waner-FHA Meeting Draws Crowd of 1,000 to OLHC Hall," *Austin News*, November 3, 1971, box 4, ANC; "Deny FHA Moratorium," *Austin News*, December 8, 1971, box 4, ANC; 5th Annual OBA Convention resolutions, May 19, 1971, folder 23, box 3, ACC. Waner lost the 1967 mayoral election to Richard J. Daley. Roger Biles, *Richard J. Daley: Politics, Race, and the Governing of Chicago* (DeKalb: Northern Illinois University Press, 1995), 136; "Waner Letter Draws Coalition Fire," *Austin News*, May 17, 1972, box 4, ANC; H.D. to editor, *Austin News*, July 23, 1975, box 4, ANC; "Two Million for Mortgages," *Austinite*, July 1, 1970, box 9, ANC; "Offer New Mortgage Policy for N-W Austin," *Austin News*, July 1, 1970, box 2, ANC.

55. McClaughry, "Troubled Dream," 24; Hayes, *Federal Government and Urban Housing*, 149, 195, and passim; Amy L. Scott, "Houses for People Not for Profit: The Housing Rights Movement in Denver, 1972–1989," paper presented at the First Biennial Urban History Conference, Pittsburgh, Pennsylvania, September 2002.

56. Brian J. L. Berry et al., *Chicago: Transformations of an Urban System* (Cambridge, MA: Ballinger, 1976), 29, 62; Gregory S. Jacobs, *Getting Around* Brown: *Desegregation, Development, and the Columbus Public Schools* (Columbus: Ohio State University Press, 1998), 156; Robert Fishman, *Bourgeois Utopias: The Rise and Fall of Suburbia* (New York: Basic Books, 1987), chap. 7, "Beyond Suburbia: The Rise of the Technoburb"; Joel Garreau, *Edge City: Life on the New Frontier* (New York: Doubleday, 1991).

EPILOGUE

1. "Overflow Crowd at UPG Meeting," *Garfieldian*, May 3, 1961; and "UPG Spurs Fight on Blight Friday," *Garfieldian* June 7, 1961. For similar expressions of disdain at the quality of suburban life, see "New Unity in Community," *Garfieldian*, May 1, 1957; and "M. Le C" to editor, *Austin News*, February 17, 1971, box 3, Austin Newspaper Collection, Special Collections and Preservation Division, Harold Washington Library Center, Chicago.

2. Letter, Richard Gaucar [?] to Dear Mr. Adams, June 21, 1967, folder 28-4, box 28, Cyrus Hall Adams III Papers, Chicago Historical Society (hereafter CHA).

3. Heather Ann Thompson, *Whose Detroit?: Politics, Labor, and Race in a Modern American City* (Ithaca: Cornell University Press, 2001), 26.

4. Chicago Industrial Study, Summary Report, Chicago Plan Commission, 1952, unprocessed box "DUR Graphics Publications," Faith Rich Papers, Special Collections and Preservation Division, Harold Washington Library Center, Chicago. On the difficulties African Americans had securing white-collar work in Chicago in the early postwar years, see the American Friends Service Committee Archives, Chicago Regional Office Files, Philadelphia, Pennsylvania (hereafter AFSC). Thomas J. Sugrue, *The Origins of the Urban Crisis: Race and Inequality in Postwar Detroit* (Princeton: Princeton University Press, 1996).

5. John R. Stilgoe, *Borderland: Origins of the American Suburb, 1820–1939* (New Haven: Yale University Press, 1988); Kenneth T. Jackson, *Crabgrass Frontier: The Suburbanization of the United States* (New York: Oxford University Press, 1985), 42–75; Mary Corbin Sies, "North American Suburbs, 1880–1950: Cultural and Social Reconsiderations," *Journal of Urban History* 27 (March 2001): 328; James L. Wunsch, "The Suburban Cliché," *Journal of Social History* 28 (Spring 1995): 643–58.

6. See Becky M. Nicolaides, *My Blue Heaven: Life and Politics in the Working-Class Suburbs of Los Angeles, 1920–1965* (Chicago: University of Chicago Press, 2002); Richard Harris, *Unplanned Suburbs: Toronto's American Tragedy, 1900 to 1950* (Baltimore: Johns Hopkins University Press, 1996); Bennett M. Berger, *Working-Class Suburb: A Study of Auto Workers in Suburbia* (Berkeley: University of California Press, 1960); Alexander von Hoffman, *Local Attachments: The Making of an American Urban Neighborhood, 1850–1920* (Baltimore: Johns Hopkins University Press, 1994), 31, 37–38, 43; Henry C. Binford, *The First Suburbs: Residential Communities on the Boston Periphery, 1815–1860* (Chicago: University of Chicago Press, 1985), 35–41, 161–63; Andrew Wiese, "The Other Suburbanites: African American Suburbanization in the North before 1950," *Journal of American History* 85 (March 1999): 1495–524; Andrew

Wiese, *Places of Their Own: African American Suburbanization in the Twentieth Century* (Chicago: University of Chicago Press, 2004); Richard Harris and Robert Lewis, "The Geography of North America Cities and Suburbs, 1900–1950: A New Synthesis," *Journal of Urban History* 27 (March 2001): 265–70.

7. Jackson, *Crabgrass Frontier*, 234–37; Robert Fishman, *Bourgeois Utopias: The Rise and Fall of Suburbia* (New York: Basic Books, 1987), chap. 7; Joel Garreau, *Edge City: Life on the New Frontier* (New York: Doubleday, 1991); Michael H. Ebner, "Experiencing Megalopolis in Princeton," *Journal of Urban History* 19, no. 2 (February 1993): 11–55; Michael H. Ebner, "Prospects for the Dual Metropolis in the USA," *Planning History* 15, no. 3 (1993): 13–21; Sies, "North American Suburbs," 346n47, citing Fishman, *Bourgeois Utopias*; Joseph A. Rodriguez, *City against Suburb: The Culture Wars in an American Metropolis* (Westport, CT: Praeger, 1999), 5–10.

8. Fishman, *Bourgeois Utopias*; Adam Rome, *The Bulldozer in the Countryside: Suburban Sprawl and the Rise of American Environmentalism* (New York: Cambridge University Press, 2001); "Why Spoil a Good Thing?" *Garfieldian*, March 3, 1965 (emphasis in the original); William H. Whyte Jr., *The Organization Man* (New York: Simon and Schuster, 1956); Richard E. Gordon, Katherine K. Gordon, and Max Gunther, *The Split-Level Trap* (New York: Bernard Geis Associates, 1960); John Keats, *The Crack in the Picture Window* (Boston: Houghton Mifflin, 1956); "More Reasons Not to Move," *Garfieldian*, December 9, 1959; "UPG Chairman Blasts Real Estate Firm's Scare Letter," *Garfieldian*, March 16, 1960; Sarafin to editor, *Garfieldian*, October 4, 1961; "No Way to Escape Racial Pressures, Says UPG Head," *Garfieldian*, February 28, 1962; "Talking It Over," *Garfieldian*, April 10, 1963; "How to PREVENT Slums—That's the Problem," *Garfieldian*, June 19, 1963; "List 71 Homes in Suburbs Open to Negro Buyers," *Garfieldian*, November 20, 1963; Bacigalupo to editor, *Garfieldian*, December 11, 1963; "Negroes Reside in 26 Suburbs," *Garfieldian*, March 3, 1965. The American Friends Service Committee ran a program to place carefully selected "pioneer" African American families in suburban homes. See AFSC Archives passim. Brian J. L. Berry, *The Open Housing Question: Race and Housing in Chicago, 1966–1976* (Cambridge, MA: Ballinger, 1979), 16, has a map showing where African Americans lived in the Chicago metropolitan area in 1968; supporting figures appear on pp. 64–65.

9. Carl W. Condit, *Chicago, 1930–70: Building, Planning, and Urban Technology* (Chicago: University of Chicago Press, 1974), 235–45; Brian J. L. Berry et al., *Chicago: Transformations of an Urban System* (Cambridge, MA: Ballinger, 1976), 17–19; David M. Young, *Chicago Transit: An Illustrated History* (DeKalb: Northern Illinois University Press, 1998), 133; Ross Miller, *Here's the Deal: The Buying and Selling of a Great American City* (New York: Alfred A. Knopf, 1996), 10, 220. For a list of the new shopping centers in the Chicago area, see Berry et al., *Chicago*, 45. On the significance of the shift in American consumer preferences from downtowns to suburban shopping malls, see Lizabeth Cohen, "From Town Center to Shopping Center: The Reconfiguration of Community Marketplaces in Postwar America," *American Historical Review* 101 (October 1996): 1050–81. On suburban shopping patterns in South Gate, California, see Nicolaides, *My Blue Heaven*, 94–96.

10. Carole Goodwin, *The Oak Park Strategy: Community Control of Racial Change* (Chicago: University of Chicago Press, 1979); Stephen Grant Meyer, *As Long as They Don't Move Next Door: Segregation and Racial Conflict in American Neighborhoods* (Lanham, MD: Rowman & Littlefield, 2000), afterword; Douglas S. Massey and Nancy A. Denton, *American Apartheid: Segregation and the Making of the Underclass* (Cambridge, MA: Harvard University Press, 1993), chap. 7.

11. Robert A. Beauregard, *Voices of Decline: The Postwar Fate of US Cities* (Cambridge, MA: Blackwell, 1993); Jackson, *Crabgrass Frontier*, 272; Paul A. Gilje, *Rioting in America* (Bloomington: Indiana University Press, 1996), 158–61; James R. Ralph Jr., *Northern Protest: Martin Luther King, Jr., Chicago, and the Civil Rights Movement* (Cambridge, MA: Harvard University Press, 1993). For examples of African Americans reluctant to perpetuate the block-

by-block pattern of change, see Howell to editor, *Garfieldian*, November 24, 1966; and activities of Meredith Gilbert, "Urban Affairs Weekly Report, for Week Ending April 2, 1967," folder "Urban Affairs Program, Reports, Weekly, Chicago Regional Office, 1966," box "Chicago R.O. 1966 (Pre-Adolescent Enrichment Prog. to Urban Affairs Prog.)," AFSC. On the social consequences of the "spatial mismatch," see William Julius Wilson, *When Work Disappears: The World of the New Urban Poor* (New York: Knopf, 1996). Berry et al., *Chicago*, 29, 62.

12. David R. Roediger, *The Wages of Whiteness: Race and the Making of the American Working Class* (New York: Verso, 1991); Peter Kolchin, "Whiteness Studies: The New History of Race in America," *Journal of American History* 89 (2002): 154–73.

13. Sugrue, *Origins of the Urban Crisis*; Arnold R. Hirsch, "Massive Resistance in the Urban North: Trumbull Park, Chicago, 1953–1966," *Journal of American History* 82 (September 1995): 522–50; William M. Tuttle Jr., *Race Riot: Chicago in the Red Summer of 1919* (New York: Atheneum, 1970). For an alternative theory of the factors that enable racial change, see Mickey Lauria, "A New Model of Neighborhood Change: Reconsidering the Role of White Flight," *Housing Policy Debate* 9 (1998): 395–424.

14. On whites' and institutional use of public policy for the purpose of removing African Americans, see Arnold R. Hirsch, *Making the Second Ghetto: Race and Housing in Chicago, 1940–1960* (Cambridge: Cambridge University Press, 1983), esp. chap. 5.

15. Charles Jaret, "Recent Patterns of Chicago Jewish Residential Mobility," *Ethnicity* 6 (1979): 238–39; Joseph Zikmund II, "Sources of the Suburban Population: 1955–1960 and 1965–1970," *Publius* 5 (Winter 1975): 27–43; *Chicago Telephone Directory* (1970), 766; press release, "Gale Cincotta, 'Mother of Community Reinvestment Act' Dies," August 15, 2001, colist-admin@comm-org.utoledo.edu, August 16, 2001.

16. For examples, see Jennifer Halperin, "Here Comes the Neighborhood," *Illinois Issues*, January 1996, 12–16; and Chicago Tribune, *The American Millstone: An Examination of the Nation's Permanent Underclass* (Chicago: Contemporary Books, 1986), 179; and Nicholas Lemann, *The Promised Land: The Great Black Migration and How It Changed America* (New York: Alfred A. Knopf, 1991), 243. In general on the rhetoric of the urban crisis, see Beauregard, *Voices of Decline*.

17. Scholarship based in the European context has established that the targets of riotous action are often carefully chosen to reflect the grievances of the rioters. See Natalie Zemon Davis, *Society and Culture in Early Modern France* (Stanford, CA: Stanford University Press, 1975), chap. 6; and E. P. Thompson, "The Moral Economy of the English Crowd in the Eighteenth Century," *Past and Present* 50 (1971): 76–136. For a periodization of rioting across United States history, see Gilje, *Rioting in America*.

18. Why the riots bypassed the South Side deserves further investigation. In some cases, the relative quiet was attributed to the presence of the Blackstone Rangers street gang.

19. "Police Head Lays Down Law to Demonstrators," *Garfieldian*, July 21, 1965; "Garfield Park Back to Normal," *Garfieldian*, August 18, 1965; "Report on Westside Riots," August 1965, folder "Urban Affairs Program, Reports, Chicago Regional Office 1965," box "Chicago R.O. 1965 (Housing Oppors. Prog.-Coms & Orgs.: Suburban Human Rels. Comm. Com. to Youth Oppors. Prog.)," AFSC. On the riot in Watts, see Gerald Horne, *Fire This Time: The Watts Uprising and the 1960s* (New York: Da Capo Press, 1997).

20. "Report on Westside Riots," August 1965, folder "Urban Affairs Program, Reports, Chicago Regional Office 1965," box "Chicago R.O. 1965 (Housing Oppors. Prog.-Coms & Orgs.: Suburban Human Rels. Comm. Com. to Youth Oppors. Prog.)," AFSC; "A Chicago Story—West Side Leadership," p. 2, folder 169-3, Chicago Urban League Records accession 76-116, Special Collections and University Archives, Richard J. Daley Library, University of Illinois at Chicago (hereafter CUL). The word "allegedly" appeared in small type above the main headline on the flyer: photostat, folder 169-3, CUL accession 76-116; "Garfield Park Back to Normal," *Garfieldian*, August 18, 1965.

21. "Report on Westside Riots," August 1965, folder "Urban Affairs Program, Reports,

Chicago Regional Office 1965," box "Chicago R.O. 1965 (Housing Oppors. Prog.-Coms & Orgs.: Suburban Human Rels. Comm. Com. to Youth Oppors. Prog.)," AFSC; "Garfield Park Back to Normal," *Garfieldian*, August 18, 1965.

22. "13 Named to Take Demands to Daley," *Garfieldian*, August 25, 1965; "Mayor Gets West Garfield 'Demands,'" *Garfieldian*, September 1, 1965; "'Unity' Heads Palos Park List of Recommendations," *Garfieldian*, March 9, 1966.

23. In general on King's sojourn in Chicago, see Ralph, *Northern Protest*.

24. *Chicago Tribune*, June 13, 14, 15, 16, and 17, 1966; Felix M. Padilla, *Latino Ethnic Consciousness: The Case of Mexican Americans and Puerto Ricans in Chicago* (Notre Dame, IN: University of Notre Dame Press, 1985), 50–51; "Talking It Over," *Garfieldian*, July 7, 1966.

25. "West Side Incidents, July 13, 14, 15, 1966," folder "July–Aug. 1966," box 4, Marillac House Records, Chicago Historical Society (hereafter MH); Urban Affairs Weekly Report, for week ending July 17, 1966, p. 2, folder "Urban Affairs Program, Reports, Weekly, Chicago Regional Office, 1966," box "Chicago R.O. 1966 (Pre-Adolescent Enrichment Prog. to Urban Affairs Prog.)," AFSC; letter, [Sister Mary William] to Sister Catherine, July 18, 1966, folder "July–August 1966," box 4, MH; Bernard O. Brown, "WSO and the Riot on the Near West Side," folder 4, box 93, Welfare Council of Metropolitan Chicago Records, Chicago Historical Society; Ralph, *Northern Protest*, 109–14; Urban Affairs Program, American Friends Service Committee, "Special Report to Chuck Henderson on VISTA Role in Recent Chicago Riots,," August 5, 1966, folder "Urban Affairs Program, Volunteers in Service to America, Chicago Regional Office, 1966," box "Chicago R.O. 1966 (Pre-Adolescent Enrichment Prog. to Urban Affairs Prog.)," AFSC; Urban Affairs Weekly Report, for week ending July 17, 1966, folder "Urban Affairs Program, Reports, Weekly, Chicago Regional Office, 1966," box "Chicago R.O. 1966 (Pre-Adolescent Enrichment Prog. to Urban Affairs Prog.)," AFSC; memo, Sister Winifred to Cottrell, July 15, 1966, folder "July–August 1966," box 4, MH.

26. Beauregard, *Voices of Decline*, 175–78; letter, Sister Mary William to Egan, April 17, 1967, p. 2, folder "April–May 1967," box 4, MH; clipping, "Why the W. Side Exploded," *Chicago Sun-Times*, April 14, 1968, folder 12, box 5, Austin Community Collection, Special Collections and Preservation Division, Harold Washington Library Center, Chicago (hereafter ACC); Urban Affairs Weekly Report, for Week Ending April 2, 1967, folder "Urban Affairs Program, Reports, Weekly, Chicago Regional Office, 1966," box "Chicago R.O. 1966 (Pre-Adolescent Enrichment Prog. to Urban Affairs Prog.)," AFSC; Marciniak to the Chicago Commission on Human Relations, April 13, 1967, p. 3, folder "April–May 1967," box 4, MH; clipping, "How—and Why—Chicago Had a 'Cool' Summer," *Chicago's American*, September 6, 1967, folder 33–1, box 33, CHA; letter, Sister Mary William to Marciniak, November 29, 1967, folder "Nov.–Dec. 1967," box 5, MH (emphasis in the original).

27. James Allen Flanery, "Chicago Newspapers' Coverage of the Major Civil Disorders of 1968" (Ph.D. diss., Northwestern University, 1971), 157, 161; clipping, "'Holding the Line' at Ashland Av.," *Chicago Daily News*, April 18, 1968, Francis X. Lawlor clipping file, Chicago Historical Society; undated Riot Report, folder 168-28, CUL accession 76-116.

28. Clipping, "Why the W. Side Exploded," *Chicago Sun-Times*, April 14, 1968, folder 12, box 5, ACC; Flanery, "Chicago Newspapers' Coverage," 155–62, 165, 175, 176, 191; undated Riot Report, folder 168-28, CUL accession 76-116; Susan Gregory, *Hey, White Girl!* (New York: W. W. Norton, 1970), 216; press release, May 1, 1968, folder "April–May 1968," box 5, MH; Cleodia O'Quinn, "opening letter," February 22, 1983, folder 3, box 1, O'Quinn Family Collection, Special Collections and Preservation Division, Harold Washington Library Center, Chicago.

29. Flanery, "Chicago Newspapers' Coverage," 167; telegram, Samuel H. Shapiro, Acting Governor, to the President, April 6, 1968, folder 14, box 81, Samuel H. Shapiro Papers, Abraham Lincoln Presidential Library, Springfield; letter, Howard W. Bartram, April 9, 1968, folder "Administration, General, Chicago Regional Office, 1968," box "Chicago Regional Office 1967 Madison Area Com. to 1968 Admin. (Convention Demonstrations)," AFSC; items in folder

"Emergency Relief forms, Jan.–April 7, 1968," box 8, MH; Roger Biles, *Richard J. Daley: Politics, Race, and the Governing of Chicago* (DeKalb: Northern Illinois University Press, 1995), 145.

30. Mike Royko, *Boss: Richard J. Daley of Chicago* (New York: Signet, 1971), 169. Mike Royko's widely read narrative has contributed to the impression that Daley made these comments at the height of the riot. For a more reliable chronology, see Biles, *Richard J. Daley*, 143–47, 150–62. David Farber, *Chicago '68* (Chicago: University of Chicago Press, 1988).

31. Chicago Tribune, *The American Millstone*; Laura S. Washington and Curtis Lawrence, "West Side Loses in Clout City," *Chicago Reporter*, December 1990; "East, West Garfield Magnets for Change," *Chicago Tribune*, May 18, 2003; Sean Zielenbach, *The Art of Revitalization: Improving Conditions in Distressed Inner-City Neighborhoods* (New York: Garland, 2000).

32. Andarb to editor, *Garfieldian*, August 25, 1965; Buck to editor, *Garfieldian*, September 21, 1966.

33. Jackson, *Crabgrass Frontier*, 272.

References to the page numbers on which figures appear are italicized.